GRAND PRIX

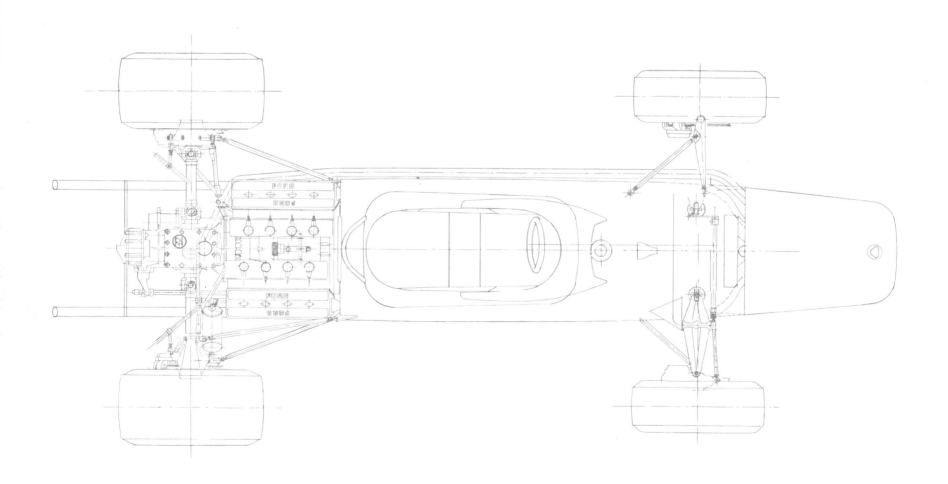

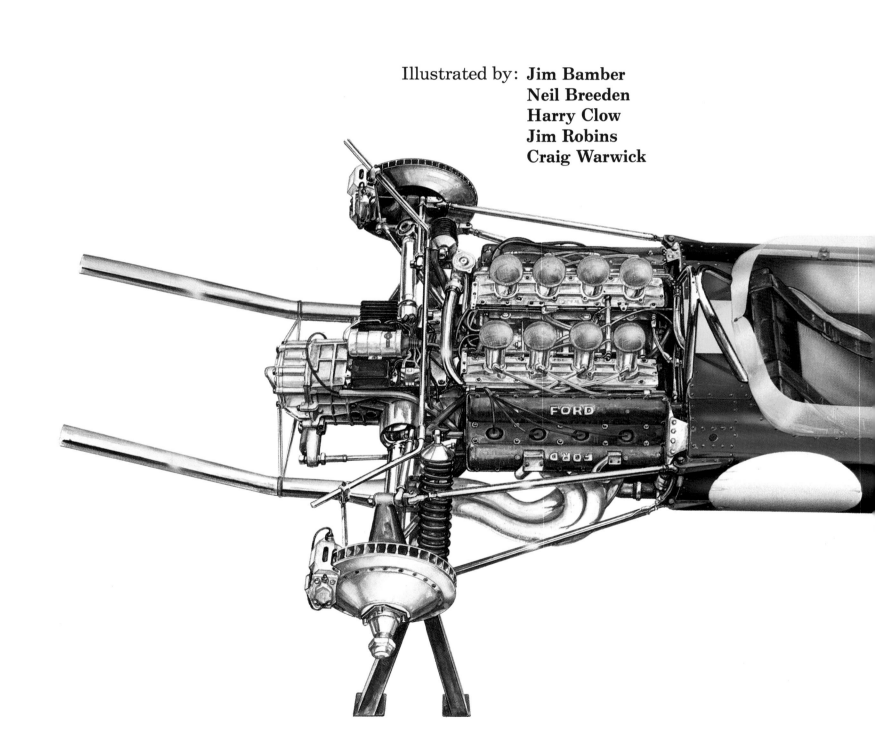

Illustrated by: **Jim Bamber**
Neil Breeden
Harry Clow
Jim Robins
Craig Warwick

GRAND PRIX

DAVID HODGES

DOUG NYE

NIGEL ROEBUCK

Michael Joseph • London

CONTENTS

Grand Prix
was conceived, edited, and designed
by Imprint Books Limited
12 Sutton Row, London W1V 5FH

First published in Great Britain by Michael Joseph Ltd.
44 Bedford Square, London WC1
1981

ISBN 0 7181 2024 8

Printed and bound in The Netherlands by
Royal Smeets Offset B.V., Weert.

INTRODUCTION

The essence of a Grand Prix is simple: a given number of drivers compete in single-seater cars which conform to a restricting set of regulations, over a given distance or time, on a circuit which meets certain requirements in terms of facilities and safety arrangements. A series of national Grands Prix in a season make up the World Championships, one for drivers and the other less well-publicized championship for the constructors of their cars.

The sport has, however, never been simple. Complexity is inherent. The cars are highly specialized, their drivers all possess rare skills. The circuits are demanding. The organization of a Grand Prix calls for executive ability to a standard not always achieved, and the governing body does not always function to the highest professional standards.

Set against the eventful story of Grand Prix racing from 1906, most of this book concentrates on twenty years, almost one-third of its total history. The basic pattern for today's racing was established in the late 1950s, when Coopers, which had their engines installed behind their drivers, began winning Grands Prix. In 1961, hoots of derision greeted John Cooper and Jack Brabham when they arrived at Indianapolis with their little rear-engined car. But by the end of that decade, the Indy establishment had, to a team, followed the Cooper's lead and put the engine behind the driver. They had hated making the change, throwing away their racing heritage, but they had no choice. Progress had decreed it.

Many changes were afoot in Europe and there was some cross-fertilization in the two worlds of Formula One and American Championship racing. Today the simplicity of racing in the late 1950s and early 1960s seems almost pastoral. The machines have become immeasurably more sophisticated, complex, and costly—and so has the whole Grand Prix circus.

"Grand Prix circus" has become a widely used term, and it perhaps has derogatory implications. As in any sport, there is a nostalgia for the past, and in that perspective it is quite possible to see a "circus" atmosphere in some of the gaudy trappings of a modern Grand Prix. But that is a distorted perspective. Under the thin veneer of commercialism, Grand Prix racing is still a deadly serious, intensely competitive, and highly professional sport.

Blatant commercialism had long been taken for granted in other types of motor racing before it came to the Grand Prix world in 1968. It had been an accepted part of American track racing since the First World War. In a sense it had been abused for nationalistic purposes in the Grands Prix of the 1930s. And Ferrari had been financially backed for politico-economic purposes since the mid-1950s. At that time, and indeed for another decade, Grand Prix cars usually ran in national colours—French cars were blue, Italian cars red, British cars green. Then in the late 1960s the flood gates to sponsorship from outside the automotive world were opened by Lotus; Team Lotus cars, previously green with a yellow stripe, were suddenly red and gold. And it became Gold Leaf Team Lotus, in return for financial backing from the British John Player tobacco company. Gasps of horror were heard in the grandstands. This simply was not playing the game.

Other teams, however, eventually followed suit, and the whole face of Grand Prix racing changed with the arrival of really big sponsorship. There seemed to be more money for everything and everybody. Drivers' earnings suddenly skyrocketed, inevitably causing many of them to become greedy. The transporters became more lavish, vividly arrayed in the sponsors' colours, spewing out spare engines in paddocks across the continent. And anybody who had even a tenuous connection with racing carried a briefcase, preferably slim and of leather. It was a time of plenty for many, and it coincided with the arrival on the scene of Bernard Ecclestone, the man who would take control of it, harness it, package it for mass consumption.

From the infusion of sponsorship money came a complete transformation in the Grand Prix scene, some of it good, some not. Mechanics, previously crammed into transporters on the long hauls through Europe, began to travel by air. For the first time, they were treated like human beings, sitting down at tables to decent meals before beginning another all-night stint, and earning at least a reasonable, if hardly generous, wage. No more cold coffee and stale sandwiches.

Today it is inconceivable that the teams would tolerate the cramped limitations of the Clermont-Ferrand paddock as it was for Grands Prix in the 1960s—a pocket handkerchief of sloping ground, where even the fuel vehicles had to be parked in a roadside area a few hundred metres along the circuit.

There also began the motor home syndrome, which had its beginnings in common sense. It was entirely understandable that a driver should want to change his clothes, talk with his engineer, relax a little, in privacy and comfort. Each team acquired a motor home, and its purpose was to provide a place of refuge. Unfortunately, however, these lavish vehicles eventually served to dehumanize the sport. The little kid, autograph book in hand, is today hard put to spot any of his heroes in the paddock, for the tendency of the driver is to step straight from the racing car and head for sanctuary behind smoked glass. And trying to enter one of these "embassies" for some frivolous purpose can often lead to a frosty response, leaving you with the feeling of having interrupted a Politburo meeting.

The sponsors' largesse has permitted a growth of the business of Grand Prix racing which would not have been otherwise possible, but the added finance has exacted its price. Drivers, ever mindful of their contracts and wallets, are far less willing to speak their minds lest they upset their source of income.

Paddock interest, however, usually centres on the machinery, for Grand Prix cars can have a total fascination simply as inert mechanical objects. It is sometimes too easy, therefore, to ignore all the other aspects of racing. Although the car is unquestionably more important than it once was, everything still depends on the skill of the drivers when the green light starts a race. Even in an age of sophistication, teams continue to build cars which call for bravery as well as skill, and there are still the brave men to drive them. Although many things have changed since the first year of the 3-litre formula in 1966, it is still possible to compare situations fifteen years apart, such as Jochen Rindt's instinctive handling of a cumbersome Cooper-Maserati in 1966 and Gilles Villeneuve's efforts to compensate for the deficiencies of an ill-behaved Ferrari in 1980. Beyond that, through most of the period, a few—a very few—outstanding drivers have been able to beat the best cars of their day with cars that might be described as marginally inferior, for the competition is such that no modern driver could hope to equal the feats of Nuvolari with a markedly inferior car. There would probably be general agreement among enthusiasts, however, that the Tyrrells which Jackie Stewart drove to World Championships were not the best cars of their days or, indeed, that James Hunt's Championship McLaren was not in the same class as other cars of its year. Motor racing, therefore, is still a sport for outstanding sportsmen. That it is much more is obvious to the most casual visitor to the paddock.

The Grand Prix paddock scene has changed enormously in twenty years. Pits, pit garages, and paddock complex are required at every circuit for the support and immediate servicing of racing cars. That function, at least, has been constant. But usage has meant that paddocks have become grander, and, in some eyes, debased by invasions of sponsors.

Trade support—support from companies in or allied to the motor industry—has always been valued. The modest retainers and bonuses paid by the trade were long a valued source of income to add to start and prize monies, while company representatives made shrewd contributions considerably beyond the mere provision of material and some money. The fuel companies have had traditional associations with racing which in some cases go back to the early days of the sport. The tyre companies, too, have always been part of the scene.

Paddocks today abound with hangers-on, many of them spawned by the multinationals which pay the bills. In the motor homes you find wall-to-wall public relations men, as well as carpet. Public relations overkill has become one of the banes of the business; many companies employ six men for the job, when, really, none are called for. It has all become terribly impersonal, the opposite of the PR man's aim, but inevitable when spontaneity is discouraged.

There is no doubt that the commercialization of Grand Prix racing has been resented, and that led in part to a bitter wrangle between Formula One factions in 1980. Weak government during the 1970s had allowed the teams, particularly those with entrepreneurial managers, virtually to take control of Grand Prix racing, through the Formula One Constructors' Association (FOCA). For reasons that were not altogether altruistic, a new president of the official governing body (FISA) set out on a campaign to regain control. The pretext was safety, with attention focussed on the issue of sliding skirts. These devices were made to permit extraordinarily high cornering speed. The expressed concern was that a skirt failure in a corner could lead to loss of control and an accident which would almost inevitably climax on the outside of that corner, where spectators are most likely to congregate. Spectators had already been driven further from the action, as concern about safety led to calls for more and more circuit modifications. Officialdom took the extraordinary view that any approach to the safety problem required alterations to the circuits rather than to the ever-faster cars. The skirts issue was apparently settled by banning them for 1981, but actually the wording of the regulations was so loose—or designers were so adept at finding loopholes—that virtually the same effect was achieved with rigid skirts in place of the old sliding devices. Lap times continued to fall.

More central to the issue was the fact that skirts were one of the means whereby the "kit-car" teams, who relied on the Cosworth engine, could match the lap speeds of more powerful cars. Those teams—the majority of which were by chance British—also formed the hard core of FOCA. In the FOCA-FISA conflict, therefore, the issue became control of the sport and its financial structure, tinged with the recurrent woolly desire to somehow set the clock back to the time when the Grand Prix were not "tainted" by a predominance of kit cars.

This philosophy ignored the very real progress in other areas made possible by the off-the-shelf availability of engines and transmission components. In the last two decades, far greater advances have been made in, for example, chassis engineering than in any other period, including the Germans' heyday of the 1930s. As the era of the rear-engined Grand Prix car opened, even Cooper, its unwitting moving force, was edging out of the artisan years, when the stress of uncalculated loads was placed upon tubular chassis members with strengths that were themselves guessed at rather than calculated. The anti-kit-car attitude was, unhappily, encouraged by an upsurge of nationalistic fervour, especially in France, when two great marque names reappeared in Grand Prix racing—Renault, in their own right and with cars that in truth broke more new ground than the much-lauded Mercedes of 1954-55, and Talbot, who took over an established kit-car team. During the same period, as the 1970s gave way to the 1980s, another great name from the past, Alfa Romeo, had also returned to the Grands Prix. Together with Ferrari, and a couple of kit-car constructors, those three seemed to hold out some promise of racing in the grand old style. In reality that was in the past.

In the hard economic times of the 1980s, with forecasts of major financial crises across the world, there is constant fear among racing people that sponsorship could dry up. Were that to happen, Grand Prix racing would still survive. The motor homes might be smaller and less lavish; there might be fewer spare engines and less testing; drivers' retainers would come down sharply, perhaps preventing thirty-year-olds from making a million and retiring; and many team owners originally attracted by telephone number cheques, would go away and make money elsewhere. There might be fewer competitive cars on the grid. But a healthy nucleus that love motor racing for its own sake should remain—like Enzo Ferrari, Colin Chapman, and Frank Williams. Racing would survive.

Many of the sport's fixtures and fittings would see it through until the next economic boom period. Several circuits came into being only in the 1970s, and all the others have been modified to the standard requirements of the period. Many of the great circuits, such as Clermont-Ferrand, Rouen, and the Nürburgring, have been lost and with them went the impossibly cramped conditions in which everybody was required to work at those places. In their stead, we have such circuits as Paul Ricard, Dijon, and Hockenheim, impersonal perhaps, but with up-to-the-minute facilities. They may gain personality with age.

Much of what has happened to Grand Prix racing in the last decade or so is distasteful to the purist, but not all of it has been to the sport's detriment. Not all of it.

THE HISTORY
DAVID HODGES

FOR SEVEN DECADES the premier international motor races have been the Grands Prix, the supreme competition among men using machines as their sports equipment. The men, the top drivers at least, have been outstanding. Through natural talent or sheer dogged dedication, they have been able to drive cars to limits well beyond the capacity of the average spectating motorist. Although, because of uncertain economic conditions or regulations which inhibited designers, the development of the cars has been uneven, the racing has continually fascinated its aficionados and interested the general public. The appeal of imaginative automotive talent wedded to top-class machinery is so strong that modern enthusiasts are as passionately interested in historic Grand Prix cars as they are in the latest World Championship contenders. Here we review the historical prelude to the modern, costly flamboyant era, which concludes as a new generation of drivers, designers, and marques began to enter Grand Prix racing.

Competitive use of the horseless carriage was inevitable, and came within a decade of the production of the first practical cars. Like the newfangled machines, the first races were simple—straightforward point-to-point events run on everyday roads. The momentum came from France, which had very early taken over the leadership of the infant car industry from Germany, the nation of its birth.

The shortcomings of these first city-to-city races became obvious long before the notorious Paris-Madrid race of 1903, which was cut short at Bordeaux after many accidents. The leader at that point, Fernand Gabriel, driving a Mors, had averaged 65.3 miles per hour over the 342 miles from Paris. He achieved this in a car that was primitive, on roads that were poorly surfaced, between uncontrolled crowds of spectators who still had little conception of the speeds at which racing cars travelled. Safety margins were slender.

The first circuit races had already been run, at Melun in 1900, but it was the 1902 Circuit des Ardennes which was perhaps the true forerunner of today's road races. In 1903 the Gordon Bennett Trophy race was run on a circuit of Irish roads, and in 1904 the Vanderbilt Trophy was raced over ten laps of a twenty-eight-mile Long Island circuit. These were all long circuits by today's standards, and although some marathon point-to-point events, such as the Carrera Panamericana, were to be run for sports cars as late as the 1950s, long road circuits were soon to become exceptions. Meanwhile, oval-track racing, which recognized the importance of spectators, was to become established in the United States, and point the way to a future schism in motor racing.

The Gordon Bennett Trophy was the first pre-eminent international race, run as a contest between national teams. The French felt it was quite unreasonable that their team should be restricted to the same number of cars as those from other nations, and in 1905 proposed that there should be five times as many French cars admitted as should be allowed from such lesser automotive countries as the United States and Italy. Understandably, that was not widely acceptable. Consequently, France effectively killed the Gordon Bennett series by refusing to organize the 1906 event, as was their right since Leon Théry driving a Brasier had won the 1905 race, and inaugurated a Grand Prix which was open to teams from any number of manufacturers. It was not the first race to carry the title Grand Prix—a local race at Pau in 1901 was the first—but until the First World War it was to be The Grand Prix, and the French would have liked it to remain so rather than have it become only one major international race in a series.

That chauvinistic Gordon Bennett episode produced a committee, and out of that came the first international governing body of motor sport—the Association Internationale des Automobile Clubs Reconnus (AIACR). It was based in Paris, and that was unfortunate. The French inevitably tended to regard it as another body for promoting French interests, as they occasionally have its successors, the 1946 Commission Sportive Internationale (CSI) of the Fédération Internationale de l'Automobile (FIA) and, from 1978, the Fédération Internationale du Sport Automobile (FISA). The supreme governing body lurks in the background throughout Grand Prix history,

setting the regulations, or formulae, and sometimes lamentably failing in its duties. But for all its many faults it was not seriously challenged until 1980.

The cars in that first Grand Prix were subject to a regulation restricting maximum weight at 1007 kg. They were stereotyped machines, similar to those run in the preceding Gordon Bennett contests. A common factor was the largest four-cylinder engine the constructors thought feasible, but multi-plate clutches were appearing and shaft drive was beginning to supplant chains. In most cases a puncture (and there were many in those early races) meant that the crew had to fit a new tyre on a wheel and inflate it beside the track, although a few cars had wheels with detachable rims.

Ahead of the thirty-two crews at Le Mans in June 1906 were twelve laps of a 64.12-mile circuit, six laps to be completed on each of two consecutive days—769 gruelling miles in cumbersome machines, in great heat, over roads that broke up under the heavy pounding. Eleven cars survived. Ferenc Szisz won for Renault at 62.88 mph, half an hour ahead of the FIAT driven by Felice Nazzaro. All but one of the other manufacturers which filled the list of finishers are long in the past: Clément-Bayard, Brasier, Panhard, Lorraine-Dietrich, and Mercedes.

In 1907 and 1908 Grand Prix results dealt heavy blows to French pride, for Nazzaro's FIAT beat Szisz's Renault over 477 miles of a circuit outside Dieppe in 1907, while in 1908 Christian Lautenschlager, a burly Swabian test driver who was racing for the first time, won for Mercedes from two Benz cars on the same course. Under the pretext of a depressed economic situation, the French automotive industry agreed to abstain from Grand Prix racing, and got a scattering of support from other countries.

This type of road racing enjoyed a brief flowering, however, in the United States, with the inauguration of the American Grand Prize at Savannah in 1908. A FIAT driven by Louis Wagner won, with Victor Hémery's Benz in second place. The last Renault run in an early Grand Prix retired. Seventy years were to pass before this famous marque returned to Grand Prix racing. In 1910 and 1911 the race was won by David Bruce Brown, a brilliant young FIAT driver, who beat a Benz driven by Hémery in 1910 and one driven by Hearn in 1911. That was the year that the Indianapolis 500 was first run, and although the Grand Prize continued until 1916 it was increasingly overshadowed by the Indy track event.

In Europe, big-car technology had largely stagnated under Grand Prix regulations which were framed first around that 1007-kg weight limit, then by a 231-litre fuel allowance, then, in 1908, by an 1100-kg weight restriction coupled with cylinder bore restrictions. But real progress had been made under the Coupe de l'Auto regulations for voiturette racing, especially when from 1911 these were framed around a 3-litre capacity limit. There had been original big-car essays—Clement Ader and Alexander Winton had built eight-cylinder racing engines as early as 1903. Franklin and Premier had actually raced eights in 1905. For the 1907 Grand Prix Walter Christie had entered one of his front-wheel drive monsters, its engine, at 19,891 cc, the largest ever seen in Grand Prix racing. Lee

Sherman Chadwick produced a supercharged car for the 1908 Savannah race. In the 1908 Grand Prix, incidentally, the first "pits" were provided. They were literally trenches with counters at track level. Although inappropriate since 1908, the term became part of motor racing.

The Grand Prix was revived in 1912, with the odd major stipulation that the maximum width of car bodies was to be 175 cm (69 in). It was won by the first "modern" Grand Prix car, a Peugeot with a high-revving twin-overhead camshaft engine, which beat a very traditional Fiat. As much to the point, Sunbeams in the concurrent Coupe de l'Auto race were third, fourth, and fifth overall. Victor Rigal, who placed third in the 3-litre Sunbeam, averaged 65.29 mph over the 956 miles at Dieppe, compared with outright winner Georges Boillot's 68.45 mph in a 7.6-litre Peugeot.

Boillot also won the low-key Grand Prix in 1913. Then the regulations for 1914 imposed a restriction on engine capacity, which has ever since been fundamental to most successful sets of racing rules. The limit was 4.5 litres, coupled with a maximum car weight of 1100 kg (2425 lb). The race attracted thirty-seven starters to a magnificent 23.38-mile circuit near Lyon. The engines were all overhead camshaft types (except the Swiss Piccard-Pictets which had sleeve-valve engines), producing up to 120 bhp, while four manufacturers' cars had brakes on all four wheels. This was the end of a brief period when competition was a very real stimulus to the design of efficient cars. The race was a Mercedes triumph, with Mercedes cars in first, second, and third places.

Many of the Grand Prix cars of the period found their way to the United States, particularly to the two-and-a-half mile Indianapolis Speedway and its increasingly magnetic 500-mile race. Ray Harroun and relief driver Cyrus Patschke had won the first 500 at 74.4 mph in a Marmon single-seater, which was quite a novelty, and Joe Dawson drove a National to victory in 1912. Then came the first "European era" at the Brickyard: Jules Goux won in a Peugeot in 1913, René Thomas in a Delage in 1914, Ralph de Palma in a Mercedes in 1915, and Dario Resta in a Peugeot in 1916. During this period, the American trend towards track racing was being accelerated by the growing popularity of board tracks, where the racing was often fast, close, and dangerous. These board tracks were to have a short life—wear and tear on their planked bankings was high, and maintenance was costly when it was properly undertaken—and they disappeared by the mid-1920s. But together with Indianapolis they contributed greatly to the American concentration on track racing to the almost total exclusion of road-course events for two decades.

When European racing resumed after the First World War it seemed little changed, although fairly soon sports car races as such were to become established, and would sometimes rival the Grands Prix. The only major events on the 1919-20 calendars were the Targa Florio and the Indianapolis 500.

In 1921 the Automobile Club de France ran its Grand Prix again. It was no longer an exclusive race, for the first Italian Grand Prix was run at Brescia in 1921. Moreover, the Italians paid starting money, whereas entry fees had always been required by the French

organizers. Oddly, the Italian race attracted only six runners, when earlier in the year the French had thirteen starters at Le Mans for their Grand Prix under the 3-litre capacity limit. The circuit, later to become famous as the venue of the 24-hour sports car race, proved to be abominably rough. Nine cars were classified, with Jimmy Murphy gaining an unexpected all-American victory in a Duesenberg. The Italian race came down to a straight contest between Ballot and Fiat, and the French gained some compensation for the defeat on their home ground as Jules Goux won in a Ballot.

That season served to revive Grand Prix racing. It entered a brilliant four-year phase under a new formula, which limited engine capacity to 2 litres and minimum weight to 650 kg (1763 lb); for the first three seasons riding mechanics were called for, but thereafter only the space for a second man in the cars was required. This formula stimulated technical progress to an unusual degree. Several outstanding cars were produced, and driving techniques developed rapidly. The first race was won by a veteran, but a new generation of drivers was to "arrive" in these 2-litre cars.

In its wanderings around France, the Grand Prix de l'ACF came to rest for a year at Strasbourg, where it was run over sixty laps of a simple 8.3-mile triangle of roads, and saw the first massed start in Grand Prix history—up to that time cars had been sent off singly or, in 1914 and 1921, in pairs. There were six teams at Strasbourg (eighteen cars), and Ballot, Bugatti, Rolland-Pilain, Aston Martin, and Sunbeam were run into the ground by Fiat. For their Grand Prix swan song, Ballot ran cars with odd barrel-shaped bodies. Bugatti

did so, too, on the T30, the forerunner of a famous line of Grand Prix cars. Although the Aston Martins were 1.5-litre cars, the other British team, Sunbeam, was confident, for their cars had been designed by Henry and were well-developed. But the thoroughbred Type 804 Fiat beat them all and Felice Nazzaro won the 499-mile race at 79.33 mph.

The Italian Grand Prix was run for the first time in the royal park at Monza that was to become its near-permanent home. The new Monza autodrome had been built remarkably quickly, and it incorporated a road circuit as well as a banked track, thus avoiding the shortcomings of many other autodromes. The superiority shown by Fiat at Strasbourg frightened off most of the would-be opposition: Type 804s driven by Pietro Bordino and Nazzaro were first and second, the sole Bugatti was flagged off fifty miles in arrears, and the only other runners—two Heims and two Diattos—retired.

The 1923 season saw the introduction of several technical novelties, above all the arrival of the supercharger in mainstream racing. The supercharger, a device to compress the fuel/air mixture, was to be an important device in the make-up of most Grand Prix engines until 1951, although the advantages it gave over normally aspirated engines were not to be recognized in the regulations until 1938.

In 1922 Mercedes ran a pair of supercharged 1.5-litre cars in the Targa Florio, and the following year they ran a team of supercharged 2-litre cars at Indianapolis with modest results (eighth and eleventh). A month after the 500, however, Allessandro Cagno drove a Fiat with a supercharged 1.5-litre four-cylinder engine to score a crushing

victory in an Italian voiturette race. That was a minor event, but even as that first European victory for a supercharged car was being celebrated, "blown" Fiat Grand Prix cars were practising for the French classic at Tours, and showing demoralizing superiority. A year later, Sunbeam was to be the first Grand Prix team to use a Roots-type supercharger to compress mixture to the carburettor. Also in 1924, the Indianapolis 500 was won by a supercharged car, but that Duesenberg had a centrifugal blower, a characteristic of which was that it made for a very narrow effective rev range in an engine—hence it was admirable for track racing, but singularly useless on road circuits; its success in the 500 served to widen the gap between track and road racing.

At Tours, the Fiats retired with engines choked by dust sucked in by their superchargers. The race fell to a British car—a rare victory, one not to be repeated in a French Grand Prix until 1960. Henry Segrave scored that victory for Sunbeam, in a car that was so nearly a carbon copy of the Fiat 804 that it was dubbed "Fiat in green paint". (Sunbeam had simply hired Vincent Bertarione, a member of the Fiat design team, to produce their 1923 Grand Prix car.) Segrave's winning speed over 497 miles was 75.3 mph, and he was followed by his team-mate Albert Divo, while Guinness took fourth place in the other Sunbeam. Between them was one of the odd Bugatti T30s, nicknamed "tank" because of its all-enveloping body. Its wheelbase and track dimensions of 78 in/40 in did not make for good roadholding. Gabriel Voisin's cars made more aerodynamic sense, and were of semi-monocoque construction, but they were underpowered with production sleeve-valve engines—one finished, fifth and last, an hour and a quarter behind the winner. Delage rushed their first V-12 to Tours, but it retired early without showing its true potential. Rolland-Pilain planned to run a cuff-valve six alongside their two outclassed eights, but that car expired during practice.

The Fiat supercharging arrangements were revised, and the cars scored a crushing one-two victory in their home Grand Prix. Jimmy Murphy was third in one of the three Millers which started at Monza, adapted for the Grand Prix role only with the addition of front-wheel brakes. Fourth and fifth were two Benz, which in conception were a decade ahead of the other cars—mid-engined and with independent rear suspension.

The 1923 season saw two Grands Prix in Spain, although neither attracted good entries. Rolland-Pilain won on the San Sebastian road circuit. Sunbeam won on the short-lived Sitges banked track, rather luckily as Zborowski's Miller had tyre failure when leading near the end.

The next year saw Grand Prix reach its peak of the decade, at Lyon. Segrave led that French Grand Prix for Sunbeam, Bordino led it for Fiat, then Guinness led it for Sunbeam, Ascari for Alfa Romeo, and finally Guiseppe Campari won it in one of the superb Alfa P2s fielded by the new team from Milan. V-12 Delages took the next two places. Contrarily, the race is as well remembered for the debut of a car that was outclassed, the Bugatti T35. Bugatti abandoned his eccentricities, and produced a most elegant little design which was to

serve motor racing well for the next five years. For a while, however, he handicapped its drivers by his refusal to use superchargers.

Oddly, all the major marques did not meet again that year. Alfa Romeo enjoyed a one-two-three-four triumph at Monza, Ascari heading the procession at 98.76 mph, but against mediocre opposition, with two outpaced cuff-valve Schmidts the only finishers (two Chiribiri and four Porsche-designed Mercedes retired). The San Sebastian Grand Prix attracted "the rest". Here Segrave won for Sunbeam from a Bugatti and two Delages on a treacherous circuit.

Racing was sliding into a decline in 1926, when the first World Championship was essayed. This was for manufacturers, and the qualifying races were the Indianapolis 500 and the Belgian, French, and Italian Grands Prix. The Grand Prix regulations now stipulated a minimum body width of 80 cm (31¾ in).

At Indianapolis, Peter de Paolo became the first 100-mph winner, averaging 101.13 mph in a Duesenberg, while the front-wheel drive Miller placed second and the Duesenberg which was third also exceeded the magic 100 mph. The limitations of the Roots-type supercharger became apparent when Bordino (relieved by Mourre) could finish no higher than tenth in a Grand Prix Fiat fitted with a monoposto body.

Only Delage challenged Alfa Romeo in the Belgian Grand Prix, ineffectually as only two Italian cars finished the race. Ascari won at an average speed of 74.46 mph.

The ACF at least attracted Bugatti and Sunbeam to their race by paying prize money for the first time. But the once-great French Grand Prix at the Montlhéry autodrome was a dreary affair, watched by a small crowd. Once again Alfa Romeo started to run away with the race, but the team was withdrawn when the great Ascari was fatally injured in a crash. Two Delages then led home a Sunbeam and the first of five Bugattis. The winners, Robert Benoist and Albert Divo, shared the winning drive (621 miles at 69.7 mph).

The last effective race of the 2-litre formula was run at Monza, where Count Brilli Peri drove the winning Alfa Romeo P2, after Kreis had briefly led in a Duesenberg. Alfa Romeo clinched the first World Championship, but the lack of interest in this was such that it ran for only one more year. Finally, the formula faded out with a lacklustre San Sebastian Grand Prix, when Delage enjoyed an almost effortless one-two-three victory.

During the 2-litre years great progress was made with racing engines. Power outputs roughly doubled between 1922 and 1925, when the supercharger and exotic fuels came into general use. Approaches to chassis and running gear changed little, apart from such experiments as Voisin's semi-monocoque or the mid-engined Benz, and there was little appreciation of the contribution which could be made to improved lap times by work on such areas as suspension. Concern had been expressed at the mounting speeds of cars, so it was inevitable that the AIACR would look first at the power of engines when framing new regulations. For 1926-27 engine capacity was restricted to 1.5 litres, and this was coupled with an increase in the minimum weight of cars to 700 kg (1332 lb).

The expectation was that most of the established teams would

contest races, but many withdrew from racing. The number of races increased, but that only served to increase entrants' costs disproportionately—outside financial support from sponsors or suppliers was not dreamed of—while the prestige rewards for manufacturers were, if anything, diminished since success in a Grand Prix was by no means as rewarding as success in The Grand Prix had once been.

The first race of the new formula was one of the great fiascos of motor sport. Only three Bugattis, supercharged T39s, appeared to contest the French Grand Prix at the featureless Miramas autodrome: one of them retired, Meo Costantini worried about suspect fuel and drove one so cautiously that he completed only eighty-five of the one hundred laps, while veteran Jules Goux won at a leisurely 68.16 mph. At least those Bugattis, the T39 derivative of the T35, had supercharged engines.

The entries for the European Grand Prix at San Sebastian totalled no more than double those for the French race, but the newcomers were straight-eight Delages, three of them in fact. This remarkable car was evidence that a small-engined formula could indeed lead to technical progress—as was also to be demonstrated by the parallel Indianapolis 91-cubic-inch regulations. The Delage was to become the outstanding car of the 1.5-litre formula. As was almost customary, chassis work on the Delage was neglected, and there was another initial fault that seems trifling: the positions of the engine and the exhaust caused the cockpit to become overheated. But it would overheat to such an extent that it was unbearable for more than a few consecutive laps. As a result of this flaw, plus the Spanish

heat, André Morel, one of the team drivers, had to be rushed to hospital with heat stroke after eleven racing laps. His car, taken over by Edmond Bourlier and Robert Sénéchal, eventually finished second between two Bugattis.

The next race was the first British Grand Prix, run over an unsatisfactory road course contrived at Brooklands. But the entry was good by 1926 standards, even though Bugatti stayed away. The last Grand Prix car from the shaky Sunbeam-Talbot-Darracq combine (a Talbot this time, designed by Vincent Bertarione and Walter Becchia and built in Paris) appeared, to challenge the Delages. The low and rakish Talbot, with a supercharged straight-eight, looked the part, but proved fragile. Robert Sénéchal and Louis Wagner (who had raced in the first Grand Prix in 1906) won the Brooklands race, in one of the Delages, from Malcolm Campbell's private Bugatti and another Delage, at a speed of 71.61 mph.

The novelty at Monza for the Italian Grand Prix was a pair of Maseratis; the disappointment was the absence of Delage and Talbot. The Maseratis retired, the factory Bugattis failed or faltered, and an amateur Bugatti driver, Charavel, won. It was ironic, for even the admission of a private entrant into a Grand Prix would have been unthinkable when the decade opened. For what little it was worth, Bugatti won the second World Championship.

That season, and to a degree the 1927 season, was more intriguing for some of the cars that did not appear as it was for on-track racing. There was the front-wheel drive Alvis (which never ran in a Grand Prix), and the even more interesting front-wheel drive

Itala Tipo 15, which was never raced anywhere. Indeed the Tipo 15 was completed only in 1100 cc voiturette form—a pity, as its specification included a supercharged V-12 designed to rev to 8000 rpm and a true monoposto body. Then there was the Fiat Tipo 451 supercharged opposed-piston engine, defeated by overheating and metallurgical problems before it got beyond bench tests. In 1927, there was to be the last Fiat Grand Prix car, the 806 with its supercharged 12-cylinder engine producing some 175 bhp for its only race, the thirty-one mile Formule Libre Milan Grand Prix at Monza where it showed enormous potential which was never to be realized.

Delage was supreme in 1927. Robert Benoist won the French, San Sebastian, Italian, and British Grands Prix, and a secondary race at Montlhéry. The car was substantially revised, with its engine offset and its head effectively turned through 180 degrees so that the exhaust was as far from the driver as possible. In this form it was to be competitive for years in Formule Libre and voiturette racing, but meanwhile in 1927 its superiority caused Bugatti to withdraw his team from the French Grand Prix. As the result of supreme confidence Delage sent only a single car to Spain and Italy. It was headed only in the French race, but briefly, by a Talbot in the last appearance of a Sunbeam-Talbot-Darracq factory team.

At Monza, the only Grand Prix OM made its only appearance. Merandi placed one second, while a track Miller driven by Cooper and Kreis was third. Finally, at Brooklands the Flatirons built by J.G. Parry Thomas, and so named for their low, flat lines, ran in their only Grand Prix. Almost inevitably powered by a straight eight, this enterprising design was never fully developed because Thomas was killed in a Land Speed Record attempt.

The 1.5-litre formula was one of unfulfilled promise. If all the cars built, let alone projected, could have been collected on one grid the outcome could have been enthralling. As it was, Formule Libre and sports car racing were healthier than Grand Prix racing. The first German Grand Prix at the Nürburgring in 1927, for example, was contested by twenty-one sports cars, before a crowd of almost one hundred thousand spectators.

The AIACR abandoned restrictions on engines in the new formula for 1928. The principal stipulation was that a car should weigh between 550 and 750 kg. But the 91-cu-in (or 1.5-litre) regulations continued at Indianapolis, and designers were kept on their toes. Sundry erstwhile Grand Prix cars appeared there, with no real success, while the two main American protagonists, Duesenberg and Miller, generally battled for honours in the 500. Duesenberg came up with a new car in 1927, with its engine mounted at an angle and the drive line running alongside the driver, while a Miller appeared with two-stage centrifugal supercharging. A "91-inch" car came close to winning at 100 mph in 1928, when Louis Meyer won in a Miller at 99.48 mph (interestingly, Varzi won the 1929 Monza Grand Prix on the banked track at 116.65 mph in an Alfa Romeo P2). Then in 1930 the so-called Junk Formula was introduced at Indianapolis, and the 500 became meaningless in mainstream racing terms until 1938.

Only Italy ran a Grand Prix to the 1928 formula, and the race was marked by tragedy, when Emilio Materassi crashed after his ex-factory Talbot touched a Bugatti. Materassi and twenty-three spectators were killed, in this the first Grand Prix accident in which members of the public died. The first three places in the race were taken by drivers soon to be aces—Louis Chiron (Bugatti), Achille Varzi (Alfa Romeo P2), and Tazio Nuvolari (Bugatti).

Louis Chiron, who was born in Monaco in 1899, started competing in local events in 1923 and was racing in Grands Prix in 1927. That year he ran against Louis Wagner, a competitor in the first Grand Prix; the joint careers of these two drivers were to span fifty years of Grand Prix racing. Chiron drove a Grand Prix car (a Lancia) in a Grand Prix (at Monaco) for the last time in 1955. Throughout his career, Chiron was an enthusiast, a stylist, and a tactician (hence two of the sobriquets applied to him—the Perfectionist and the Wily Fox). He tended to drive French cars, although in common with most leading men of the period he also raced Alfa Romeos; his experience with the ill-fated 1936 Mercedes led to a brief semi-retirement, but he re-emerged as a major contender in postwar Grands Prix.

Achille Varzi started his racing career on motorcycles, turning to cars in 1927 and making his name with a privately run P2 Alfa. During the 1930s he raced Bugattis, Alfa Romeos (for the factory team and for Ferrari), Auto Union, and Maserati, gaining a reputation as a shrewd, sometimes even ruthless, driver whose style was smooth and clean. Throughout his long career he had only two serious accidents; the first left him unscathed, but the second, in an Alfa Romeo at Berne in 1948, was instantly fatal.

Tazio Giorgio Nuvolari was the greatest driver of the inter-war decades. A quiet, modest little man who was transformed in a car, he drove with extraordinary skill coupled with the ardour and passion expected of an Italian. He, too, was a motorcyclist who turned to cars in the mid-1920s, and although he was to drive a wide variety of cars he is still best remembered for his exploits in P3 Alfa Romeos, when by virtuoso driving he compensated for horsepower deficiencies. The British tended to recall him with particular affection, quite simply as the Great Little Man.

Fuel consumption regulations were tried in 1929 and 1930. Only the French and Spanish Grands Prix were run under them in 1929, being won by Bugatti drivers Williams and Chiron, while in 1930 only the Belgian Grand Prix was run as a formula race, again won by Chiron in a Bugatti.

However, 1929 had seen the first running of an improbable event, but one which was to prove astonishingly durable—the Monaco Grand Prix. This was the first race to be run on a circuit completely within a town, and it was greeted with scepticism. It worked, however, and until the 1950s was widely imitated, especially in France, Italy, and Switzerland; except for the Pau event, safety considerations and sheer inconvenience doomed other street races, at least until the 1970s, when a street race in the United States, almost as improbable as that first Monaco event, succeeded at Long Beach.

Monaco's 1929 race was a Formule Libre event, and there were sixteen starters, by no means a poor field at that time. The race was between William Grover Williams, an expatriate Englishman, in a Bugatti T35B and Rudolf Caracciola in a 7.1-litre SSK Mercedes-Benz. The German actually led the race in his apparently quite unsuitable car, but after a slow pit stop finished third behind Williams and Bouriano also in a Bugatti.

Caracciola was another driver whose career was to peak in the 1930s. In the preceding decade he had made his name with sports cars, before starting his long association with Mercedes in the mid-1920s and proving his worth in their big supercharged cars. He drove one to victory in the first German Grand Prix in 1926 (the first of his six victories in the event) and put in perhaps his greatest drive to win the 1931 Mille Miglia. In 1932, he turned to an Alfa P3, a dainty car compared with the big Mercedes. A crash at Monaco in 1933 put him out of racing for a season, but despite misgivings about his fitness he answered the Mercedes call when they returned to Grand Prix racing in 1934, and was to become their team leader for the next six seasons.

Racing slowly recovered from its nadir in the first seasons of the new decade. Most of the impetus came from Italy, where new designs began to appear. Available teams and drivers tended to set the pattern, for the simple requirement that cars have two-seater bodies and that national Grands Prix should be of at least ten hours duration—to all intents and purposes a free formula—led to mixed fields of pure racing cars and stripped sports cars. Then, for 1932, a more realistic five-hour duration was agreed, and at last the two-seater body requirement was buried.

That opened the door for the first definitive monoposto Grand Prix car, the Alfa Romeo Type B (P3). As it came on the scene, many of the lesser entrants, and their hotchpotch of cars from the turn-of-the-decade seasons, were disappearing and the fields made up of

Monza Alfas, Maseratis, and Bugattis were much more purposeful. In 1932, Bugatti had a reasonable season with the T51 although, apart from its twin-overhead camshaft 2.3-litre engine, this was a straight derivative of the T35 family. But it was by no means dominant, and at the end of the season the T54 was introduced; its engine produced 300 bhp, but it could seldom be fully exploited and the car soon gained a reputation for dubious handling qualities. Maserati simply revamped their straight-eight. So 1932 was Alfa Romeo's season, for their handsome cars were beaten only twice.

Alfa Romeo withdrew at the end of the season, leaving Scuderia Ferrari to uphold their honour with 2.65-litre versions of the erstwhile sports Monza. This move led, unintentionally, to near-parity among the three principal marques and to a very good racing year, albeit one marred by several fatal accidents. The first major race was at Monaco, where for the first time in Grand Prix history grid positions were decided by lap times recorded in practice, not by the luck of a draw. Achille Varzi became the first driver to gain a pole position by his own efforts. That Grand Prix saw one of the most sustained duels of racing, between Varzi in a factory Bugatti and Nuvolari in a Ferrari Alfa. They were locked in battle from start almost to finish, Varzi leading at the end of thirty-four laps, Nuvolari at the end of sixty-six. On the one-hundredth and last lap both drivers over-revved their engines. The Bugatti eight withstood this abuse, an oil pipe split on the Alfa eight.

Varzi won the next race, too, on the very fast Mellaha circuit at Tripoli, but there was a furore over the result. In conjunction with this race there was a well-funded lottery, and the leading drivers "came to an arrangement" with gamblers who had drawn their names. (The system was changed in 1934.) The final order in 1933 was Varzi, Nuvolari, and Sir Henry Birkin. At that time Birkin was one of only two British drivers of real Grand Prix calibre. It was tragic that he contracted septicaemia from an exhaust burn at Tripoli, which later proved fatal.

The French Grand Prix fell to the burly Giuseppe Campari, driving a Maserati, ahead of Phillipe Etancelin and George Eyston in private 2.35-litre Monza Alfas. Three other Monzas completed the list of finishers; after having promised much—primarily the debut of his new T57—Bugatti withdrew his factory team. Ferrari entered three Alfas, and Nuvolari's fiery driving proved too much for all of them—the engine of his own blew up in practice, he started the race in Borzacchini's car, but its transmission wilted as did the transmission of Taruffi's Alfa which he took over. For the next race, the Belgian Grand Prix, Nuvolari was in a Maserati, and he won from Varzi and Réné Dreyfus who were driving T51 Bugattis. When he won the next two secondary events, Alfa Romeo dusted down the P3s and handed them over to Scuderia Ferrari. The reward was three secondary victories, then a win in a climactic Italian Grand Prix, when Fagioli's Alfa led the Maseratis driven by Nuvolari and Zehender to the flag.

Later that same day the Monza Grand Prix was marked by tragedy. In the first heat, the crankcase of a Ferrari-entered Duesenberg split, and spread oil over one hundred yards at a curve. It was not cleared when the second heat started, and on the first lap

FIAT

Fiat was very active in the first Grand Prix era and until the mid-1920s. Then came two seasons' absence. In 1927 Fiat had one outing, which ended in victory, and then abruptly withdrew and destroyed their racing equipment. That act fed the story that the management had tired of seeing their cars compete with replicas of Fiats, or run against cars designed by former Fiat employees. Beyond that there was little glory to be gained in the years of the Grand Prix doldrums, while there was advantage (and state encouragement) in applying research resources to aero engines and the Schneider Trophy.

The FIATs (for Fabbrica Italiana Automobili Torino), run in the first Grands Prix, retained all the outward archaic appearance of cars from the age of city-to-city races. Indeed their 1906 entries were reworked 1905 cars. The 1912 Grand Prix FIATs were the last big bluff chain-drive monsters. But they had some advanced features, notably in their engines, with overhead valves, hemispherical combustion chambers, and, from the S61 of 1910, overhead camshafts. In general they were successful cars. Second and fifth in the 1906 Grand Prix proved to be an appetizer for the triumphant year of 1907 when the combination of Felice Nazzaro and FIAT was unbeatable. They won the French Grand Prix, the Kaiserpreis, and the Targa Florio. Although all the FIATs in the 1908 French Grand Prix retired, there was the consolation of first and third places in the American Grand Prize at Savannah.

The thundering 14.1-litre S74s were the fastest cars in the French Grand Prix when that race was revived in 1912, and Wagner survived the 956-mile marathon to take second place in one. The company then ceased racing for a year. In 1914 they reappeared with the four-wheel-braked S57 for that year's Grand Prix. Only one of their cars lasted the distance, finishing in eleventh and last place.

The S57s were brought out again after the war, and in 1921 Count Giulio Masetti drove one to victory in the Targa Florio. That year the 801 was first raced with an interim four-cylinder engine; its straight-eight was not ready in time for the French Grand Prix. The definitive form of this car made its debut in the Italian Grand Prix at Brescia, one of the team finishing a disappointing third.

The real revival came in 1922, when the sleek red 804 set a standard for the 2-litre formula. The 804 design team was headed by Guido Fornaca and included Vincent Bertarione and Vittorio Jano who were both later enticed to join other companies. The 804's straight-six initially produced 95 bhp, and that was enough for the Fiat drivers to run away from the rest in the French Grand Prix. Although accidents accounted for two of the Fiats, Nazzaro won in the third by no less than fifty-eight minutes.

For 1923 Fiat joined the straight-eight movement and, moreover, the engine of the 805 was supercharged. The 805s had the legs of a strong field in the French Grand Prix, but all three retired as their engines choked on dust pumped in by the Wittig vane-type super-chargers. These were replaced by Roots-type superchargers, still delivering compressed air to the carburettor, but with adequate filtering, and output increased by some 15 bhp over the initial 130 bhp. Thus revised, the 805s were first and second in the Italian Grand Prix—the first Grand Prix victory for a supercharged car.

In 1924, the 805s were withdrawn after a total team failure in the French race. One was sent to America in 1925, where Bordino won a couple of minor races as a warm up for Indianapolis. In the 500 itself the 805 was disappointing, finishing the race in a lowly tenth place.

Experiments continued, and an opposed-piston two-stroke engine was built for the 1.5-litre formula. It was tested but never raced. Its power output was exceeded by the twin six used in the 806, designer Tranquillo Zerbi extracting 187 bhp from its 1.5 litres. This compact low car was raced only once, Bordino winning the 1927 Milan Grand Prix at Monza in it. Then Fiat withdrew from racing.

Campari and Borzacchini crashed at that point. Both were killed. Incredibly, it had still not been cleared when the final was run, and on the eighth lap Count Czaikowski also crashed at that curve and was killed. The oil flag was not then in use, and it seems that efforts to clear this oil were confined to sweeping.

There remained the Czech Grand Prix, which Chiron won for the third time, driving a Ferrari Alfa P3, and the Spanish Grand Prix, which also fell to Chiron. That last race of 1933 also saw the belated debut of the Bugatti T59, the last new Grand Prix car on "classic" lines. It was an outstandingly elegant machine in the old tradition, but, lacking even the refinement of independent suspension, it was to all intents and purposes obsolete as its first full season approached.

While Grand Prix racing reached one of its perodic peaks in 1933, in car design and racing philosophies it was a peak carried over from the vintage years. During 1933 the regulations which were to come into effect in 1934 had been known, and their stipulations were a maximum dry car weight of 750 kg, minimum body dimensions at the cockpit (85 cm wide, 25 cm deep), and a minimum race distance of 500 km (312 miles). This formula was intended to run for three years. It had been conceived with stability in mind, in the knowledge of cars that had raced in 1932, with the assumption that speeds would be restrained to roughly the level of that year.

The Italian and French teams decided that their existing cars would serve, with minor modifications. But two German constructors started with clean sheets of paper, and within the new rules came up with advanced new designs; the formula which was expected to

maintain the status quo failed in that respect before its first races were run. Auto Union and Mercedes-Benz had been offered government inducements to demonstrate international technological superiority through racing, in the form of a prize and, more importantly, advantageous contracts for other work, and both took new approaches. They had engines producing around 300 bhp—that would be doubled during the life of the formula—but those engine power outputs were not the key to faster lap times. It was their approaches to chassis and running gear design that were to give Auto Union and Mercedes-Benz enormous advantages in roadholding and handling. Both teams were to suffer teething problems, but as the 1934 season moved into its second half it became only too obvious that the Italians had few answers to this new challenge, and France had none at all. Even leading drivers were to be humbled by little-known Germans in the new cars, for although both teams had to employ some foreign drivers, their nationalistic *raisons d'être* meant that German heroes were to be preferred.

A full confrontation between new and old did not come until July, at the French Grand Prix. Earlier in the year, the Ferrari team had enjoyed a one-two-three at Tripoli and a one-two at Monaco. Auto Union first raced in the Avusrennen, and had to be content with third place behind Guy Moll in a streamlined Alfa track special and Varzi in another Alfa. The Mercedes debut was at the Nürburgring, where von Brauchitsch won in a W25 from Stuck's Auto Union and Chiron's Alfa. The French Grand Prix at Montlhéry turned out to be an Alfa Romeo triumph, Ferrari's cars finishing one-two-three with

FIAT 1907

In 1907 FIAT, in an effort to give Giovanni Agnelli the victory he wanted, contested and won all three major races. The regulations for the three races varied, so stock-based cars were used for the Targa Florio and Kaiserpreis, while for the Grand Prix it was felt that a revamp of the 1906 cars would serve and would not be troubled by the fuel consumption formula. This formula allowed 231 litres of fuel per car and

this required a consumption of no less than 3.3 km per litre or about 9.4 mpg.

Guido Fornaca and Carlos Cavalli modified the impressive engine, which was advanced with its overhead valves operated by pushrods and rockers. This led to a contemporary comment "all engine and a flimsy vehicle" (each piston weighed more than ten pounds). The engine revved faster than in 1906, and its power was up from 110 bhp to 130

bhp. This was transmitted through a fluid clutch to a four-speed gearbox and chain final drive.

Wooden artillery wheels with detachable rims were fitted, with the spares—so essential on the poor roads of the Dieppe circuit—piled horizontally above the fuel tank, located low at the rear of the car. Braking was to the rear wheels and transmission only. Overall, this was a car that typified the "age of monsters".

SPECIFICATIONS
FIAT 16.3-litre   1907

Engine
Four-in-line
Bore × stroke: 180 mm × 160 mm
Capacity: 16,286 cc
Pushrod overhead valves
Maximum power: 130 bhp at 1600 rpm

Transmission
Four-speed; chain final drive

Chassis
Channel section side members

Front and rear suspension
Rigid axle, semi-elliptic springs, and friction shock absorbers

Brakes
Drum (rear wheels only) and transmission

Dimensions
Wheelbase: 112 in 2845 mm)
Front track: 53 in (1346 mm)
Rear track: 53 in (1346 mm)

only a misfiring Bugatti left of the rest of the field. The complete Mercedes team went out before half distance, and only one of the Auto Unions survived into the second half of the race. Above all, that Grand Prix belonged to Louis Chiron, who first matched the German cars and then drove on to an easy victory. But it was a result that misled. There would be only one other major victory for an Alfa Romeo P3, very few for any other Italian cars, and none at all for France.

Although the retirement rate of the German cars remained high for the rest of the year, they got on top and were to stay there until 1939. After the Montlhéry debacle, Stuck's Auto Union headed Fagioli's Mercedes in the German Grand Prix, then the challenge was carried to Italy, to the Coppa Acerbo. This was a tragic race for Ferrari—Moll was killed when he crashed, Chiron's Alfa was destroyed when it caught fire, and Varzi broke two Alfas in his efforts to stay with the German cars. The Scuderia did not recover for the rest of 1934. Fagioli won the race for Mercedes, then Auto Union took the first two places in the first Swiss Grand Prix, at Berne's tricky Bremgarten circuit. Chicanes were introduced at Monza for the Italian Grand Prix, in the hope that the German cars would be slowed to level terms, but Mercedes won from Auto Union. Fagioli won the Spanish Grand Prix from his team leader Caracciola, then Stuck rounded off the year by winning the Czech Grand Prix from Fagioli.

The German cars were revised for 1935, both teams using larger engines and, as much to the point, paying greater attention to getting more of their power on the road. Ferrari uprated the P3, with a larger engine and independent front suspension, and put together a pair of the ferocious *Bimotore* for Formule Libre races on fast circuits. The *Bimotore* used P3 components, with two engines (one ahead of the cockpit, one behind) whose output was transmitted through a central gearbox to the rear wheels. Power of the order of 540 bhp was put through the rear tyres, and these seldom lasted long. Meanwhile, Alfa Romeo started work on a V-12, while the Maserati brothers turned to a V-8, as an interim measure enlarging their straight-six. Bugatti was in eclipse and French enthusiasts were exhorted to support the SEFAC project. In Italy, Count Trossi tested his Monaco-designed front-wheel drive car, powered by a two-stroke radial engine ahead of its front wheels, but it was never raced.

In racing, a Mercedes driven by Fagioli won at Monaco, Achille Varzi, the new Auto Union driver, won at Tunis, and Caracciola won at Tripoli. At Avus, Stuck raised the lap record to 161.88 mph while Fagioli won. Then in the Eifelrennen at the Nürburgring, former motorcyclist Bernd Rosemeyer raced a car for the first time. He actually led in an Auto Union and eventually finished second behind Caracciola. Mercedes were first and second in the French Grand Prix, where the chicane ploy was tried again on fast stretches, but without success. They then won again in Belgium.

The 1935 German Grand Prix was an extraordinary race, with both German teams out in force (Mercedes had five cars, Auto Union four) to race for the honour of a home victory. The virtuosity of Nuvolari denied them both. At ten laps he led in a P3. A bungled pit

PEUGEOT

The Peugeot marque is almost as old as the motor car. During the period leading up to World War I it made major contributions to top-level racing, notably in turning the evolution of Grand Prix cars away from the dead end of muscle-bound, chain-driven monsters towards sophistication. Peugeots were run in the earliest races. The then recently absorbed Lion-Peugeot company had gained an excellent voiturette racing record when two drivers, Georges Boillot and Jules Goux, and technician-driver Paul Zuccarelli, persuaded Robert Peugeot to embark on a more ambitious programme for a projected 1911 Grand Prix car.

That design was developed as the L76. In it Boillot scored a fortunate and significant victory in the 1912 French Grand Prix. Later that year, the dashing Georges won the secondary Sarthe Grand Prix at Le Mans. In 1913, Goux drove a slightly modified version to win the Indianapolis 500 by no less than thirteen minutes—the first 500 victory for a foreign car. Meanwhile, a 3-litre Peugeot had been run unsuccessfully in the Coupe de *l'Auto* race concurrent with the 1912 Grand Prix. Out of this smaller and lighter car, Peugeot designer Ernest Henry developed a 5.6-litre Grand Prix car for 1913, using an engine with similar twin-overhead camshaft valvegear and with its bore exactly half the stroke (78 mm x 156 mm). In the 1913 French race, Boillot and Goux gained first and second places in Peugeots. One of these cars also came fourth in the 1914 Indianapolis 500, two places behind a 3-litre Peugeot. The success of an improved 3-litre car in the 1913 Coupe de *l'Auto*, when its engine produced 90 bhp at 2950 rpm (30.2 bhp per litre), was another nail in the coffin of side-valve engines for top-line racing.

Peugeot, Boillot, and France expected much of the 1914 Grand Prix Peugeot, a shapely car with the refinement of four-wheel brakes. Its failure was a bitter disappointment. The team cars were driven into the ground and, finally, had only a fourth place behind three Mercedes to show for the effort. There was a half-hearted racing car attempt after the war, but for most of the 1920s Peugeot turned to sports cars. But their superb twin-overhead camshaft engines had set new racing standards and inspired a generation of designers.

stop dropped him to fifth. He flogged the Alfa back to second place as the last lap started, and it seemed no less than justice when race leader von Brauchitsch, in a Mercedes, suffered tyre failure and the fiery Italian won.

Auto Union won the Coppa Acerbo and the Italian and Czech Grands Prix. Mercedes won the Swiss and Spanish Grands Prix. The most significant victory among the late-season races came in Czechoslovakia, where the winning Auto Union was driven by Rosemeyer.

The next season was Rosemeyer's. Mercedes's new short-wheelbase car won two early-season races, but its best placing for the rest of the year was a second, behind Nuvolari's Alfa in the Penya Rhin Grand Prix in Spain. Rosemeyer won the Eifelrennen, German Grand Prix, Coppa Acerbo, Swiss Grand Prix, and Italian Grand Prix. At Bremgarten, where he headed an Auto Union one-two-three, young Rosemeyer set a lap record at 105.42 mph. Although the circuit was used for the Swiss Grand Prix until 1954, the year before the Swiss banned racing, this record stands unbeaten.

Alfa Romeo enjoyed a brief resurgence, with cars better suited to twisty circuits: Nuvolari won the Hungarian Grand Prix, Circuit of Milan, Coppa Ciano, and the Vanderbilt Cup, revived none too successfully on a "Micky Mouse" circuit at Roosevelt Field. The French Grand Prix did not take place because the ACF decided that if there were no Grand Prix cars to which French honour could be entrusted, they would run their premier race for sports cars. A Bugatti won that event, and the French proclaimed a victory for

reason. France was a spent force—the SEFAC had completed a few hesitant practice laps before the 1935 French Grand Prix, and an inelegant Bugatti monoplace (4.7-litre T50 engine in a T59 chassis) had made an ineffectual appearance. France waited for a new formula.

That new formula should have come in 1937. Regulations coupling capacity to a sliding scale of weights were announced in the autumn of 1936, too late for new cars to be designed and built. The life of the 750-kg formula was extended for a season. Both German teams, especially Mercedes, found more power, producing the most powerful engines to be used in road racing until the CanAm cars of the early 1970s.

While Auto Union increasingly relied on the talents of Rosemeyer in 1937, Mercedes's redoubtable team manager Alfred Neubauer carried out extensive tests, hoping to find an all-German team. Caracciola and von Brauchitsch were naturally retained, seemingly none too pleased with the third front-line choice, former mechanic Hermann Lang. As reserves, Neubauer selected Richard Seaman, an Englishman with a brilliant voiturette record, Christian Kautz, a Swiss, and Geofredo Zehender, an Italian.

Mercedes's considerably greater resources, added to the superior power of their engine, tilted the balance back in their favour. There were twelve races considered sufficiently important for the German teams to contest in earnest; seven fell to Mercedes that year and five to Auto Union. In those twelve principal events the best result for a non-German car was one third place, scored by Rex Mays in an

Peugeot L76

Ernest Henry was the fourth member of the team responsible for this milestone car, and is generally credited with putting the ideas of Boillot, Goux, and, above all, former Hispano-Suiza man Paul Zuccarelli, on paper.

The regulations for the 1912 Grand Prix did not restrict engine capacity, but in the Peugeot engine the principle of achieving more power by increasing capacity was set aside in favour of efficiency. The 7.6-litre unit, despite the handicap of a long stroke inherited from the stillborn 1911 Peugeot engine, produced 130 bhp at 2250 rpm compared with the 140 bhp at 1600 rpm obtained from the 14.1-litre engine in the Fiat, which finished second in the Grand Prix at Dieppe.

It was the first racing engine with two overhead camshafts operating four 45-degree valves per cylinder, and was combined with efficient hemispherical combustion chambers and good aspiration through generous valve overlap. Its block and head were integral, cast in iron. This engine was mounted in a separate subframe in the L76, while the transmission and running gear were orthodox.

SPECIFICATIONS
Peugeot L76   1912
Engine
Four-in-line
Bore × stroke: 110 mm × 200 mm
Capacity: 7598 cc
(113 mm × 184 mm, 7384 cc for Indianapolis in 1913)
Carburettors: one Claudel
Maximum power: 130 bhp at 2250 rpm

Transmission
Four-speed

Chassis
Pressed steel side members

Front suspension
Rigid axle, semi-elliptic springs, and friction shock absorbers

Rear suspension
Rigid axle, semi-elliptic springs, and friction shock absorbers

Brakes
Drum (rear wheels only) and transmission

Dimensions
Wheelbase: 108 in (2743 mm)
Front track: 54 in (1371 mm)
Rear track: 54 in (1371 mm)

eight-cylinder Alfa Romeo in the Vanderbilt Cup. There were just two minor successes for Alfa Romeo: Pintacuda beat the sole Auto Union in a race at Rio de Janeiro, and Auto Union sent only their number four driver Rudolf Hasse to the Milan Grand Prix, where he was soundly beaten by three Alfa drivers. The first of these was Nuvolari, but he was beginning to despair of ineffectual Alfas and late in the year, at the Swiss Grand Prix, he was to be seen in the cockpit of an Auto Union.

Lang gained his first victory at Tripoli, then won the Avusrennen in a streamlined Mercedes at the astonishing speed of 162.61 mph. Then Rosemeyer won the Eifelrennen and the Vanderbilt Cup, while Hasse won the Belgian Grand Prix from Stuck. But that result has to be seen in perspective. Only seven cars started and Mercedes had a bad day; those German cars may have been mightily impressive individually, but too often there was little obvious racing as a few of them spread around long circuits.

The grid for the German Grand Prix was unusually full, however, while the Eifel forests around the Nürburgring had their hordes of young campers, anticipating another German triumph, apparently orchestrated by Korpsfuhrer Huhnlein and his brownshirt cohorts. The race was bound to fall to one of five Mercedes or five Auto Unions, and the other sixteen cars were no more than grid fillers. The final order was indeed Caracciola, von Brauchitsch, Rosemeyer, but Ernst von Delius died after his Auto Union crashed. (He was actually the first driver to be killed in a racing accident in one of those German Grand Prix cars of the 1930s, which is quite remark-

able, since they had to be driven on the edge of loss of control, on narrow high-pressure tyres which were not forgiving of errors.)

Mercedes team-mates von Brauchitsch and Caracciola duelled at Monaco. Von Brauchitsch won and Caracciola set a lap record that stood for eighteen years. Rosemeyer won the Coppa Acerbo. Caracciola drew on all his artistry to win on a damp Bremgarten circuit, won again at Leghorn where the Italian Grand Prix was run, and then won again in the Masaryk Grand Prix.

Then the 750-kg formula ran out in England. Donington enterprise brought front-rank Grand Prix cars to England for the first time since the curious Grands Prix at Brooklands. (There simply had not been a road circuit available on the British mainland until Donington came into existence.) This Formule Libre event was one of the best races of the year. Rosemeyer won it, and it was his last race.

The formula which came into effect in 1938 attempted for the first time to equate supercharged and unsupercharged engines, allowing capacities of 3 and 4.5 litres respectively. This ratio was too close; the gap could not, for example, be bridged by the better fuel consumption and, therefore, fewer pit stops of the unblown cars, but it was a move in the right direction. It encouraged the French to return and the Italians to make another effort. Mercedes were well prepared. Auto Union were in disarray for they had considered withdrawing from motor sport after Rosemeyer's death in a speed record attempt. Delahaye and Talbot started to develop unsupercharged Grand Prix cars based on sports models. Delahaye was spurred on

MERCEDES

The name Mercedes recurs through the early years of racing. In 1906, when Grand Prix racing began, there were three Mercedes cars in the French Grand Prix. These 14,432 cc cars were 115 bhp, chain-drive monsters which achieved little (two placed tenth and eleventh) although Camille Jenatzy later finished fifth in the Vanderbilt Cup with one. In the 1907 Grand Prix developed versions, with engines producing 130 bhp, ran even less effectively. Victor Hémery finished tenth in the only one of the three cars to run the distance.

Something had to be done to restore a tarnished image, and for 1908 Paul Daimler designed a new car which was thoroughly tested before the Grand Prix. Its engine still followed the inlet over exhaust pattern, with its four cylinders cast in blocks of two, and its 12,781 cc producing 135 bhp. Christian Lautenschlager, driving his first race, won the 477-mile event at 69.05 mph. Two of these cars later went to the United States where Ralph de Palma won the 1912 Vanderbilt Cup and Elgin Trophy. In 1913, Pilette ran two in the secondary Grand Prix de France, where they were outclassed, but were of historical interest as the last mainline cars to race with chain drive.

In the 1908 French Grand Prix Mercedes's sternest opposition had come from Benz, a firm which was desperate to slough off the ultraconservative mantle conferred upon it by Carl Benz. Technically, their cars were more advanced than the Mercedes and if their leading driver, Victor Hémery, had not suffered eye injuries early in the race, Benz could well have beaten their German rival. As it was, their cars finished second, third, and seventh. The two marques did not meet at this level in Europe again. In 1926, they merged as Daimler-Benz, their cars being marketed as Mercedes-Benz.

Mercedes returned to Grand Prix racing in force in 1914. Full use was made of the Daimler company's aeroengine technology. Possible new features were tried in the cars, run by Pilette in 1913, and the Lyon circuit to be used for the 1914 race was painstakingly assessed—an approach which heralded a coming technical age of racing. Mercedes succeeded almost beyond expectation, the team scored a crushing one-two-three victory. But a decade was to pass before Mercedes ventured to contest a Grand Prix again.

Mercedes 1914
This was by no means an adventurous or advanced car. The design team under Daimler and Nallinger produced a sound machine within the capacity limit of 4.5-litres. The engine was made up of individually machined cylinders welded together, with an integral head, each with four 60-degree valves operated by rockers from a single overhead camshaft. It was rated at 115 bhp—the same power being extracted from its 4.5 litres as the 14.5 litres of the first Mercedes Grand Prix engine produced.

Transmission was through a separate four-speed gearbox to a live rear axle, with twin driving pinions to reduce wheelspin. The engine was mounted directly to the frame, which dropped between the wheels and was cross-braced at the cockpit. Overall, the car was low and purposeful, ideal for the daunting Lyon and Targa Florio circuits and for American tracks.

SPECIFICATIONS
Mercedes 4.5-litre   1914
Engine
Four-in-line
Bore × stroke: 93 mm × 165 mm
Capacity: 4483 cc
Single overhead camshaft
Maximum power: 115 bhp at 3200 rpm
Transmission
Four-speed
Chassis
Pressed steel side members, cross-braced
Front and rear suspension
Live axle, semi-elliptic springs, and face-cam shock absorbers
Brakes
Drum (rear wheels only) and transmission
Dimensions
Wheelbase: 112 in (2845 mm)
Front track: 52.5 in (1334 mm)
Rear track: 53 in (1346 mm)

by an early-season triumph when Réné Dreyfus beat the solitary Mercedes at the Pau season opener—in a snowstorm. The SEFAC qualified under the new rules, with its 2.8-litre supercharged engine, and was actually to complete two laps in a race. Completely out of touch with reality, Bugatti reworked the 1936 monoplace with a 285 bhp 3-litre engine to combat 400 bhp plus of the German cars. Alfa Romeo essayed three cars, an eight, a V-12, and a V-16, but lost Nuvolari for good when his 308 caught fire during practice at Pau. Maserati introduced their 8CTF which, given development resources, could well have challenged the German cars more often than it did.

Mercedes was dominant again in 1938, but only to the extent that they began to encourage their opponents to race lest the triumphs were too hollow. As it was, the Italians increasingly looked to the 1.5-litre voiturette class and in 1939 were to run such prestigious events as the Tripoli Grand Prix to its regulations. Moreover, international politics could hardly be ignored. During 1938, for example, Italian teams decided—or were directed—not to race in France.

The Tripoli Grand Prix finishing order was Lang, von Brauchitsch, Caracciola. That order was neatly reversed in the next event on the abbreviated 1938 calendar, the French Grand Prix. This race returned to the classic Reims circuit which had been used in 1932. But it was hardly a race: nine cars started, and by the third lap only three Mercedes and a pair of outpaced Talbots were still running.

At the German Grand Prix, Auto Union managed to muster four cars. One was driven by Nuvolari as the team began to put together an effective challenge to Mercedes. The race turned out to be the

only Grand Prix in the whole decade to be won by an English driver. Richard Seaman headed Lang (who was fast supplanting Caracciola as the leading German driver).

Lang and Caracciola won two Italian secondary races, but remarkably Giuseppe Farina placed an Alfa Romeo 316 second in both races. Once again Caracciola was master in a wet Swiss Grand Prix. Then at Monza, Nuvolari romped away with the Italian Grand Prix, winning by a full lap from Farina's Alfa while the only Mercedes to finish was third. The great Italian then wound up the season with another virtuoso drive, at Donington, where he beat Lang and Seaman.

There were still fewer races in 1939, and Lang confirmed his growing stature by winning four of them (the Belgian and Swiss Grands Prix, the Eifelrennen, and the Pau Grand Prix). Caracciola scored his last major victory in the German Grand Prix. Sadly, the Mercedes team also lost its most promising driver when Seaman was killed in a Belgian Grand Prix accident.

Auto Union took the other two races: H.P. Muller won at Reims as the field was decimated and Nuvolari won the Yugoslav Grand Prix a few hours after the outbreak of the Second World War. There were consolations for other marques: Talbot's unblown cars finished third and fourth in the French Grand Prix; Paul Pietsch actually led the German Grand Prix in a Maserati and finished third; and Farina, driving a 1.5-litre Alfa 158 voiturette, ran second for several laps of the Swiss Grand Prix.

The Alfa 158s were raced again in 1940, and were to become full-

DUESENBERG

Fred and August Duesenberg entered the automotive world designing and building Mason cars, then set up on their own in 1912, intending to concentrate on racing cars. In 1913, Duesenbergs, albeit still named Masons, placed ninth and thirteenth in the Indianapolis 500. A year later, Duesenbergs were tenth and twelfth. In 1915, Eddie O'Donnell took fifth place, and in 1916 Wilbur d'Alene was runner-up.

The practical straight-eight racing engine owed much to wartime aircraft engine work, and the experience gained by the Duesenberg brothers was shared by others, including Ernest Henry, former Peugeot designer. At Indianapolis in 1919, the Henry-designed straight-eight Ballots confronted the first straight-eight Duesenberg. Ballot got the best of that encounter; Albert Guyot placed one fourth while Tommy Milton's Duesenberg retired.

Duesenberg reworked their eight for the 1920-23 183-cu-in capacity limit (which coincided with the 1921-22 3-litre Grand Prix regulations). The result was a car which placed third, fourth, and sixth in the 500. Duesenbergs were second, fourth, sixth, and eighth in the 1921 500. That year there was another confrontation in the French Grand Prix. The other entries could be discounted. To the chagrin of the French, Duesenbergs led for twenty-three of the thirty laps. Jimmy Murphy eventually won by fifteen minutes from Ralph de Palma in a Ballot.

A refined version of the 183-cu-in, eight-cylinder engine came in 1922, ironically the year Jimmy Murphy won at Indianapolis in a Miller-engined 1921 Duesenberg (but a 100 per cent Duesenberg was second, followed by a Ballot and five more Duesenbergs).

In 1923, only one of three Duesenbergs even qualified at Indianapolis. The next year the brothers bounced back with a trio of supercharged cars, and one lasted the 500 miles to win. Peter de Paulo won the last 122-cu-in Indianapolis for Duesenberg in 1925, exceeding 100 mph (101.13 mph) at Indianapolis for the first time.

The brothers continued to build racing cars after Erret Lobban Cord bought their company in 1926. Duesenberg enjoyed a last Indianapolis victory in 1927, although their cars continued to gain places in the top ten at Indianapolis until 1934.

Duesenberg 3-litre
This was a most elegant car, mechanically novel in some details, but generally a sound racing machine. The straight-eight engine had only a single overhead camshaft and three valves per cylinder (the two exhaust valves were operated by a forked rocker). A twin-overhead camshaft version was produced in 1923. Initially, the car had cable-operated brakes (in some track races on the rear wheels only), but hydraulic four-wheel brakes were introduced almost immediately, and were the first to be seen in Grand Prix racing. The advantage these brakes gave drivers into corners was complemented by the flexibility of the engine when accelerating. These qualities more than compensated for the three-speed gearbox, which betrayed the track racing origins of this car.

SPECIFICATIONS
Duesenberg 3-litre 1921
Engine
Straight-eight
Bore × stroke: 63.5 mm × 117 mm
Capacity: 2997 cc
Single overhead camshaft
Maximum power: 115 bhp at 4250 rpm
Transmission
Three-speed
Chassis
Cross-braced channel side members
Front suspension
Rigid axle, semi-elliptic springs, and friction shock absorbers
Rear suspension
Live axle, semi-elliptic springs, and friction shock absorbers
Brakes
Drum
Dimensions
Wheelbase: 106 in (2692 mm)
Front track: 51 in (1295 mm)
Rear track: 51 in (1295 mm)

blown Grand Prix cars after the war. Meanwhile, Alfa Romeo built the first (and only) 162, with a 490 bhp V-16, which was never raced.

Inevitably, early postwar races were Formule Libre events for any machinery that had survived and was raceworthy. The first meeting was organized in the Bois de Boulogne in September 1945. The main event of the day provided a last noteworthy victory for Bugatti, a 4.7-litre monoplace driven by Jean-Pierre Wimille beating a pair of Talbots. Then, in 1946, the Alfa Romeos were brought out again and set the standard for front-line cars. They failed in their first race, but in the Grand Prix des Nations at Geneva they began a fabulous run of success.

The 158s were run by Alfa Corse (for in 1938 Ferrari had struck out on his own) and their immediate supercharged rivals were built by Maserati, while Talbot fielded the most effective unsupercharged cars. There was a variety of attempts to break into Grand Prix racing with projects which turned out to be lost causes. France had the CTA-Arsenal, with an engine designed by Lory of Delage fame, which broke its back axle at its only start, in the 1947 French Grand Prix. There was the ill-conceived BRM—those initials did not earn respectability for many years. Cisitalia resources were ludicrously overstretched in the 360 project; designed by the Porsche Buro, this was a mid-engined car in which two- or four-wheel drive could be selected by its driver, and had it run competitively anywhere (let alone dismally in an obscure Argentine event after the Cisitalia company had failed) it could have changed the course of racing car design. The E-type ERA made no impression at all. Alfa Romeo did

not develop or race their rear-engined 512—they had no need to.

Some of the familiar old circuits appeared on the calendar again—wide-open Reims, for the 1948 French Grand Prix, Monza and Monaco in the same year, Bremgarten, tricky in good conditions and highly dangerous in bad weather (the 1948 Swiss Grand Prix meeting cost the lives of Kautz and Varzi). The British discovered redundant airfields, with perimeter tracks which made acceptable quasi-road circuits. Among these, Silverstone was to become the most permanent and famous, and by the second half of the 1970s was to be the least-changed of all World Championship circuits.

The simple availability of racing venues in England, where before the Second World War there had been so few, coincided with an enormous upsurge of interest in motor racing, which transformed a sport that had been secondary and had never attracted a wide following. From the late 1940s, a whole generation of new drivers could enter a sport that was in tune with the times and no longer exclusive. Their need for events in which to compete led to an unprecedented growth in the national calendar, whereas Continental countries simply continued where they had left off.

The demand for cars led to the foundation of a racing machinery industry in Britain that was to supplant the existing Continental constructors. Moreover, a straightforward practical approach to building cars for a low-cost minor class was to lead to a revolution in racing car design: by the time the World Championships were firmly established, the first Formula Three was flourishing, and with few exceptions its cars were mid-engined.

ALFA ROMEO

The name is fundamental to forty-five years of Grand Prix history, so that when Alfa Romeo returned to World Championship racing in the late 1970s they could hardly be regarded as just another Formula One constructor's team. The image of the dark red cars of earlier years lingered long after each was outmoded.

Giuseppe Merosi designed a Grand Prix ALFA to the 1914 regulations, but this car was destined never to run in a Grand Prix. As Alfa Romeo, the company returned to racing immediately after World War I, but did not enter the Grand Prix arena until 1924. The Merosi-designed twin-cam six-cylinder P1 was completed in 1923, but discarded after Ugo Sivocci's fatal crash during practice for the Italian Grand Prix.

On behalf of Nicola Romeo, Enzo Ferrari was instrumental in persuading Vittorio Jano to leave Fiat to design the P1's successor. This P2 was to become the dominant car of the last two years of the 2-litre formula, 1924 and 1925, and did not fade away until 1930.

The Tipo A "twin-six" appeared in 1931, with two parallel straight-six engines, two linked gearboxes, and twin propeller shafts. It was potentially fast, but hardly practical, and while Campari did win the Coppa Acerbo in one, another factory driver, Luigi Arcangeli, was killed in a Tipo A accident. The 2.35-litre Monza version of the famous 8C sports car was turned to as an alternative for Grand Prix racing—Campari and Nuvolari shared victory in the 1931 Italian Grand Prix with one, private entrants gained some successes in secondary races with them, and in 1931 Scuderia Ferrari did their best to represent Alfa with 2.55-litre bored out versions—until it became only too obvious that they were no longer competitive.

In 1932, Alfa Romeo fielded the Tipo B, the supreme Grand Prix car of the traditional school. It won its first race, the Italian Grand Prix, and was defeated only twice during the rest of that season. Then, in 1933, Alfa Romeo was nationalized and withdrew from competition. Ferrari continued to represent the marque on a quasi-factory basis, and only when the 8Cs were being beaten too often were the Tipo Bs released to the Scuderia, to resume their winning ways. These seemed set to continue through 1934, when the cars

were only slightly modified to comply with the 750-kg formula. Win they did—in the absence of the German teams, and even against those teams when they first raced outside Germany—in the French Grand Prix. But inevitably Mercedes and Auto Union began to crush their opponents.

Nuvolari's victory in the 1935 German Grand Prix owed everything to his brilliance in overcoming the handicap of driving a Tipo B. Ferrari ventured the Bimotore derivative of the Tipo B, with one engine ahead of the cockpit and another behind it, in an attempt to match the power and speed of the German cars, but succeeded only at the expense of self-defeating tyre wear.

The first half-litre cars had been built by the Coopers, father and son, in 1946. They were totally unpretentious in design terms, and in their spindly appearance and conception those early Coopers looked like throwbacks to the cycle cars of a much earlier generation, and their design evolved only slowly. But they were built in surprising numbers; 500 cc racing became a forcing ground for drivers, and this British national class became an international formula, the first Formula Three, in 1950. Although Cooper-Norton domination was eventually to lead to a loss of interest, the ladder principal of three international formulae—One, Two, and Three—was established, and with minor variations (as when Formula Junior briefly took the place of Formula Three) has held good ever since.

Continental attempts to establish 1100 cc "voiturette" classes foundered, but the 2-litre Formula Two which came into effect in 1948 was a success. It was contested by thoroughly conventional front-engined cars, until the 1.5-litre Formula Two came in in 1957, when rear-engined Coopers set the pace. Again, and again unwittingly, this unpretentious little firm pushed designers towards a fundamental new approach to racing car layout.

Another change with the times came as America rediscovered road racing in the postwar years. At the time, this meant sports car racing. Track racing was inviolate, its pattern from short-oval midgets to Indy roadsters apparently set to continue forever. European Grand Prix cars were occasionally run at Indianapolis, none making any impression until Jack Brabham drove a mid-engined Cooper into ninth place at Indy in 1961. Ironically, two

World Champions, Jack Brabham and Mario Andretti, served their racing apprenticeships in the short-oval midgets, which are almost as far from the Grand Prix circus as the racing spectrum allows. There was, however, one even more improbable background for a future World Champion. That was the long-distance open-road races for modified production cars (almost invariably American sedans) in South America. This rough and tough brand of point-to-point racing centred on Argentina, and was in decline in the 1940s. But Juan Manuel Fangio, one of its leading drivers, was to become one of the three great World Champions. The widely varied forms of racing were beginning to relate as never before.

Meanwhile, the lordly Alfa Romeo 158s ruled the Grands Prix, the Maseratis, Talbots, and Ferraris breathless in their wake to pick up crumbs of results. Alfa Corse ran the 158s only four times in 1948 and invariably won. Trossi won the Swiss Grand Prix—his last victory—while Jean-Pierre Wimille won the French race, the Italian Grand Prix in Turin's Valentino Park, and headed an Alfa Romeo one-two-three-four in the full-length Grand Prix which marked the reopening of the Monza autodrome. A British Grand Prix was run at Silverstone, and was won by Luigi Villoresi in a Maserati 4CLT/48 at 72.28 mph. The revived Monaco Grand Prix fell to Giuseppe Farina in a Maserati at 59.74 mph, from a motley field. In Holland the Zandvoort circuit was opened with a race meeting organized by the British Racing Drivers Club. There was racing again at the Pedrables circuit in Spain, where Villoresi headed Reg Parnell in a Maserati triumph at the Penya Rhin Grand Prix. Villoresi also won

Alfa Romeo persisted, with the Tipo C in 1935, then with the V-12-engined 12C-36, in which Nuvolari beat the Germans in secondary races, but not in the Grandes Epreuves. The final fling under the 750-kg regulations was the 4.5-litre 430 bhp 12C-37, Jano's racing car swan song for Alfa Romeo—and a failure. In 1938, the company took its racing back under direct control, with Alfa Corse. Three cars were built to the 3-litre formula, with straight-eight-, twelve-, and sixteen-cylinder engines (308, 312, and 316). None was successful in mainline events, but meanwhile, at the behest of Ferrari, the most successful of all Grand Prix Alfas was unwittingly being created.

Alfa Romeo P2

The heart of this first successful Grand Prix Alfa was a twin-over-head camshaft straight-eight, with a gear-driven Roots-type super-charger. When it was introduced in 1924, it produced 134 bhp—fractionally more than the 2-litre Fiat 805 engine which it closely resembled. The following season this was increased to 154 bhp. The straight-forward chassis and semi-elliptic suspension were no more than adequate for this power output and were considerably modified when the cars were brought out again to run in Formule Libre events in the late 1920s.

Antonio Ascari drove a P2 to victory in its first race, at Cremona. Campari won the major race of 1924, the French Grand Prix at Lyon, and the team went on to gain a one-two-three victory in the Italian Grand Prix. Ascari set a 104.24 mph lap record at Monza that was to stand until 1931. In 1925, the P2s took first and second places in the Belgian and Italian Grands Prix, and were leading the French race when the team was withdrawn following Ascari's death. The P2s were successful in secondary events late in the decade. They became the first cars of a new team, Scuderia Ferrari, in 1930, the same year that Achille Varzi rounded off the P2's career with a flourish by winning the Targa Florio.

SPECIFICATIONS
Alfa Romeo P2
Engine
Straight-eight
Bore × stroke: 61 mm × 85 mm
Capacity: 1987 cc
Twin overhead camshafts
Roots-type supercharger
Maximum power: 154 bhp at 5500 rpm
Transmission
Four-speed
Chassis
Pressed steel side members
Front and rear suspension
Rigid axle, semi-elliptic springs, and shock absorbers
Brakes
Drum
Dimensions
Wheelbase: 103 in (2616 mm)
Front track: 51 in (1295 mm)
Rear track: 49 in (1245 mm)

secondary events at Albi, Pau, and Comminges and—with fellow Maserati driver Baron de Graffenried—headed Raymond Sommer's Ferrari in the Grand Prix des Nations at Geneva.

In hindsight, the French Grand Prix at Reims should have been the most memorable race, for the great Tazio Nuvolari raced a Grand Prix car for the last time (sharing with Villoresi the Maserati which finished seventh), while Fangio raced in a major Grand Prix for the first time (he retired), and, incidentally, Alberto Ascari drove in a third-placed Alfa Romeo 158 in his only race for the team which his father had led in the 1920s.

Alfa Romeo withdrew from racing in 1949. Funds were low (and there were mutterings about the misapplication of American aid), the experimental department was fully occupied with development work on production models, and three great Alfa drivers had died—Varzi in that crash at Berne, Count Trossi of cancer, and Wimille in a Simca-Gordini during practice for a secondary race at Buenos Aires.

Fangio took three early-season races in Maseratis and one in a Simca-Gordini. Then came the first British Grand Prix to use the Silverstone circuit in the form that has been so little changed ever since. It was won by de Graffenried in a Maserati at 77.31 mph. The Belgian Grand Prix attracted a much better entry, and was won by Louis Rosier in a Talbot, from the Ferraris driven by Villoresi, Ascari, and Whitehead. Then Ascari won for Ferrari at Berne, Chiron for Talbot at Reims, and Villoresi for Maserati at Zandvoort. Ascari won the Italian Grand Prix at Monza by a lap from Etan-

celin's Talbot, and the last race of the season was the Czechoslovakian Grand Prix, run over a shortened eleven-mile Masaryk circuit and won by independent Ferrari driver Peter Whitehead, the first Englishman to win a Grand Prix since 1938.

The 1949 season was the last in which some of the older cars were competitive—Cuth Harrison actually took sixth place at Monza with a prewar ERA—and as the competition was perhaps less intense and speeds were generally lower, it was a season overshadowed by the absent Alfa Romeo team.

Alfa was back in 1950, with more power extracted from the engine of the 158, and balanced strength in a trio of regular drivers, the famous three Fs: Giuseppe Farina had a relaxed straight arm style and was known as the perfectionist; fifty-two-year-old Luigi Fagioli was the veteran, less temperamental than he had been in the 1930s and accepting his number two role; Fangio was not an immediately popular choice for Italians, for there was still abundant national talent, but his nationality was soon to be forgiven, or forgotten. Once again the Alfa team won every race in which it was entered, and in 1950 the new World Championship ensured much more consistent support for the races which became scoring events than had been the case. (There were still many regional events for Grand Prix cars, which were sometimes contested by leading teams, as when Fangio took a single Alfa to San Remo at the beginning of the season, and duly won.)

Maserati and Talbot were fading and Ferrari was in the interim period of change from supercharged to unsupercharged engines.

ALFA ROMEO

The 1.5-litre voiturette class (equivalent to Formula Two in modern terms) was increasingly favoured by Italian constructors who were unable to break the German grip on the Grands Prix. Jano's erstwhile assistant, Gioacchini Colombo, was despatched to Modena to design an Alfa Romeo contender, and there the first Alfettas, Tipo 158s, were built, although they were never to be raced

by Scuderia Ferrari. In 1947, the 158 automatically became a Grand Prix car under the new regulations. The 158 had won its first race as a voiturette, and—albeit under the designation 159—it won its last race as a Grand Prix car thirteen years later. As a Grand Prix car it had an unbroken run of twenty-six victories. Alfa withdrew for the 1949 season, and in 1951 their cars were at last matched—by Ferrari.

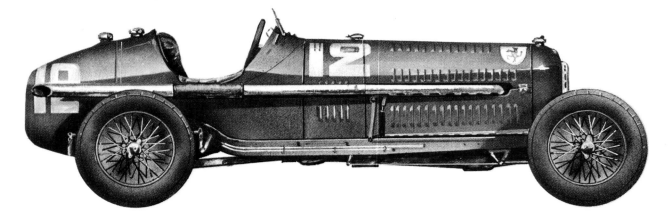

SPECIFICATIONS
Alfa Romeo Tipo B 1935
Engine
Straight-eight
Bore × stroke: 71 mm × 100 mm
Capacity: 3165 cc
Twin overhead camshafts
Twin Roots-type superchargers
Maximum power: 265 bhp at
5400 rpm
Transmission
Four-speed
Chassis
Pressed steel channel section
side members, cross-braced
Suspension
Front: Dubonnet independent
Rear: rigid axle, reversed
quarter-elliptic springs, and
friction dampers
Brakes
Drum
Dimensions
Wheelbase: 104 in (2640 mm)
Front track: 55 in (1400 mm)
Rear track: 53 in (1350 mm)

Alfa Romeo Tipo B P3
Few racing cars rate the overworked term "classic" as unquestionably as Vittorio Jano's Tipo B Alfa Romeo, known as the P3 to all but the most pedantic. It was at once in the Italian tradition, yet a forward-looking Grand Prix car—the first genuine single-seater, monoposto, in Grand Prix racing.

In a period of economic astringency, Jano necessarily followed proven lines in design. Effectively, he used an existing sports car engine, a straight-eight in two blocks of four cylinders, separated by a central

train of gears driving the overhead camshafts and twin superchargers (one on each side). In its initial 2.65-litre form, this produced 180 bhp and was eventually rated at 215 bhp; the 1934 B-2900 version gave 255 bhp, and the 1935 3165 cc version developed 265 bhp.

The final drive was highly original, with two angled propeller shafts taking the drive from a differential immediately behind the gearbox to twin bevels towards the outer ends of the rear axle. This arrangement reduced unsprung weight and made for easier access to the differential

for ratio changes. Chassis, running gear, and brakes derived from the Monza. The complete car had the virtue of light weight.

The lovely Tipo B became obsolescent when the formidable German cars of 1934 became raceworthy, but it was modified in attempts to meet this severe new challenge. As well as enlarged engines, Dubonnet independent front suspension, hydraulic brakes, and quarter-elliptic rear springs came in 1935. But there was little reward on the circuits, beyond Nuvolari's legendary victory in the 1935 German Grand Prix.

France had hopes for Amédée Gordini, who was building his first full Grand Prix cars, though these were to be overstressed and fragile. BRM completed the first of its ridiculously overcomplex Type 15s, in time for it to be exhibited at the British Grand Prix meeting.

The season saw the Ferrari challenge to Alfa Romeo steadily gaining strength. Alfa Romeo started with a one-two-three at Silverstone. Then Fangio saved the day for the team at Monaco by avoiding the wreckage of an extraordinary chain-reaction accident on the first lap, and finishing a lap clear of Ascari's Ferrari. In Belgium, Switzerland, and France the Alfas were first and second, although Raymond Sommer actually led the Belgian race in a Talbot, while the Alfas made their refuelling stops.

At Geneva, Ascari had a 4.1-litre car and emphatically served notice that the 158 was no longer invincible as he held second place for sixty-two of the sixty-eight laps, before retiring with engine failure. So for the all-important Italian race at Monza Alfa Romeo entered five cars—no team had been entered in such strength since the German Grands Prix of the 1930s—and moreover two of their cars were 159s, a still further developed version of the Alfetta. Ascari attacked the Alfas remorselessly throughout the race, first in his own 4.5-litre Ferrari then in Serafini's which he took over, and this only just lacked the all-out speed to enable him to catch Farina's Alfa in the closing laps.

Farina was the first World Champion, his team-mates Fangio and Fagioli were runners-up, and the scene was set for an Alfa Romeo-Ferrari battle in 1951. The other teams were to play

supporting roles, and even cars which looked promising on paper, such as the 4.5-litre V-12 Osca built by the Maserati brothers, were to be disappointing. The much-heralded BRMs were to run in just one championship race, finishing fifth and seventh at Silverstone.

Ferrari did little work on unsupercharged cars. Alfa Romeo did what they could with a design that was basically thirteen years old; the team relied on Farina and Fangio, had Sanesi and Bonetto as second strings, and Fagioli in reserve. Ferrari had Ascari and Villoresi, the vastly experienced Piero Taruffi, and a new man from Argentina, Froilan Gonzalez, who had made a great impression in local off-season races, driving a 2-litre Ferrari to defeat soundly a team of W163s, which Mercedes had overhauled and misguidedly sent out to contest Formule Libre events.

The first ranking Grand Prix of 1951 was run at Berne, where Fangio was master of the wet track, but Taruffi placed a Ferrari second. Farina won the Belgian race, from Ascari and Villoresi. The French result was similar, except that the winning Alfa was shared by Fagioli and Fangio. (The traditional and accepted practice of a leading driver taking over a team-mate's car if his own became unhealthy during a race continued until the World Championship arrangement no longer awarded half points for shared drives, when in any case the delays caused by stopping, changing driver, and restarting would have been an unacceptable handicap in faster, shorter races.)

The turning point came at the British Grand Prix at Silverstone, where the drivers of supercharged cars could not fully exploit the

There was a sports car effort in the early 1950s, and another more sustained sports racing campaign by Autodelta, the new competitions subsidiary, in the late 1960s and 1970s. That led to their cautious re-entry into Grand Prix racing, initially supplying engines to British constructors before another full Alfa Romeo Grand Prix team appeared.

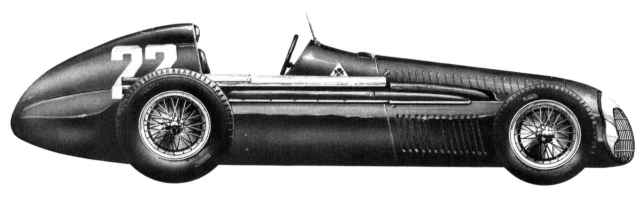

Alfa Romeo 158/159

Colombo's 158 (1.5 litres, eight cylinders) was an uncomplicated design, elegant and well-balanced. Its engine was a straight-eight, effectively half of the 316 V-16 Grand Prix engine, with the gear drive for its camshafts and ancillaries at the front (a departure for Alfa Romeo), and a single supercharger on the left. When first bench tested, it produced 180 bhp. When it was first raced (at Leghorn in 1938) it gave 195 bhp and in 1939 its output was raised to 225 bhp.

The 158 Alfetta was raced ten times before Italy entered the war. The cars, together with much Alfa

Corse equipment, spent the last two years of World War II hidden in the village of Melzo. They were then brought out and run almost as soon as racing resumed—and suffered, at St. Cloud, the only total team failure in the career of the 158. From 1947, however, they began the long run of success with a two-staged supercharger and 175 bhp as Grand Prix cars. By 1948, the 158/47 engine was producing 350 bhp.

When the 158s were raced again in 1950 and 1951, chief designer Orazio Satta and team manager Battista Guidotti faced an escalating challenge—simply to maintain a competitive edge with their ageing

design. More and more power was squeezed from the engine—370 bhp early in 1950, as much as 425 bhp on the bench in 1951, at ever greater costs in power absorbed by the supercharger drive (up to 125 bhp) and an eventual fuel consumption of 1.6 mpg. The frame was beefed up, brakes had to be improved (with this came the designation 159), and the de Dion axle, first tried experimentally in 1941, took the place of the swing axle arrangement at the rear. In the 1951 Spanish Grand Prix, the 159s—still looking much like the original Alfetta—were raced for the last time, winning and clinching their final championship.

SPECIFICATIONS
Alfa Romeo 158/159

Engine
Straight-eight
Bore × stroke: 58 mm × 70 mm
Capacity: 1479 cc
Twin overhead camshafts
Roots-type supercharger
Maximum power: 195 bhp at 7000 rpm in 1938, 225 bhp at 7500 rpm in 1947, 425 bhp at 9300 rpm in 1951

Transmission
Four-speed

Chassis
Tubular side members, four cross members

Front suspension
Independent by transverse leaf spring, trailing arms, and friction/hydraulic shock absorbers (hydraulic on 159)

Rear suspension
Swing axle, transverse leaf spring, friction/hydraulic shock absorbers (de Dion axle, radius arms, and hydraulic shock absorbers on 159)

Brakes
Drum

Dimensions
Wheelbase: 98½ in (2502 mm)
Front track: 50 in (1270 mm)
Rear track: 52 in (1321 mm)

maximum speed potential of their cars, while the torque characteristics of the Ferrari V-12 were well-suited to the circuit. Gonzalez rose to the occasion, and once Fangio stopped to refuel, the burly Froilan consolidated his lead, winning for Ferrari at 96.11 mph. So ended the incredible run of the Alfa 158, unbeaten since 1946. And Ferrari had effectively vanquished his old team, building the car which eventually beat the classic Alfa which he had conceived in a very different era of racing and for a very different purpose.

That year Grand Prix racing returned to the Nürburgring. Three Alfas retired early in the race and Fangio fought the Ferraris alone. Ascari won at 83.76 mph, while Fangio was second ahead of four more Ferraris. Each team then won a secondary race, Ferrari at Pescara, Alfa at Bari, before the Italian Grand Prix.

Ascari led, Fangio led, Ascari led again and ever more commandingly as the Alfas wilted at Monza. Eventually, only Farina was left, fighting a gallant but hopeless battle as a split tank streamed fuel behind his Alfa. Ascari won at 115.53 mph, from Gonzalez. Farina was third, followed by Villoresi and Taruffi. There was one more race, in Spain, where the Ferrari team lost before the start, choosing to use small rear wheels and thus overloading their tyres. Fangio won, gaining the World Championship, and took the record of the Alfa Romeo 158/159 to thirty-one victories in thirty-five races contested. It was to be the last Grand Prix victory for a supercharged car. And not until 1980 did an Alfa Romeo lead a Grand Prix again.

That Spanish Grand Prix was also the last race of any consequence under the first Formula One regulations. Alfa Romeo withdrew and race organizers opted for a Formula Two World Championship rather than face the prospect of an unbroken succession of Ferrari victories.

Ironically, the first year of Formula Two World Championship racing saw an unbroken succession of Ferrari victories. In summary, the Type 500 failed the team only once (in the 1953 Syracuse Grand Prix) and was beaten fairly and squarely only twice in two years. It was a relatively simple car, basically a Lampredi-designed four-cylinder engine in a chassis derived from the supercharged V-12 cars of earlier seasons. Ascari drove it to win two World Championships and contributed such a score of championship race victories to Ferrari's credit that this has never been matched.

In the overall Grand Prix story, these were years of technical sterility, but they were years full of racing interest. The possibility of success with relatively unsophisticated cars had already been shown to be attractive to a much more varied group of entrants than could aspire to Formula One racing. Ferrari had taken it seriously throughout, his cars initially challenged by A6G Maseratis, stripped sports Oscas and Cisitalias from Italy, and Gordini's Simca-based cars from France. The sports BMW 328 was the basis of the OBM in Britain, and of the first postwar German racing cars, built by Ernst Loof and known as Veritas in Germany, Meteor in other countries, and the AFM. Alta was the basis of John Heath's HWM. In 1952, HWM was to become the first British team in Grand Prix racing since the 1920s to run in Continental events.

Some of these efforts faded before Formula Two had Grand Prix

BUGATTI

Ettore Bugatti built exquisite racing cars, but few gained outstanding racing records, for his artistry was not complemented by an advanced technical philosophy. Few Bugattis stand out in Grand Prix history. However, one, the T35, is archetypal and vital, for with its derivatives it was a mainstay of racing through the late 1920s.

Bugatti had entered Grand Prix racing in 1922 with the odd "barrel-bodied" T30, powered by the eight-cylinder engine that had been taking shape through the preceding years. This engine, which was used with production running gear, was to become famous. The next season saw the odder "tank" variant essay into streamlining, with full-width bodywork and handling quirks to further handicap its drivers. The T35 made its debut in the 1924 French Grand Prix at Lyon. Aesthetically pleasing it may have been, successful it was not, so long as other major teams contested the Grands Prix, although in 1925 it won the first of five consecutive Targa Florio victories. It was, however, the first production Grand Prix car. In its T39, T35B, and T35C variants it was enormously successful through the years of racing's doldrums. These Bugattis won sixty-eight major races and hundreds of minor events.

The successor to the T35, in 1931, was the outwardly similar T51, notable as the first Grand Prix car with a twin-overhead-camshaft version of the Bugatti straight-eight. It won six prominent races, but the subsequent T54 and a four-wheel drive variant were failures. In 1933, to counter the growing Italian force in Grand Prix racing, Bugatti produced the T59. This was perhaps the last car of an age that was already past, an offset single-seater in the first monoplace decade. Although the T59 gained some respectable placings, its only Grand Prix victory came in Belgium in 1934. Derivatives with central cockpits did appear later, but Bugatti's Grand Prix effort had faded away in the face of the new German technological wave. In the late 1930s he concentrated on sports cars, although a single-seater was brought out to win a race in Paris in 1945 at the first postwar meeting.

In 1956, the name Bugatti appeared once more on a Grand Prix entry list, at Reims. The car was the T251, an advanced rear-engined spaceframe design by Gioacchino Colombo. It was underdeveloped—the effort behind it was woefully underfinanced—and it completed only eighteen undistinguished laps in the French Grand Prix. To purists it was hardly a Bugatti. The marque is best remembered for the elegant cars with horseshoe radiators of the vintage era.

status conferred on it in 1952, but others appeared. The main challenge to Ferrari was still to come from Maserati, with the A6GCM designed by Gioacchino Colombo and Alberto Massimino; this car was not ready until late in 1952. Meanwhile Enrico Platé's team was to campaign converted 4CLT/48s as Maserati-Platés. The Maserati brothers produced a neat little Osca, but lacked the resources to develop it fully.

That problem haunted Amédée Gordini, who had severed his last Simca connections. He claimed up to 180 bhp from his engine; that would have matched Ferrari, but about 155 bhp seemed to be the best actually achieved. Gordini's use of a live rear axle and torsion bars proved a false economy as it contributed to a high rate of transmission failures. Gordini tried hard to preserve a French presence in Grand Prix racing, but he would enjoy just one marked success.

A potentially more promising French car never even ran. The Sacha-Gordine was designed by Cesare Vigna and had a rear-mounted twin-overhead camshaft V-8 in a tubular chassis with independent torsion bar suspension all around. Like the Cisitalia 360 it owed much to Porsche practices, and, except in the detail that not even one car was quite finished, was a remarkably similar stillborn but prophetic exercise.

The British contribution was now to be reckoned with. HWM was in the forefront, with developed cars, powered by the Alta engine, which was naturally also used in the Alta car. Connaught had the Type A, a sound car in all respects except for its under-powered overhead-valve pushrod engine based on a Lea-Francis unit. There was the last of the ERAs, the G-type powered by a Bristol engine, which proved unsuccessful. There was a Frazer Nash, which really was a "special", and there was the ingenious Aston-Butterworth with its opposed-piston air-cooled four-cylinder engine. Above all, there was the Cooper T20, significant less for what it was than for its achievements when young Mike Hawthorn drove it with rare verve. It, too, used the pushrod overhead-valve Bristol "six" which derived from a BMW design, and unusually for Cooper this was mounted ahead of the cockpit. The T20 was light and handled well, which in the hands of Hawthorn went a long way to compensate for the modest 127 bhp produced by its engine. Hawthorn gained the best Grand Prix placings for a British car for many a year, third in the British Grand Prix, fourth in the Dutch and Belgian Grands Prix, in these Coopers.

There were also fourth and fifth places for Connaught in the British Grand Prix, fifth for Frazer Nash in Switzerland, and fifth for HWM in Belgium. There were even victories in secondary events—Paul Frère's in an HWM in the Grand Prix des Frontières, Lance Macklin's in an HWM in the Silverstone International Trophy.

These were not harbingers of a decisive swing against the un-broken domination of the three Continental nations, but the growing stature of British drivers could hardly be ignored. Hawthorn and Collins perhaps belonged to the old tradition of the hard-playing sporting amateur, but in Stirling Moss there was a professionalism which was not universally admired at that time.

Bugatti T35

This classic inherited its mechanical features from the T30. The single-overhead-camshaft three-valve (two inlet, one exhaust) straight-eight was developed from an optimistic claimed power output of 90 bhp in the T30 to 95 bhp at the introduction of the T35. In itself that was hardly adequate, but the T35 was light and compact, had excellent handling and roadholding qualities, which in part compensated for its power deficiency. The frame was rigid, with main members varying in depth according to anticipated loadings, and stiffened transversely by the engine and cross tubes at the rear. Bugatti used a tubular axle and semi-elliptics at the front, reversed quarter-elliptics and radius arms at the rear, integral brake drums, and unique light alloy wheels with flat spokes. While the basic car changed little, the engine was substantially uprated during the next five years, especially when Bugatti adopted supercharging, introducing it on the 1.5-litre T39 and retaining it in the T35B (2.3 litres) and T35C (2 litres).

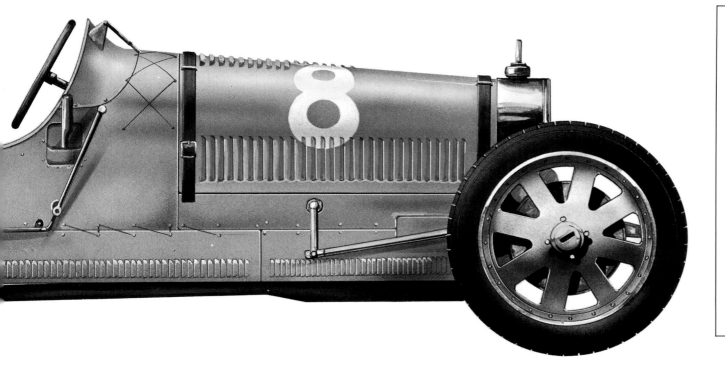

SPECIFICATIONS
Bugatti T35 1924
Engine
Straight-eight
Bore × stroke: 60 mm × 88 mm
Capacity: 1991 cc
Single overhead camshaft
Carburettors: two Zenith
Maximum power: 95 bhp at
5000 rpm on introduction,
later with Roots-type supercharger,
135 bhp at 5300 rpm

Transmission
Four-speed

Chassis
Channel side members, cross-braced

Front suspension
Rigid axle and semi-elliptic springs

Rear suspension
Live axle, quarter-elliptic springs and radius arms, and friction shock absorbers

Brakes
Drum

Dimensions
Wheelbase: 94 in (2388 mm)
Front track: 49 in (1245 mm)
Rear track: 47 in (1194 mm)

French prospects hardly looked rosy, although there was one triumph. Most of the series of eight Grands Prix de France, of which the Rouen race was *the* French Grand Prix, were run at slow circuits to which the Ferrari Tipo 500 was admirably suited. But Reims was potentially as fast as ever, as the village of Geux and its right-angle corner were bypassed. That Grand Prix was led from flag to flag by Jean Behra in a Gordini, unchallenged by Farina in a Ferrari, who finished a distant second. That victory, albeit not in a World Championship race, was the last for an all-French equipe for two decades.

The seven World Championship Grands Prix in 1952 fell to Ferrari. Ascari won in Belgium, France, Britain, Holland, Germany, and Italy, while Piero Taruffi won the Swiss Grand Prix. Only at Monza did the team really have to fight, against an on-form Gonzalez in a Maserati. He led until he had to stop for fuel, then battled back up the order to finish second. Race speeds were naturally lower than in 1951, although not much lower at the more sinuous circuits. (Ascari's winning speed of 82.2 mph at the Nürburgring in 1952 compared with his speed of 83.7 mph over a slightly longer distance in 1951.)

Driving strengths were evenly matched in 1953 as the Maserati challenge to Ferrari built up. Ferrari had Ascari, Farina, Villoresi, and Hawthorn. Maserati had Fangio, Gonzalez, Marimon, and Bonetto. Those eight names are interesting. Apart from Ascari, the Italians were ageing. Maserati relied on three Argentines, while Mike Hawthorn was the first English driver to be regularly contracted by one of the leading Continental teams since the 1930s.

There were other teams, to be left behind by the battling Italian marques to pick up the minor placings or the minor races—Elie Bayol won at Aix-les-Bains with an Osca, and the evergreen Louis Chiron gained two second places in non-championship events with a revised Osca. Gordini still lacked resources, while HWM had to race wherever and whenever possible to balance their budget and thus had no time for development, and little even for between-races overhauls (and it showed in their results). Cooper refined their design in the T23, which in the hands of Moss sometimes challenged the Italian teams, but was unreliable.

Ferrari had reliability, while for Maserati Gioacchini Colombo had concentrated on engine development rather than the car's rudimentary suspension, so that it was not an all-rounder but suited to the better-surfaced and faster circuits.

Ascari won both the early-season Argentine races, and when the championship season got under way, he won with ease at Zandvoort. But he took the lead at Spa only after Gonzalez and Fangio had retired, for their Maseratis had the best of the Ferrari on the fast Belgian circuit. (Ascari's winning speed was 112.47 mph.)

Reims was the setting for the first of the two outstanding races of the Formula Two Grands Prix, indeed of any postwar Grands Prix to that time. The Maserati ploy of starting Gonzalez with half-filled tanks—perhaps to gain a sufficient lead to allow time for refuelling, perhaps in the hope he could lure the Ferrari drivers to overstress their engines—failed and his pit stop dropped him to fifth place.

DELAGE

Louis Delage committed his company to racing in secondary classes in the first decade of the twentieth century, and to Grand Prix racing in 1913, when his cars finished fourth and fifth in the French Grand Prix. (Only a bizarre incident after a tyre failure cost one of his drivers victory—Guyot's riding mechanic jumped out before the car stopped and was run over by one of his own rear wheels.) Two of these 1913 cars then finished first and third in the 1914 Indianapolis 500, but the more advanced 1914 Grand Prix Delage, with twin-overhead camshaft, desmodromic-valve engines, and four-wheel brakes, was unsuccessful.

Delage returned to the Grands Prix in 1923 with a remarkable 2-litre V-12, which was developed to a competitive state through the next two seasons. That was followed by Albert Lory's superb 1.5-litre straight-eight, successful in Grands Prix and later in private hands; Chiron placed one seventh at Indianapolis in 1929, and in 1936 Richard Seaman drove this car to several voiturette victories. Delage abandoned racing in 1928 and after the company had merged with Delahaye in 1935 its name was applied to sports cars which enjoyed some race success.

Delage 1.5-litre
Delage abandoned their V-12 for the 1926-27 formula. Lory designed a supercharged straight-eight in its place. The engine was efficient despite its weight, with a one-piece crankshaft running in ten split roller races, while there were no less than sixty-two ball and roller bearings in the complete unit. It was installed in a light, flexible chassis, and in the 1926 version its exhaust made the cockpit unbearably hot. Consequently, for 1927 the whole engine was turned 180 degrees. In this form it proved unbeatable. Louis Delage then sold these exquisite cars, which he had commissioned regardless of cost.

SPECIFICATIONS
Delage 1.5-litre   1926
Engine
Straight-eight
Bore × stroke: 55.8 mm × 76 mm
Capacity: 1488 cc
Twin overhead camshafts
Carburettor: one Cozette
Roots-type supercharger
Maximum power: 170 bhp at 8000 rpm
Transmission
Five-speed
Chassis
Channel section, cross-braced frame
Front suspension
Rigid axle, semi-elliptic springs, and shock absorbers
Rear suspension
Live axle, semi-elliptic springs, and shock absorbers
Brakes
Drum
Dimensions
Wheelbase: 99 in (2502 mm)
Front track: 53 in (1346 mm)
Rear track: 53 in (1346 mm)

From the time he stopped, Fangio and Hawthorn locked into a duel for the lead, and with two laps to go they crossed the line wheel to wheel. Then the experience of Fangio seemed to tell, but he slid wide out of the last corner and as the Maserati's second gear was inoperative Hawthorn beat him on acceleration. He held on to the finishing line, winning by an official second after two and a half hours of racing, while Gonzalez was third, less than a second behind Fangio.

The Ferrari drivers fought off the Maserati challenge at the next three championship races. Ascari won at Silverstone (at 92.97 mph) from Fangio, Farina, Gonzalez, and Hawthorn; Farina won the German Grand Prix (at 83.89 mph) from Fangio and Hawthorn; Ascari led his team-mates Farina and Hawthorn to a Ferrari one-two-three in the Swiss Grand Prix.

The championship season reached its end in a Monza climax—a ferocious Ferrari versus Maserati battle over the entire race distance. The lead changed many times, but as at Reims the result was decided in the last corner. Ascari led into it and under such pressure that he had to try to change his line in the corner to go around a back marker. His Ferrari was already at the limit of adhesion, and it slid, half spun, and was rammed by Marimon's lapped Maserati. Fangio took to the grass to try to avoid them, and he slipped through from third place to win. Farina recovered to finish second, Villoresi and Hawthorn followed, and then came two Gordini drivers (Trintignant and Mieres), lapped but giving Gordini his best championship result of the year.

The two years of Formula Two Grands Prix had been more successful than many thought possible when this formula was brought in as a poor substitute for "the real thing". In most respects the racing had been better than in preceding years, so that the surprisingly slight drop in speeds was noticeable only to avid stopwatch handlers. The new Formula One regulations were known, of course, and both Ferrari and Maserati seemed well prepared. Gordini had little option but to continue his shoestring operation towards Formula One oblivion. The British teams were for the moment down and out and their participation in the first year of the new formula was to be negligible. However, there were two heavyweight newcomers, Mercedes-Benz and Lancia.

The regulations were deceptively simple: maximum engine capacity was 2.5 litres in unsupercharged form or 750 cc in supercharged form; race distance 300 kilometres (186 miles) or three hours. Only one supercharged car ever started in a race, where its performance was abysmal and it was never seen again. As if to contradict the simplicity of the regulations, the most successful car was anything but simple. But stunning though the technology of that Mercedes W196 was, there was nothing fundamentally new in its conception, and a more conscious effort to push on the frontiers of racing car design was Vittorio Jano's Lancia D50 which appeared late in the 1954 season.

The Italians had good reason to worry about Mercedes, for the German team had already shown its strength in sports car events. Their Grand Prix car, the W196, had much in common with a new sports racer. In fact, when the W196 first appeared, it looked

MILLER

Between the World Wars, Miller was one of the magic names of United States track racing, although the true identity and sheer proliferation of Miller cars were too often lost under sponsors' names. The occasional performances of his cars on road circuits suggested, however, that with more sustained effort Harry Armenius Miller could have had great influence in Grand Prix racing. He was one of the rare innovative racing car designers—laying down outlines to be translated into metal by his talented partners, Leo Goosens and Fred Offenhauser. The first Miller racing engine, a 4.7-litre four, appeared in 1916. The first of his famous eights was built six years later. This was a 2999 cc unit, and for the 122-cu-in formula, which came in at the beginning of 1923, Miller designed the classic 1983 cc engine. That year six of the first seven cars at Indianapolis were Millers. This was followed by the world's first successful front-wheel drive racing car which was also the first with a de Dion axle, and the exquisite 1.5-litre 91 engine. Although he failed as a businessman, Miller continued to design unorthodox racing machinery through the 1930s.

Miller 91
The heart of the 91 was a highly refined 1478 cc supercharged straight-eight which initially developed 154 bhp, but was uprated during its life to produce more than 250 bhp, which was advanced by world standards.

The engine was installed in a slim, single-seater body. Most unusually, the 91 was offered in rear-wheel or front-wheel drive forms, since the engine could be turned through 180 degrees and the gearbox was positioned to suit either arrangement. The 91 dominated the 1926 Indianapolis 500 and was used in United States track racing for many years, although the centrifugal supercharger, three-speed gearbox, and inadequate brakes limited its road circuit potential.

SPECIFICATIONS
Miller 91   1929
Engine
Straight-eight
Bore × stroke: 55.5 mm × 76.2 mm
Capacity: 1478 cc
Twin overhead camshafts
Carburettors: Miller or Winfield
Miller centrifugal supercharger
Maximum power: 154-250 bhp at 7200-8000 rpm

Transmission
Three-speed

Chassis
Channel section cross-braced frame

Front and rear suspension
Rear wheel drive: rigid axle, semi-elliptic springs, and shock absorbers front and rear

Brakes
Drum, front and rear

Dimensions
Wheelbase: 100 in (2540 mm)
Front track: 52 in (1320 mm)
Rear track: 52 in (1320 mm)
Dry weight: 1415 lb (642 kg)

Tyres
Firestone

Variants
Front wheel drive: front de Dion type axle, quarter-elliptic springs and friction dampers, rigid rear axle, semi-elliptic springs, and friction dampers

like a sports car to many people, for it had enclosed wheels. Aerodynamics still meant no more than "streamlining", hence the *stromlinienwagen,* and as far as frontal area was concerned, the Stuttgart design team had reduced it about as far as possible with a front-engined car. The engine was not outstandingly powerful, but Mercedes made much greater efforts than the Italian designers to ensure that power was put on the road efficiently through swing-axle suspension, and used inboard brakes to reduce unsprung weight.

Vittorio Jano was not a design team, yet through engineering intuition this great designer came up with a car that equalled the Mercedes in novelty and in racing and development potential (although events were to conspire to prevent this being carried through). His D50 design was the first Grand Prix car to be built by Lancia. It had an ultralight chassis of small-diameter tubes and the engine crankcase and block were stressed to play a load-bearing role. Fuel and oil were carried in outrigged sponsons between the wheels on each side, so that this variable weight was within the wheelbase and handling did not change through a race (as it did with the traditional tail fuel tank), and the airflow in the notoriously turbulent area between the wheels was smoothed.

During the early-season absence of Lancia the Italians closed ranks against the threat from north of the Alps, and contracted Lancia drivers Ascari and Villoresi were "loaned" to Maserati. Meanwhile, Fangio was free to drive a Maserati in the early-season races while he waited for the Mercedes to which he was committed.

The first Grand Prix of the new formula was run in Argentina and was won by its champion, Fangio, from the Ferraris driven by Farina and Gonzalez. Back in Europe, only fourteen cars started in the Belgian Grand Prix, won by Fangio from Trintignant (now a Ferrari driver) and Stirling Moss in a private Maserati 250F.

Mercedes chose Reims for their return, and this was devastating for the other teams. Fangio took the pole position with ease, a whole second faster than Ascari in the best Italian car; between them on the front row of the grid was Karl Kling in another Mercedes. Confidence in the W196 was such that although there were no front-rank German drivers, preference could be given to Germans to support Fangio, the team's one ace. Although Hans Herrman soon retired the third Mercedes as its engine trailed smoke across the shimmering fields, Fangio and Kling dominated the race, taking the flag in team order one-tenth of a second apart. Behind them the field was shattered. Only seven of the twenty-one starters finished, with third-placed driver Manzon a lap down in a Ferrari.

The next race, however, showed that this Mercedes team was not going to be all-conquering. On a damp day at Silverstone the drivers of the W196 found handling a little uncertain and the enclosed front wheels meant that they could not place their cars precisely in corners marked by oil drums. Fangio fought hard, but gained only a fourth place at the end behind Gonzalez, in a Ferrari 625, Hawthorn, and Marimon.

That could not be allowed to happen at the Nürburgring, and one of the four cars Mercedes lined up for the German Grand Prix was an open-wheel W196, for Fangio. Nevertheless, Gonzalez led the race in

MERCEDES-BENZ

Mercedes maintained their interest in racing in the early 1920s, using the old 1914 cars, building new 1.5-litre and 2-litre competition cars, and developing the supercharger. A factory team was run at Indianapolis in 1923 and gained eighth and eleventh places. The company re-entered the Grand Prix arena in 1924 in Italy, although their cars did not start after Zborowski's fatal accident during practice. Benz were less ambitious over the whole period, but in 1923 they produced the astonishing Tropfenwagen—rear-engined with an inadequate twin-overhead camshaft six-cylinder engine, swing axle independent rear suspension, and inboard rear brakes. It was run in only one Grand Prix, at Monza, where the team gained fourth and fifth places.

The initial Mercedes-Benz accent was on ponderous sports cars, in which drivers of the calibre of Rudolf Caracciola achieved great feats, but which were increasingly outmoded by the early 1930s. In mid-1933, ideas about Grand Prix cars took shape as a programme got under way and a design team headed by Dr. Hans Niebel started work. The Grand Prix world, which had become too set in its ways, was about to be dragged into a new era.

The designers rejected the Benz experiment and, unlike Auto Union, their rivals, they were consequently to experience problems with excess frontal area and, more significantly, keeping within the 750 kg maximum weight limit. Once the white paint had to be scraped off to achieve this, hence was born the "Silver Arrow" appellation beloved of the popular press. In January 1934, the first W25 was completed. It was a clean, uncluttered car. After the bedding-in problems of car and team were resolved it was a winner. It did in fact win its debut race, the 1934 Eifelrennen, then the team failed completely in the French Grand Prix and won only three more races that year, the Italian and Spanish Grands Prix and at Pescara.

In 1935, however, Mercedes were beaten only four times. Rudi Caracciola won the Eifelrennen and the Belgian, French, Spanish, Swiss, and Tripoli Grands Prix. Luigi Fagioli won the Monaco Grand Prix, Penya Rhin, and the Avus races. Then the pendulum swung again, for the 1936 car with its short wheelbase and 4.7-litre

M25E engine was a disaster. Only the Monaco and Tunis Grands Prix fell to Mercedes, for handling was poor, and the engine was overstressed. In midseason the team was withdrawn. The legend of Mercedes-Benz invincibility is brittle. They were back on top in 1937. Otto Schilling had taken over when Hans Niebel died late in 1934, and Rudolf Uhlenhaut, a brilliant young engineer, was drafted into the team as a troubleshooter. He was to be closely associated with all high-performance Mercedes for the next three decades.

The W125 had a longer wheelbase and revised suspension, to improve roadholding and get more of the power onto the road. The engine was from the F-series (or M125) straight-eight with its revised supercharger layout. Actual output depended on compression ratio and fuel "brew" used: 575 bhp was realistic in a late-1937 race engine, and 600 bhp quite feasible with a more exotic fuel blend, while 646 bhp was once achieved, albeit not in a racing car. With a streamlined body and high gearing for track racing at Avus, the W125 had a top speed of 210 mph. With this formidable machine, Mercedes-Benz regained the upper hand, and won seven 1937 races to Auto Union's five; Caracciola won the German, Swiss, Italian, and Czechoslovakian Grands Prix, Hermann Lang, a rising star, won at Avus and Tripoli, and a mildly disgruntled Manfred von Brauchitsch won at Monaco.

For the 3-litre formula in 1938-39 Mercedes's opposition was weaker than for many years, so that the W154 was seldom beaten in 1938 despite its shortcomings. It was beaten only twice in 1939 (by Nuvolari in an Auto Union D-type), when it had become an outstanding combination of power and efficiency. The team went record breaking and put a bigger effort into hill climbing as the number of races dwindled. Races that developed into demonstrations of German superiority (often with little visible racing) were no longer popular with race organizers. And there were squalid political overtones.

One of the 1939 cars turned up at Indianapolis in 1947 and 1948, but its complexities defeated its American crew. Two were restored to raceworthy condition and sent to contest Argentine Formule

its early stages, but he had been demoralized by the death of his compatriot Onofré Marimon in practice, and so he stopped to hand his Ferrari over to Hawthorn. By that time Fangio was in the lead, and he duly won, from Hawthorn, Trintignant, and Kling. The winning speed, 82.77 mph, was actually slower than in 1953, but the race was four laps longer.

The front of the grid for the last Swiss Grand Prix showed that Mercedes could not be complacent—Gonzalez, Fangio, Moss; Ferrari, Mercedes, Maserati. Fangio led from flag to flag, though, from Moss, then Hawthorn, then Gonzalez at the end as the other two retired. Monza demanded a great effort from the Italian teams, of course, and surprisingly the streamlined Mercedes enjoyed little or no advantage on this fast circuit. Ascari led in a Ferrari. When he retired, Moss—his Maserati now under the wing of the factory team—took command of the race. It was only his engine failure that let Fangio through to a lucky win, from Hawthorn and a Ferrari shared by Gonzalez and Maglioli. And Peter Collins drove a car called a Vanwall through to a seventh place.

There remained only the Spanish Grand Prix, where the Lancia D50 at last appeared, and Ascari drove it away from the field for nine laps. He retired, as did his team-mate Villoresi, but the racing world was impressed. The driver who inherited Ascari's lead was not one of the aces, but Harry Schell in a Maserati; he lost the lead to Trintignant, and when that Ferrari expired Mike Hawthorn went through to win the race. Luigi Musso was second in a Maserati, Fangio a struggling third.

On the evidence of 1954, Mercedes could not look forward with confidence to the new season, and could no longer indulge in the luxury of uncompetitive German drivers. Neubauer therefore signed Moss to give Fangio the sorely needed backing of another top-line driver. That was a blow to Maserati, who recruited Jean Behra. Ferrari's four-cylinder cars were outclassed and there was dissension within the Scuderia (not for the first time, nor the last). Lancia engaged one of the few up-and-coming Italians, Eugenio Castellotti, as number two to Ascari.

The prospect was for a great season, with Lancia, Maserati, and Mercedes all "in the hunt", Ferrari, Gordini, and perhaps even Vanwall in contention for the lesser placings, while Connaught was showing promise (and like Vanwall used disc brakes) and even a new BRM was at last taking shape. Yet the most significant car of the year was little noticed at the time—after all, it started from the back of the British Grand Prix grid and retired before half distance. It was a Cooper, an adapted sports car with all-enveloping bodywork and a none-too-powerful 2.2-litre engine. But it was the first mid-engined car to start in a Grand Prix since 1939. Its driver was Jack Brabham, an Australian with a rather odd style.

Until June the season was normal. Fangio was one of the few drivers not affected by the intense heat in Argentina and duly won his home Grand Prix again. The customary early season races were run in Europe. Ascari won for Lancia at Naples and Turin, factory or private Maserati 250Fs elsewhere (Behra at Bordeaux and Pau, Simon at Albi, Collins at Silverstone). The Monaco Grand Prix was

Libre events in 1951: Fangio and Kling drove the cars, but were defeated by Gonzalez in a 2-litre Ferrari. So they were reserved for demonstrations, while Mercedes's postwar comeback was concentrated on sports cars, despite the existence of a car which, like the Alfa 158, had been designed as a prewar voiturette and fitted the postwar Grand Prix regulations. That 1.5-litre V-8 W165 had been created to beat the Italians in the 1939 Tripoli Grand Prix. It did, but was never raced again.

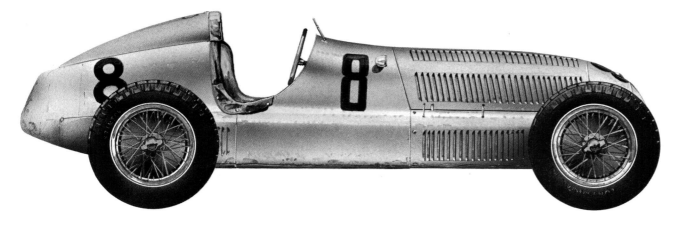

Mercedes-Benz W25

The target for the W25 design team was the known quantity of the early-1930s Italian cars, and this was more than met. Outwardly, their car was far less unconventional than the Auto Union, but the design brought together for the first time in a conventional, front-engined, Grand Prix car the elements of independent front and rear suspension, a gearbox

and differential attached to the frame and therefore sprung weight, and hydraulic brakes. The M25 straight-eight followed orthodox Mercedes practice, in that individual cylinders, in two pairs, were combined with a welded-on water jacket. It proved to have great development potential: in its first 3.36-litre form it gave 325 bhp early in 1934; 354 bhp late that year; the 3.71-litre

M25AB developed 398 bhp, and the 3.99-litre M25B later in 1935 gave 430 bhp; the 4.3-litre M25C had a 462 bhp maximum output, and in the 4.7-litre M25E this was up to 494 bhp in 1936. Keeping ahead in the power race was simple compared with meeting the weight limit. Wherever possible holes were drilled in the chassis and ancillary components for lightness.

SPECIFICATIONS
Mercedes-Benz W25 1934
Engine
Straight-eight
Bore × stroke: 78 mm × 88 mm
Capacity: 3360 cc
Twin overhead camshafts
Maximum power: 325 bhp at 5800 rpm

Transmission
Four-speed

Chassis
Box section main members, cross-braced

Front suspension
Independent by wishbones, coil springs actuated by cranks, and friction shock absorbers

Rear suspension
Swing axles, quarter-elliptic springs, and friction shock absorbers

Brakes
Drum

Dimensions
Wheelbase: 107 in (2718 mm)
Front track: 58 in (1473 mm)
Rear track: 55 in (1397 mm)

revived in May, when Fangio and Moss both led and retired, Ascari crashed into the harbour and swam away from his Lancia, and Maurice Trintignant was the surprise winner in a Ferrari, from Castellotti. Then Fangio and Moss took first and second places for Mercedes in Belgium.

By then the season had started to go sour. Four days after his Monaco accident, "Ciccio" Ascari attended a Ferrari sports car test session at Monza. He was still on good terms with Ferrari, and his request to try a car could not be denied. After two laps he crashed and was thrown from the cockpit. He died in an ambulance, as his father had. Alberto Ascari's death left a void in Italian racing and it was the last straw for the Lancia Grand Prix team, already in jeopardy because of Lancia's desperate financial position. The D50 raced as a Lancia just once more, when Castellotti borrowed one to run independently in the Belgian Grand Prix. Later in the year the cars were handed over to Ferrari, together with a shrewdly arranged Fiat subsidy guaranteed for five years.

Motor racing's blackest day came at Le Mans on June 11, when Pierre Levegh crashed into a spectator area, his sports Mercedes disintegrating upon contact with the banking, which launched it into the crowd. This tragedy sent shock waves through the world of motor sport. The French, German, Spanish, and Swiss Grands Prix were abandoned—indeed all forms of motor racing were banned in Switzerland, which has since seen only hill climbs and a "Swiss Grand Prix" run at Dijon in France—while all racing in France was cancelled for the rest of 1955. Several secondary regional Grands

Prix were never run again and the American Automobile Association revoked its control of the sport in the United States.

There was obviously concern about circuit safety, although with hindsight the reviews were probably not deep enough. Contrarily, those British circuits contrived on redundant airfields, which were part way to autodromes and which blinkered purists like to decry because they were not, and are not, "the real thing", now appeared in a much better light.

Although Mercedes's cars were reckoned to have a five-year development life, the company decided to withdraw from racing at the end of the season. As far as Grands Prix were concerned, that meant after three more championship races. In Holland, only a week after the Le Mans Tragedy, Fangio and Moss were first and second. Then the British Grand Prix was run for the first time on a curious circuit at Aintree, and the Mercedes team finished one-two-three-four. Diplomatically, Moss was allowed to win this one, from Fangio, Kling, and Taruffi. Then it was Monza time, for the first Grand Prix on the combined banked track and road circuit, where the D50s should have appeared as Ferraris, but were withdrawn after throwing tyre treads in practice. Fangio won that Italian Grand Prix at 128.42 mph in a streamlined Mercedes, from Taruffi in another Mercedes, Castellotti (Ferrari), and Behra (Maserati).

There was an autumn flurry of activity on British circuits. The two main races, at Aintree and Oulton Park, were won by Roy Salvadori and Moss, both driving Maseratis. But the new BRM P25 driven by Peter Collins showed surprising speed at Oulton Park,

MERCEDES-BENZ

Mercedes-Benz W154
This was the most sophisticated front-engined car of the prewar era, a distinction it shared with its little W165 brother until the W196 appeared in 1954. For their 3-litre power unit, Mercedes turned to a V-12, with its supercharger compressing the fuel/air mixture rather than just air to the carburettor as had previously been Mercedes practice, and with two-stage supercharging in 1939.

The M154 initially produced 425 bhp, rising to 470 bhp in its highest state of tune in 1938. Piston trouble was persistent, however, and this engine did tend to ooze oil. It was still used in 1939, together with the interchangeable M163 which had a new block and crankcase, numerous beefed-up details and in-series two-stage supercharging, with the larger of the two Roots-type units blowing

into the smaller. The peak power of the M163 was 483 bhp.

The W125 chassis and suspension were carried over to the W154, which was notably soft by previous racing standards. With the intention of reducing overall height, the engine was mounted at an angle to the centre line of the car and canted down towards the rear, from where the transmission ran alongside the driver to a five-speed gearbox/final drive (transaxle). In 1939, the brakes were "turbo-finned" to assist cooling and so remedy another 1938 deficiency. The 1938 bodies were neither handsome nor outstandingly effective, and the 1939 version (dubbed but not designated W163) had much sleeker lines, which concealed a revised weight distribution achieved by using two small, side fuel tanks as well as the saddle and tail tanks of 1938.

The Grand Prix comeback was in 1954, the first season of 2.5-litre formula racing, with a well-prepared team, a sensational car, and just enough misjudgement to encourage the others to keep trying. The W196 was costly and complex, but adequately backed financially and technically. It went to its first race, the French Grand Prix, wearing all-enveloping bodywork. That was fine for Reims (Mercedes were first and second), but it proved to be a handicap on circuits where drivers needed to see the wheels to judge their corner lines with absolute accuracy. Consequently, it was abandoned after the next race, save for the high-speed tracks of Avus and Monza.

There was a general feeling that Fangio carried Mercedes-Benz to the championship in 1954, for he won the French, German, Swiss,

SPECIFICATIONS
Mercedes-Benz W154   1938
Engine
60-degree V-12
Bore × stroke: 67 mm × 70 mm
Capacity 2962 cc
Twin overhead camshafts
(per bank)
Maximum power: 483 bhp at
7500 rpm

Transmission
Five-speed

Chassis
Tubular main side members

Front suspension
Independent by wishbones, coil
springs, and hydraulic shock
absorbers

Rear suspension
De Dion axle, torsion bars, and
hydraulic shock absorbers

Brakes
Drum

Dimensions
Wheelbase: 107 in (2718 mm)
Front track: 58 in (1473 mm)
Rear track: 55 in (1397 mm)

where Desmond Titterington took third place behind Hawthorn's Lancia-Ferrari in the Gold Cup. Then Harry Schell won a couple of minor Formule Libre races in a Vanwall at Castle Combe.

At the end of the season there was a real surprise. Connaught sent two cars to Sicily, to contest the Syracuse Grand Prix against front-rank Italian opposition. That seemed no more than another outing in the "jolly good sporting effort" spirit. But Tony Brooks—then virtually unknown outside British national racing—took one of the Connaughts into the lead sixteen laps before the end, and won the race by three-quarters of a minute from Maserati drivers Musso and Villoresi. That was the first victory for a British driver in a British Grand Prix car since 1924. The world of racing was astounded.

There was to be no overnight revolution, and the marvel of 1956 was that racing recovered from the heavy blows of 1955. The retirement of Mercedes did not lead to a drop in standards—the apparently less sophisticated cars actually proved faster and competition was as intense as racing entered a new phase, with the British challenge to the Italians becoming very real. Ferrari started to transform the D50s out of all recognition, so that they inevitably became known as Lancia-Ferraris. And Ferrari managed to capture Fangio, with the formidable trio of Castellotti, Musso, and Collins to back him up. Maserati refined the 250F, had Moss, Jean Behra (who was somewhat disgruntled at being "demoted") and Cesare Perdisa. Hawthorn and Brooks joined BRM for a frustrating spell; the car was light and compact, and when it was right it was very fast, but in 1956 it was so seldom right. All Vanwall needed was reliability and

front-rank drivers, for neither Schell nor Trintignant was really more than a good number two. Connaught dubbed its B-type the Syracuse, but were forced by lack of finance to concentrate their programme on British racing.

Gordini found some reliability, but never speed, in his eight-cylinder car. An honourable French name was to reappear fleetingly, at the French Grand Prix—Bugatti, and Trintignant was released by Vanwall to drive it *pour la gloire*. Alas, the sole outing for this ingenious Colombo-designed T251 was inglorious—eighteen seconds off the pace in practice, retired after eighteen back-of-the-field racing laps. A decade later, a French government would inject substantial sums of money into restoring the racing blue of France to the forefront.

Once again Fangio opened the year with a victory in Argentina, in Musso's car after he had twice spun his own, and after Carlos Menditeguy, Musso, Moss, and Behra had all led. Before the championship season opened in Europe, Ferrari went to Syracuse to score a one-two-three, Moss took his 250F to New Zealand to win at Ardmore, then took three minor races in England. Then, for the more important International Trophy at Silverstone, he agreed to drive a Vanwall and once Hawthorn (BRM), the early leader, had retired, he won it at an average speed faster than the old lap record, trouncing Fangio and Collins.

At Monaco, Moss led from start to finish, while behind him Fangio demonstrated some of the evil qualities of the transitional Lancia-Ferrari, battering his own car against kerbs and straw bales

---

and Italian Grands Prix, drove the highest-placed W196 in Britain (fourth) and Spain (third), and ran second to Kling in the Avus "demonstration race".

In 1955, however, Fangio had a strong team-mate in Stirling Moss, who usually ran behind him to team orders, and the W196s lost only one of the races contested. Fangio won the Argentine, Belgian, Dutch, and Italian Grands Prix (and the non-championship Buenos Aires Grand Prix), while Moss headed a Mercedes one-two-three-four in the British Grand Prix at Aintree.

At the end of the season Daimler-Benz quit racing. Mercedes have since dabbled in other forms of motor sport, but never in mainline racing. Yet the reputation of the Silver Arrows lingers.

Mercedes-Benz W196

The racing world was dazzled by the advanced technology evident in the W196, yet some of its features which drew most attention, such as the desmodromic valve gear, were never adopted for the mass of competition cars, and within a short time of the team's withdrawal W196 times were being equalled by much simpler machines. But it was a mighty example of technical overkill.

The engine was the last effective straight-eight in Grand Prix racing. Its cylinders were in two blocks with integral heads and central timing gears, with Bosch fuel injection and that cam-driven positive valvegear. It was laid over at 37 degrees in the spaceframe. The gearbox was integral with the final drive, and the swing rear axles were jointed and located to give a low roll centre. Enormous ATE drum brakes were finned to aid cooling, and mounted inboard front and rear (except on the short wheelbase variant built for Monaco in 1955, which had outboard front brakes).

That a team of special cars should be built for just one Monaco race speaks volumes for the thoroughness of the Mercedes-Benz approach to Grand Prix racing. The racing world was the poorer for the disappearance of a design with such great potential after just two seasons.

SPECIFICATIONS
Mercedes-Benz W196 1954
Engine
Straight-eight
Bore × stroke: 76 mm × 68.8 mm
Capacity: 2496 cc
Twin overhead camshafts
Maximum power: 290 bhp at
8500 rpm

Transmission
Five-speed

Chassis
Tubular space frame

Front suspension
Independent by wishbones, torsion bars, and hydraulic shock absorbers

Rear suspension
Swing axles, torsion bars, and hydraulic shock absorbers

Brakes
Drum; inboard front and rear

Dimensions
Wheelbase: 1954: 93 in (2362 mm)
1955: 87 in (2210 mm)
Front track: 52 in (1322 mm)
Rear track: 53 in (1346 mm)

before taking over Collins's car to finish second. The Belgian Grand Prix fell to Collins, as Fangio and Moss retired their cars; Frère was second for Ferrari. Moss took over Perdisa's car to finish third. Schell was fourth in a Vanwall.

Vanwall had a rumbustious time at Reims, first when their two stand-in drivers Hawthorn and Chapman collided in practice. (That was the first and only time Colin Chapman was entered to drive in a Grand Prix, and he did not start.) Schell over-revved his Vanwall engine early in the race, took over Hawthorn's car, and startled Ferrari by fighting through to second before falling back again to tenth. Collins won, from Castellotti and Behra, and he took the lead in the World Championship.

Fangio soon regained that, winning at Silverstone by a clear lap from Collins/de Portago, Behra, and Jack Fairman in a Connaught. He won at the Nürburgring, by a clear minute from Moss and breaking Lang's 1939 lap record in the process. The banked track at Monza battered cars in practice for the Italian Grand Prix—tyres failed, suspension components failed, and steering arms broke as the uneven surface and heavy "g" loadings took their toll. Castellotti and Musso started the race with spirit, but without much sense, and were in the pits after three laps, leaving it to Fangio, Moss, and Schell to fight for the lead. The steering on the Ferrari failed, an oil pipe broke on the Vanwall, Musso put in another sprint and paid the penalty again, and Moss's lead seemed secure. Peter Collins voluntarily pulled into the pits and in a quite extraordinary gesture of sportsmanship handed his healthy car to Fangio. Collins felt that

Fangio deserved the championship, but he could well have won the race and the championship if he had stayed on the circuit, for with five laps to go Moss's Maserati slowed, down to its last drops of fuel. A thoughtful nudge from another Maserati driver, Piotti, helped Moss to the pits for a swift refuel. Moss won, by just five seconds, from Fangio, who became World Champion. And a Connaught driven by Ron Flockhart was third in the Italian Grand Prix.

The next season was the last great one for Maserati, barren in terms of Grand Prix victories for Ferrari, and, at last, the British teams arrived in force. Red versus green. Fangio left Ferrari with relief, to lead the rival Italian team in updated 250Fs. Jean Behra remained loyal to Maserati and Schell and Menditeguy joined the team. The Lancia lines finally disappeared from Ferrari's cars, although the V-8 engine stayed; Hawthorn rejoined, with Collins and the only front-rank Italians, Castellotti and Musso. The team suffered a setback when Castellotti was killed in a test accident.

It was a sign of the times that Stirling Moss, who could have had the pick of teams, chose to move to Vanwall and was joined by Tony Brooks and later by Stuart Lewis-Evans. BRM had an engine which produced as much power as the Vanwall and Ferrari units—about 280 bhp—and suspension reworked on the advice of Colin Chapman, but the team was dogged by its reputation and had no topflight drivers for 1957. Connaught, whose B-types had to serve, also lacked top drivers and neither the C-type derivative nor a mid-engined project came to fruition.

Rear-engined—or more properly, mid-engined—cars were coming,

AUTO UNION

Until the moment the first Auto Union appeared, the established world of motor racing hardly seemed to appreciate the significance of the first reports of the P-Wagen or to comprehend the freedom that the 750-kg formula gave to designers. This car, from the drawing board of Dr. Ferdinand Porsche, a talented and original designer, took shape with the stimulus of an obsessive spirit of nationalism, and with the contemporary Mercedes it was to make nonsense of preconceived ideas about Grand Prix cars.

The Auto Union consortium of minor manufacturers—Horch, Audi, Wanderer, and DKW—was formed in 1932. Late in that same year, Dr. Porsche began work on an independent design for a P-Wagen racing car for the Hockleistungs Fahrzeugbau offshoot of the Porsche Büro, which in turn was heavily involved in design work for Auto Union. In mid-1933, Auto Union committed itself to this racing car project, which thus was to become the Auto Union A-type. Later that year the first car was completed at the Horch factory.

The A-type was thoroughly unorthodox. It was not the first mid-engined Grand Prix car (Benz had essayed their Tropfenwagen in 1923) but it was to become the first mid-engined car to win a Grand Prix. That success did not come instantly, nor was it to be prolific in the first two seasons. Hans Stuck was the team's leading driver. Better known at first as a leading hill climb exponent than as a racing driver, he perhaps had fewer ingrained seat-of-the-pants inhibitions about this mid-engined racing car, and certainly he was the only driver to come to terms with it in its first season. His convincing victory in the 1934 German Grand Prix quashed contemporary speculation about the roadholding shortcomings of the Auto Union. These did exist, but owed more to the rear suspension than to the position of the engine in the chassis, and were perhaps inspired by a mistrust of novelty. Stuck went on to win the Swiss and Czech Grands Prix in 1934. The team also went hill climbing and record breaking. (Stuck won the European Mountain Championship, and his victory at Mont Ventoux in 1934 was the first for a German Grand Prix car in France since 1914.) These were important sidelines for both German teams in the 1930s. Stuck actually set the world

one-hour and sundry distance records at Avus before the Auto Union was first raced, and set the seal on its first season with five more records.

In 1935, the B-type was usually runner-up to Mercedes, winning only one Grande Epreuve, at Monza, and two secondary events. But in the last of these, the Masaryk Grand Prix over the long Brno circuit, the winning Auto Union was driven by a brilliant newcomer, Bernd Rosemeyer. He took the hill climb title from Stuck and in 1936 won the German, Italian, and Swiss Grands Prix, as well as two secondary races, while Varzi won the Tripoli Grand Prix. Thus Auto Union outscored Mercedes.

however, despite misgivings lingering from the Auto Union days. The virtues of centralized weight distribution and lower frontal area were still thought to be negated by the forward cockpit position. Overlooked was the fact that Auto Union had combined over 500 bhp with narrow-tread tyres suspended on swinging half axles. Under power, these swing axles would up-edge their tyres, dramatically reducing contact area with the road, and this was a major factor in making the Auto Unions notoriously demanding to drive. Formula Three was considered irrelevant, as the engines used were light and compact, and by no means powerful. Larger engines, it was felt, positively demanded front mounting. But in 1957 a new Formula Two (1.5 litres) came into effect and the previous year Cooper had run spindly mid-engined cars to its regulations. The T41 stemmed directly from the Formula Three cars, with a simple tubular frame and transverse leaf/wishbone suspension. Power came from the Coventry Climax and the twin overhead camshaft FPF in 1957. That year a 1.9-litre version of the FPF was prepared at the request of the Coopers and Rob Walker, and slipped into the back of a T41. Jack Brabham drove this at Monaco, running fifth at half-distance and pushing the car across the line at the finish to be classified sixth. This did not convince the traditionalists. Yet within three years the "traditional" postwar ideas about Grand Prix car design were to be totally outmoded, and soon after that a Cooper was to introduce a revolution to the hidebound establishment at Indianapolis.

Fangio won in Argentina, as a matter of course, and he won again at Monaco, after Moss, Collins, and Hawthorn had crashed at the chicane in the opening laps. Brooks was second, Gregory third, and Lewis-Evans was fourth in a Connaught. This was the marque's last finish in a points-scoring position as it went to the wall when Kenneth McAlpine withdrew his support and race cancellations cut into the modest income from starting money.

Fangio won again at Rouen, heading a Ferrari trio (Musso, Collins, and Hawthorn) in the French Grand Prix. The British Grand Prix at Aintree was an exciting race in itself and its ending led to British euphoria. Moss led, then stopped with an ignition fault. He took over Brooks's Vanwall—Brooks was still unwell after a Le Mans accident—and started to work his way up the field. It seemed that third place would be as high up the order as he would get. Behra led, but his clutch burst and Hawthorn, in second place, punctured a tyre on the debris. So Moss and Brooks shared the triumph of the first all-British win in a World Championship Grand Prix, beating three Ferraris (Musso, Hawthorn, and Trintignant). All Tony Vandervell looked for after that was his cars defeating the red cars on their home ground.

Before that there was the German Grand Prix, and Fangio's greatest race. Maserati knew their tyres would not last the race distance and, therefore, started Fangio with half-full tanks (the last time this ploy was tried in a Grand Prix). When Fangio stopped, Hawthorn and Collins passed into an apparently safe lead, and their pit signalled them to maintain pace. But Fangio gained astonishingly, and two laps of the long Nürburgring had to be completed before the Ferrari pair got the message. By then it was too late, and with a final

---

Auto Union A-Type

The A-type was a rare car, as novel under the skin as it was in outward appearance. It had a tubular frame, with its main side members initially used to carry coolant between the nose radiator and engine. The body was mainly in light alloy, but some unstressed side "panels" were doped fabric at first, to save weight. The engine was located behind the cockpit, and fuel was carried between cockpit and engine so that handling remained constant whatever the fuel load. The independent front suspension tor-

sion-bar system had been introduced on a Porsche-designed Wanderer. At the rear, a swing axle and transverse spring arrangement was to prove one of the weak design features because the inherent swing-axle cornering tuck-in aggravated problems encountered by drivers seated so far forward in the chassis. In the 1935 B version, torsion bars were substituted for the transverse springs.

The engine was a light, compact, and narrow V-16, with a single camshaft in the 45-degree vee which

operated the inlet valves directly and the exhaust valves by pushrods which passed over the cylinder heads. The arrangement proved acceptable in a unit that was relatively slow-revving. It had excellent torque qualities, however, and thus was unusually flexible for a racing engine. The Roots-type supercharger was mounted at the back. Drive was taken to a five-speed gearbox behind the rear axle line, and from there forward to the differential.

For the B-type, the engine was bored out to 4.95 litres, and then to

5.6 litres. The car was further revised as the C-type, the most successful Auto Union in terms of race results, with a longer wheelbase and the capacity of the engine increased to 6 litres, still without an increase in weight. In addition to the standard racing versions of each type, various special models were prepared. Streamlined bodies, some with enclosed cockpits, were built for record cars, while the hill climb car had twin rear wheels. "Sprint" engines were also made for use in these cars.

SPECIFICATIONS
Auto Union A-type   1934
Engine
45-degree V-16
Bore × stroke: 68 mm × 75 mm
Capacity: 4360 cc
Single camshaft
Roots-type supercharger
Maximum power: 295 bhp at 4500 rpm

Transmission
Five-speed

Chassis
Tubular

Front suspension
Independent by trailing links, torsion bars, and shock absorbers

Rear suspension
Independent by swing axles, transverse leaf spring, and shock absorbers

Brakes
Drum

Dimensions
Wheelbase: 112 in (2845 mm)
Front track: 52 in (1321 mm)
Rear track: 52 in (1321 mm)

fastest lap Fangio was past them. That lap raised the record to 91.51 mph, Fangio's race average of 88.79 mph being faster than the old lap record. It was his twenty-fourth championship victory, and it was to be his last.

The Pescara Grand Prix on the long-established Adriatic coast circuit was elevated to championship status, for with the cancellation of the Dutch and Belgian races there were too few ranking events in 1957. (This was the first time that two championship races were run in one country and the last time that Grand Prix cars raced at Pescara.) Ironically, Ferrari sent only one car to this Italian race, for Musso, who was indulging one of his spasmodic threats to give up racing, usually a guaranteed method of getting his way with whichever Italian or international body needed persuasion. Vanwall triumphed again—Moss beat Fangio by almost three minutes.

Even so, the Monza *tifosi* were astonished when the three fastest cars in practice for the Italian Grand Prix were Vanwalls. Only Fangio was remotely in touch with Moss at the end of the race and the Ferrari driven into third place by Count Berghe von Trips was two laps behind the winning Vanwall.

The season ended on a note of change, with the non-championship Moroccan Grand Prix at Casablanca. In the preceding Modena Grand Prix, Ferrari had run two Dino 246 cars with 1.8-litre V-6 engines; now these appeared in 2417 cc form, the last front-engined Grand Prix car to make an impact. The Moroccan race was also the last for a full Maserati factory team, and it was fitting that Behra should win the race in a 250F. BRM had two secondary successes

behind them in 1957, at Caen and Silverstone, and now they ventured out of England to face front-line opposition for the first time since the French Grand Prix. They were rewarded when Trintignant gained third place for them in Morocco, behind Lewis-Evans's Vanwall.

At that race was assembled what appeared to be the 1958 cast and the uncertainty for the coming season centred on the "pump" fuel which became obligatory, for only Ferrari had an engine designed to run on it. It had to be defined as 100-130 octane aviation fuel—not quite what the average motorist could buy at the pumps, but considered sufficient to sustain oil companies' publicity claims. It meant better fuel consumption, and coupled with shorter races (300 km maximum distance, or two hours duration), a pit stop would almost rule out a driver's chance of victory. More fundamentally, designers could allow for lower variable weights and hence the design revolution that was imminent was abetted.

Almost incidentally, the shared points arrangement in the championship was discontinued, so that only one driver could score in a car. Effectively that put an end to the practice of shared drives.

But the cast was not complete with Ferrari, BRM, Vanwall, and left-over Maseratis or the lightweight 250F. There were Coopers, with 1.96-litre Coventry Climax engines, later as part of the growing process with 195 bhp 2.2-litre versions. The cars were more than adapted Formula Two models, sturdier and with disc brakes, light and with a low frontal area, and while their circuit behaviour might seem crude in retrospect, at the time it was of an order to instil

AUTO UNION

Mercedes was back in the ascendancy in 1937, when Auto Union resources were stretched. They contrived, for example, only one "special" for the prestigious Avusrennen, albeit that car was a beautiful streamlined track machine. Among Rosemeyer's four victories were the Vanderbilt Cup at Long Island's Roosevelt Raceway and the last race of the 750-kg formula, the Donington Grand Prix in England.

There was a sad postscript to the 1937 season. The Oberste Nationale Sportbehorde für die Deutsche had ruled that German cars should attack records on German soil, and in an October speed week Rosemeyer soundly defeated Mercedes by taking two world records and several lesser ones. Mercedes pulled strings to arrange a counterattack in January 1938 and Auto Union insisted on a right to reply. On his first run, at an autobahn venue which was inadequate and in conditions which Rosemeyer reportedly recognized were unfavourable, he crashed and was killed instantly.

Auto Union was left uncertain and unready for the new racing season under new regulations. When their cars did race they seemed to be no match for Mercedes. But in mid-season, Werner persuaded Nuvolari to join the team. Before the end of the season, he became accustomed to the mid-engined cars, won the Italian Grand Prix by a clear lap and the Donington Grand Prix by a wide margin.

In 1939, the D-type matched the Mercedes in terms of speed, but few races were won by the team. A new driver, Herman Muller, won the French Grand Prix by a lap. Stuck won at Bucharest. Nuvolari won the Yugoslav Grand Prix at Belgrade, which was run hours after Britain and France had declared war on Germany.

The Auto Union base had been at Zwickau, now in East Germany, and that is perhaps the main reason why so few Auto Unions survive. It was two decades after they had last been raced that the mid-engine layout was to become conventional in road racing cars.

unusual confidence in their drivers. A new marque to Grand Prix racing was Lotus, like Cooper relying on 1.96- and 2.2-litre Coventry Climax engines. But Chapman still mounted his engines ahead of the cockpit, tilted to cut down frontal area, in "mini-Vanwall" bodies.

The British teams decided not to go to Argentina, where there were six Maseratis, three Ferraris, and the lone Cooper entered at the last moment by Rob Walker for Stirling Moss. He drove a clever tactical race; the other teams were misled into expecting that the Cooper would have to stop to change tyres, but Moss conserved them to run the distance and won by 2.7 seconds from the Ferrari driven by Musso and Hawthorn. That was the first Grand Prix victory for a mid-engined car since 1939. Fangio was fourth in that race, and two weeks later gained his last victory in a Grand Prix car, in the Formule Libre Buenos Aires Grand Prix.

There was an unusually widespread flurry of non-championship races, in New Zealand where Brabham won the Grand Prix in a Cooper, and in Europe where each of the Ferrari drivers won a race—Hawthorn at Goodwood, Collins at Silverstone, Musso at Syracuse. That Sicilian race also saw the first woman driver to make a serious effort in modern Grand Prix racing; Maria Teresa de Fillipis looked tiny and frail in the cockpit of a Maserati 250F, but was by no means ineffectual (her best Grand Prix placing was tenth, in Belgium in 1958).

Walker's Cooper won again at Monaco, this time driven by Maurice Trintignant, heading Musso and Collins in Ferraris, Brabham in a Cooper, Schell in a BRM, and Cliff Allison in a Lotus—

this marque scored a point in its first Grand Prix. Allison finished in the same position at Zandvoort, where the results list was at least more "normal" so far as the configuration of the leading cars was concerned, however unusual their nationality in view of the then-recent past: Vanwall (Moss), BRMs (Schell and Behra), Cooper (Salvadori), and Ferrari (Hawthorn).

The Belgian Grand Prix demonstrated one result of the changed regulations: it was won in one hour and thirty-seven minutes, the shortest full Grand Prix to run to that time. Tony Brooks won it, but the outcome might have been so different—his gearbox was failing as he won, second man Hawthorn coasted over the line with a piston blown in his Ferrari, third man Lewis-Evans passed the flag with the front suspension of his Vanwall collapsing. Only Allison's Lotus, in fourth place, appeared to be healthy enough to complete another lap.

The French Grand Prix at Reims was fast, relatively long, tragic, and nostalgic. Mike Hawthorn won it from Moss and von Trips, showing that Ferrari could never be discounted. But Musso crashed early in the race and was fatally injured. He was trying to stay with Hawthorn through the long full-throttle 150 mph bend past the pits, and was perhaps out of his depth, for he was not a driver of Hawthorn's calibre. Ferrari said, "The price was too high. I have lost the only Italian driver who mattered."

In the final laps at Reims, Hawthorn was in a position to lap Fangio, but in a delicate compliment he eased so he would not lap The Old Man in his last race. For Fangio was at Reims only to honour an agreement. He had decided to retire at the end of 1957 and

---

Auto Union D-Type

Ferdinand Porsche's successor, Eberan von Eberhorst, elected to retain the basic Auto Union layout in the car for the 3-litre formula, but this D-type was considerably more sophisticated than its forerunners. Its V-12 engine had three camshafts, the central one operating the inlet valves, and was a faster-revving engine than the V-16. It was more a "racing engine", but in terms of

power it never matched the rival Mercedes power unit, even when two-stage supercharging was adopted in 1939.

The D-type was a more compact car, and the use of side fuel tanks meant that the cockpit could be further back in the chassis. Coupled with a de Dion suspension layout at the rear, this made for a car which was much more controllable than the Porsche-designed Auto Unions.

Despite its power handicap, it could equal Mercedes lap times on most circuits. Had development of the D-type not been laggardly, and if the team had had driving strength in depth instead of relying essentially on one man, Tazio Nuvolari, this car could have consistently out-performed the more conventional Mercedes, and thus set an example which constructors might more readily have followed in the postwar years.

SPECIFICATIONS
Auto Union D-type   1938-51
Engine
60-degree V-12
Bore × stroke: 65 mm × 75 mm
Capacity: 2990 cc
Roots-type supercharger
Three overhead camshafts
Maximum power: 485 bhp at
7000 rpm
Transmission
Five-speed
Chassis
Tubular
Front suspension
Independent by trailing links,
torsion bars, and shock absorbers
Rear suspension
De Dion with longitudinal torsion
bars and shock absorbers
Brakes
Drum
Dimensions
Wheelbase: 112 in (2845 mm)
Front track: 55 in (1397 mm)
Rear track: 55 in (1397 mm)

to contest only the Argentine and French events. Hawthorn's gesture was in perfect accord with the respect in which Fangio was held during his career, and with the deference accorded to no other past champion since his retirement.

Peter Collins won at Silverstone, from Hawthorn, but when the Ferrari pair were trying to counterattack Brooks at the Nürburgring two weeks later Collins crashed and was fatally injured after being flung out of his Ferrari. So there was little joy in that Vanwall victory, and the Cooper placings were perhaps overlooked—Salvadori second, Trintignant third, and a Formula Two car driven by a young New Zealander, Bruce McLaren, fifth overall.

The Portugese Grand Prix was a championship race for the first time, run on a street circuit on the outskirts of Oporto. Moss won, but misread a pit signal informing him that runner-up Hawthorn had set the fastest lap. Hawthorn gained another second place, behind Brooks, in the Italian Grand Prix, while Phil Hill, the American newcomer to the Ferrari Grand Prix team, was third and Graham Hill scored his first championship point when he finished sixth in a Lotus.

Moss scored maximum points in the last championship race, in Morocco, with a victory and fastest lap. Hawthorn did all he needed to secure the championship, scoring six points by finishing second. Vanwall convincingly won the new Constructors' Championship. But in that black season, this was another race overshadowed by a fatal accident, this time to fast-rising driver Stuart Lewis-Evans; there was strong feeling that his burns might not have been so

severe had "commercial petrol" not then been the mandatory fuel.

The 1959 season opened without a reigning World Champion, for Mike Hawthorn died in a road accident soon after announcing his retirement—and without the team which had won the Constructors' Championship, for the Vanwall team was virtually wound up. This was the season that really marked the end of the front-engined Grand Prix car, although the message had become crystal clear in 1958. Those early-season Cooper victories might have been dismissed as flukes, and the Nürburgring result attributed to the peculiar suitability of the circuit, but there were also significant Cooper placings at fast circuits: Salvadori was third at Silverstone and Monza, Brabham sixth at Reims, and if that could be achieved with underpowered cars, what might result if Cooper enjoyed power parity? In 1959 they did, as the Coventry Climax engine "grew" to a full 2.5 litres, giving up to 240 bhp. Moreover, the modest Cooper team had two particularly talented drivers, Brabham and McLaren, who were most definitely not in the old mould. They were both practical men, as well as top drivers, capable of translating cockpit sensations into car improvements, who brought to the fore the art of chassis tuning. The time was not far off when Jack Brabham was to persuade the surprisingly conservative Coopers to abandon their transverse spring suspension and adopt coil springs "all round", and that was no mean achievement. Later both he and his Cooper team-mate of 1959-60, Bruce McLaren, were to launch their own highly successful marques.

Like other teams in the 1950s—Ferrari, Maserati, and

MASERATI

Almost from first to last, Maserati's Grand Prix efforts were built on shoestring budgets. Even in the heady days of the mid-1950s when the team was a serious championship contender, it was run with resources that seem ludicrously inadequate by modern standards. Maserati was in reality much like an imagined Italian racing car constructor of a past age of the sport—a performance machinery boutique run by men with flair and a dedication to racing cars. Ironically, the best-remembered Grand Prix Maserati came long after the brothers who had founded the company had gone their own characteristically independent way.

Five of six brothers who had been involved in Italian motor sport from its earliest days set up their first enterprise, manufacturing spark plugs, before the First World War. Alfieri Maserati had raced before the war and soon after it competed in a "special" of his own concoction. It was a natural step for Officine Maserati to edge towards competition cars. In the early 1920s the brothers undertook first Diatto development work, then the construction of a straight-eight for a Diatto Grand Prix car. When Diatto failed, the brothers acquired that car, and modified it to meet the 1.5-litre regulations which came into effect in 1926. It became the first Maserati, and it was successful first time out, in the Targa Florio, when Alfieri took a class victory. Further successes were few, and modest, but the marque was established. Derivatives of that car followed and then there was the first twin-engined essay. This V-4 of 1929 had two 2-litre straight-eights side-by-side on a common crankcase, producing around 300 bhp. Although it had a reputation for insanitary handling it gave Umberto Borzacchini a victory in the 1930 Tripoli Grand Prix. This car was followed by the 4.9-litre V-5, which was spasmodically raced between 1932 and 1934 and gained some secondary successes.

These twin-engined cars were outside the mainstream, however—Maserati's 1930 to 1932 car was the 8C-2500 and 8C-2800 (designations simply indicating cylinders and capacity). Although these

8C cars were utterly conventional behind their raked noses, they were new cars heralding the racing revival, and were campaigned by some of the leading drivers. They led to the 8C-3000 of 1933, a narrow-bodied single-seater with the novelty of hydraulic brakes to all four wheels (a European first). It was faster than contemporary Alfa Romeos, if less reliable, and was driven by men of the calibre of Giuseppe Campari and Tazio Nuvolari.

Maserati attempted to match the German cars of the mid-1930s with the Tipo 34, which had 3.3- and 3.7-litre engines, and with the 1935 V-8RI, which had a 4.8-litre V-8 in a new chassis and all-round independent suspension. But, increasingly, the brothers turned to

Vanwall—Cooper built a streamlined car for the Reims circuit and like those others it was used only in practice. It was some 15 mph faster than the open version on the flat-out straights, but at the expense of cornering speed and stability as the front end tended to lift—at an officially timed 190 mph. "Streamlining" was still equated with "wind cheating", for designers had yet to think positively about aerodynamics.

The name Cooper increasingly recurred in entry lists, as independent entrants realized that these straightforward cars were ideal. Even such Italian teams as Scuderia Centro-Sud used them, perhaps with local encouragement, as Italian engineers could thereby gain an insight into their workings. Attempts, however, to use alternative power units, such as Ferrari or Maserati, in Cooper chassis were hardly rewarding.

Ferrari was now on the defensive. The Dino 246 had the most powerful engine (producing more than 290 bhp) and disc brakes, since Hawthorn had persuaded Ferrari to try a set from a road car in 1958 and there had been no denying their effectiveness. The leading Italian team now had to look outside Italy for all its drivers—Brooks, Phil Hill, and Behra, until he quarrelled with the team manager and was replaced by Allison, while sports car men Gendebien and Gurney were also called on to drive in some Grands Prix.

Colin Chapman had reworked the BRM suspension again, and that ill-starred team now seemed well placed, for the car handled well and in terms of engine power was second only to Ferrari. But before the end of the year one of their front-engined cars was to be cut up and rebuilt as a mid-engined prototype. Harry Schell was joined in the team by Jo Bonnier, while Ron Flockhart was reserve driver and a car was loaned to the British Racing Partnership for Moss to drive on appropriate circuits. Chapman also revised his own 16 to accept the 2.5-litre Coventry Climax engine, but his team (Graham Hill and Innes Ireland) was to be less successful than it had been in 1958.

Aston Martin entered Formula One with the classically handsome DBR4/250, heavy as it derived from a sports car, with impeccable manners and up to 280 bhp in its six-cylinder engine, but late and suddenly obsolete in its conception. Salvadori placed one second to Brabham's Cooper in the International Trophy at Silverstone, but after that promising debut the car was never competitive.

The Argentine series lapsed, and a few teams made the trip to New Zealand, where the Grand Prix saw a Cooper one-two-three (Moss in Walker's car heading Brabham and McLaren) and the Lady Wigram Trophy fell to Ron Flockhart in a BRM from the Cooper factory pair. The only early-season non-championship races in Europe were run in Britain. Cooper won at Goodwood and Silverstone and Ferrari at Aintree after the leading Coopers retired.

The season opened in earnest at Monaco, where seven of the sixteen starters were mid-engined, and where four of those cars finished in the first six. Brabham won, from Brooks, Trintignant, Phil Hill, McLaren, and Salvadori. Then came the Dutch Grand Prix and BRM's first championship victory, won by Jo Bonnier from Brabham and Gregory, with Innes Ireland taking fourth place to gain Lotus their best result of the season.

voiturette racing, notably with the 4CM and 6CM, which became category leaders until the Alfetta arrived. Maserati's less-than-successful response was the 4CL of 1939.

By that time, Cavallieri Adolfo Orsi had taken over the company—attracted by its spark plug business, although his son Omer was to see Maserati through to a troubled period two decades later—retaining the services of the brothers for ten years as part of the deal. He underwrote Maserati's return to Grand Prix racing with the 8CTF, which, given development time and resources, could perhaps have been a competitive Grand Prix car, and in any case proved its worth in the United States.

Maserati 8CTF

Orsi made a small budget available for a 3-litre Grand Prix car, and within that restriction Maserati ingenuity produced an effective car; in Grands Prix, hard driving almost invariably overstressed its straight-eight, but generated occasional speed which frightened the dominant German teams. As if to underline the difference in standards, however, it was a highly successful track car in the United States, rudely upsetting the established order at Indianapolis.

In many respects, this 8CTF was a scaled up 4CM voiturette, with torsion bar independent front suspension and quarter-elliptics and rigid axle at the rear. It also had a similar chassis, albeit with the novelty of a cast X-bracing at the rear which also served as an oil tank and fuel tank support, and an elegantly simple body. The engine was effectively two 4CM fours with a single cylinder head; the first long-stroke version was superseded by a square (78 x 78 mm) engine in the 8CL of 1940, but this variant achieved little.

In that year, all the 8Cs then built, three 8CTF and one 8CL, ran at Indianapolis. Wilbur Shaw gained his second victory in the Boyle Special 8CTF; Theodore Horn was third in this car in 1946 and 1947, fourth in 1948.

SPECIFICATIONS
Maserati 8CTF 1938
Engine
Straight-eight
Bore × stroke: 69 mm × 100 mm
Capacity: 2992 cc
Twin overhead camshafts
Two Roots-type superchargers
Maximum power: 365 bhp at 6400 rpm
Transmission
Four-speed
Chassis
Box section, cross-braced
Front suspension
Independent by wishbones, torsion bars, and shock absorbers
Rear suspension
Live axle, quarter-elliptics, and shock absorbers
Brakes
Drum
Dimensions
Wheelbase: 107 in (2718 mm)
Front track: 53 in (1346 mm)
Rear track: 54 in (1372 mm)

Ferrari won the French Grand Prix. In practice at Reims the fifteen fastest drivers lapped faster than the official lap record, but the race field was decimated by the extreme heat—over 110°F—as much as by normal racing failures. Brooks, Phil Hill, and Gendebien placed three Ferraris in the first four, Brabham splitting them in third place. Brabham took the British Grand Prix at Aintree from Moss and McLaren.

For largely political reasons, the German Grand Prix was run at Avus, used by modern Grand Prix cars only for a Mercedes "demonstration race" five years earlier. This was not the full flat-out Avus of the 1930s. Obviously a circuit running into the Russian Zone of Berlin was out of the question, so it was cut short at that end, where a 180-degree hairpin bend linked the parallel main straights, but the steeply-banked brick-surfaced north curve of the prewar track remained. There was an old tradition of streamlined specials for Avus races, but in 1959 these were banned and that prompted a requirement for open-wheel cars to be written into the international formula regulations. The two-part race was a gift for Ferrari's strong and powerful cars. Brooks duly won, at 146.71 mph, from the team's two American drivers, Dan Gurney and Phil Hill.

Almost as predictably, Coopers finished first, second, and third in the Portugese Grand Prix, Moss heading Gregory and Trintignant. The pendulum might have been expected to swing in Ferrari's favour again at Monza. The Ferraris did indeed lead that Italian Grand Prix, but only until they stopped for tyre changes. Moss, who had shadowed them, ran through nonstop, and won from Phil Hill,

Brabham, then Gurney, Allison, and Gendebien in three Ferraris.

There was one more race that season, the first United States Grand Prix, contested by eighteen cars at the Sebring airfield circuit. Moss's championship chances disappeared when he retired after six laps. Brabham ran out of fuel within half a mile of the finish, but he pushed his Cooper across the line to finish fourth. That sealed his first World Championship. Bruce McLaren won the race, and at the age of twenty-two became the youngest driver to win a World Championship event. Trintignant was second and Brooks third, almost a lap behind McLaren.

Cooper had won the Constructors' Championship, and the reality the Grand Prix world had to face in 1960 was the mid-engined car. The 1960 Cooper T53 was a substantial yet lithe car, better-engineered and more sophisticated than its predecessors. But for all their shortcomings, the performances of those cars virtually forced every other constructor to adopt the mid-engined layout. Ferrari persisted with outmoded Dino 246s, but also used their V-6 behind the driver in a car first raced at Monaco, and the Scuderia felt its way into the new era with a mid-engined Formula Two car. The first mid-engined BRMs were not as handsome as their front-engined predecessors, but had obvious potential. The most interesting "convert" was Colin Chapman, and he did much more than imitate the basic Cooper layout. His Lotus 18 was an original, with a multi-tubular spaceframe and ingenious suspension with geometry giving a very low roll centre, low frontal area and signalling a trend towards a reclining position for the driver.

MASERATI

In 1941, the company was moved from its home city of Bologna to Modena. The surviving brothers, Bindo, Ernesto, and Ettore, remained with it. While the 4CLT was prominent on early postwar grids, they set in motion the two-stage supercharged 4CLT development for 1947, and of course for Grand Prix use. Then, as the 4CLT San Remo, after its debut race victory in the hands of Ascari, the design was substantially revised with coil spring front suspension, a tubular frame, and engine development which produced up to 260 bhp. That was simply not enough to match the Alfa Romeos, or the rising new challenge from Ferrari. These 4CLTs, however, were to gain numerous victories in Alfa's absence. Sufficient power could never be wrung from the four-cylinder unit, and although Scuderia Milano claimed that their developed version delivered about 300 bhp in 1949 and 1950, that was mainly achieved by increased supercharger pressures, and at the cost of drastically reduced reliability.

The Maserati brothers had also laid down a sports car design before they left to found Osca. This car was hardly exploited, but its unsupercharged six-cylinder engine was substantially reworked as the basis of the A6GCM and A6SSG Formula Two cars of 1952-53, which became eligible for World Championship events in those years as Formula One collapsed. These cars were consistently improved, but were runners-up to Ferraris until the final race of 1953, when Fangio won the Italian Grand Prix for Maserati.

That augured well for the new 2.5-litre formula, and Gioacchino Colombo's 250F. Fangio won the first two Grands Prix of 1954 in the 250F, but his departure to Mercedes was the largest single factor against Maserati winning another championship race in that season (250Fs did win secondary events). The model gained justifiable favour among leading independent entrants. Consequently, later in its life it was not uncommon to see as many as ten of them on a grid. Moss took two championship races in 250Fs in 1956, when Maserati developed the outright speed potential of the car to match the ruling Lancia-Ferraris. Then Fangio returned to lead the Maserati team in

1957, winning four Grandes Epreuves and the Constructors' Championship, for the marque. But that was its golden year. Maserati was deep in financial trouble, in large part because of sports racing excesses, and the factory team was no more.

Maserati racing cars were still built, for example a 250F-based "special" with a 4.2-litre engine for the Monza Race of Two Worlds, and a lightweight 250F3, which Fangio drove in his last Grand Prix, at Reims in 1958. This car might have pointed the way to a promising line of development—indeed, a car completed as a Tec Mec but run in only one race showed how this could have progressed. Grand Prix racing, however, was in a period of radical change, so although Scuderia Centro-Sud persevered with the 250F, this outstanding car almost suddenly became obsolete.

Odd attempts were made to use Maserati engines during the last 2.5-litre years, and even sports car units appeared in 1.5-litre single-seaters. Then in 1966 a more serious effort was made, with Cooper. Tailormade 3-litre engines were not commonly available to the "kit-car" constructors for the first season of the new formula, and Cooper turned to Maserati. They had a V-12, which had first seen the light of day as a 2.5-litre unit, and in 1957 had raced occasionally in factory 250F chassis, producing a great noise but no tangible results. Now, suitably enlarged and subjected to some development, it powered the factory Coopers and some independent Coopers. This combination enjoyed some success in the first two seasons of 3-litre Grands Prix; then new power units—especially the Cosworth DFV—showed it up for what it was; an old, bulky, none-too-powerful and outclassed engine. Development was not pursued, and in any case the Orsi family sold Maserati.

The name survives as a manufacturer of high-performance road cars, but the lasting monument to the marque in racing is the number of 250Fs which have appeared in historic events. The popularity of this outstanding car also has been underlined by the construction of near replicas.

As well as the Ferraris, other front-engined cars flitted across the scene. Aston Martin made an odd ineffectual appearance, as did a lone lightweight Vanwall. Lance Reventlow introduced the last new Grand Prix car on conventional lines, the beautifully made Scarab; it proved heavy and with a 230 bhp four-cylinder engine it was underpowered. After a few attempts to qualify, and only one race start, the Scarab team returned to the United States.

Many drivers remained faithful to their 1959 teams. Brabham and McLaren drove the factory Coopers, and Coopers were the mainstay of the independent teams. Ferrari could call on Phil Hill, von Trips, Allison, Mairesse, and Ginther. BRM had Graham Hill, Bonnier, and Gurney. Lotus started the year with Ireland and Alan Stacey. Two notable newcomers made their Grand Prix debuts in Lotus 18s—John Surtees at Monaco and Jim Clark at Zandvoort.

The Argentine Grand Prix was revived for a year and won by McLaren in a 1959 Cooper from Allison in a Ferrari. Brabham and McLaren finished first and second in both New Zealand races, then attention switched to the British warm-up races. Almost suddenly, Lotus were winning Formula One races. Ireland beat Moss and Bristow in Coopers at Goodwood, Brabham and Graham Hill at Silverstone. Rob Walker and Stirling Moss turned to a Lotus 18.

Moss took pole position at Monaco, where all sixteen drivers who qualified to start had to lap in times under the fastest 1959 race lap just to get on the grid, and he won the race. So an independent team scored the first World Championship victory for Lotus.

At the Dutch Grand Prix Jack Brabham began a run of five victories which gained him a second championship. At Zandvoort he headed Ireland, Graham Hill, and Moss, and at Spa he won at 133.62 mph from McLaren and Gendebien to give Cooper a one-two-three. But that Belgian meeting was overshadowed by tragedy, for Alan Stacey (Lotus) and Chris Bristow (Cooper) died in accidents. Moss crashed in practice when a stub axle failed and was out of racing until the autumn. These accidents led to stories of Lotus fragility, which have recurred at intervals. Then, and later, these rumours often stemmed from an inability to equate component strength with anything but visible bulk.

In 1960, the Cooper was clearly fastest in practice at Reims, where Brabham lapped at 135.75 mph and won the French Grand Prix at an average speed of 131.93 mph, faster than the old lap record. Coopers took the first four places in that race, Lotus the next three. Graham Hill provided most of the excitement in the British Grand Prix, for he stalled his engine as the race started and then drove his BRM through the field to take the lead, only to lose it again near the end when he made a slight error. So John Surtees followed Brabham past the flag, then came Ireland, McLaren, Brooks in a Cooper, and the first of the Ferraris, driven by von Trips and lapped twice.

Surtees led the Portugese Grand Prix for most of its distance. His retirement let Brabham through to win from McLaren and Clark. The German Grand Prix was downgraded to a Formula Two race, for with Porsche in the field that made for a German victory. The Italians took the only course which might lead to a Ferrari

Maserati 250F

This was a no-nonsense Grand Prix car, classic in its proportions and workmanlike in its mechanical make-up, wholly competitive in the hands of factory drivers and the mainstay of independent entrants through the front-engined years of the 2.5-litre formula.

The 250F derived in part from the Colombo-developed A6SSG 2-litre Formula Two car of 1953, with a new tubular spaceframe, the earlier car's wishbone and coil spring independent front suspension, and a de Dion type layout at the rear—at last Maserati had abandoned the rigid axle. The combined transverse gearbox and final drive unit was mounted to the chassis; four-speed gearboxes were considered sufficient in the early cars, but five-speed units were soon introduced. The straight-six was effectively an enlarged version of the A6SSG engine, initially developing 240 bhp but continuously improved, with revised cylinder heads, camshafts, and so on, to produce some 270 bhp by 1957. Development of the mainline 250Fs was logical and extended beyond mechanical parts.

Progressively, the chassis was made lighter, the body became sleeker, the massive drum brakes were continually uprated in a vain effort to match the discs which other marques were introducing (and which were tried to good effect on independent 250Fs). Maserati built thirty-two 250Fs, and two of them were fitted with V-12 (88.5 x 56 mm, 2449 cc) engines and run without success in 1957, the last year when a team was fielded.

SPECIFICATIONS
Maserati 250F 1954
Engine
Straight-six
Bore × stroke: 84 mm × 75 mm
Capacity: 2493 cc
Twin overhead camshafts
Maximum power: 270 bhp at
8000 rpm

Transmission
Five-speed

Chassis
Multi-tubular spaceframe

Front suspension
Independent by wishbones, coil
springs, and hydraulic shock
absorbers

Rear suspension
De Dion axle, transverse leaf
spring, and shock absorbers

Brakes
Drum

Dimensions
Wheelbase: 90 in (2286 mm)
Front track: 51 in (1295 mm)
Rear track: 49 in (1245 mm)

victory at Monza—they ran the Italian Grand Prix on the combined road circuit and banked track. Mindful of the problems, not to say dangers, of running cars with suspension and tyres intended for road circuits on the bumpy banking, the British teams stayed at home. A sixteen-car field of Formula One and Formula Two cars started. Ferraris finished first, second, and third (Phil Hill, Ginther, Mairesse), two laps ahead of Giulio Cabianca's Cooper-Ferrari and the Formula Two Ferrari driven by von Trips. That was the last championship Grand Prix victory for a front-engined Grand Prix car, but for the last such victory in a fully representative race on a road circuit it was already necessary to look back more than a year, to the French Grand Prix in 1959.

Stirling Moss won the last Grand Prix of the 2.5-litre formula, the American event at Riverside from Ireland, McLaren, Brabham, Bonnier, and Phil Hill in a Cooper. Ferrari recognized the futility of sending a team. The crowd was small—the American race did not gain any stature until it was moved to Watkins Glen—and the team which had most consistently supported Grand Prix racing was absent. Thus the formula died on a subdued note.

But there was a postscript, which hardly rated headlines at the time, but proved far-reaching; after the Riverside race, Jack Brabham took a Cooper to Indianapolis to run some test laps. He lapped at 144 mph, with 252 bhp behind him and the car in road racing trim. The 1960 500 had been won at a record 138.76 mph, by a roadster powered by an Offenhauser engine with more than 400 bhp.

Nothing new had been seen at Indianapolis for years; the last radical novelties had been the mid-engined Gulf-Millers of 1939, the supercharged Novi eights which seldom lasted five hundred miles, or the front-wheel drive Blue Crown Specials which won in the late 1940s. The USAC and Indianapolis establishments liked their anachronistic roadsters, the "specials" named for sponsors, and the settled all-American nature of the race, with its gently rising speeds, occasional spectacular accidents, unfailingly large crowds, and technical stagnation. There was apparently nothing in Europe to upset the status quo. Only one of the four Ferraris entered for the 1952 500 had qualified, and that failed to last the distance. Five-hundred-mile races had been run at Monza in 1957-58 to exploit the banked track, and these had fallen to USAC roadsters, while the "specials" prepared by Ferrari and Maserati and driven by leading Grand Prix aces had been beaten. (Jim Rathman's winning speed in 1958 was 166.72 mph, which made it the fastest race ever run, for at last Lang's 162.61 mph in the 1937 Avusrennen was beaten.)

The Cooper-Climax was too easily dismissed as a "funny car" in 1960. Cooper and Brabham were back at the Speedway in 1961, this time to race. Their car was slightly offset, and had a 2.7-litre version of the Coventry Climax FPF. Brabham qualified it for the fifth row, and placed it ninth in the race at 134.116 mph. Some roadster owners were apprehensive, seeing a distant threat to their investment. Some even welcomed the possibility that they might be forced to try something new. Generally, the USAC establishment saw little significance in the one-off Cooper entry. However, that side trip after the United States Grand Prix in 1960 gave a foretaste. The changed

TALBOT

In the mid-1930s the ramshackle Sunbeam-Talbot-Darracq combine broke up, and Antonio Lago took over control of its weakest company, Automobiles Talbot. He looked to high-performance cars and competition to underpin his programme to rescue the company, and in 1936 Talbot re-entered racing, with sports cars.

The Grand Prix regulations which came into force in 1938 admitted 4.5-litre unsupercharged engines, and thus appeared attractive to French constructors. Two stripped sports Talbots were entered for the French Grand Prix, and Carrière placed one fourth. This encouraged the construction of three new cars for the 1939 Grands Prix—two offset single-seaters on sports chassis, and a central-cockpit car which was the forerunner of the postwar Lago-Talbots. The first two gained third and fourth places in the all-important French Grand Prix and were later shipped to the United States, where attempts to qualify them at Indianapolis were unsuccessful.

Fortunately for Lago, whose resources were meagre, the maximum capacity for unsupercharged engines remained unchanged in the first postwar Grand Prix regulations. Carlo Marchetti, who had taken Walter Becchia's place as chief engineer, reworked the sports-based straight-six and mounted it in a straightforward chassis to create the "proper" Grand Prix Lago-Talbot. The only unusual feature of the car was its Wilson gearbox. This car was to carry French hopes through the years of the first Formula One.

Meanwhile, as motor sport picked up again through Europe, the earlier cars were raced and, indeed, were to serve private owners into the 1950s. There were several successes in secondary French events. A high point came when Louis Chiron won the first postwar French Grand Prix at Lyon in 1947, while other Talbots gained third, fourth, and sixth places.

The Lago-Talbot made its debut in the 1948 Monaco Grand Prix. It was heavier than its Italian rivals, and the engine was considerably less powerful, but the car was reliable and strong, and, above all, its fuel consumption was economical (9 mpg, compared with about 3 mpg of the supercharged Italian cars). This meant that Lago-Talbots could race in a 500-kilometre Grand Prix with at most one fuel stop, against the two or three required for the 1.5-litre cars. The hope was that even Alfa Romeo 158 drivers might be provoked into over-stressing their engines. This seldom happened. The most Lago-Talbot drivers could hope for were honourable placings. But in 1949 Alfa Romeo withdrew for a season, and on the more open circuits the big blue cars could match the less reliable Maseratis and the uncertain early Ferraris. Louis Rosier won the Belgian Grand Prix and Louis Chiron triumphed in the Grand Prix de France at Reims, while there were good second places in the Czech and Italian Grands Prix, and victories in three secondary races.

Then the Alfas returned, Ferrari got down to serious development of an unsupercharged Formula One car, and the writing was on the wall for Talbot. Any ideas which Lago had for more advanced cars never progressed beyond the drawing board. Nevertheless, the hare and tortoise principle almost held good for one more season, with secondary victories and good Grand Prix placings falling to Lago-Talbots. But the car's obsolescence increasingly affected the spirit of its drivers; in 1951 Talbot won only the Dutch and Bordeaux Grands Prix, and in 1952 won only two very obscure events.

Lago continued with sports cars, but that effort slowly faded, and in 1959 the company was absorbed by Simca. Two decades later, a very different Talbot company was once again represented in Grand Prix racing.

concept of a racing car evolved in the Grand Prix world was to come to track racing as a revolution, and for a while that would bring the two worlds of racing together again.

Meanwhile, in itself the 2.5-litre formula had been a success, to the extent that the British newcomers fought through 1960 to extend its life, for as in the past the CSI had decided to upgrade an existing Formula Two to become the new Grand Prix formula. That meant 1.5-litre Grand Prix racing, and that prospect was by no means universally welcomed.

Safety, too often overlooked in the past, was now a major consideration, and to a degree safety was equated with lower speeds. First and foremost, the capacity limit was 1.5 litres. A minimum dry car weight of 450 kg (992 lb) was specified, hopefully to counter the use of costly alloys or flimsy components. Replenishment with oil during a race was forbidden; thus it was hoped that spillage on circuits would be minimized. Self-starters became obligatory and it was hoped that this would obviate the inherent danger of a stationary car with a stalled engine, although it introduced a potential fire hazard in the form of a battery. Dual braking systems were required, as were roll-over safety bars. (The strength and dimensions of these hoops behind drivers' heads were not specified, however, and it is doubtful if some would have supported the weight of an inverted car.) "Pump" fuel was defined as 100-octane fuel, and standards were applied for fuel system components.

When these regulations were announced in draft form in 1958, the reaction was predictably hostile, particularly in Britain where there was a substantial lobby intent on seeing that they were not put into effect, bolstered by the knowledge that in framing them the CSI had been far from unanimous. The dispute became increasingly acrimonious in 1960, but it never became as serious as the 1980-81 conflict. The CSI stood firm.

Underlying the clamour about the dull racing 1.5-litre Grands Prix would provide, and that true driving skill would count for little in 1.5-litre cars, there was considerable self-interest, for apart from BRM the British constructors had come to rely on Coventry Climax engines. Much valuable time was wasted, which both BRM and Coventry Climax could have spent designing and developing 1.5-litre engines in good time.

A parallel Intercontinental formula was instituted, to all intents and purposes to extend the life of 2.5-litre racing, for it admitted single-seaters with engines of between 2 and 3 litres. This hardly got off the ground, and while the British teams waited for British 1.5-litre V-8s, they had to contest the Grands Prix with mildly uprated Formula Two Coventry Climax four-cylinder power units, and thus were severely handicapped through 1961. For while Ferrari paid lip service to the Intercontinental idea, the Maranello technicians produced new cars with V-6 engines giving a power advantage of up to 40 bhp. That advantage was overcome only twice, by Stirling Moss at Monaco and the Nürburgring. So much for the theory that all drivers would be reduced to the same level of mediocrity, which was forgotten almost as quickly as the theory that the Intercontinental formula would attract American constructors.

Talbot 4.5-litre

In concept the Lago-Talbot was dated when the first Formula One came into effect, and it was to be the last Grand Prix car with semi-elliptic rear suspension. In essence, it derived from Talbot sports cars, using identical suspension and a similar but narrower chassis frame carrying a neat body. Front-mounted oil coolers were its only unusual outward characteristic. The engine was a long-stroke six, in which the single camshaft of the sports unit was replaced by two camshafts mounted high, one on either side of the block, operating large overhead valves through short pushrods and rockers, an arrangement that was efficient, avoided the complication of overhead camshafts, and saved weight. Lago had been general manager of the Wilson Self-Changing Gear Company before he joined STD, and a Wilson epicyclic preselector gearbox, which had the advantage of being extremely rugged, was standard. With a Wilson gearbox, a driver selected a gear before he needed to change, the actual change being effected by stabbing the clutch pedal. Behind the gearbox, spur gears offset the transmission to the right and drive was carried to a similarly offset differential; this allowed a low cockpit seat.

Such development as Talbot finances permitted was concentrated on the engine. In three years, output was increased by about 40 bhp and some of the excess weight was pared from later cars.

SPECIFICATIONS
Lago-Talbot 4.5-litre   1948

Engine
Straight-six
Bore × stroke: 93 mm × 110 mm
Capacity: 4482 cc
Carburettors: 3 Zenith
Maximum power: 240 bhp at 4700 rpm (1948) to 280 bhp at 5000 rpm (1950)

Transmission
Four-speed preselector

Chassis
Channel-section cross-braced frame

Front suspension
Independent by wishbones, transverse leaf spring, and shock absorbers

Rear suspension
Rigid axle, semi-elliptic springs, and shock absorbers

Brakes
Drum

Dimensions
Wheelbase: 98 in (2489 mm)
Front track: 54 in (1372 mm)
Rear track: 51 in (1295 mm)

A 2.5-litre racing class survived through the 1960s in Australia and New Zealand, but the 2.5-litre Grand Prix formula which ushered in the modern age of racing was over. The formula had run for seven years—which seemed an extraordinarily long span, although it was to be handsomely surpassed by the 3-litre formula which came in 1966—and it had seen vast changes.

Those affecting car design had been reviewed, and were spreading to other major categories such as sports car and USAC racing. True manufacturer representation in Grand Prix racing had dwindled: there was Ferrari—it seems that there has always been Ferrari, and it will be a sad day if the marque ever disappears from Grands Prix—Porsche and Honda were to come and go, Ford were to appear "by proxy", and Alfa Romeo and Renault would eventually return. But the era of the kit car had come, for many small constructors who could never have aspired to Grand Prix racing in earlier periods were able to do so as major components, such as engines and gearboxes, became available "off the shelf"; the time was coming when organizations existed just to build and run teams, having no other automotive commitments.

The five years of the 1.5-litre formula was a period of accelerating change. Although traditionalists deplored the prospect of "puny little cars", by the end of the formula these were the fastest Grand Prix cars in lap times around circuits. In addition, unprecedented progress was made in terms of efficiency, chassis design, and road-holding. The racing was good through those years.

The first season, 1961, seemed to run true to predictions in that Ferrari engine power secured the championship. Late in the season the first Coventry Climax V-8 appeared, followed by the first BRM V-8, although neither became raceworthy until 1962. When Dunlop produced "high-hysteresis" tyres it was suddenly realized that tyre technology was entering a period when much more than tread patterns was involved.

Ferrari approached the season uncertainly, but realized they had a winner when a car was loaned to Formula One novice Giancarlo Baghetti for the Syracuse Grand Prix and he clearly beat full British and German teams. Whether the Ferrari V-6s achieved their claimed power outputs was almost academic; their cars were only beaten twice, and then by Stirling Moss in Rob Walker's Lotus 18. Porsche came close to victory in the French Grand Prix when all the factory Ferraris retired and Baghetti won in his nominally independent car. At the end of the season, with championships secured, Ferrari did not contest the United States Grand Prix and Innes Ireland scored the first championship victory for Lotus. Ferrari won at Zandvoort, Spa, Reims, and Aintree. The championships were settled on a sombre day at Monza, where von Trips and fourteen spectators were killed in an accident. Moss's brilliance triumphed at Monaco and at the Nürburgring, where he won his last Grand Prix.

The British race was the only Grand Prix to be contested by the Ferguson P99, a "development car" for the Ferguson four-wheel drive system, which, incidentally, was also the last front-engined car to run in a Grand Prix. It was disqualified at Aintree, but later in the year Moss drove it to win the Oulton Park Gold Cup. That was the

VANWALL

Frustration is a not uncommon return for an investment of enthusiasm and participation in Grand Prix racing, and it accrued in generous measure to anybody involved with the original BRM enterprise. One of these people, G.A. "Tony" Vandervell, an industrialist and patriot of an old-fashioned school, had the will and resources to go it alone. He found that this road to success was by no means quick or easy. Effectively, the Vanwall project was born in 1949 when Vandervell acquired a Ferrari 125. The intention was that this car should be used for test purposes and to give the infant BRM team some racing experience. It was run as a Thinwall, that being a Vandervell Products trade name. The second Thinwall, in 1950, was also a supercharged Ferrari, but in 1951 this was rebuilt around a 4.5-litre unsupercharged Ferrari V-12. This car was steadily improved with, for example, disc brakes, and it led into another 4.5-litre car which was raced on in Formule Libre events for some time after racing to the 1.5-litre supercharged/4.5-litre unsupercharged Grand Prix formula collapsed in 1952.

By that time, Vandervell was thoroughly exasperated with BRM. He had the nucleus of a team—it had been running the Thinwalls—drawing office, and tool room, and he had enormous influence with potential component suppliers. So Vandervell set out to beat not just BRM, but the Grand Prix world. He was also involved with the Norton motorcycle company. Joe Craig and Leo Kuzmicki, of Norton, became committed in the design of a twin-overhead camshaft car engine, which Kuzmicki continued to work on after the Vandervell-Norton association ended.

In many respects, this unit consisted of four Norton engines made into one unit, with its four separate cylinder barrels spigotted to a light-alloy crankcase and cylinder head, valves closed by exposed hair springs and four Amal motorcycle-type carburettors. These carburettors were used on the first 2-litre unit and an interim 2.3-litre engine, but in 1955 were replaced by Bosch fuel injection on the definitive 2.5-litre engine. This basic engine was to serve for the rest of Vanwall's career. It was first used in a straightforward chassis built by Cooper, with Ferrari-type suspension, and initially distinguished by its ugly surface radiator.

Only in 1956 did Vanwall begin to become a Grand Prix force, with a car which really stood out on the grids. Driven by Stirling Moss (in a "guest appearance", as Maserati did not contest the race) it had a debut victory in the International Trophy race at Silverstone. The rest of that season was marked by promise, and frustration. Harry Schell did succeed in getting among the leaders in the French and Italian Grands Prix, but the best placing was a fourth in Belgium. Too often there were minor problems, with, for example, the throttle control. In the next year Vanwall driving strength was formidable, but the problems persisted until the British Grand Prix at Aintree, where Moss took over the car in which an unwell Tony Brooks had started, and drove it to a famous victory. Even more telling victories fell to Vanwall at Pescara and Monza, the home ground of the then-dominant Italian teams.

Ironically, the first year of Grand Prix racing on "petrol", which caused more problems for Vanwall than for most teams, was also their best. Moss won the Dutch, Portugese, and Moroccan Grands Prix, Brooks won the Belgian, German, and Italian, and Vanwall took the championship. Unhappily, Stuart Lewis-Evans, the third team driver, was fatally injured in the last race of the season, at Casablanca.

Early in 1959, Tony Vandervell had to give up his personal involvement in the team for medical reasons. A new car was run for Brooks in the 1959 British Grand Prix. For 1960 a new light and low Vanwall ran in the French Grand Prix, but it was out of its time for by then the mid-engined era had arrived. Low-key research continued. A Vanwall-engined Lotus was tested and then for the abortive Intercontinental formula a 2.6-litre mid-engined Vanwall was built. John Surtees raced it at Silverstone. It finished fifth. That marked the end of the Vanwall racing effort. Although the rest of the team had been highly professional, the power had come from the top, and without Tony Vandervell there was effectively no reason for Vanwall.

only Formula One victory for a four-wheel drive car; three years later BRM tested a four-wheel drive car, but did not race it.

The 1962 championship was fought out between BRM and Lotus. And BRM, under threat of closure if they did not win, took the championship. Until their last race, in South Africa, Lotus could have won with the combination of Clark and the trend-setting monocoque 25. A failed bolt, and consequent loss of oil, cost Clark that last race which he had led for three-quarters of its distance. The race, and the championships, fell to Graham Hill and BRM.

The rest? Cooper won at Monaco, and gained a distant third place in the championship. Porsche gained a lucky win in France, which only served to underline the company's disappointment with their Grand Prix venture, and they quit at the end of the year. Porsche was even a point behind Lola (for whom Surtees gained two second places) in the points table, in equal fifth place with Ferrari. The Italian cars' handling was no better than it had been in 1961; their power advantage gone, the team was riddled with dissent. The outcome was a breakaway group, headed by Carlo Chiti, who set up ATS (Automobili Turismo e Sport, unrelated to the late-1970s team with the same initials). They produced an ineffectual Grand Prix car, which served only to drag down the careers of Phil Hill and Baghetti. Ferrari started on the road to recovery with John Surtees, who won his first Grand Prix at the Nürburgring and was fourth in the championship table. Graham Hill won two races for BRM, at Monaco and Watkins Glen. The rest of the season belonged to Jim Clark and Lotus. He won the other seven races, including the new

Mexican Grand Prix, and he led five of them from start to finish.

Technically, most teams spent a season just trying to keep up. BRM moved to semi-monocoque construction, yet Brabham's spaceframe cars promised much, so the chassis debate continued. Coventry Climax looked to fuel injection, and Ferrari turned to V-8s. Grand Prix technology was about to arrive at Indianapolis, where in 1963 the old order just fought off the new in the form of Jim Clark in a Ford-powered Lotus. Safety was still much in mind, and trackside Armco barriers increasingly displaced the traditional straw bales, while a "dummy grid" system was brought in to reduce the possibility of start-line accidents.

Uniquely, any one of three drivers could have won the 1964 championship at its last race, in Mexico. Graham Hill went to it with a point's lead, and with victories at Monaco and Watkins Glen behind him; John Surtees was second, and had won at the Nürburgring and Monza; Jim Clark was third, in a position to equal Hill's score only if he won in Mexico and the BRM driver retired, for if that happened the title would be his by virtue of a greater number of victories in the Dutch, Belgian, and British events. In the race Hill was sidelined, and Clark did lead, until the penultimate lap when his V-8 seized. While Dan Gurney went through to win the race in a Brabham, Lorenzo Bandini slowed to let his Ferrari team leader John Surtees through to second place and the six points which secured the title.

Earlier in the season, Dan Gurney had scored Brabham's first Grand Prix victory, in France, while Bandini had won his only

SPECIFICATIONS
Vanwall 2.5-litre   1954
Engine
Four-in-line
Bore × stroke: 96 mm × 86 mm
Capacity: 1490 cc
Twin overhead camshafts
Maximum power: 285 bhp at 7300 rpm

Transmission
Five-speed

Chassis
Tubular spaceframe

Front suspension
Independent by wishbones, coil springs, and hydraulic shock absorbers

Rear suspension
De Dion, coil springs, and hydraulic shock absorbers

Brakes
Disc; inboard at rear

Dimensions
Wheelbase: 91 in (2311 mm)
Front track: 56 in (1422 mm)
Rear track: 52 in (1321 mm)

Vanwall 2.5-litre

The Vanwall which won the Constructors' Championship in 1958 was partly the end product of an evolutionary process. It was a striking car in contemporary Grand Prix company, big and high, and it gave an impression of aerodynamic efficiency. That impression did not mislead, for in the main the low-

drag body by Frank Costin was effective. It clothed a spaceframe designed by Colin Chapman—yet to become a Formula One designer in his own right when this definitive Vanwall appeared in 1956—who had also worked his magic on the suspension.

The engine remained an oversquare four, with power output up to 285

bhp in 1957, its peak year. There was, however, some loss of power resulting from the mandatory use of "commercially available" AvGas fuel in 1958. On the other hand, the Vanwall bogy of unreliability, which too often stemmed from the inability of minor components to live with vibrations, was by then completely eliminated.

championship Grand Prix, at Zeltweg in Austria. New names had included Mike Hailwood, driving a full season after a couple of Grands Prix in 1963, while at the other extreme Maurice Trintignant drove a BRM in four races, in his last season. Honda made an exploratory debut in the German Grand Prix, with an original and complex car and American Ronnie Bucknum driving his first single-seater race. Honda worked hard, engaging experienced Richie Ginther for 1965. Until the last race of that year, and the last of the 1.5-litre formula, the team had a disappointing time. At Mexico City, however, Ginther led from start to finish. That victory was significant for a Japanese car and was also the first of many for Goodyear, ending Dunlop's near-monopoly through the 1.5-litre years.

Overall, the 1965 season was quite simply Clark's and Lotus's. The Scot won the South African, Belgian, French, British, Dutch, and German Grands Prix, and he gained the first non-American victory at Indianapolis since 1916, the first for a mid-engined car, and the first at 150 mph average (150.686 mph), and he broke a succession of records for Offenhauser-powered cars that went back to 1947. Meanwhile, Hill won again at Monaco and again at Watkins Glen. Third in the championship was his new BRM team-mate, Jackie Stewart, who drove his first Grand Prix as the season opened in South Africa (and scored his first point), was third at Monaco, second at Spa and at Clermont-Ferrand, and rounded off the European part of the season with victory in the Italian Grand Prix.

The once-derided 1.5-litre formula had run its course, and oddly the British teams which had overwhelmingly made up its Grand Prix fields faced the 3-litre future as uncertainly as they had the first 1.5-litre year—and basically for the same reason. Only BRM made their own engines, and although these were used by some other teams, the majority had used the Coventry Climax V-8. Now, although a 2-litre version of that engine was to be made available for Jim Clark, Coventry Climax abandoned motor racing. Coventry Climax engines had powered the winning cars in twenty-five 1.5-litre Grands Prix, their availability had become taken almost for granted, and it had encouraged the kit-car constructors even more than the 2.5-litre four-cylinder Climax engine.

The real solution to the dilemma, at least for one team, came in the second year of the formula. In November 1965, Ford of Britain agreed to back a Grand Prix engine. Because designer-designate Keith Duckworth had never undertaken a complete engine, the Ford-Cosworth Grand Prix project was approached through the FVA for Formula Two; when this was completed late in 1966, work began on a 3-litre V-8, the DFV. Five months later, the first DFV was handed to Colin Chapman. By comparison with the Grand Prix engines raced in 1966, the overall impression of the DFV was of compactness and neatness, with no ancillaries apparently hung on as after-thoughts. Nobody saw it as potentially the single most important piece of racing machinery ever designed.

Vast changes were to come when the 3-litre formula was established. Meanwhile, as it opened there were hardening professional attitudes throughout the Grand Prix world, among promoters and organizers as well as teams. There was still fun in racing, and was to be into the next decade. However, the time when amateur or playboy drivers could achieve good Grand Prix results had passed. Stirling Moss had been the archetypal modern professional racing driver, and there was little room for drivers who did not match his standards of professionalism in the 1960s, even less in the 1970s.

The secondary, or non-championship, races for Grand Prix cars were disappearing, too. The last to survive on a regular basis were run in England—the Race of Champions at Brands Hatch and the International Trophy at Silverstone, a race with a longer history than most Grands Prix of the late 1970s, and one with a real sense of tradition. But history and tradition counted for little in a sport that was also big business, as in truth it had to become, in view of the vast investment a successful team represents, and in line with other prominent international sports.

In the first year of 3-litre racing it was forcibly demonstrated that sheer engine power is not all-important, for the championship fell to Brabham, the simplest and lightest car, with the least powerful 3-litre engine. Jack Brabham and Ron Tauranac showed the way to go with the BT19 and BT20, while Chapman really pushed racing car development ahead with the Lotus 49. Still the obsession with power, and getting that power onto the road, led to a rash of four-wheel drive cars in 1969, encouraged by the showing of the turbine-powered four-wheel drive Lotus at Indianapolis in 1968. But all abandoned it as too complex and heavy, and demanding techniques drivers found alien. The true way forward was in chassis and running gear refinement, and in aerodynamics. In addition to the contributions made by designers, the parts played by the proprietary component manufacturers (notably the Hewland gearbox company) and the tyre technicians were substantial.

The 1966 Brabhams used front wheels with 8 in wide rims, rear wheels with 10 in wide rims; in 1980 respective rim widths were generally 11 in and up to 19 in. Thus, at some cost in frontal area and straightline speed, the amount of tyre in contact with the road surface was greatly increased, and that played a part in the rapid rise in cornering speeds. Tyre compounds multiplied, and costs soared. This forced Dunlop out of Grand Prix racing at the end of 1970; Firestone soon followed, leaving Goodyear in a monopoly position that was not altogether welcome until Michelin came into racing in the late 1970s. Then Goodyear departed as the Grand Prix world was plunged into turmoil at the end of the 1980 season. By that time, a degree of reality had prevailed, and some of the more costly tyre absurdities, such as short-life "qualifiers", were forgotten.

Aerodynamic aids developed rapidly from little trim tabs on the noses of Brabhams, through the first exploratory "wings" over the gearboxes of Ferraris and Brabhams in the spring of 1968, to high-mounted aerofoils later that year. These were abruptly restricted in size and height following accidents in the 1969 Spanish Grand Prix. Within those restrictions, aerodynamic aids became more and more sophisticated, until Colin Chapman took another quantum leap forward in 1978, by effectively utilizing the flow of air under a car, to produce downforce which enabled cornering speeds to be enormously increased. This ground-effects idea was rapidly refined by other designers, until efforts were made to curb it by regulation for 1981, and thereby it was piously hoped that the alarmingly high cornering speeds would also be reduced.

During the years of the 3-litre formula, for lack of resources or success, a few apparently well-established teams collapsed, among them Cooper and BRM. New solidly founded teams appeared. Tyrrell was a "kit-car" example from the middle period, Renault at the other extreme coming in the late 1970s. Independent entrants failed to survive (or were just not admitted to entry lists), although Williams, the championship team of 1980, had it roots in that once-fertile soil. There were also attempts to break into Grand Prix racing by would-be constructors, whose impact on even the fringes was hardly noticed.

Resources became vital, and the key to the treasury of resources was sponsorship. Colin Chapman opened the door in 1968, his cars appearing "painted like cigarette packets" and with a later attempt to name them John Player Specials, in an apparent apeing of American track practice which appalled the traditionalists. In the 1970s, however, it became universal practice.

Motor racing is a sport that cannot stand still. More professional racing has meant harder, closer racing, and modern spectators would find it difficult to accept some of the professional races of the past, headed by lordly Mercedes or Alfas. The gaudy colours of the sponsors have meant money that has enabled technical inspiration to be put into effect in ever more efficient machinery. And Grand Prix racing would be nothing if it was not competition between examples of advanced automotive engineering driven by men with great ability.

THE CARS

DOUG NYE

IN ERAS PAST racing cars were often pushed to Grand Prix grids by their mechanics, with the driver walking alongside. In recent years the general practice has been for the cars to be driven a lap from the pit lane to the grid, where they are then surrounded by their crews. There is much to be said for the old routine, however, for it focussed a spotlight on the team. In an age when star billing is everything, it is all too easy for popular presentation and reporting to concentrate on the man in the cockpit, while in reality Grand Prix racing is a team effort which involves many people, from the sponsors to the factory gofer.

It is often said that the most important element of a team is its budget. Superficially, this might seem to be reflected in the drivers' real or reputed earnings or in lavish paddock trappings, but these costs are only the tip of the iceberg, and in any case they may be the ostentation of a sponsor who hopes by entertainment or display to win a return on his investment.

The real depth of Grand Prix teams, and the real costs, are hinted at in the pits. They are in the transporters, in the pits garages, and, of course, in the cars. They are the products of high automotive technology, designed for a special task within restricting regulations, with materials and workmanship of aerospace standards taken for granted. It all requires deep wells of financial resources, and while it is not axiomatic that a generous budget automatically leads to success on the circuits, it is true that no modern team can hope to succeed on a shoestring.

Team resources have to span the best possible plant, access to the best research, development, and test facilities, the best designers and the best mechanics, and a high degree of management skill. The motivations are perhaps obvious, and dedication is necessary at all levels, for hours can be long and irregular—"all-nighters" before a race are well-known in the lore of team mechanics—and demanding standards must be met in conditions that can be most difficult.

The men in the cockpits on a grid are at the apex of complex pyramids. The teams they represent follow a broad pattern, but their varying backgrounds, different approaches, successes, and failures, driving forces and dominant personalities contribute greatly to the fascination this twentieth-century sport holds for millions of enthusiasts the world over.

The technical development of the Grand Prix car, just like all other technological advances, has progressed considerably since 1906 when that first Grand Prix race was held. Effectively, there have been three groups of cars produced: the early machines of the heroic age—high-built, big-engined, and often chain-driven with minimal bodywork to protect the crew; the cars built from the 1920s to the close of the 1950s with their mainly front-mounted engines and bodies providing smooth aerodynamic protection; and, finally, the rear-engined (or more properly mid-engined) cars which have reigned supreme since 1959, using ever wider tyres and continuously evolving aerodynamic performance aids.

Obviously, there are myriad subsidiary groups of detail development within these broad classes, but no class has seen so much, or such rapid detail development as the modern mid-engined cars. Looking further back into the past a number of development stepping stones are apparent. The change from chain-drive to shaft-drive before the First World War was one notable advance. This was followed closely by the introduction of high-revving, high specific power-output engines which no longer relied upon sheer size to produce competitive power. The earliest pioneers generally considered that the larger the engine the better. Their cars' engine capacities mushroomed from about 3 litres to 12, 14, and even 19 litres in capacity. Peugeot and Delage then developed high-efficiency 3-litre voiturette engines into power plants of about 5 litres, which in lighter chassis proved capable of humbling the giant cars of the old régime.

Continuous revision of the regulations for each annual Grand Prix race forced development. After World War I, formulae catered in turn for 3-, 2-, and 1.5-litre Grand Prix cars. Consequently, the shape of the Grand Prix car changed. It became lower and sleeker, small capacity engines became supercharged, and suspension systems were more refined although still relying heavily upon the traditional "cart spring".

The years of the Depression, at the turn of the 1920s and 1930s, saw the few manufacturers and private individuals who could afford to go racing use a motley armoury of cars. Some were left from earlier formulae plus a few mind-boggling monster cars specially built with high-efficiency supercharged engines of up to 7 litres capacity. In some cases two engines were used, side by side in the front, or one at either end.

By 1933, international financial structures had stabilized sufficiently for a new 750-kilogramme maximum weight formula to be applied to Grand Prix racing from 1934 until 1936. It was later extended to include the 1937 season as well. This was the famous formula which attracted money from the German Third Reich in the ultra-modern shapes of Mercedes-Benz and Auto Union. With state aid these large and sophisticated companies advanced technical development as never before. The engine had always been the most important feature in the mind of every Grand Prix car designer. The chassis and suspension system was virtually a bothersome necessity, unworthy of creative thought. The Germans changed all that, confirming the value of a properly stressed tubular ladder-frame chassis in place of the accepted channel-section "steel girder" frame. They combined sophisticated and relatively soft long-travel springing with a stiff chassis so that the road wheels would follow road undulations more faithfully than in the past. Earlier cars, as well as contemporary machines from Italian, French, British, and American constructors, tended to rely upon stiff leaf-spring suspensions hung from flexible channel-section chassis. These machines gave their drivers a bone-shaking ride, but could be made to slide fairly accurately through corners without assuming alarming angles of body roll. Certainly they tended to hop and skip from bump to bump, but that was the way competition cars had always been. The German engineers sought to change all that with their new suspension systems. By allowing their cars' road wheels to stay in contact with the road surface for more of the time they reaped enormous advantages in improved traction under power. Similarly

they enjoyed better braking. One aspect of the modern Grand Prix car was thus appreciated and applied successfully.

In 1937, when Mercedes-Benz dominated the scene with their W125, the company introduced a new suspension refinement which was to hold sway for two decades. The W125's front suspension employed double wishbone members linking the road wheels to the chassis, sprung by a coil spring. The rear wheels were maintained parallel to one another by a so-called de Dion tube beam. This linked their hubs and was arched to clear a chassis-mounted final-drive unit and universally jointed swinging drive shafts.

Still the supercharged engine held sway. Mercedes went for peak power while Auto Union concentrated more on massive torque for vivid acceleration even when the engine was running slowly. World War II chopped almost ten years out of Grand Prix car development. The cars which resumed racing in 1945 and 1946 were relics surviving from prewar days and the new models of 1947 to 1949 drew heavily on prewar practice. Ferrari proved that a good unsupercharged engine had the legs of a supercharged unit which was limited by the regulations to only one-third the unsupercharged capacity. The first true postwar Grand Prix cars were those designed for the new 2.5-litre unsupercharged Grand Prix formula introduced in 1954. This new formula ran until 1960. Supercharged engines were restricted to a mere 750 cc, which rendered them totally uncompetitive. Mercedes-Benz reappeared in racing with a straight-eight-cylinder engine of great sophistication mounted in a lightweight multi-tubular spaceframe chassis. This chassis showed other Formula One manufacturers how to produce a stiff structure without the penalty of excessive weight.

Spaceframe chassis structures had been "borrowed" from aviation fuselage construction methods and had found their way into racing through Trossi and Waddy specials in the 1930s, Cisitalia's *vettureti* in the 1940s, and budding British minor-formula work in the early 1950s. Actually Grand Prix racing was beginning to draw upon aviation knowledge and experience to an ever greater degree. In World War I, military aero engines had drawn from the French Grand Prix-winning Mercedes racing engine. Now, after a second war which had boosted aviation achievement to undreamed of heights, the technology flow was reversed. Already Jaguar had built their D-type sports racing car on aeronautic monocoque chassis principles, which replaced the traditional steel tube, girder, or lattice-work, frame with a stressed skin homogeneous structure. This structure's sheet panelling and internal formers gave the necessary rigidity in an elegant and lightweight, yet immensely stiff, form. Colin Chapman's Lotus sports cars were amassing a huge number of race wins using ultra-lightweight tubular spaceframe chassis, which he was to use as a launching pad for his own Grand Prix racing ambitions.

The 1954 formula saw huge advances made in the production of horsepower without forced induction. In Britain a number of companies became capable of building racing engines not for use in their own cars, but for sale to outside chassis constructors. Such companies as Mercedes-Benz, Ferrari, Maserati, and Lancia all built road cars which would sell upon the success of their Grand Prix machinery. In Britain at the same time a number of specialist firms appeared, interested purely in competition. Cooper, Connaught, HWM, and BRM were early runners in this new game, buying their engines from such outside sources as Alta, Bristol, JAP, or, later, Coventry Climax, or in BRM's case attempting to do it themselves at enormous cost and with modest success. In 1956, when Vanwall came on the scene seriously, they used the best available chassis designer—Colin Chapman—the best available aerodynamicist—Frank Costin—and the best available engine—their own—to produce what became a World Champion car.

Fuel injection replaced carburettors, and disc brakes were used, while all other British manufacturers, led by BRM, had introduced this notable advance into international single-seater racing. Less time spent braking means more time can be spent under power. In turn, average lap speeds rise, lap times fall, lap records are broken, and the sophisticated car proves harder to beat. Saving weight means less mass to be accelerated and braked, less load for the tyres to heave around a corner, and when 2.5-litre Formula One races were shortened and heavy alcohol fuels banned in favour of lighter AvGas aviation fuel for the 1958-60 seasons, the door was opened to lighter, smaller, and more nimble cars than ever before. The British stepped in, with Cooper using fundamentally uprated versions of their 1.5-litre Coventry Climax mid-engined Formula Two cars. Driven by such skilled drivers as Stirling Moss and Jack Brabham, the little Coopers with their forgiving cornering characteristics, light weight, and minimal frontal area—allowing them to compensate for the handicap of low power—heralded the outbreak of the rear-engined revolution.

In 1959, when Coventry Climax made full 2.5-litre engines, Cooper proved unbeatable on the more tortuous race circuits and BRM, Lotus, and Ferrari rapidly began mid-engined experiments of their own. The traditional front-engined racing car was soon set aside, never to be used again. Simultaneously, the fully adjustable chassis was beginning to evolve. Formerly a Grand Prix car would be designed, built, and tested until its handling was considered adequate and would then be raced more or less in its proven form for the rest of the season. When stringent new 1.5-litre capacity limits were applied for the Grand Prix Formula of 1961 to 1965, teams had to make do with minimal power, between 160 and 200 bhp. By this time, too, wheel-enveloping bodywork had been banned.

Consequently, easily adjustable suspension became standard. Mechanics would tinker with wheel cambers, castors, toe-in, spring rates, ride height, and roll resistance until lap times improved during practice and before each race. Colin Chapman popularized the monocoque construction method for single-seater cars and when regulations later demanded metal fuel tank sheathing the old spaceframe concept finally died. The monocoque became universal.

During the 1960s Dunlop, Goodyear, and Firestone found themselves in bitter competition on the Grand Prix scene. Tyres grew wider. Tread patterns developed and were finally erased when rubber compounding made it possible to run a completely "bald" tyre to place the maximum area possible in contact with the road without losing grip. The aerodynamic resistance of these wider tyres slashed straightline speeds. The narrow-tyred 1960 2.5-litre Cooper hit 190 mph on the long straights at Reims. The 1966 wide-tyred 3-litre Repco Brabham could hardly exceed 180 mph, yet lapped much more quickly. The Cooper averaged 135 mph and the Brabham, slower on the straights, 140 mph for the lap. This was because the Brabham did not need to slow down so much for the corners, simply wafting through them at speeds which would have been suicidal in the Cooper, due to its primitive tyres and suspension. This art of going ever faster through the turns has been refined through the late-1960s and 1970s into the 1980s. From 1967 strutted wings added aerodynamic download to force tyres down into firmer contact with the road. Regulation changes killed the tall wings, but low-set wing designs improved and downloads increased. Then, in 1977, Colin Chapman's Lotus team introduced the ground-effects system. The sliding skirts increased adhesion as never before.

From 1967 to 1974 and well into 1980 the off-the-shelf Cosworth-Ford DFV engine dominated Grand Prix racing. Renault emerged in 1977 with their 1.5-litre turbocharged Formula One programme in which outputs of 550-565 bhp became usual. Into the 1980s turbocharged engines began to be produced for Formula One by Ferrari and Alfa Romeo as well as Renault. The turbos had begun to threaten the normally aspirated Cosworth-engined brigade.

The Cosworth DFV
Keith Duckworth designed this engine initially for Team Lotus, with sponsorship from Ford of Britain. It was designated DFV ("double four valve", since in part it derived from the "four valve" FVA). The initial power output of this straightforward V-8 was 412 bhp; fourteen years later it exceeded 480 bhp. The DFV was first raced in the Lotus 49s in the 1967 Dutch Grand Prix and Jim Clark won with it first time out. By June 1981 over one hundred and forty World Championship victories had been scored by DFV-powered cars, and teams using the DFV had won the Constructors' Championship eight times. The DFV has also won the Le Mans 24-Hour Race and other endurance events, while derivatives have been highly successful in other categories. Most notably, the DFX, a smaller capacity (2.6-litre) turbocharged derivative became dominant in USAC racing in the second half of the 1970s and powered three Indianapolis 500 winners. From 1967 through 1981 the design of the DFV was fundamentally unchanged, although there were many detail modifications; during that period more than three hundred and sixty DFVs were built and the engine became a mainstay of Grand Prix racing.

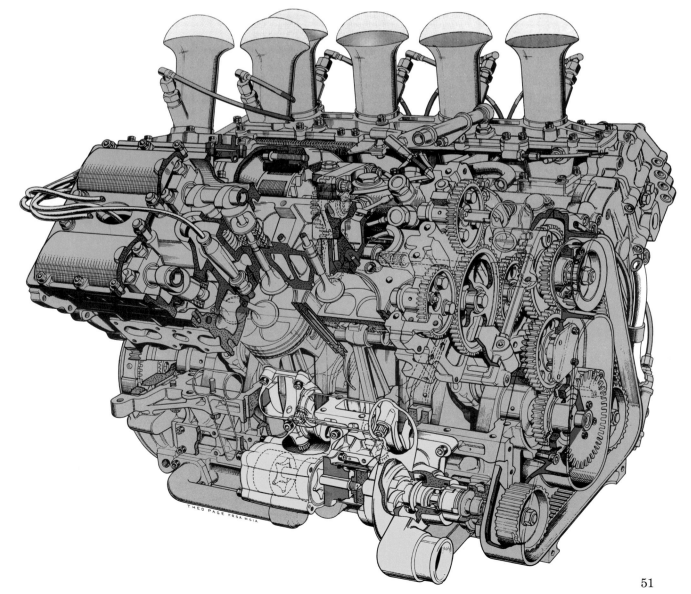

ALFA ROMEO

In the spring of 1979, Bruno Giacomelli drove a tubby, maroon, Formula One car in the Belgian Grand Prix at Zolder. It was the Alfa Romeo Tipo 177, and its appearance marked the return of the world-famous Portello factory to Grand Prix racing, which it had dominated at various times in the 1920s and 1930s and in the decades after the war.

In October 1951, Alfa Romeo had won their last Grand Prix race and their last Formula One World Championship title at Barcelona. In the ensuing years, Alfa were never entirely divorced from racing, competing with sports saloons, Gran Turismo cars, and in 1955-56 with the legendary Disco Volante, the Flying Saucer, sports roadster.

In September 1964, Dr. Orazio Satta Puliga, Alfa's chief engineer, set his team to work on a completely new V-8, mid-engined, sports racing car intended for the 2-litre class. This prototype was completed by late 1965 at Portello and was then turned over to Autodelta, the new company which was responsible for defending Alfa's honour in racing. In March 1967, the new car, the Alfa Romeo T33, won on its debut at the minor Fléron hill climb in Belgium. Its first serious races were unsuccessful, but in February 1968 new coupé versions came first and second in their class at the Daytona 24-Hours in Florida. Although first, second, and third in its class at the 1968 Le Mans 24-Hour Race, the T33 was seen too often as an unreliable also-ran.

The type eventually matured, through an interim 2.5-litre version, as the full 3-litre V-8 T33/3, which in 1969 won at the Zeltweg and Enna circuits. Alfa Romeo and Autodelta learned much from their experiences with this 32-valve, four-cam, V-8 engine and in the autumn of 1970 they produced a new lightweight, multi-tubular, spaceframe chassis to carry it. This car was known as the 33/3 TT, for *telaio tubolare,* tubular chassis. In 1972, it took second place in the Constructors' World Championship.

Encouraged, the management of Alfa Romeo authorized Autodelta's chief engineer, Carlo Chiti, to produce for 1973 a completely new 3-litre, flat-12, sports racing engine similar to the Ferrari flat-12, a proven Formula One winner which had been adapted to Ferrari sports racing cars. But this new Alfa Romeo 33TT/12 sports car was outclassed by Ferrari and Matra-Simca in 1973. When Ferrari withdrew from sports car competition in 1974, Matra-Simca proved unbeatable. The French company withdrew in 1975, however, and that season the flat-12 Alfas annihilated the feeble opposition, winning seven of eight major races contested.

By 1977, Alfa Romeo had developed and produced the 33SC/12 cars, which won every race in a poorly supported World Championship. Meanwhile, the low profile and high power output of the 3-litre, flat-12 sports car engine had attracted Formula One interest, first from Graham Hill's private team and then from Bernie Ecclestone's Brabham company. The prototype, Martini-sponsored, Brabham-Alfa Romeo Grand Prix car was unveiled to the press in October 1975. After a troublesome first season it began to show promise. The significance of its achievement was not lost upon the Alfa Romeo management. Their Grand Prix racing ambitions were rekindled.

It had become apparent that Renault were returning to Grand Prix racing. Fiat were deeply involved, financially, with Ferrari and there were strong rumours of Formula One entries from Porsche and BMW. These would be worthy opponents. In 1977, Chiti and Autodelta were authorized to begin development of their own complete Alfa Romeo Formula One car. The new prototype flat-12 Formula One car was designated the 177-001. The *quadrifoglio,* Alfa's famous four-leafed clover racing symbol, was coming back to Grand Prix racing—a quarter of a century after its withdrawal.

SPECIFICATIONS
Alfa Romeo 179   1979

Engine
Alfa Romeo 1260, 60-degree V-12
Bore × stroke: 78.5 mm × 51.5 mm
Capacity: 2991 cc
Lucas fuel injection
Marelli Dinoplex electronic ignition
Maximum power: c 525 bhp at c 10,500 rpm

Transmission
Alfa Romeo, six-speed and reverse

Chassis
Three-quarter length monocoque nacelle employing engine as stressed member at rear

Front suspension
Top rocker arms actuating inboard coil spring/damper units, bottom wishbones

Rear suspension
Parallel top links, twin radius rods, inboard coil spring/damper units, bottom wishbones

Brakes
Disc; inboard, front and rear

Dimensions
Wheelbase: 108 in (2743 mm)
Front track: 67.7 in (1720 mm)
Rear track: 61.8 in (1570 mm)
Wheel rim width: 11 in front, 19 in rear
Formula weight: 1313 lb (595 kg)

Tyres
Goodyear

The aged flat-12 engine of the 177 was rapidly replaced by the new 1260 V-12 unit in a Tipo 179 chassis from the 1979 Italian Grand Prix, when Bruno Giacomelli and Vittorio Brambilla were driving for the team. During 1980 Patrick Depailler joined the team and, until his tragic death while testing at Hockenheim, he and Giacomelli proved the V-12 cars' competitiveness. After a wild period, Giacomelli's driving improved rapidly and at Watkins Glen his Alfa led for many laps before retirement. A 1.5-litre turbocharged V-8 engine was developed for 1981 and Mario Andretti joined Giacomelli in this "proper" factory Formula One team.

Alfa Romeo 177

This prototype 3-litre, Formula One Alfa Romeo was completed essentially as a test vehicle during 1977 and was numbered 177-001. It mated a sizeable monocoque chassis to a flat-12 engine and featured an unusually bulky aerodynamic body design. Due to internal political problems—Alfa Romeo had a strong Communist union opposed to "rich men's sport"—the 177 was not actually raced until 1979, when Bruno Giacomelli drove it in the Belgian Grand Prix. It ran in midfield before colliding with Jody Scheckter's Ferrari. The 177 reappeared in the Italian Grand Prix when Vittorio Brambilla finished twelfth in it. The same race saw the debut of the new Tipo 179 V-12-engined car, and subsequently the ugly flat-12 177 prototype was withdrawn. There was no Tipo 178.

Carlo Chiti was born on December 29, 1924, in Pistoia, Italy. This heavily built, droll Tuscan graduated from Pisa University in 1951 with a degree in aeronautical engineering. Cars were his first love and in 1952 he joined the Alfa Romeo experimental department, where he remained for five years. In 1957, he went to Ferrari and was responsible for their 1961 World Championship-winning cars. Chiti left in 1962 to found ATS (Automobili Turismo e Sport), a company which produced a disastrous Formula One car in the hopes of beating Ferrari. Late the following year, Chiti, in partnership with Ludovico Chizzola, formed Autodelta SpA with Alfa's blessing. Alfa Romeo owe their return to motor racing prominence to this hard-working engineer's dedication and resolve.

Team Drivers
Mario Andretti • Vittorio Brambilla • Patrick Depailler • Bruno Giacomelli

ARROWS

Few Grand Prix teams have had such a controversial birth as the British Arrows organization. Arrows was conceived in 1977 by disgruntled members of the Nichols Advanced Vehicles Systems Shadow team, who had grown tired of living almost literally from hand to mouth, scraping by from race to race on start money, occasional winnings, and bonus prizes after the team had lost its major sponsors.

In October 1977, Arrows was formed. An acronym of the initials of its founders' names, the letters AR stood for former Shadow Italian sponsors Franco and Christina Ambrosio, R for Alan Rees, ex-March founder member and team manager, O for Jackie Oliver, a former Formula One driver and now sponsorship-finder, W for Dave Wass, an engineer, and S for Tony Southgate, Arrows's chief designer.

They found premises to house the team just outside London, in Milton Keynes, moved in on November 28th, and set themselves the target of producing their new car in time for the Brazilian Grand Prix in January 1978. The car had to be ready to run no later than January 21st, when it had to be put on the Formula One teams' flight to Rio de Janeiro. By working day and night, Arrows's loyal personnel built the prototype FA1 in just sixty days.

The Ambrosios persuaded Riccardo Patrese, the promising Italian driver, to join the team. He drove the FA1 car for the first time in the Brazilian Grand Prix. In the next race, at Kyalami in South Africa, a skilful tyre choice enabled Patrese actually to lead until, sadly, his engine exploded. This was indeed a sensational start to the team's first season, but numerous problems loomed ahead. They had contracted former Lotus driver Gunnar Nilsson as Patrese's team-mate, but that winter he became desperately and, as it transpired, terminally ill with cancer. Franco Ambrosio was jailed in Italy on financial charges. On top of this, Don Nichols of the Shadow team took umbrage at Arrows's production of what he felt had been the 1978 Shadow DN9 design. Litigation ensued and in August the British High Court found in Nichols's favour, estimating that 40 per cent of the drawings from which the Arrows FA1 had been constructed actually belonged to Shadow. The car was banned and ordered to be destroyed.

Once again the Arrows men began from nothing and contrived not to miss a race. This time they built a new A1 model in just fifty-two days. The car was ready for the Austrian Grand Prix, but it could not quite reproduce the form of the competitive, if rather unreliable, FA1 which had preceded it. The German Rolf Stommelen joined the team as Patrese's partner in Nilsson's place and spent the rest of the season with them. Then in the Italian Grand Prix, at Monza, Patrese was accused of triggering the multiple accident which resulted in Ronnie Peterson's tragic death. After a season in which the young Italian driver had carved a wild reputation for himself, he was barred by other drivers from competing in the United States Grand Prix at Watkins Glen. As if this was not sufficient trouble for one season, the Formula One Constructors' Association then announced that Arrows would not be admitted as a member in 1979 because of the findings in the Shadows court case. This resulted in vastly increased travelling costs as well as other problems for 1979.

Arrows remained undeterred, and although the ground-effects A1 design had proved itself less than competitive, the A1B, used until the bullet-nosed A2 design made its debut in the middle of 1979, was better, but never a potential winner. During the 1978 season, Patrese achieved one second, a fourth, and two sixth places in the World Championship series and ended the year with a total of eleven points for eleventh-equal place alongside Alan Jones in the Drivers' Championship.

Much was hoped for the A2, but it quickly proved to be a failure. Although its futuristic aerodynamics performed well in the wind tunnel, on the racetrack they could not compensate for what was considered to be a heavy and bulky Formula One car. In 1979, Patrese scored just one fifth place with the A1B for two championship points and nineteenth-equal championship place with the German Hans Joachim Stuck. Actually, the young Italian's new team-mate Jochen Mass was more successful. He gained three unimpressive

sixth places during the year, to accumulate three championship points and fifteenth-equal place in the championship alongside Nelson Piquet, Jacky Ickx, and Elio de Angelis.

This was poor recompense for the intense effort put into the Arrows programme by engineers as talented as Southgate and Wass, both of whom, but particularly Southgate, had considerable reputations. But by its very nature, Grand Prix racing success is fickle and cyclical, and with enthusiastic and substantial sponsorship from the

Arrows FA1
The British High Court found that 40 per cent of the drawings for this car originated as those for the projected Shadow DN9. Indeed, the car clearly showed its pedigree. Formula One car design is idiosyncratic and Tony Southgate's unmistakable signature was evident in the sleek lines of this balanced and aesthetically pleasing ground-effects car. Its shaped, stressed-skin monocoque carried the Cosworth DFV engine as an integral load-bearing member in the usual way, while the suspension was sophisticated yet conventional, with wishbones, links, and coil springs. Certainly in its behaviour, if not its provenance, the original Arrows was a pleasant, honest car.

German Warsteiner brewery Arrows always had potential for greater things. It took them too long to recover, however, from the heavy blows of 1978 which shattered their early promise.

In the 1980 season Arrows built reliability into their A3 ground-effects cars. Nevertheless, Patrese and Mass could do no better than inherit two second places, in California and Spain. Dissension within the team led to Southgate leaving. But Arrows had proved their resilience so often before that the team seemed sure to survive.

Arrows FA2

This startling design attracted much attention when it made its debut in 1979, in the French Grand Prix at Dijon. Quite apart from its advanced bullet-nosed aerodynamic form, it was notable for its use of vast ground-effects side pods through which direct airflow was positively encouraged. This system of harnessing airflow beneath the car to enhance cornering power had been popularized by Lotus in 1977-78. At their leading edge, these pods compressed the airstream against the road surface while internally their chamber space enlarged towards the rear where the air was given a clear exit. In effect, the enlarging venturi section in these pods promoted a drop in air pressure beneath the car, and, since sliding skirts in contact with the road sealed off this area on either side, the chassis was effectively sucked down to the road and in theory would have a huge advantage in cornering power. But the Arrows FA2 was not a car which could emulate Lotus well enough to be competitive. Nevertheless, it remained perhaps the most exciting looking car on the circuits.

Tony Southgate, like so many Formula One engineers, simply liked making things in general and cars in particular. An instinctive engineer, with a feel for what was right, he began with a 750 Formula club racing special in England, powered by a prewar Austin 7 engine, and progressed through jobs with Lola and Brabham to become Eagle's chief designer in the United States. He then moved back home from California to join BRM, and from them to Shadow, then Lotus, back to Shadow, and then to Arrows. Late in 1980 he moved again, this time back to the Theodore team which was being built out of Shadow by Teddy Yip, a Hong Kong racing enthusiast.

SPECIFICATIONS
Arrows A3 1980

Engine
Cosworth-Ford DFV
90-degree V-8
Bore × stroke: 85.7 mm × 64.8 mm
Capacity: 2993 cc
Lucas fuel injection
Lucas electronic ignition
Maximum power: c 480 bhp at
c 10,750 rpm

Transmission
Hewland FGA400, five-speed and reverse

Chassis
Slender stressed-skin three-quarter monocoque employing engine and transmission case as structural members at rear

Front suspension
Top rocker arms, wide-based lower wishbones, inboard coil spring/damper units

Rear suspension
Top rocker arm, wide-based lower wishbones, inboard coil spring/damper units

Brakes
Disc; outboard front and rear

Dimensions
Wheelbase: 103 in (2616 mm)
Front track: 71 in (1803 mm)
Rear track: 64 in (1626 mm)
Wheel rim width: 11 in front,
18 in rear
Chassis weight: c 85 lb (38 kg)
Formula weight: c 1275 lb (578 kg)

Tyres
Goodyear

Team Drivers
Rupert Keegan • Jochen Mass •
Riccardo Patrese •
Rolf Stommelen

BRM

At the end of 1961, Sir Alfred Owen, head of the mighty Owen Organisation, one of Britain's largest engineering combines and owner of the BRM racing team, could look back on a decade of BRM racing in which only one World Championship Grand Prix victory had been won. The original BRM V-16 1.5-litre supercharged Grand Prix car had been a much-publicized flop in 1950-51 when British Racing Motors was still being run as a cooperative venture, employing finance and services from about two hundred sponsors from within the British motor industry. BRM was founded by Raymond Mays and the Owen Organisation had been one of his most enthusiastic supporters. When the original trust was terminated in 1952 Sir Alfred Owen took on all the team's assets—and its many liabilities.

After the 1.5-litre supercharged Formula One had died, the V-16-cylinder cars had been raced successfully in Formule Libre events. Peter Berthon, chief engineer of BRM, and his collaborators then produced a four-cylinder, unsupercharged, 2.5-litre car for the new Grand Prix Formula which ran from 1954 to 1957 and was later extended into 1960. This car proved immensely fast, but almost as unreliable as the V-16 before it. In 1957, however, it began winning minor races and in 1959, with Joachim Bonnier at the wheel, it won the Dutch Grand Prix.

During the 1959 and 1960 seasons BRM was the first "proper" Formula One constructor to follow Cooper-Climax's lead and build rear-engined cars. When it became obvious that the unpopular new "Half-Ton" Formula—for 1.5-litre unsupercharged cars with a minimum weight limit of five hundred kilogrammes—really was going to be applied in 1961, Peter Berthon and his men set about producing a suitable new V-8 engine.

The prototype P56 V-8 engine did not appear until the end of the 1961 season, and in the meantime new ultralight spaceframe chassis P57 cars were produced. They were ready to accept the new engines when available, but in the interim they were powered by simple straight-four, twin-overhead camshaft, Coventry Climax FPF engines. These BRM-Climax cars handled particularly well, but were underpowered and unreliable. After another hopeless season, Sir Alfred Owen issued an ultimatum to his racing team staff: "Win the World Championship in 1962 or I shall be forced to close down BRM."

The original P56 V-8 engine proved to have great potential; it also, however, suffered from immense development problems. It was originally designed as an extremely high-revving power unit, intended to make the most of Lucas fuel injection and electronic ignition. The P56 engines which ended that 1962 season were very different from the original design. New crankcases, blocks, pistons, connecting rods, and crankshafts were produced in a few hectic months by Tony Rudd, the new chief engineer, and his colleagues.

New P578 multi-tubular spaceframe chassis were produced to carry the compact, high-revving V-8 engines. They were to be driven for the factory team by Graham Hill and the former Ferrari chief tester, Californian Richie Ginther. In original form the V-8 used individual stub pipes which curled skywards from each exhaust port, and won the car the nickname "The Stackpipe BRM". The stacks were extremely fragile and shattered and fell off with remarkable ease. As each one disappeared, more and more noise, and less and less power, would emanate from the engine.

Nevertheless, Graham Hill proved that here, finally, was a race-winning BRM when he won the first heat of the non-championship Brussels Grand Prix, and then the Glover Trophy at Goodwood. At Silverstone he featured in a truly epic virtual dead heat with Jimmy Clark's Lotus-Climax V-8, to win the British Racing Drivers Club International Trophy by the first inch or so of his car's nose cone.

The first World Championship Grand Prix of the 1962 season was the Dutch race, at Zandvoort, where BRM had scored their only victory in 1959. There Hill drove an excellent race to notch his maiden Grande Epreuve success. The stackpipe exhausts were replaced by a low-level system for the Belgian Grand Prix and for subsequent races. Hill drove brilliantly in pouring rain to win the German Grand

Prix, and he and Ginther placed first and second at Monza on a joyful day for BRM. The season had developed into a straight fight for the championship between Graham Hill in the BRM and Jimmy Clark in the Lotus-Climax.

The deciding race was in South Africa. Clark surged into the lead with Hill a strong, but apparently hopeless, second. Then a bolt worked loose from the Climax V-8 engine and let its oil out; Clark retired and Hill screamed home to win the World Championship title for which Sir Alfred Owen, Raymond Mays, and all the men of BRM had waited so long.

The spaceframe BRM P578s raced on through 1963, when Hill and Ginther chased Clark and his Lotus-Climax home in the World Championships. In 1964, a new monocoque-chassised car, known as the P61 Mark 2, or more popularly as the P261, was introduced to carry further developed versions of the P56 V-8 engine. These P261s became truly classic racing cars without winning a World Championship. In 1964, Hill won two more Grands Prix and together he and Ginther took five second places. Graham only lost the World title halfway through the final qualifying race that year. In 1965, he was joined by young Jackie Stewart. Between them they won three more Grandes Epreuves and Graham achieved a memorable hat-trick at Monaco. In 1966 and 1967, with 2-litre engines, the P261s were victorious in the Tasman Championship. Stewart used one to win yet another Monaco Grand Prix for BRM. It was the toughest race in the calendar. At last nobody could say that BRMs were unreliable.

The 3-litre H-16 engine, which was developed for the 1966 and 1967 seasons was a failure, however, and it was replaced in 1968 by a more conventional V-12. But the design of BRM's chassis was now dated and it was not until 1970-71, with new P153 and P160 cars designed by Tony Southgate, that BRM won again. Thereafter, it was all downhill. At the end of 1974, the Owen Organisation withdrew support. In private hands the team spluttered on. Then, in 1977, virtually unnoticed, its serious racing days reached their ignominious end.

Team Drivers

Dick Attwood • Jean Behra • Jean-Pierre Beltoise • Jo Bonnier • Tony Brooks • Peter Collins • Piers Courage • Vic Elford • Jack Fairman • Juan Manuel Fangio • Ron Flockhart • Mackay Fraser • Howden Ganley • Peter Gethin • Richie Ginther • Froilan Gonzalez • Dan Gurney • Mike Hawthorn • Graham Hill • Niki Lauda • Les Leston • Helmut Marko • François Migault • John Miles • Jackie Oliver • Reg Parnell • Larry Perkins • Henri Pescarolo • Clay Regazzoni • Pedro Rodriguez • Roy Salvadori • Harry Schell • Vern Schuppan • Jo Siffert • Mike Spence • Jackie Stewart • John Surtees • Maurice Trintignant • Peter Walker • Ken Wharton

BRM P261

This monocoque-chassised car differed from the bathtub open-top monocoques introduced by Colin Chapman of Lotus in 1962, for it used stressed-skin sections which more completely enclosed the driver, wrapping around his legs at the forward end of the nacelle, and arching into a 360-degree stressed section immediately behind his shoulders. Two projecting rear horns supported the V-8 engine. The car used rocker-arm inboard front suspension with a sophisticated outboard coil-spring system at the rear. The frame had been intended for a centre-exhaust V-8 engine, in which the pipes emerged within the engine vee, but when this was slow in appearing tunnels were cut through the rear chassis horns to accommodate low-level exhausts. When the centre-pipe engines did appear, the old tunnels were plated over.

BRM P153

In the 3-litre formula years, BRM tried and failed with Tony Rudd's complex H-16-cylinder configuration power unit which was based on the idea of two 1.5-litre V-8s opened out to lay their cylinder banks horizontally and coupled together, one above the other. A conventional 3-litre V-12 engine, originally intended for sports car use, superseded the H-16 in 1968, but it did not become competitive until 1970, when, in a new P153 chassis designed by Tony Southgate, it was driven to victory in the Belgian Grand Prix by that fiery Mexican driver Pedro Rodriguez. The P153 used a broad, low, "onion" planform, bathtub monocoque chassis and handled superbly.

SPECIFICATIONS
BRM P57   1962

Engine
BRM 90-degree V-8
Bore × stroke: 68.5 mm × 50.8 mm
Capacity: 1497 cc
Lucas fuel injection
Lucas electronic ignition
Maximum power: *c* 190 bhp at
10,500 rpm

Transmission
BRM, five- or six-speed and reverse

Chassis
Lightweight multi-tubular
spaceframe

Front suspension
Double wishbones with interposed
coil spring/damper units and
anti-roll bar

Rear suspension
Top wishbone, reversed lower
wishbone and radius rod with
co-axial coil spring/damper units

Brakes
Disc; outboard front and rear

Dimensions
Wheelbase: 89.8 in (2281 mm)
Front track: 52½ in (1333 mm)
Rear track: 52¼ in (1327 mm)
Wheel rim width: 5 in front,
6.5 in rear
Chassis weight: *c* 85 lb (38.5 kg)
Formula weight: *c* 1102 lb (500 kg)

Tyres
Dunlop

Raymond Mays was an amateur racing driver as a Cambridge undergraduate immediately after World War I. The creator of commercial sponsorship for motor racing, he persuaded many companies to support his private racing through the 1920s and in 1934 he won backing for English Racing Automobiles Ltd. Their ERAs put Britain on the international racing map. In 1946 Mays set out to repeat the trick with the British Racing Motors project.

Tony Rudd was a schoolboy in 1938 when he was introduced to racing by the Siamese Chula-Bira team and their ERAs. He served an engineering apprenticeship with Rolls-Royce, and became wartime chief of their Merlin aero-engine fault-investigation unit. After the war he helped Bira race Maserati and OSCA cars before joining BRM as a development engineer. He became chief engineer and team manager in 1962. In 1969 he left BRM to become engineering director of the Lotus group.

Constructors' Championship
1962

BRABHAM

Jack Brabham, an Australian, came into racing the hard way. Although he drove Coopers to two consecutive World Championship titles in 1959 and 1960, his ambition was not limited to driving glory. He wanted to be his own master, and to build his own cars.

In 1955, Jack went to England to seek his fortune. Four years later he returned to Australia in triumph as World Champion Driver and persuaded Ron Tauranac, an engineer, to join him in England as his business partner. Ron arrived in the spring of 1960 and began designing a new Formula Junior car, which the two men planned to put into production.

In 1961, Jack spent his last season driving for Cooper, while Ron, virtually single-handed, built the new Formula Junior car. They called it the MRD after the initials of their new company—Motor Racing Developments Ltd. When it was pointed out that an excited French commentator's pronunciation would make the name sound like a French expletive, Jack reluctantly bestowed his own name on the car. Thus the Brabham racing car was born.

In the winter of 1961-62 Jack drove a private Lotus in Formula One races, while Ron constructed a pilot batch of twelve production Formula Junior cars. When they were delivered Ron designed his first Grand Prix car—the Brabham-Climax V-8 BT3. It was completed in August and by the end of the season Jack Brabham had scored his first World Championship points in a car bearing his own name.

In 1963, Jack established the Brabham Racing Organisation as his Grand Prix team. It was independent of MRD, whose aim was to manufacture customer cars for the minor formulae. Although MRD was also to produce Formula One equipment for BRO, as far as Tauranac was concerned this was not of prime importance.

Jack signed Dan Gurney, the lanky Californian, as his Grand Prix team-mate. Gurney was a potential winner in any class of racing, but the Brabham team was plagued by unreliability until the middle of 1964, when Dan's car survived to bring him victory, first in the French Grand Prix at Rouen, and then in the Mexican Grand Prix at Mexico City.

During those three seasons, from 1963 until 1965, when Gurney left to build his own Eagle cars, the Brabham team epitomized the realities of Grand Prix racing. The demands of the sport are total. It is sometimes difficult for the public to appreciate the exhausting physical and mental concentration and application, as well as the sheer hard work that is hidden behind the glamour. Jack Brabham, Ron Tauranac, Dan Gurney, and their chief mechanics, Tim Wall and Roy Billington, worked every hour they could.

Formula One was not Brabham's only target. In 1964 he had become deeply involved in Formula Two racing with smaller-engined cars. And in 1966, when Ron's new 3-litre Formula One cars brought Jack his third World Championship title, MRD's Honda-engined Formula Two cars dominated that class as well.

When the 3-litre Grand Prix formula had been introduced in 1966, Brabham and Tauranac turned to the Australian Repco company for a suitable power unit. Repco produced a simple two-cam V-8 engine based on an obsolete Oldsmobile production engine block. Ron built a typically practical, good-handling chassis designed to make the most of the Australian engine's modest power. With it Jack won the French Grand Prix in July—the first time a Grand Prix had been won by a driver in a car bearing his own name. Jack thereafter won three more Grands Prix in rapid succession. In 1967, Ron produced Formula Two-based BT24 cars which exemplified compact and practical Formula One packaging, and Denny Hulme, the New Zealander who had replaced Dan Gurney in the team in 1966, took the Driver's title narrowly from his team chief to give Repco-Brabham their second consecutive Formula One Constructors' Championship.

Nevertheless, more power was vital for the 1968 season when the new Cosworth-Ford V-8 engine was to be used by McLaren and Tyrrell-Matra, as well as by Lotus who had introduced it the previous season. Repco produced for Brabham a four-cam true racing engine which was to prove an almost total disaster for Jack and his new team-mate Jochen Rindt. In 1969 Brabham adopted the Cosworth V-8, but lost Rindt to Lotus.

Brabham-Climax BT3

When the Formula Junior Brabham BT2s triumphed in 1962, Ron Tauranac modified this design to accommodate a 1.5-litre Coventry Climax V-8 engine. The result was the BT3 Formula One car—the first Grand Prix Brabham. Its multi-tubular spaceframe chassis was suspended on coil springs at front and rear, with independent suspension by double front wishbones and by reversed wishbones, links, and radius rods at the rear. The driver reclined in a custom-made cockpit, flanked by aluminium fuel tanks on either side, and with the engine just behind his shoulders. A Hewland five-speed and reverse gearbox and final drive unit was bolted to the engine in the car's tail. The bodywork was moulded in thin fibreglass, and included a neat engine cover and streamlined tail fairing. Driven by Jack Brabham, the BT3 performed nobly at the end of 1962, and Jack retained it in the new BRO livery of dark green and gold for much of the 1963 season. In it he won the non-championship Formula One races at Solitude, near Stuttgart, and at Zeltweg in Austria.

SPECIFICATIONS
Repco-Brabham BT19   1966

Engine
Repco RB620, 90-degree V-8
Bore × stroke: 88.9 mm × 60.3 mm
Capacity: 2995 cc
Lucas port fuel injection
Coil and distributor ignition
Maximum power: *c* 285 bhp at
c 7250 rpm

Transmission
Hewland DG300, five-speed and reverse

Chassis
Multi-tubular spaceframe

Front suspension
Double wishbones and outboard coil spring/damper units

Rear suspension
Reversed lower wishbones, single top links, and twin radius rods with outboard coil spring/damper units

Brakes
Disc; outboard front and rear

Dimensions
Wheelbase: 92 in (2337 mm)
Front track: 53½ in (1359 mm)
Rear track: 56 in (1422 mm)
Wheel rim width: 10 in front,
8 in rear
Unladen weight: 1142 lb (518 kg)

Tyres
Goodyear

The Brabham Badge

Repco, the Replacement Parts Company, made otherwise unobtainable parts for imported cars in Melbourne, and Jack Brabham and Ron Tauranac were among its customers. Tauranac built MRD's first Formula Junior production cars in premises provided by Repco in England and these cars were officially known as Repco-Brabhams. The V-8 engine later gave World Championship significance to the name.

Ron Tauranac's years as engineer with MRD were characterized more by dedication than by great ambition. Born in England in 1925, Ron was four when his family emigrated to Australia. At fourteen he became apprenticed to the Commonwealth Aircraft Company and after World War II he worked widely in engineering. In the late 1940s Ron and his brother Austin Lewis became hooked on motor racing and began building Ralt specials, the name of the cars formed from their initials. In 1954, Ron, a quiet, often prickly man, defeated Jack Brabham in the New South Wales Hill Climb Championship. Five years later, he was preparing to lay down a production run of Ralt cars, when he was persuaded to go into partnership with Jack, a relationship which endured for eleven years. After selling MRD, Ron established Ralt, a new racing car production company producing successful Formula Two and Three racing cars.

Constructors' Championship
1966 • 1967

BRABHAM

By this time, Ron Tauranac was the only Formula One designer still producing multi-tubular spaceframe chassis, although his BT26/26A cars were among the best-handling. In 1969, Jacky Ickx, the Belgian driver, joined the team and when Jack was hurt in a mid-season testing accident, Ickx rose to the challenge and won both the German and Canadian Grands Prix. At the end of the season, however, Ickx left to rejoin Ferrari.

In 1970, Jack Brabham decided he would retire at the end of the year. He was forty-four and in his last racing season he drove Tauranac's first monocoque Formula One car, built from sheet alloy instead of steel tubes, in deference to a change in the regulations. This car, the BT33, proved immensely competitive, and Jack won on its debut in the South African Grand Prix, only to lose both the Monaco and British Grands Prix at the last moment.

Jack retired at the close of that season to return to Australia. Ron Tauranac bought his shares in MRD and, in the 1971 season, ran Formula One cars for Graham Hill and Tim Schenken. Beyond one minor non-championship event, success eluded them, and the taciturn, introverted Tauranac seemed to miss Jack terribly. Then Bernie Ecclestone made an offer to buy the company and Ron accepted it. He thought he could stay on and that things would continue as before, but it seemed the Australian and the South Londoner could not work together. Four months later Ron left.

Ecclestone personally financed the Motor Racing Developments team. He closed the production racing car side of the business and encouraged Gordon Murray, one of Ron's former assistant engineers,

to design new Grand Prix cars. He retained Hill and brought in Wilson Fittipaldi and then, in 1973, Carlos Reutemann. In 1973, Gordon's BT42, driven by Reutemann, made a competitive debut. In 1974, Reutemann, in the improved BT44, won the South African and Austrian Grands Prix. Success continued into 1975, but Brabham reliability could never match that of the dominant Ferrari.

In 1976, Ecclestone went to Alfa Romeo for a flat-12 Italian engine, in the hope of combating the supreme Ferrari flat-12s. That season was a difficult one and in 1977, just as the Brabham-Alfas seemed to be reaching their peak, Carlos Pace, Brabham's new lead driver, was killed in a flying accident. Niki Lauda helped focus team development in 1978 and 1979 and with the Murray-developed BT46B fan-car he won the Swedish Grand Prix. The BT46B had a large, gearbox-driven fan at the rear, which sucked air from the peripherally sealed engine bay, to create an area of low pressure which gave the car far greater road adhesion than other Formula One cars. The fan was judged a rule-bending device and was banned immediately afterwards, although the Swedish result stood.

New V-12 Alfa Romeo engines were adopted in 1979, but proved uncompetitive. At the end of that season, Lauda retired abruptly and Brabham returned to Cosworth V-8 power. It had become clear, however, that Lauda's 1979 team-mate, the young Brazilian Nelson Piquet, was a star in the making. And at Long Beach in 1980 his Brabham-Cosworth BT47 set fastest practice time, fastest race lap, and led all the way to victory. It was the perfect performance, truly worthy of his car's honoured name.

Brabham BT26

Most teams had begun to build sheet-metal monocoque Formula One cars by 1966, but Ron Tauranac was still convinced that his lightweight, good-handling spaceframe could be competitive. In 1968 his BT26 design was a compromise between the pure tubular spaceframe and the stressed-skin monocoque, with aluminium sheathing used on the main tubes in place of tubular triangulation. The biplane wing arrangement was introduced for the last three Grands Prix of that season. Although the Repco engine was unreliable, the chassis was excellent. In 1969 the same chassis carried the Cosworth V-8 engine and the type number BT26A. The BT26 handled superbly with its conservative, though well-developed, all-independent suspension, which featured bottom wishbones front and rear with top links and long radius rods. The BT26A became visually distinctive in 1969 with strap-on side tanks and undershot nose section.

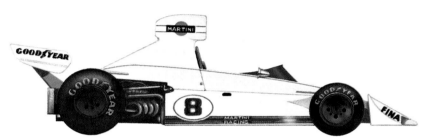

Brabham BT44

Ralph Bellamy, the Australian MRD engineer, had sketched a pyramid-section Formula One chassis before he left MRD in the winter of 1972-73. Gordon Murray made the idea work in the tiny BT42 car of 1973, and the next season the much-improved, still pyramid-section BT44 and BT44B models with Martini & Rossi sponsorship brought Brabham back into the winner's circle. The unusual section concentrated the fuel load close to the road, punched a small hole in the air, and offered useful upper surfaces to promote aerodynamic downthrust. To keep the noseline clean, Murray used two small water radiators, one ahead of each front wheel.

Team Drivers
Andrea de Adamich • Jack Brabham • Luis Bueno • Wilson Fittipaldi • Dan Gurney • Graham Hill • Denny Hulme • Jacky Ickx • Niki Lauda • Carlos Pace • Nelson Piquet • Carlos Reutemann • Jochen Rindt • Tim Schenken • Rolf Stommelen • Hans Stuck • Ricardo Zunino

---

SPECIFICATIONS

Brabham-Alfa BT45
1976-77

Engine
Alfa Romeo flat-12
Bore × stroke: 77 mm × 53.6 mm
Capacity: 2995 cc
Lucas-Spica fuel injection
Marelli Dinoplex electronic ignition
Maximum power: c 510 bhp at 12,000 rpm

Transmission
Hewland/MRD FG400, six-speed and reverse

Chassis
Stressed-skin three-quarter monocoque employing engine and transmission case as structural members at rear

Front suspension
Double wishbones, semi-inboard coil spring/damper units

Rear suspension
Parallel lower links, single top links, and twin radius rods with outboard coil spring/damper units

Brakes
Disc; outboard front, inboard rear

Dimensions
Wheelbase: 98 in (2490 mm)
Front track: 56 in (1420 mm)
Rear track: 60 in (1525 mm)
Wheel rim width: 10 in front, 19 in rear
Chassis weight: 110 lb (50 kg)
Formula weight: 1370 lb (622 kg)

Tyres
Goodyear

Bernie Ecclestone studied to be a chemist, but instead established a huge motorcycle dealership in South London. In the 1950s he raced 500 cc Formula Three cars with some success and later entered a team of Connaught Grand Prix cars. Ecclestone dropped out of racing when his friend Stuart Lewis-Evans, a Vanwall driver, was killed in 1958, but returned about ten years later as Jochen Rindt's business manager. In 1970, Bernie bought MRD and their Brabham marque name. He rapidly rose to head the Formula One Constructors' Association, and thus became one of the most important men in Grand Prix motor racing.

Gordon Murray is South African born, tall, modishly dressed, and quiet. "I found him standing in a corner under a dust-sheet," says Bernie Ecclestone, hinting that at MRD, before his own arrival, Murray's talents had gone unrecognized. Ecclestone gave Murray a free hand and the engineer returned his trust by building a line of exceptionally handsome and competitive Grand Prix Brabham cars.

COOPER

The Cooper Car Company evolved from humble beginnings to spearhead one of the most significant technical developments that Grand Prix racing has ever seen. This was the change from classical, front-engined racing car design to rear-engined—or, more properly, mid-engined—configuration.

Cooper's racing designs, centred upon mounting the engine behind the driver, had roots in the company's earliest history. In 1946, Charles Cooper, a former prewar racing mechanic, built a 500 cc motorcycle-engined racing car for his son, John. A second car quickly followed for John's friend Eric Brandon. JAP Speedway motorcycle power units were used for simplicity with power. Since chain-drive was retained it was necessary to mount the units close against the driven rear axle, and to move the cockpit in front of the engine. The Coopers cut the front suspensions from a pair of Fiat Topolino saloons and turned one around to support the rear end of their new single-seater. Both John and Eric drove well, and the fast-growing 500 cc racing movement in Britain quickly recognized the potency of these new cars. Several customers were attracted, and so the Cooper Car Company became established. They built 500 cc Formula Three cars in considerable numbers for private customers and established domination in their class.

In the early 1950s, Cooper diverged from their mid-engined theme with small production runs of their famous front-engined Formula Two Cooper-Bristol single-seaters. They also produced a small number of sports cars which used MG and Jaguar engines, in addition to the relatively inexpensive but competitively powerful, 2-litre Bristol six-cylinder unit. Nevertheless, mid-engined, single-seater design was close to the hearts of Charles and John Cooper. The only reason the Formula Two car had carried its Bristol engine in front of the driver was that unit's inordinate six-cylinder length.

At that time, the handling of the prewar, 16-cylinder Auto Union Grand Prix cars was recalled with a horror which tainted all discussion of the virtues of centralized weight distribution and the mounting of engine between cockpit and the rear axle. It was felt there was something wrong with a far-forward cockpit. Clearly, many people had forgotten that Auto Union had attempted to combine something like 550 horsepower with narrow-tread tyres suspended on swinging half-axles. Since, under power, the swing-axles would up-edge their tyres, dramatically slashing contact area with the road, it was hardly surprising that the Auto Union A- to C-Types were notoriously demanding to drive and tricky to control. With the light and compact motorcycle engines employed in Formula Three, neither space nor power was a problem. Many engineers considered, however, that larger engines demanded front mounting, and that Cooper could never build a competitive large-engined car using their 500 cc configuration.

After several seasons of gradual and logical development, however, Cooper did just that. In 1955, Charles and John produced a series of lightweight, central-seat, mid-engined, sports racing cars, powered by 1098 cc and 1460 cc Coventry Climax four-cylinder engines. Then Jack Brabham built one with a two-litre, six-cylinder Bristol engine in the back and ran it in the British Grand Prix.

During 1956, dress rehearsal races were held in Britain in preparation for the new 1500 cc Formula Two class which was to come into effect in 1957. In these races Cooper ran a grown-up version of their highly successful Formula Three chain-driven designs. They mounted a 1.5-litre Climax engine centrally in a rugged, multi-tubular spaceframe chassis, driving to the rear wheels through an about-faced and modified Citroën front-wheel drive production gearbox.

The new Cooper-Climax Formula Two prototypes dominated both preview Formula Two races, and in the 1957-58 season, driven by such men as Jack Brabham, Bruce McLaren, and Roy Salvadori, they led the new class. Into 1959 Cooper-Climaxes won virtually everywhere in Formula Two, despite strong opposition from Porsche and the occasional appearance of Ferrari's powerful Dino V-6.

During 1957, a few tentative Formula One Grand Prix race appearances were made by the factory with Formula Two cars suitably enlarged for the occasion. It was quickly apparent that the nimble little Coopers could outhandle the classic, front-engined designs, but lacked their power. For 1958, Rob Walker, a private owner, commissioned a special, enlarged engine from Coventry Climax. With this engine installed in a basic Formula Two chassis, Stirling Moss defeated Ferrari in the Argentine Grand Prix. Maurice Trintignant won in the same car at Monaco, and although Ferrari and Vanwall recovered to clinch the World titles, the rear-engined revolution was clearly coming.

With the determined driving of Jack Brabham, factory team Cooper-Climaxes employed full 2.5-litre Climax FPF twin-cam, four-cylinder engines in the 1959 World Championship series. With 240 bhp in such a light and nimble chassis, Brabham could hardly be

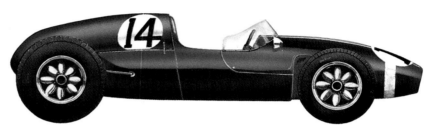

Cooper-Climax T43
The first grown-up, mid-engined, single-seat Coopers were built for 1500 cc Formula Two racing in 1956 and 1957 and were powered by four-cylinder Coventry Climax engines developed from a wartime Civil Defence fire pump engine design. Some of these cars were uprated with 1960 cc power units to participate in 1958 Formula One races against full 2.5-litre (but front-engined) cars. On the debut of the interim 1.9-litre Cooper-Climax

Formula One "special", entered by Rob Walker and driven by Stirling Moss in that season's Argentine Grand Prix, it won—running non-stop to beat Ferrari. The little car had outhandled and outbraked the traditional front-engined machines. Its nimble handling and a 2.1-litre engine proved victorious again at the next Grand Prix, at Monaco, where Maurice Trintignant drove for the private Walker team. These successes marked the dawn of the so-called rear-engined revolution.

beaten. He won the Monaco and British Grands Prix. When Brabham's car ran out of fuel while leading the deciding United States Grand Prix at Sebring, his team-mate, Bruce McLaren, went by to win—and to assure both Brabham and Cooper of the World Championship titles.

In 1960, new, low-line cars were built and Brabham drove to five consecutive Grand Prix victories while McLaren won the opening race of the season in Argentina. Cooper had established the mid-engined racing car as the design of the future, but when Lotus, BRM, Ferrari, and others followed their lead they proved more innovative and certainly far more sophisticated. Cooper Cars were soon eclipsed. Cooper had a minor resurgence in 1966 with their first monocoque car, the T81 Cooper-Maserati, but in 1967 the Italian engine proved too big and too thirsty. A BRM V-12 was adopted for 1968. At the end of that season, however, the marque died.

The Indy Cooper-Climax T54

After their double World Championship success in 1959 and 1960 the Cooper Car Company had firmly established the mid-engined configuration in top-class road racing. In 1961, they mounted an assault upon the Indianapolis 500, using a specially enlarged, 2.7-litre version of their Coventry Climax FPF Grand Prix engine mounted in a lengthened-wheelbase Formula One-based-

chassis. This project was sponsored by Bill Kimberley, the Kleenex millionaire. Jack Brabham drove the little green car to ninth position in the 500-mile race to rock the conservative USAC establishment. Having the engine in the wrong place was heresy enough for them, but to run the colour green at the Speedway was just too much, for tradition had made that colour taboo at Indianapolis.

SPECIFICATIONS

**Cooper-Climax T53
1959-60**

Engine
Coventry Climax FPF
straight-four
Bore × stroke: 94 mm × 89.9 mm
Capacity: 2495 cc
Lucas ignition
Two Weber carburettors
Maximum power: c 240 bhp at
6750 rpm

Transmission
Cooper-Knight, four- or five-speed
and reverse

Chassis
Large diameter tubular
spaceframe

Front suspension
Double wishbones, outboard coil
spring/damper units, and
anti-roll bar

Rear suspension
Double wishbones, outboard coil
spring/damper units

Brakes
Disc; outboard front and rear

Dimensions
Wheelbase: 91 in (2311 mm)
Front track: 46½ in (1181 mm)
Rear track: 48 in (1219 mm)
Wheel rim width: 5 in front,
6½ in rear
Formula weight: c 1120 lb
(522 kg)

Tyres
Dunlop

John Cooper, one of the most popular men in Formula One racing, built himself a reputation not only as a good racing driver in 500 cc Formula Three events, but also as a practical engineer and an understanding team manager. John's straightforward good humour and enthusiasm, combined with his father's business acumen and experience as a racing mechanic, took his team to the top of their field. In 1965, at the age of forty-two, John was seriously injured in a road accident while driving an experimental, twin-engined Mini-Cooper. Subsequently, he sold his company to outside commercial interests. He is now the proprietor of a large and successful car dealership in Ferring, Sussex, on the south coast of England.

Team Drivers
Cliff Allison • Lucien Bianchi •
Jo Bonnier • Jack Brabham •
Tom Bridger • Chris Bristow •
Tony Brooks • Ivor Bueb •
Vic Elford • Paul Frère •
Olivier Gendebien • Masten Gregory •
André Guelfi • Hans Herrmann •
Phil Hill • Guy Ligier • John Love •
Tony Maggs • Bruce McLaren •
Stirling Moss • François Picard •
Brian Redman • Alan Rees •
Jochen Rindt • Pedro Rodriguez •
Roy Salvadori • Ludovico Scarfiotti •
Jo Siffert • John Surtees •
Henry Taylor • Maurice Trintignant •
Robin Widdows

Constructors' Championship
1959 • 1960

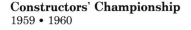

COYOTE

American track racing as run by the United States Automobile Club since 1956 seems rather peculiar to European aficionados who are accustomed to road racing. The idea of running single-seater racing cars around essentially left-turn-only oval tracks would not seem particularly demanding, nor exciting, despite speeds of about two hundred miles per hour. Since the mid-engined revolution in car design was forced upon the ultra-conservative USAC establishment, beginning in 1961 with Cooper and Lotus, however, American championship racing has undergone enormous changes.

Anthony Joseph Foyt Jr. was a successful young pillar of the establishment in the late 1950s and early 1960s, driving front-engined cars, but in 1964 he rapidly adapted to the road-racing style mid-engined machines. He bought Ford V-8-engined Lotuses and for the 1966 Indianapolis 500 had a Lotus-like car of his own built in Long Beach, California. It was a slender monocoque car with a Ford V-8 engine and suspension designed by Foyt. He christened it the Coyote, but sadly crashed it on the first day of qualifications. It was too severely damaged to be rebuilt in time for the race.

In 1967, the Foyt family moved to Houston, Texas, where two new full-monocoque cars were constructed for the Indianapolis track classic. Having won the 500 in front-engined cars in 1961 and 1964, Foyt was poised to join Louis Meyer, Wilbur Shaw, and Mauri Rose as the race's only three-time winners. He won in the Coyote at a record speed of 151.21 mph. Having won the race three times, Foyt then determined to be the first four-time winner, and Coyote construction efforts were therefore maintained at a high level of practical sophistication. Joe Leonard, his team-mate, had placed third in that 1967 500 in the rebuilt prototype Coyote, and later that season Foyt scored the marque's first one-mile track victory in the Trenton 200.

Two more Coyotes appeared in 1968, and both cars, plus one of the 1967 models, qualified easily for the 500 driven by Foyt, Carl Williams, and Jim McElreath. But none survived to the finish. Foyt won the Continental Divide 150-mile road race and the Hanford 250 that season. The Coyote was always to be taken seriously.

For the 1969 season, Foyt turned to a reduced capacity 2.6-litre turbocharged Ford V-8 engine, and his revamped Coyote qualified on pole position for the Indy 500 at a staggering 170.57 mph—a new track record for piston-engined cars. He led the race for one-third of its distance before a broken manifold forced him to drop back. His team-mate Roger McCluskey set fastest race lap at 166.51 mph (boost pressure and therefore outright engine power being reduced to survive race distance).

Jim McElreath, driving a Coyote, won the 1970 Ontario race in California, and in 1971 Foyt, in a Coyote, was third at Indianapolis and Pocono, second at Milwaukee, and first at Phoenix. In 1972, Foyt became a loner, building only one car for his own use. Then for 1973, assisted by his father, A.J. Foyt Sr., Jack Starne, Eddie Kuzma, and Pete Werner, he built two new cars to his own design. During Indianapolis tyre testing, the new, flat-profiled Coyote lapped at more than 194 mph. The 1974 car was fine-tuned with a Coyote-Foyt Ford-based V-8 which slowly developed form until the end of 1978. In this car Foyt achieved his record-breaking fourth Indy 500 victory in 1978. He then continued to race it into obsolescence.

Throughout this period Foyt remained faithful to what had been the four-cam Ford V-8 engine, the rights to which he had purchased late in 1969 when Ford bowed out of USAC involvement. Known thereafter as the "Foyt V-8" the turbocharged power units were supplied to many of A.J.'s competitors until the turbo-Offenhauser forged far ahead. Finally, the advent of the Cosworth DFX turbo V-8 rendered the old Detroit engine uncompetitive. At the end of 1978, A.J.'s Coyote-Foyt V-8 won at Silverstone in England. This was its swan song, a thoughtful, tactical, road race victory by The Man of USAC racing.

SPECIFICATIONS
Coyote-Foyt 1977

Engine
Ford-Foyt 90-degree V-8
Bore × stroke: 91 mm × 48.2 mm
Capacity: 159 cu in
Fuel injection with Schwitzer/
Garrett AiResearch turbocharger
Mallory electronic ignition
Maximum power: c 650-900 bhp
(dependent upon boost pressure
selected) at c 8800 rpm

Transmission
Hewland LG or Weissman,
three-speed

Chassis
Broad shallow (8 in) monocoque
nacelle, with engine supported by
tubular subframe at rear

Front suspension
Top rocker arms, bottom
wishbones, inboard coil spring/
damper units, and sway bar

Rear suspension
Single top links, parallel bottom
links, twin radius rods, outboard
coil spring/damper units, and
sway bar

Brakes
Disc; outboard front and rear

Dimensions
Wheelbase: 104 in (2642 mm)
Front track: 66½ in (1689 mm)
Rear track: 64½ in (1638 mm)
Chassis weight: 135 lb (61 kg)
Unladen weight: 1500 lb (680 kg)

Tyres
Goodyear

Coyote 1967

The barrel-chested 1967 Coyote-Ford V-8 gave A.J. Foyt his third victory in the prestigious and highly lucrative Indianapolis 500-Mile track classic. Following the fashion set by Lotus in 1963, the Coyote had a monocoque chassis and offset suspension with shorter links on the left side than on the right to create asymmetric weight distribution through the left-turn-only corners. The cars were sponsored by Sheraton-Thompson, and it was an unusual 500 because, for the first time since 1915, the race was stopped by rain after only eighteen laps. It was restarted the next day, and Foyt established himself in second place, unable to do anything about Parnelli Jones's revolutionary STP Turbocar which was in the lead. Then, just seven and a half miles from the finish, the turbine-engined car failed, and Foyt was victorious, his Coyote a 500-Mile champion.

A.J. Foyt Sr., is the father of a famous racing driver, but nevertheless has considerable racing distinction of his own. He shares with George Bignotti and Jim Hall the distinction of having run winning cars in each of the three big USAC 500-mile races, at Indianapolis, Ontario, and Pocono. Tony Foyt became his son's crew chief in 1966 and played a major part in the careful design and construction of the line of Coyote cars and the Ford-derived engines which powered them. Tony Foyt's garage business in Houston, Texas was turned into the Coyote construction shop. This great American success story was very much a family affair.

Team Drivers
A.J. Foyt Jr. • Joe Leonard •
Roger McCluskey • Jim McElreath •
George Snider • Carl Williams

EAGLE

It is relatively rare for a racing driver to become a racing car constructor. In 1961 Jack Brabham, twice World Champion, did just that. Felice Nazzaro, the great Italian Grand Prix driver, had constructed cars before the First World War, but few followed in his footsteps. Brabham's example, however, was to be followed in quick succession by an American and a New Zealander, both of whom had been deeply influenced by him. They were Dan Gurney, the tall and friendly epitome of the all-American sportsman, and Bruce McLaren. Dan actually led Jack's Formula One team from 1963 until 1965 while Bruce had been Jack's team-mate at Cooper in 1959 and 1960. Carroll Shelby was another driver-constructor. This Texan, a former Aston Martin factory driver, was the 1959 Le Mans 24-Hours winner. He had originated the Cobra sports car project in 1962, and it was with his cooperation that Gurney founded his own Eagle team to contest United States Auto Club Championship track races in America, and the Formula One World Championship series internationally.

Gurney first established his own small team in 1964 to race a Lotus 19B sports racing car in the American West Coast Professional series, the forerunner of the famous CanAm Championship. Shelby was running his Cobra cars successfully in World GT Championship events at that time, using Goodyear tyres and sponsorship. When he heard of Goodyear's ambition to topple Firestone's supremacy in Indianapolis-style track racing (which Firestone had dominated since 1911) he introduced Gurney to them.

Dan, sponsored by Goodyear, founded All-American Racers Inc., AAR, based in Santa Ana, California. After a USAC track session with a Lotus and two Halibrand Shrike cars in 1965, he masterminded a new car building programme for the 1966 season. And he chose Eagle, after America's national symbol, as the name for his new cars.

While Dan was eager to fulfill Goodyear's ambition and win the Indianapolis 500, the world's most lucrative race, he was essentially a road racing Formula One man at heart. With additional sponsorship he was able to start a British subsidiary of his team, again using the

AAR initials, although this time they stood for Anglo-American Racers Ltd. Gurney hired Len Terry, the designer of the 1965 Indy-winning Lotus 38, to produce his new cars. They emerged early in 1966—the 4.2-litre Ford V-8-powered T1G for Indy racing, and the Formula One T2G with a temporary 2.7-litre Climax four-cylinder engine until a full 3-litre Eagle-Weslake should become available. Both cars were beautiful in their metallic dark blue and white Eagle livery with "beak" nose section styling.

Although the track cars were unlucky, the four-cylinder interim Formula One gave Dan his first World Championship points in his own car, with a fifth place in the French Grand Prix that year. The remarkably compact Weslake V-12 engine appeared at Monza for the Italian Grand Prix. In 1967, with his compatriot Richie Ginther as the number two driver, Dan gave Eagle its first victory in the Brands Hatch Race of Champions. Unfortunately, when Richie failed to qualify at Monaco he decided to retire from racing. Dan continued with temporary number two drivers and won the Belgian Grand Prix at Spa. It was the first "all-American" Grande Epreuve victory since Jimmy Murphy's French Grand Prix success for Duesenberg in 1921.

In America that year, Dan won the Rex Mays 300 USAC road race at Riverside. In 1968, his factory USAC Eagle with a "stock block" 5-litre Ford V-8 engine was second at Indy behind a privately entered sister car driven by Bobby Unser, which used a 2.8-litre turbocharged Offenhauser four-cylinder engine. Denny Hulme was fourth in yet another Santa Ana car.

But 1968 also saw AAR's underfinanced Formula One programme stumble and fall. Dan drove a McLaren in the later Grand Prix races of the season, and plans for a new 1969 car—possibly Cosworth V-8-powered—were shelved. Eagle were not to return to

SPECIFICATIONS
Eagle-Weslake T2G 1967

Engine
Eagle-Weslake 60-degree V-12
Bore × stroke: 72.8 mm × 60 mm
Capacity: 2997 cc
Lucas fuel injection
Lucas electronic ignition
Maximum power: c 415 bhp at 10,000 rpm

Transmission
Hewland DG300, five-speed and reverse

Chassis
Stressed-skin full-length monocoque supporting engine and transmission on horns at rear

Front suspension
Top rocker arms operating inboard coil spring/damper units with bottom wishbones

Rear suspension
Single top links, reversed lower wishbones, twin radius rods with outboard coil spring/damper units

Brakes
Disc; outboard front and rear

Dimensions
Wheelbase: 96.5 in (2451 mm)
Front track: 61 in (1549 mm)
Rear track: 61 in (1549 mm)
Unladen weight: c 1200 lb (545 kg)

Tyres
Goodyear

Formula One. Instead they prepared themselves for a high tide of USAC track racing success from 1972 to 1975 with staggeringly fast new cars designed by Roman Slobodynskyj, a Ukrainian-born engineer. Bobby Unser's factory USAC car won four major events in 1972, took pole position for all three classic 500-mile races (at Indy, Pocono, and Ontario, California) by setting fastest qualifying time, and smashed eight track records. The Eagle team's luck at Indianapolis was always atrocious, until 1975 when they won at last, with Bobby Unser driving. Dan Gurney had accomplished his aim. Later, however, things went badly for his formerly tight-knit team, which disintegrated and found times very hard as Dan fought to keep it going with new personnel and new cars. He seemed to have failed when, in 1980, Eagle withdrew from racing, but it proved to be temporary. A new Eagle, which used a highly modified Chevrolet "stock block" engine, was produced for 1981 USAC racing.

The AAR Eagle
The Eagle emblem was designed by Dan Gurney's father John, a leading singer with the New York Metropolitan Opera. Dan's original intention had been to call the Indianapolis cars Gurneys and the Formula One cars—which would take American pride abroad—Eagles. But since the early cars were so similar they were all called Eagles.

USAC Eagle 1975
Roman Slobodynskyj's basic 1972 track car design proved so successful that for the next three years it was subjected merely to logical development and regulation changes. Dan Gurney said, and could prove, that it was "hard to improve on a master-piece", and the USAC Eagles remained the fastest cars in their class. It was only unreliability that cheated them of greater success. The cars did well commercially, and twenty-eight 1972 cars were built and sold, followed by numerous updates on existing chassis, six completely new 1973 cars, and fifteen more in 1974. This was the high tide of Eagle success and a proud time for American racing.

Roman Slobodynskyj emigrated to America from the Ukraine in 1950 when he was nine years old. He worked as a draughtsman on aerospace projects, progressing rapidly to concept design. He joined Dan Gurney's AAR team in 1969. Demonstrating a shrewd and meticulous grasp of the complex problems of motor racing, his daring and effective designs were a crucial contribution to the success of the team for many years.

Team Drivers
Donnie Allison • Bob Bondurant • Duane Carter Jr. • Richie Ginther • Jerry Grant • Dan Gurney • Mike Hiss • David Hobbs • Denny Hulme • Gordon Johncock • Mel Kenyon • Joe Leonard • Bruce McLaren • Mike Mosely • Sam Posey • Swede Savage • Ludovico Scarfiotti • Bobby Unser • Bill Vukovich Jr.

ENSIGN

Morris Nunn, like so many retired racing drivers, could not keep away from the sport he loved after he retired in 1970. With backing from a friend, Bernard Lewis, he built his own Formula Three car in the garage at his home. The prototype Ensign LNF3 was technically interesting as the first significant non-Formula One single-seater to house its radiators in pods on each side of the cockpit. Nunn had adopted this feature from the Lotus 72 Grand Prix car and he matched it to a neat monocoque forward chassis with a tubular engine truss at the rear. With chisel-nose bodywork the Ensign was extremely pretty, and proved an almost instant success.

Driven by Bev Bond, the prototype was second in the first important international race for the then new 1600 cc Formula Three, and second time out Bond won. Orders were taken for more Ensign cars, complying with Formula Atlantic and Formula Two as well as Formula Three. In 1972, Nunn was approached by Rikki von Opel, the scion of the German car manufacturing family, who wanted to buy a factory Formula Three team drive. He was sponsored by Iberia airlines and joined in the team by Mike Walker, a young English driver. The 1972 Ensign Formula Three car was as sleek as the 1971 original, with an aerodynamic fairing over the engine bay. It became the fastest car in its class along straights, but lost ground to the opposition under braking. The Ensign was the best looking of the small-engined single-seater racing cars, but supplying outside customers stretched Nunn's limited resources, and results suffered.

Then von Opel, who had ambitions to race Formula One cars, offered to finance the construction of an Ensign using the conventional 3-litre Cosworth-Ford V-8 engine and Hewland transmission package. Nunn jumped at the opportunity. He decided to leave the production side of the business to an outside company while he concentrated upon the von Opel Grand Prix "special".

This first Formula One Ensign-Cosworth was completed in seven months from a clean sheet of paper and was given the type number N173 and the chassis number MN01, after Mo Nunn's initials. The distinctive car, with flared aerodynamic bodywork, made its debut at the 1973 French Grand Prix at Ricard-Castellet. Von Opel finished the race, albeit in last place. Effectively, this set the tone for the rest of the season, for such a small team and such an inexperienced driver could realistically hope for little more. Von Opel realized that he might be wiser to buy into one of the major teams for 1974, and he rented a drive with Brabham. This left Nunn with a Formula One car, a lot of ambition, but no driver.

Then Theodore Yip, the Hong Kong racing enthusiast, bought the Ensign drive for Vern Schuppan, his Australian protégé. The MN01 was updated to N174 trim and two later chassis, MN02 and MN03, were completed as the season progressed. Then in mid-season Yip and Schuppan drifted away. Once again Nunn was rescued, this time by Mike Wilds, who brought sponsorship from Dempster Developments, a property company, for the late races of 1974.

Mo continued to struggle on in Formula One and Ensign survived into 1975 with the N175 model, chassis MN04, which carried the unlikely livery of a Dutch alarm systems company, H.B. Bewaking. The Dutch drivers were the inexperienced Roelof Wunderink and Gijs van Lennep, a former Le Mans winner. Neither could set the Formula One world alight. Nunn then persuaded Chris Amon to try the car. In 1976, Nunn split from H.B., who took the MN04 with them to race as the Boro-Cosworth.

Nunn obtained the services of Dave Baldwin, a former Team Lotus designer, and the new 1976 Ensign N176, chassis MN05, was genuinely adventurous, the type of car which would have been widely acclaimed had Lotus built it. Despite months of partial retirement, Amon drove it with much of his old fire, but all his usual ill-fortune; the car continually failed while in contact with the leading group, if never actually challenging for the lead. Its unreliability was structural as well as mechanical and Chris had some frights. After witnessing Niki Lauda's fiery accident in the German Grand Prix, Chris decided to retire from Formula One for good and the Belgian ex-Ferrari driver Jacky Ickx completed Ensign's season.

In 1977, Nunn was still afloat, with enthusiastic backing from

SPECIFICATIONS
Ensign N176   1976

Engine
Cosworth-Ford DFV
90-degree V-8
Bore × stroke: 85.7 mm × 64.8 mm
Capacity: 2993 cc
Lucas fuel injection
Lucas electronic ignition
Maximum power: c 486 bhp at
c 10,500 rpm

Transmission
Hewland FGA400, five-speed
and reverse

Chassis
Three-quarter length monocoque
nacelle employing engine as
load-bearing member at rear

Front suspension
Double wishbones, inboard coil
spring/damper units, anti-roll bar

Rear suspension
Parallel lower links, single top
links, twin radius rods, outboard
coil spring/damper units, later
inboard coil spring/damper units

Brakes
Disc; outboard front and rear

Dimensions
Wheelbase: 102 in (2591 mm)
Front track: 58 in (1473 mm)
Rear track: 62 in (1575 mm)
Formula weight: c 1312 lb
(595 kg)

Tyres
Goodyear

Chuck Jones, a California businessman. Baldwin had begun work on a new N177 car, but left to join Fittipaldi before it was completed. He built virtually the same car for them. John Baldwin (who was no relation) completed the new Ensigns MN07, MN08, and MN09 for Clay Regazzoni—who brought sponsorship from Tissot watches—and as a semi-factory entry for the promising Frenchman Patrick Tambay, who was backed by Teddy Yip. These cars were driven in 1978 by Ickx, whose performances were half-hearted, and Derek Daly, who made the most of an uncompetitive car to establish his name.

In 1979, Nunn built a new car with Shahab Ahmed, the former Surtees and Tyrrell engineer. It was a flop. Daly left and Patrick Gaillard and Marc Surer had little better fortune. The future looked bleak until in 1980 Nunn got Unipart sponsorship, Regazzoni as driver, and new engineers and mechanics. Then, at Long Beach, there was an accident. The car was destroyed and Clay was badly injured. During the rest of the season three drivers struggled just to qualify an Ensign to start, not always successfully, and the team slithered towards extinction. In 1981, however, a backer purchased the assets, and enabled the irrepressible Nunn to continue.

Ensign N180

In keeping with most 1980 Formula One cars, the Ensign-Cosworth followed closely the ground-effects aerodynamic trend pioneered by the Lotus 79 in 1978. The car had a slender sheet-aluminium monocoque chassis encompassing the cockpit area and a single-cell fuel tank behind the driver. To this cell's rear bulkhead was attached the 3-litre Cosworth DFV V-8 engine and Hewland gearbox; these components were rigidly mounted to act as structural chassis members and to accept rear suspension loadings. Aerodynamic pods on either side enclosed the radiators and carried extending skirts to control airflow beneath the car and so promote a suction effect to aid cornering adhesion. The Ensign was unusual in having a narrow rear track, which minimized its frontal area, enabled it to cut a smaller hole in the air through which it was travelling, and in this way improved its maximum straight-line speed.

Morris Nuffield Nunn was born in Walsall, England, in 1939. In 1962, at the age of twenty-three, he looked into a local garage owned by the racing Ashmore Brothers and emerged owning a 1959 Formula Two Cooper. He had never even seen a race before when he drove it for the first time at Mallory Park. Predictably, he finished last. In 1963 he gained experience although the Cooper was uncompetitive, and in 1964, with backing from Bertie Bradnack, a former driver, he began to win with a Lotus 23B sports car. In 1965 Bernard Lewis helped him race a Formula Three Lotus. In 1966 he was a regular Formula Three frontrunner with his always immaculate red Lotus 41. Seasons of quick driving, with flashes of occasionally lurid racing, won him a Lotus factory Formula Three and occasional Formula Two drives, but Mo never quite had the edge to establish himself in the major league. He was universally well liked and found his metier when he began building the Ensigns. His friendly little team was always hospitable and his wife Sylvia always ready with the inevitable pot of tea. During the 1970s the Nunns became an integral part of the Formula One scene.

Team Drivers
Chris Amon • Hans Binder • Bev Bond • Derek Daly • Harald Ertl • Patrick Gaillard • Jacky Ickx • Jan Lammers • Gijs van Lennep • Lamberto Leoni • Brett Lunger • Tiff Needell • Patrick Neve • Danny Ongais • Rikki von Opel • Nelson Piquet • Clay Regazzoni • Vern Schuppan • Marc Surer • Mike Wilds • Roelof Wunderink

FERRARI

Within the sprawling Ferrari compound at Maranello, nestling against the foot of Italy's Emilian Appenine mountains, there are a number of tiny engine test cells, their brick walls stained with a film of oil. Each diminutive cell played an important role in motor racing history, for it was here that Ferrari first ran many of the most successful racing engines of the postwar period. To Enzo Ferrari, the engine was always of paramount importance. Until 1963, the chassis which carried it was merely a secondary consideration.

In 1946, the first Ferrari V-12 appeared, designed by Gioacchino Colombo, the ex-Ferrari and Alfa Romeo engineer, who had difficulty finding work in the postwar period because of his vociferous wartime allegiance to Mussolini. It was Enzo Ferrari who finally hired Colombo to produce a new engine which would give competitive power to a new range of Ferrari sports and Grand Prix cars. This new engine had to have greater power potential than the currently supreme straight-eight supercharged Alfa Romeo 158—initiated by Ferrari himself in 1937—and had to be sufficiently low-stressed to provide a firm foundation for extensive future development.

Colombo produced a 1500 cc V-12, unusual at that time not only for its multiplicity of tiny cylinders, but in their use of a greater bore than stroke. The engine had single overhead camshafts in each cylinder bank. It was used in a series of Ferrari sports racing cars built between 1946 and 1947. In 1948, a single-stage Roots-type supercharger was added and this engine appeared in a prototype Ferrari single-seater which made its debut at Turin, in the first postwar Italian Grand Prix.

In theory, Colombo's calculations showed that the engine would rev to an unprecedented 10,000 rpm, but in practice it could not exceed 7500 rpm safely. Consequently, its power output was restricted to a disappointing 225 bhp. To make the most of this modest output, the new V-12 was installed in a light, low-profile, short-wheelbase car. This squat build, combined with swing-axle rear suspension, made

the car nervous and intensely demanding on its drivers, because it was liable to spin at the slightest provocation.

During 1949, in the absence of the Alfa Romeo Grand Prix team, these new Ferraris and their developed successors proved quite successful, particularly when they were driven by Alberto Ascari and his mentor Luigi Villoresi. In 1950, however, when Alfa Romeo returned to the fray, the better-handling, long-wheelbase, twin-stage-supercharged, 1.5-litre Ferraris were simply outgunned for power.

Meanwhile, Ferrari had employed a new engineer, Aurelio Lampredi, who believed that the team should turn to the unsupercharged 4.5-litre option in Grand Prix regulations. Instead of combating Alfa's 1.5-litre supercharged straight-eight cars with a 1.5-litre supercharged V-12, he suggested a redesigned V-12, unblown and making use of those extra three litres. As a result, the big 4.5-litre V-12 Ferrari 375 was developed from smaller-capacity unblown

SPECIFICATIONS
Ferrari 375 1951

Engine
Ferrari 60-degree V-12
Bore × stroke: 80 mm × 74.5 mm
Capacity: 4494 cc
Three Weber carburettors
Marelli magneto ignition
Maximum power: c 350 bhp at 7000 rpm

Transmission
Ferrari, four-speed and reverse

Chassis
Twin-tube ladder frame

Front suspension
Double wishbones, transverse leaf spring, and hydraulic dampers

Rear suspension
De Dion axle, transverse leaf spring, and hydraulic dampers

Brakes
Drum; outboard front and rear

Dimensions
Wheelbase: 92 in (2337 mm)
Front track: 50 in (1270 mm)
Rear track: 51 in (1295 mm)
Wheel rim width: 4½-5½ in front and 7 in rear
Formula weight: c 1850 lb (839 kg)

Tyres
Englebert

versions. During 1951 it proved it could run with the supercharged Alfas, and then—when it was driven by Froilan Gonzalez—it beat the previously insuperable Alfa team in the British Grand Prix at Silverstone. Ascari won the next race, the German Grand Prix, at the Nürburgring, and this proved it was the car, not merely the driver, which had succeeded in Britain. Alfa Romeo were fortunate to emerge at the close of the season with Juan Fangio as World Champion Driver. They promptly withdrew, acknowledging that their 158/159 had reached the end of its long development life. The equally fast and more economical unsupercharged Ferraris pointed the way for future development. The thirsty Alfa Romeos lost their races because they needed two or three pit stops compared to the Ferraris' one, or two at the most.

Enzo Ferrari has always believed in spreading his risks. While the 4.5-litre unsupercharged Grand Prix engine had been developed he had produced a parallel sports car line ready to accommodate that engine. He also had an unsupercharged 2-litre, four-cylinder in-line engine emerging in the background. Alfa Romeo's withdrawal from Formula One left only Ferrari with modern competitive machinery. Consequently, for 1952-53 the FIA permitted Grand Prix organizers to run their World Championship-qualifying Grand Prix races to 2-litre Formula Two regulations. And there was Ferrari, prepared with the competitive four-cylinder Tipo 500.

Alberto Ascari proved conclusively how well-prepared they were by winning the World Drivers' Championship in both seasons. He took first place in all six Grands Prix that he started in 1952 and in five of his eight starts in 1953. The only major Grand Prix he did not contest in 1952 fell to his team-mate Piero Taruffi in another Ferrari 500. In 1953, Mike Hawthorn, a newcomer, won for the team in France, and Farina won for them in Germany. To this magnificent success story must be added all the non-championship Formula Two races won by Ascari for Ferrari at Syracuse, Saint-Gaudens, la Baule, Marseilles, and Pau. It took Fangio to break Ferrari's stranglehold on the formula by winning the last 2-litre Championship Grand Prix at Monza in September 1953. When the Ferraris were beaten it was headline news. Maserati were overjoyed at their Monza success on Italian soil, and in 1952, at Reims, when Jean Behra's little Gordini led the Ferrari fleet to the line, many believed his car must have had a 2.5-litre engine.

Il Cavallino Rampante
On June 17, 1923, twenty-five-year-old Enzo Ferrari won a race at the Savio circuit, near Ravenna, in an Alfa Romeo. Ravenna was the home town of the Baracca family, whose son Francesco had been Italy's leading fighter pilot in World War I. Baracca's squadron had carried a prancing horse emblem on its aircraft. Enzo's elder brother Alfredo had served with the squadron as ground crew before contracting a fatal illness. Baracca's parents met Enzo Ferrari at the Savio race, kept in contact with him, and eventually presented him with their late son's symbol of courage and audacity—*Il Cavallino Rampante*, the Prancing Horse—for his personal use. Enzo Ferrari added the yellow background, the colour of Modena, to the shield, and his cars have carried the symbol into battle ever since.

FERRARI

The new 2.5-litre Grand Prix formula actually took effect on January 1, 1954, and Ferrari simply developed their 500 2-litre design into the 2.5-litre Tipo 625. These Ferrari classifications are interesting; they are derived from the capacity in cubic centimetres of one engine cylinder. Thus a single cylinder of a 1.5-litre 12-cylinder Ferrari 125 has a displacement of 125 cc, because 125 x 12 = 1500. Equally, the Ferrari 500 was a 2.0-litre, four-cylinder car, and the 625 was a 2.5-litre, four-cylinder car because 625 x 4 = 2500.

This rather half-hearted Ferrari 625 Grand Prix car was no match for the potent new Maserati 250F and Lancia D50 designs in 1954-55, while the Mercedes-Benz W196 proved itself in a class of its own. Only Lancia's financial problems, which led to the collapse of their Formula One hopes, and Gianni Lancia's cession of six of his cars, material, and designer Vittorio Jano to Ferrari, gave the Maranello team suitable armament for the 1956 and 1957 seasons. In 1957, the old Lancia-Ferrari V-8 cars were becoming antiquated, and Jano evolved a new V-6 power unit initially for 1500 cc Formula Two racing. Towards the end of 1957, its capacity was increased to 2.4 litres for Formula One racing. From 1958 to 1960 it powered the Dino 246 and Dino 256 cars, carrying the name of Enzo Ferrari's dead son to World Championship laurels for Mike Hawthorn in that first full season.

When Jano retired, Carlo Chiti, the former Alfa Romeo technician, took over as Ferrari's chief engineer. In 1960, he developed a new 120-degree V-6 power unit for 1500 cc Formula Two racing. A new Formula One with a 1500 cc capacity limit was to take effect from January 1, 1961. Once again Enzo Ferrari was prepared. The predominantly British opposition had tried too long to perpetuate 2.5-litre racing and were left with a year's hiatus until their new 1.5-litre V-8 power units from BRM and Coventry Climax could be fully developed.

During that first season of 1.5-litre Formula One racing, the V-6 Ferraris were again in a class of their own. Phil Hill won the World

Drivers' Championship for Ferrari at the tragic Italian Grand Prix which witnessed the deaths of Wolfgang von Trips, the Ferrari driver who was leading the World Championship, and fourteen spectators as his car crashed into the crowd.

The V-6 continued to be raced into 1964, until a new Ferrari V-8 engine gave John Surtees another World Championship. Then, in 1966, the new 3-litre Grand Prix formula took effect. Of course, Ferrari was well-prepared—using a 3-litre V-12 engine developed from the

Ferrari Dino 246

This was the car which carried Mike Hawthorn to his World Drivers' Championship in 1958, the first time a British driver had won. It was a narrow victory which Hawthorn took by just one point from Stirling Moss, driving for Vanwall. Moss won more Grands Prix that season, but Hawthorn achieved his title as the result of just one victory and a string of second places and fastest laps. Vanwall, however, stole the Formula One Constructors' Championship title from Ferrari. The Dino used an unusual 65-degree four-cam V-6 engine with standard dimensions of 85 mm x 71 mm to displace 2417 cc. In 1958, this compact engine produced more than 280 bhp at 8500 rpm, but its crude chassis made it daunting to drive; both Peter Collins and Luigi Musso lost their lives in these wickedly fast cars.

SPECIFICATIONS
Ferrari Tipo 156   1961

Engine
Ferrari Dino 120-degree V-6
Bore × stroke: 73 mm × 58.8 mm
Capacity: 1477 cc
Three Weber carburettors
Marelli or Bosch ignition
Maximum power: c 190 bhp at 9500 rpm

Transmission
Ferrari, five-speed and reverse

Chassis
Large diameter multi-tubular spaceframe

Front suspension
Double wishbones with interposed coil spring/damper units and anti-roll bar

Rear suspension
Double wishbones with coil spring/damper units and anti-roll bar

Brakes
Disc; outboard front, inboard rear

Dimensions
Wheelbase: 90.6 in (2301 mm)
Front and rear track: 47.2 in (1198 mm)
Wheel rim width: 5 in front, 6 in rear
Formula weight: c 1102 lb (500 kg)

Tyres
Dunlop

age-old 12-cylinder engine armoury at Maranello which had been continuously prominent in international sports car racing since the mid-1950s. Strength in depth had always been Ferrari's aim. But in 1966, the perennial politics and infighting of his team lost him John Surtees. The less powerful Repco Brabham V-8 stole the Formula One championships. The V-12 was at the end of its dominant period in Formula One, and Ferrari would have to start anew before major success could return to Maranello.

Ferrari V-12

In 1961, in a new 1.5-litre Formula One, Ferrari won the World Championship. He had the perfect opportunity to repeat this success in 1966, when the 3-litre formula was introduced. There were shelves of 3-litre V-12 sports car engine parts at Maranello, well-proven after many years of endurance race success. Engineer Mauro Forghieri designed a monocoque chassis for the new Grand Prix car and fitted it with a V-12 of 77 mm bore x 53.5 mm

stroke, displacing 2989 cc, with double overhead camshafts per bank actuating two valves per cylinder. With Lucas fuel injection this unit produced 375 bhp at 10,000 rpm. Driven by John Surtees, it won the fast Belgian Grand Prix at Spa. In mid-season Surtees left and one of the team's greatest assets was lost to them. The new car never went so well again except for Ludovico Scarfiotti's emotive home-ground victory in that year's Italian Grand Prix at Monza.

Team Drivers
Andrea de Adamich • Cliff Allison •
Chris Amon • Mario Andretti •
Alberto Ascari •
Giancarlo Baghetti •
Lorenzo Bandini • Jean Behra •
Derek Bell • Bob Bondurant •
Ernesto Brambilla • Tony Brooks •
Piero Carini • Eugenio Castellotti
Peter Collins •
Juan Manuel Fangio •
Giuseppe Farina • Paul Frere •
Olivier Gendebien •
Richie Ginther • Ignazio Giunti •
Froilan Gonzalez • Dan Gurney •
Mike Hawthorn • Phil Hill •
Jacky Ickx • Niki Lauda •
Umberto Maglioli •
Willy Mairesse • Robert Manzon •
Arturo Merzario • Luigi Musso •
Mike Parkes • Andre Pilette •
Didier Pironi • Alfonso de Portago •
Clay Regazzoni •
Carlos Reutemann •
Pedro Rodriguez •
Ricardo Rodriguez •
Ludovico Scarfiotti •
Jody Scheckter • Harry Schell •
Dorino Serafini • André Simon •
Raymond Sommer • John Surtees •
Piero Taruffi • Maurice Trintignant •
Wolfgang von Trips •
Nino Vaccarella •
Gilles Villeneuve • Luigi Villoresi •
Jonathan Williams

Mauro Forghieri was born in 1935. After he got his engineering degree from the University of Bologna he immediately went to work as an instructor at the Ferrari training school at Maranello. In 1960 he was called in to assist Carlo Chiti in his racing programme. At the end of the 1961 season Chiti left the company and Forghieri was appointed to take his place. He was never afraid to learn from leading chassis designers. He adopted for his 1963 V-6 Formula One Ferraris British-style lightweight multi-tubular spaceframes, radius arm suspension, and cast-alloy road wheels plus the added sophistication of Bosch fuel injection in place of the almost traditional Weber carburettors. Mauro was also responsible for the modern line of World Championship sports and GT Ferraris produced during the 1960s. Once concentration upon Formula One became total, Forghieri's Ferraris began to win World Championships. He was temporarily displaced as head of race engineering at Maranello only to be hastily recalled when his would-be successors failed. Niki Lauda once described him as "a madman, but also a genius. . . ." His histrionic displays combined with the performances of his cars lend weight to this observation.

Constructors' Championship
1961 • 1964 • 1975 • 1976 •
1977 • 1979

73

FERRARI

During the latter years of their 3-litre Formula One V-12 engine programme, from 1966 to 1969, Ferrari achieved only sporadic success. Although Chris Amon often looked set for excellent results, particularly during 1967, he was always cheated by some mechanical malady or sheer misfortune. In 1968, Jacky Ickx won the French Grand Prix in the rain at Rouen, and was still in the running for the World Championship when he crashed during practice in Canada and broke a leg. The 1969 season was catastrophic for Ferrari, for their obsolete and overweight V-12-engined Formula One car was effectively outclassed by the predominantly Cosworth V-8-powered opposition.

Attempts to extract more power from the old, if often rejuvenated, V-12 had impaired its reliability. During 1969 Ferrari's major effort was concentrated on the development of a new flat-12 horizontally opposed, or boxer, engine for Grand Prix use. The new power unit should have made its debut at Monza in the 1969 Italian Grand Prix, but Chris Amon's prototype burst behind him during private testing and that prompted his decision to abandon Ferrari immediately. But it was a grievous error on his part, for the new flat-12 was to become a force to be reckoned with in Grand Prix racing during the early 1970s.

This type of engine had a long development background at Maranello, dating from 1962 when engineer Mauro Forghieri became part of the racing team hierarchy. He replaced Carlo Chiti who had walked out during the great "palace revolution" at Ferrari at the end of the 1961 season. Enzo Ferrari had detailed two of his promising young engineers, Forghieri and Angelo Bellei, to develop multi-cylinder Formula One engines to replace the Dino V-6. Bellei's relatively simple 1.5-litre V-8 was produced in time to be tested late in 1963 and in 1964 it powered John Surtees and Ferrari to World Championship titles.

Forghieri's much more radical and sophisticated 1.5-litre flat-12 was a longer term project. It appeared first at Monza in September 1964, and in 1965, the last 1.5-litre Grand Prix season, it was raced extensively, although without major success. Forghieri became established as the racing team's technical director during this period while Bellei was made responsible for production road car developments. In 1969, the idea of the old 1.5-litre flat-12 was retrieved, developed to 2-litre capacity, and mounted in an ultra-lightweight sports racing car chassis for the European Mountain Championship hill climb competition. The car was designated the Tipo 212E (Europeo) and driven by the Swiss driver Peter Schetty it utterly dominated the championship. The next step was a further redesign of the proven basic concept, which yielded the full 3-litre Formula One flat-12.

This new engine was dimensionally "oversquare", with a bore size of 78.5 mm and an ultra-short stroke length of 51.5 mm, displacing 2991 cc. Gear-driven twin overhead camshafts were used on each opposed cylinder bank, the heads containing four valves per cylinder. To minimize frictional losses the crankshaft ran in only four main bearings, rather than the conventional seven of most 12-cylinder engines. (Combinations of plain and roller bearings were tested.) After early failures and development troubles the flat-12 or 312B boxer engine became a truly formidable proposition.

The initial 1970 312Bs started winning in that season's Austrian Grand Prix, where Ickx and Regazzoni placed first and second. Regazzoni won at Monza. In Canada Ickx was first and Regazzoni was second, and the Mexican Grand Prix result was the same. When the 312Bs won the first races of 1971 people talked of the "death of the Cosworth engine". Such speculation was premature: the 1971 312Bs flopped. The cars won three championship rounds in 1971-72, but by 1973 Ferrari were in real trouble. Forghieri had been temporarily set to work on other projects and the 312B3 cars, which were redesigned to comply with new deformable-structure chassis regulations, proved uncompetitive. Ferrari actually withdrew from Formula One to sort matters out.

In 1974 they returned, stronger than ever with Niki Lauda joining Regazzoni in the team. It was only Lauda's inexperience and bad luck

that robbed them of championship honours that season, although he won two Grands Prix and Regazzoni won a third. During the 1975 season the Italian team achieved full stature with its square-cut and extremely powerful 312T (the T standing for *transversale*, a reference to the transverse-shaft gearbox). Lauda won four Grands Prix and Regazzoni a fifth—the Italian—to bring Maranello another Formula One Constructors' Championship after a gap of no less than ten seasons. In 1976 the uprated 312T2 cars proved less manageable than their predecessors. Lauda nevertheless won six Grands Prix. After recovering from his horrifying Nürburgring accident he put himself out of the World Drivers' Championship by withdrawing on safety grounds from the deciding race, in Japan, where James Hunt took the drivers' title. McLaren could not, however, break Ferrari's grip on the constructors' crown.

In 1977 Lauda won two Grands Prix and Carlos Reutemann took a third. A string of reliable second places confirmed Lauda's second Drivers' Championship and Ferrari's hat trick of constructors' titles.

In 1978 the new generation of "wing cars" took off with the Lotus 78/79 series. Nevertheless, the further updated 312T2s and T3s won Ferrari five Grands Prix, four gained by Reutemann, one by his new team-mate Gilles Villeneuve. These cars ran on French-made Michelin tyres with great success. In 1979, Jody Scheckter, the new team leader, shone in the 312T4 cars, which were the ugliest yet. He gained another World Championship, with victories in three Grands Prix, while Villeneuve won another three.

Unfortunately, the protruding cylinder heads of the flat-12 engine made it very difficult for Ferrari to achieve adequate ground effect from airflow management devices as used on the V-8, V-12 (Alfa Romeo), and V-6 turbo opposition. And in 1980, when Michelin lost their way, Ferrari's 312T5 proved disastrously uncompetitive.

The flat-12 engine had apparently had its day in Formula One, and its successor for 1981 was a 1.5-litre turbocharged and much modernized version of the 1961 120-degree V-6 engine. The recast

block was mounted as a stressed chassis member in the rear of the new car and the four-cam V-6 carried its exhausts within the vee. This provided short, straight manifolds leading directly into German KKK turbocharger impellers which were mounted directly above the engine. The two compressor stages were immediately ahead of these impellers feeding the induction via air-charge intercoolers. A transverse-shaft gearbox developed from the one used successfully on the 312T series cars was employed. Suspension consisted of rocker arms and coil spring/dampers front and rear. There were large ground-effects pods on either side of the slender monocoque. This new-generation Ferrari was designated the Tipo 126C, which Enzo Ferrari insisted meant *competizione*, rather than *compressore*. One era had ended, and a whole new era was just beginning.

Ferrari 312B

The beautifully sleek and low-built 312B cars of 1970 employed a fascinatingly original semi-monocoque chassis design. The three-quarter-length forward nacelle was formed from stressed skins riveted and bonded to a lightweight multi-tubular internal spaceframe. This nacelle terminated behind the cockpit. From the top of the rear bulkhead there projected a backbone beam from which the flat-12 engine was suspended to accept gearbox and major suspension loads. The only bodywork comprised a fibreglass nose cone and vestigial cockpit surround which incorporated the windscreen. There were also various air scoops around the engine bay, and the front and rear wing sections. The 312B was, and remains, one of the handsomest of all mid-engined Grand Prix cars.

SPECIFICATIONS
Ferrari 126C   1980-81

Engine
Ferrari 126C 120-degree V-6
Bore × stroke: 81 mm × 48.4 mm
Capacity: 1496 cc
Lucas-Ferrari fuel injection; twin-turbochargers by Kuhnle, Kopp & Kausch
Marelli Dinoplex electronic ignition
Maximum power: c 540 bhp at 11,000 rpm

Transmission
Ferrari transverse, five- or six-speed and reverse

Chassis
Three-quarter length monocoque nacelle employing engine as load-bearing member at rear, ground-effects pods on either side

Front suspension
Top rocker arms, wide-based lower wishbones, inboard coil spring/damper units and anti-roll bar

Rear suspension
Top rocker arms, lower links, inboard coil spring/damper units and anti-roll bar

Brakes
Disc; outboard front and rear

Dimensions
Wheelbase: 107 in (2719 mm)
Front track: 69⅓ in (1760 mm)
Rear track: 64 in (1626 mm)
Wheel rim width: 11 in front, 18 in rear
Chassis weight: c 100 lb (45 kg)
Formula weight: c 1322 lb (600 kg)

Tyres
Michelin

Enzo Ferrari is a remarkable man who has been involved in racing for more than fifty years. During the 1920s he was a racing driver, car distributor, and competition entrepreneur for Alfa Romeo. For 1930 he established the Scuderia Ferrari, with the support of enthusiastic, wealthy partners, to race Alfa Romeo cars in Italy and Europe. The Scuderia took over Alfa Romeo Grand Prix commitments in the mid-1930s and raced on their behalf until 1938. In 1940, two straight-eight 1.5-litre sports cars were built by Ferrari in Modena for that year's Mille Miglia. In 1945 the first 1.5-litre V-12 Ferrari cars appeared, carrying The Old Man's prancing horse insignia. Since that time Ferrari has supported motor racing longer and in greater depth than any other marque in history—all at Enzo Ferrari's personal insistence. This autocratic Italian maestro built his reputation as a formidable businessman, adept at making maximum use of his employees' talents and at developing strength in depth. There has been no smarter man in motor racing history.

HESKETH

The luxury yacht lying in the harbour at Monte Carlo throbbed with music, laughter, the pop of champagne corks, and the clinking of glasses. The Monaco Grand Prix would take place in a few days and Hesketh Racing were in town. It was the same wherever Lord Alexander Hesketh's youthful and exuberant team travelled during its first Grand Prix racing season, 1973, although its extravagance was to fade. Beneath the lavish veneer of playboy fun—typified by their teddy bear symbol—there was a serious group of men who reached the top—and built a car capable of winning Grands Prix.

When Hesketh first came into minor prominence, running a Formula Three Dastle for Anthony "Bubbles" Horsley, a fun-loving friend, they seemed destined to go nowhere. When they hired James Hunt, an accident-prone driver just fired by March, few people took notice.

The Hesketh team bought a Formula Two Surtees for 1973. This looked a little more serious. James destroyed it while testing at Goodwood. Hesketh then rented a Formula One Surtees for Hunt to drive in the Brands Hatch Race of Champions. Hunt finished third. Hesketh promptly ordered a new March 731 and managed to convince their development chief, Dr. Harvey Postlethwaite, that his team's racing ambitions really were serious. Postlethwaite moved to the Hesketh family home at Easton Neston—within earshot of Silverstone—together with the new Formula One car. That season his modifications made the car fiercely competitive on Firestone tyres, at a time when it was believed Goodyears had to be used to win.

Hunt was ninth in his first Grand Prix at Monaco. In the French Grand Prix he was sixth and scored his and Hesketh's maiden championship point. He bettered this with a fourth place and the fastest lap in the British race, a third place in the Dutch Grand Prix, and, finally, was second to Ronnie Peterson's Lotus in the United States Grand Prix, where he again set the fastest race lap. Clearly, Hunt was a driver of great promise, Hesketh Racing was capable of working as well as living hard, and Postlethwaite was a gifted engineer.

Inspired by these performances, Lord Hesketh authorized for 1974 the construction of new Hesketh cars powered by the Cosworth-Ford V-8 engine. The prototype Hesketh 308 appeared in April 1974 and delighted Hesketh's home crowd by winning the Silverstone International Trophy. It was in this Hesketh 308 that Hunt began his fierce rivalry—despite their close friendship off the track—with Niki Lauda, Ferrari's number one driver.

Although the Hesketh proved fast and competitive, it lacked essential reliability. Not until the Dutch Grand Prix in 1975 did the team's preparation, their tactics, and Hunt's highly competitive driving bring a 308 to victory in a Grand Prix. This race at Zandvoort was a half-wet, half-dry event with cars making pit stops to change from wet-weather tyres to dry-weather slicks. Hesketh timed their change superbly. It was enough to enable Hunt to hold Lauda off until the end.

This was to be the zenith of the Hesketh team's career, for Lord Hesketh had run his cars completely unsupported by commercial sponsors. His other business interests were not proving as successful at that time, and the financial strain of running a Grand Prix team began to prove too great a burden for one man. Moves were made to find a suitable sponsor for the 1976 season. Postlethwaite had introduced a new car which was intended to reach full development during that year. This Hesketh 308C was one of the lowest and flattest Formula One cars yet seen. It started a new trend towards engine air intakes designed integrally with the general body shape, rather than stuck on later, virtually as an afterthought. The suspension looked conventional, but it used rubber blocks in compression to save weight and complication.

For once Postlethwaite's calculations were incorrect, however, and in its early outings, although it showed undeniable promise, the latest Hesketh was also found to be an unpredictable car. While the team were grappling with these problems, financial matters suddenly became critical. Lord Hesketh was unable to reach agreement with would-be commercial sponsors, for he did not want to dilute his own identity and certainly would not submerge it beneath a sponsor's commercial brand name. Just as prospects were beginning to look promising for the new season, Hesketh abruptly called together his staff and told them that the team was finished.

Frank Williams, who had won backing from Walter Wolf, an Austrian-born Canadian businessman, bought the cars and also took on some Hesketh personnel. In 1976, the Hesketh 308C became the first Wolf-Williams car. The project proved disastrous, however, and never came close to fulfilling the original Hesketh promise.

Meanwhile, the entrepreneurial skills of Bubbles Horsley, the Hesketh racing manager, salvaged something from the wreck and kept the team running through 1976-77 by operating a rent-a-drive scheme for young drivers with personal sponsorship. Initially, they used the Hesketh 308B cars, updated now to D-type specification. Then for 1977 Frank Dernie, the Hesketh design engineer, produced an all-new 308E model which was a practical middle-of-the-field car, but enjoyed limited success. Hesketh Racing survived into the 1980s with an engine rebuilding workshop caring for the Cosworth DFV engines of many top teams.

Hesketh 308B

When Harvey Postlethwaite produced his first Hesketh 308 in 1974, it was necessarily based closely upon his March 731 variant, developed during the preceding year. He attempted to produce a car which would be fast in a straight line, yet which also generated high aerodynamic downforce to assist its cornering capabilities. In the wind tunnel, he developed a shape which produced increasing downforce as it yawed—slid sideways—through the air. In this way, the car had an inbuilt tendency to correct itself, to find the aerodynamic path of least resistance. This made it pleasant to drive, and very fast. In the 1975 308, Postlethwaite sought a more slippery shape by removing the radiator from the nose and replacing it with twin coolers amidships on either side, leaving the wide nose clean and uncluttered. With well-developed, although conventional, coil and wishbone suspension the car proved highly competitive and won the Dutch Grand Prix.

Team Drivers
Eddie Cheever • Guy Edwards •
Harald Ertl • James Hunt •
Alan Jones • Rupert Keegan •
Brett Lunger • Torsten Palm •
Alex Ribeiro • Rolf Stommelen

SPECIFICATIONS
Hesketh 308C   1975-76

Engine
Cosworth-Ford DFV
90-degree V-8
Bore × stroke: 85.7 mm × 64.8 mm
Capacity: 2995 cc
Lucas fuel injection
Lucas electronic ignition
Maximum power: c 470 bhp at
c 10,500 rpm

Transmission
Hewland FGA400, five-speed and
reverse

Chassis
Stressed-skin three-quarter
monocoque employing engine and
transmission case as structural
members at rear

Front suspension
Double wishbones, inboard coil
spring/damper units

Rear suspension
Parallel lower links, single top
links, double radius rods,
outboard rubber springs or metal
coil spring/damper units

Brakes
Disc; outboard front, inboard rear

Dimensions
Wheelbase: 102 in (2590 mm)
Front track: 55 in (1397 mm)
Rear track: 57 in (1448 mm)
Wheel rim width: 10 in front,
19 in rear
Chassis weight: c 100 lb (45 kg)
Formula weight: c 1323 lb
(600 kg)

Tyres
Goodyear

Alexander Fermor-Hesketh was still in his teens when he became involved with racing and was just twenty-one years old when his team began to look greedily to Formula One. His father had died while Alexander was still a child, and he grew up to enjoy and augment his inherited wealth. Heavily built and extrovert, he could be the life of the party, but his jovial exterior hid genuine racing ambition, which emerged in the professional way his team worked, despite their jet-setting high jinks when they relaxed so enthusiastically. Lord Hesketh's personal collection of cars included a Maserati "Birdcage" sports racing car, and a pre-World War I Grand Prix Benz. He was also an enthusiastic motorcyclist, as became evident in 1980, when he announced the completion of the vee-twin Hesketh SuperBike, built at Easton Neston, in the stables from which his Grand Prix cars had once emerged.

THE CARS
HONDA

In 1964, intense excitement gripped the Grand Prix racing world when it became known that the Japanese Honda company, who dominated international motorcycle racing, was turning their attention to Formula One. Their first car, painted off-white with the rising sun emblem on its nose, made its debut in the German Grand Prix at the Nürburgring that year driven by Ronnie Bucknum, an American. The car was technically fascinating, if not outstandingly competitive.

This Honda RA271 model used a transverse, 1.5-litre V-12 engine designed and developed by a special team; Yoshio Nakamura was development coordinator. Each miniscule cylinder contained four valves, and the engine could rev to 13,000 rpm. It was slung in a tubular subframe bolted to a central monocoque nacelle. The car used American Goodyear tyres.

After an accident at the Nürburgring when the steering failed, Bucknum reappeared with the car at Monza for the Italian Grand Prix. Fuel injection had replaced the original Keihin motorcycle-type carburettors. The car proved unreliable and retired in Italy and in the United States. But in 1965 new RA272 cars were constructed. Richie Ginther left BRM to drive with Bucknum.

That season these revised new cars excelled on the faster circuits, although they lacked the reliability to be in leading positions at the finish. It was not until the United States Grand Prix in October that both cars finished, and then seventh and eleventh. But at the high-altitude Mexico City circuit for the last Grand Prix of the 1.5-litre formula, both Hondas shone, and Ginther led all the way to score a unique Japanese victory in Formula One. At last the Honda V-12s had found true form. But it was too late. The formula changed and the little white cars could only become interesting museum pieces.

Encouraged, however, by this last-ditch success, Soichiro Honda authorized the construction of a new car to contest the 3-litre Formula One races in 1966. This machine was a massive device with a roller-bearing, 3-litre V-12 engine of enormous potential, but grossly overweight. It was another four-camshaft, four-valve-per-cylinder design, and on its debut the new RA273 car was said to have scaled 243 kg over the 500 kg minimum weight limit. Nevertheless, the 78 mm by 52.2 mm, 2992 cc power unit delivered more than 400 bhp at 10,000 rpm, a lot at that time. Ginther survived an horrendous crash during its first race at the 1966 Italian Grand Prix. In Mexico, Ginther was fourth and set fastest lap, while Bucknum finished eighth in a sister car.

For 1967, Nakamura persuaded John Surtees, the former motorcycle World Champion, to join the team. John believed that since Honda had started badly in motorcycle racing but then established total domination, they could be expected to do the same in Formula One. The RA273 was developed, but it never shed the burden of its overweight and oversized engine. Surtees finished third in the South African Grand Prix, fourth in the German, and sixth in the British before appearing in a new RA300 car at Monza. This car used many Indianapolis Lola chassis parts and had been built around the Japanese V-12 engine in Surtees's British workshops. On its debut, John won the Italian Grand Prix and then placed fourth in Mexico.

For 1968, a team which included Surtees, Nakamura, Eric Broadley of Lola, and Derrick White developed the RA301 light-weight monocoque, but late delivery delayed its development. Honda politics produced an air-cooled V-8 3-litre car at this time, and work lagged on the water-cooled V-12. The Honda-built, air-cooled RA302 was a fascinating design with four camshafts and four valves per cylinder, fuel injection, and a 120-degree V-8 layout with dimensions of 88 mm by 61.4 mm for 2987 cc. This was a very light unit and delivered some 430 bhp at 10,000 rpm. But the chassis was underdeveloped and early in its debut race, the 1968 French Grand Prix at Rouen, it crashed and its driver Jo Schlesser was killed. Surtees was second in this race in the RA301 and also set fastest lap—a new record—at Spa that year. A second RA302 appeared later in the year, but at its close Honda withdrew to ponder their mistakes, after failing to match their motorcycle achievements in Formula One racing.

Honda RA273
Big, bulky, and noisy are perhaps the three most apt adjectives to describe the Japanese company's first 3-litre Grand Prix car. It was a massive affair, its bulky monocoque chassis design dictated largely by the gross outline of its engine. The V-12 power unit was huge, due to the choice of low-friction roller bearings to support its crankshaft in place of the efficient, lightweight plain bearings used by most other manufacturers. Roller bearings were standard components in racing motorcycle engines with which the Japanese engineers had become so accomplished, and they saw no reason to change. It was a grievous error, from which their prototype 3-litre Grand Prix cars could not recover.

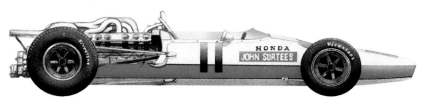

Honda RA301

By 1968 the 3-litre Honda had profited from John Surtees's knowledge of and involvement in British racing car chassis design. While the engine was still bulky, weight had been trimmed by the use of lightweight, cast-magnesium crankcases. To approach the legal minimum weight limit more closely they then needed the lightest possible monocoque chassis structure conducive to sufficient strength and rigidity. The Anglo-Japanese RA301 was the result. But it was of course a compromise, and the competition of Formula One racing is unrelenting—compromises seldom succeed.

SPECIFICATIONS
Honda RA272   1964

Engine
Honda 60-degree V-12
Bore × stroke: 58.1 mm × 47 mm
Capacity: 1495 cc
Six Keihin carburettors
Honda coil and battery ignition
Maximum power: c 220 bhp at 11,000 rpm

Transmission
Honda, six-speed and reverse

Chassis
Lightweight aluminium sheet monocoque centre section with tubular engine bay subframe at rear

Front suspension
Top rocker arms, lower wishbones and inboard coil spring/damper units and anti-roll bar

Rear suspension
Double wishbones with interposed coil spring/damper units, twin radius rods and anti-roll bar

Brakes
Disc; outboard front and rear

Dimensions
Wheelbase: 90 in (2289 mm)
Front track: 53 in (1346 mm)
Rear track: 65.9 in (1674 mm)
Unladen weight: 1155 lb (523 kg)

Tyres
Goodyear

Team Drivers
Ronnie Bucknum • Richie Ginther • David Hobbs • Jo Schlesser • John Surtees

Yoshio Nakamura's angular features became familiar in Formula One circles in 1964. This gifted development engineer, who had played such an important role in the postwar growth and burgeoning success of Soichiro Honda's company, won universal respect. Always correct and evidently accomplished, Nakamura had a massive work load thrown upon him by the relative failure of the Formula One car designs. In 1965, when Richie Ginther led the field in the British and Dutch Grands Prix, and eventually won the final 1.5-litre Grand Prix race at Mexico City, it was wonderful to see Nakamura's usually inscrutable expression light up with delight. Nakamura is now a Honda development engineer "at large".

LIGIER

Guy Ligier's Formula One team has done more than any other except Matra to put France back on top of motor racing after years in the doldrums. Ligier, a former Rugby International and self-made millionaire with a highly successful road construction business, drove his own private Cooper-Maserati and Repco-Brabham Formula One cars in 1966 and 1967. In 1968 he then teamed with his friend, Jo Schlesser, in a brace of Formula Two McLarens. When Schlesser was killed in the air-cooled Honda that year in the French Grand Prix, Ligier withdrew from driving and concentrated on the GT car project which he had founded.

The first car, the Ligier JS1 (thus initialled in memory of Schlesser), was designed by Michel Tétu and used a body styled by the Italian house of Frua. The engine was a 1.6-litre Cosworth-Ford FVA. The Ligier GT cars progressed through 2.6-litre Ford and 3-litre Maserati V-6 engines. Citroën supported the JS2-Maserati competition programme and the cars were actually distributed through Citroën dealers in France until production ceased in 1976.

In 1971, Guy Ligier and Patrick Depailler drove a Ligier JS3 in the Le Mans 24-Hour race. In 1975, when Cosworth DFV V-8 engines were fitted, a second place was achieved at Le Mans. Gitanes, the French cigarette company, sponsored the 1975 sports car programme and were eager to enter Formula One in 1976. Ligier responded enthusiastically. Matra Sports—who had withdrawn from racing at the end of 1974—supported this French effort by loaning Ligier the services of team manager Gerard Ducarouge and engineers Michel Beaujon and Paul Carillo. Ligier had intended to build a monocoque Formula One car powered by the British DFV engine. Ducarouge, however, persuaded Matra to extend development of their old 3-litre V-12 engine for Ligier's use to make it as nearly as possible an all-French project. During testing Jacques Laffite, a Formula Two and

budding Williams Formula One driver, proved quicker than Jean-Pierre Beltoise, who had been Matra's Formula One star, and it was Laffite who won the drive.

The Ligier-Matra JS5 proved a remarkably competitive car, the wail of its V-12 exhaust genuinely pleased the crowds, and although it was never a sure-fire candidate for Grand Prix victory, on occasion it showed remarkable pace. And on occasion, Laffite, a hard-fighting driver of Gallic spirit and considerable charm, displayed remarkable skill. Some observers believed that if he would take his driving more seriously he would become one of the top six men.

In the 1976 Italian Grand Prix at Monza, Laffite, driving the JS5, qualified on pole position. It was a considerable triumph for the tight-knit and remarkably popular one-car French team. Then, in 1977, Ligier built a modernized JS7 car. In the Swedish Grand Prix at Anderstorp, Laffite drove it to victory after the Lotus had retired. It was the first Grand Prix to be won by a Frenchman, driving a French car, powered by a French engine since the inception of the World Championship series in 1950.

During 1978, the old Matra engine began to show signs of age and although the Ligier JS9 remained competitive it never seriously looked as if it would win another race. Matra opted out at the end of that season. Ligier were left to turn to the Cosworth DVF engine for 1979. This they did to remarkable effect with the JS11 model, support on a two-car basis from Gitanes, and Matra resources in the background for technological and, especially, aerodynamic development. The new ground-effects Ligier proved a sensation when Laffite won on the type's debut in Argentina and then afterwards in Brazil. Patrick Dapailler—his new team-mate—took second place in Brazil and won the Spanish Grand Prix. Clearly, the Ligier was the car to beat and French blue was riding high. The French Government set aside two million francs to capitalize a research and development department for the team. During the summer of European Grand Prix racing, however, Ligier had trouble. Depailler smashed both legs in a hang-gliding accident and was replaced by Jacky Ickx. The Ligier

SPECIFICATIONS
Ligier-Cosworth JS11 1979

Engine
Cosworth-Ford DFV
90-degree V-8
Bore × stroke: 85.6 mm × 64.8 mm
Capacity: 2993 cc
Lucas fuel injection
Lucas electronic ignition
Maximum power: *c* 480-490 bhp
at 10,800 rpm

Transmission
Hewland FG400, five- or six-speed and reverse

Chassis
Three-quarter length monocoque nacelle employing engine as load-bearing member at rear with bodywork suction pods slung either side

Front suspension
Top rocker arms, bottom wishbones, inboard coil spring/damper units and anti-roll bar

Rear suspension
Top rocker arms, bottom wishbones, inboard coil spring/damper units and anti-roll bar

Dimensions
Wheelbase: 110 in (2800 mm)
Front track: 68.4 in (1738 mm)
Rear track: 63.3 in (1608 mm)
Wheel sizes: 13 in diameter front and rear, 11 in wide front rims, 19 in wide rear rims
Chassis weight: *c* 88 lb (40 kg)
Formula weight: *c* 1290 lb (559 kg)

Tyres
Goodyear

team lost their performance edge, particularly over the Williams team, their main late-season rivals alongside Ferrari.

In 1980, the uprated JS11-DFVs were still remarkably competitive and proved more consistent winners driven by Laffite and Didier Pironi, his more determined new team-mate. The new season actually saw a battle between the Ligiers and their Williams rivals with the French state-backed Renault team creating problems for both on the faster circuits where their turbocharged engines could out-gun any Cosworth. Pironi proved himself the slightly quicker driver of the Ligier pair by leading races and winning in Belgium, but Laffite's experience and flair brought him success with a string of good finishes and a popular victory in the German Grand Prix.

For 1981 the Ligier team attracted Talbot support and planned to revive the Matra V-12 engine until engineer Georges Martin could complete a new Talbot 1.5-litre turbocharged power unit.

Guy Ligier started work at the age of fourteen as a butcher assistant. When he saved enough money he bought a second-hand digger and went into the earth-moving business, an undertaking which eventually employed hundreds of people and was responsible for building many of the French autoroutes. The competitive nature of this approachable, self-made man was evident when he played international rugby. During a recession, he sold his business interests and invested his fortune in motor sports. He raced motorcycles before trying Formula Junior in an Elva-DKW. He then turned to GT racing in a Porsche 1600 and 904. He first raced in Formula One in 1966. Ligier is experienced at motor racing and business, and the success of his team is, therefore, not surprising.

Ligier JS5

When it was first unveiled to the press in late 1975 with its enormous ram intake for the engine induction, the Ligier-Matra JS5 was likened to a giant teapot on wheels. It proved itself—as expected from Matra engineers—to be a remarkably well-built and sound design based upon a strong aluminium-sheet monocoque chassis. Its suspension was conventional mid-1970s Formula One while the V-12 engine dimensions of 79.7 mm x 50 mm displaced 2993 cc and delivered a claimed 500 bhp at 11,600 rpm. It certainly sounded like it. Two JS5s were built. They were handsome cars after the tall airbox had been banned from the Spanish Grand Prix of 1976.

Team Drivers
Patrick Depailler • Jacky Ickx •
Jean-Pierre Jarier • Jacques Laffite •
Didier Pironi

LOLA

Eric Broadley's Lola company first achieved international prominence in 1959 with a line of lightweight, front-engined sports racing cars powered by the ubiquitous 1098 cc Coventry Climax four-cylinder engine. Broadley was an architect by training and a racing car designer by vocation. He ran a tiny factory in Bromley, South London. Building upon the success of his Lotus-beating sports racing cars, he produced a front-engined Formula Junior single-seater—the Lola Mark 2—in 1960. This was followed a year later by a mid-engined Mark 3 Formula Junior car.

The first mid-engined Lola Juniors showed tremendous promise. They were light and well-made and, as in all Broadley designs, employed sophisticated, all-independent suspension systems which endowed them with excellent cornering capabilities. In 1962, John Surtees and Bowmaker, a finance house, approached Broadley to build them a Formula One car. Bowmaker would finance it for Surtees and Roy Salvadori to race. The car, the Mark 4, was a frontrunner in the 1962 World Championship, but in 1963 Surtees went to Ferrari and Lola did not build another Grand Prix car until 1974. Eric Broadley had found more attractive commercial fields to conquer elsewhere.

In 1963, Broadley designed a mid-engined, long-distance racing coupé, using the then current 4.2-litre Ford V-8 engine. This car was known as the Lola-Ford Mark 6 GT. It ran at Le Mans and attracted the attention of the American Ford company. They were at that time preparing an assault upon the promotional prize of the French 24-Hour race. Broadley was taken on as a design consultant for the Ford GT40 project. When his part in that ultimately successful venture was concluded, he returned to Lola Cars Ltd., which was reconstituted in former Ford-financed premises at Slough in Buckinghamshire, England.

From that time onward, Lola Cars became one of the most prolific racing car manufacturers of all time, and certainly the largest in modern times. The marque became famous for its massively powerful, American-engined, sports racing cars. Driven by John Surtees, these cars won the first CanAm Championship in 1966 and were extremely

successful internationally in the latter seasons of that decade. Lola also built single-seater racing cars for almost every formula except Formula One. Their Formula Two efforts were seldom successful, but they excelled in Formula Ford, Formula Vee, and Supervee, and in the big, American-engined, 5-litre class of Formula 5000.

The American customer market had always played a vitally important role in the success of Lola cars. Following Lotus's lead in 1965, Broadley turned his attention to the lucrative Indianapolis 500 race. In 1966, drawing upon his earlier experience, he designed and built Ford-engined T90 track cars for John Mecom, a Texas oil millionaire. Driven by Graham Hill, one of these cars actually won that classic race.

By 1968, Eric was building four-wheel drive Indianapolis cars. In 1969, an Indy Lola placed third in the prestigious 500. In 1970, another Lola was second. Since 1970, the company have operated from a new factory in Huntingdon, concentrating exclusively on the manufacturing of cars for customers.

In 1973, Graham Hill approached Broadley for a new Formula One car, to be raced in 1974 by his private team which was sponsored by Embassy cigarettes. Based upon extensive Formula 5000 single-seater experience, Broadley produced an appropriate version of his Type 370 design. Although nothing much was expected of the cars, they did provide the former double World Champion with a practical season's racing.

In the late 1970s, Lola again found themselves involved with Indianapolis cars, this time with the remarkably successful T500 USAC track-racer. This car was built for Jim Hall's Chaparral team and was developed to give Al Unser victory in the track-racing Triple Crown. To achieve this honour, he won all three 500-milers of 1978 at Indianapolis, Ontario (California), and Pocono. The years of sports car development, and the courting of American customers, had paid off in the biggest possible way.

Lola-Climax Mark 4A

The multi-tubular spaceframe Formula One Lola of 1962 was light and functional, good to look at, and fast, but it did not handle particularly well in early outings. John Surtees persuaded Eric Broadley that chassis stiffening was required. With typical efficiency the design was race-proven as the season progressed. The Lolas were re-engined with 2.5-litre Climax FPF four-cylinder engines in place of the Formula One 1.5-litre V-8s for the Tasman Championship. During 1963, the private Parnell team ran Formula One-trim Mark 4s for Amon, Hailwood, and Revson, alongside Lotus 24s.

Eric Broadley became renowned in racing as the astute businessman and immensely gifted engineer behind the success of Lola Cars Ltd. This British company became the world's largest manufacturer of specialist racing cars during the 1960s and 1970s. Eric trained as an architect, but racing in 750 Motor Club specials was his prime interest. In 1958, he and his cousin put into production a svelte 1100 cc sports racing car, named the Lola Mark 1 after the popular song *Whatever Lola Wants, Lola Gets*. The car was immensely successful, setting new handling standards in its class, and upon that basis Lola Cars was founded. Into the 1980s Lolas have raced and won in almost every formula, including Formula One, Two, Three, A and 5000, Junior, Vee, Supervee, the various Ford-engined classes, plus CanAm Group 7 World Championship sports cars, and, of course, Indianapolis-style USAC racing. Eric Broadley's intense study of suspension and chassis design has been instrumental in the success of his cars.

Lola-Cosworth T370

Towards the end of 1973, it became apparent to Graham Hill and his sponsors that the Shadow DN1 which he had been racing had little future. In looking about for a new car Graham forged a link with Lola Cars. Eric Broadley's design staff produced their T370 design for Graham's Embassy team, adapting proven single-seater Formula 5000 parts to 3-litre Cosworth V-8 Formula One engines. The white and red T370s were raced by Graham, Guy Edwards, and Rolf Stommelen, but were never truly competitive.

SPECIFICATIONS
Lola-Cosworth T500   1978

Engine
Cosworth-Ford DFX
90-degree V-8
Bore × stroke: 85.7 mm × 57.3 mm
Capacity: 158 cubic in
Mallory magneto ignition
Hilborn fuel injection with turbocharger
Maximum power: c 580 bhp at 9500 rpm (dependent upon boost pressure)

Chassis
Three-quarter monocoque nacelle using engine as load-bearing member at rear

Transmission
Hewland LG500, four-speed

Front suspension
Top rocker arms, bottom wishbones, inboard coil spring/damper units, and driver-adjustable sway bar

Rear suspension
Parallel links, twin radius rods, outboard coil spring/damper units, and driver-adjustable sway bar

Brakes
Disc; outboard front and rear

Dimensions
Wheelbase: 110 in (1794 mm)
Front track: 62 in (1575 mm)
Rear track: 60 in (1524 mm)
Formula weight: c 1500 lb (680 kg)

Tyres
Goodyear

Team Drivers
John Surtees (After 1962, the factory did not campaign an official team, and all subsequent Lolas were privately entered.)

LOTUS

Beginning in 1960, Colin Chapman's Lotus company and team developed into the single most potent force in Formula One racing. Chapman's designs repeatedly threw back the frontiers of modern racing knowledge to set new performance standards and design trends.

After establishing himself with a series of lightweight sports racing cars with spaceframe chassis in 1956, Chapman embarked upon his first single-seater, the Lotus Type 12. It was aimed at the forthcoming 1500 cc Formula Two. The spidery Lotus 12 and its vastly more sophisticated successor, the 1958-59 Type 16, were fast, fragile, and unsuccessful. Eventually, Colin grew tired of patching the 16s when their chassis cracked and their handling misbehaved. It was then, he says, "we went mid-engined and did it properly."

This "proper" mid-engined Lotus Type 18 made its shattering debut in 1960. It immediately set new standards and dominated not only Formula Junior and Formula Two but also Formula One. In 1960, Lotus won more Formula One races than Cooper, but Cooper won more of the all-important World Championship Grands Prix which the fragile Lotus 18s often led, but equally often failed to survive. A new, private Formula One Type 18 was sold to Rob Walker's team for Stirling Moss. On their debut Moss won the Monaco Grand Prix giving Lotus their maiden Grande Epreuve victory. At the end of the season it was Moss, again in the Walker 18, who scored the second Lotus Grand Prix victory, at Riverside in the United States.

In 1961, a much developed version of the 18 was produced for the new 1.5-litre Formula One. This car—the Type 21—proved immensely competitive driven by Innes Ireland and Jimmy Clark, despite their enforced use of stopgap former Formula Two Climax engines against Ferrari's powerful V-6s. Ferrari powered their way to a World Championship which the excellent handling, light Lotuses would surely otherwise have taken. Ireland won the United States Grand Prix to score Team Lotus's first major success, while Moss's updated, but essentially obsolete, Walker 18 won at Monaco and the Nürburgring, the two most demanding circuits of the series.

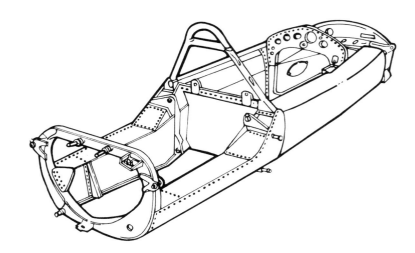

The Monocoque Chassis

When Colin Chapman introduced the Lotus 25 monocoque chassis to Formula One racing in the 1962 Dutch Grand Prix at Zandvoort he was setting a trend which today has become universal in all major single-seater racing car formulae. The thinking was simple: Why bother with a tube chassis and separate aluminium sheet fuel tanks when you can make a large fuel tank strong enough and with sections cut out to carry the driver, cockpit, and engine bay? The result was the so-called "bathtub-type" Lotus 25 monocoque chassis, illustrated above, with stressed sheet aluminium torsion boxes housing rubber-bag fuel tanks on either side of the driver. Two extension horns were formed at the rear on which the engine and rear suspension were mounted. A combination fibreglass nose cone and cockpit surround body panel enclosed the cockpit when complete. The new type of chassis was stiffer than any previous multi-tubular spaceframe and protected its fuel load and the driver more effectively. Its drawbacks were poor general accessibility and the difficulty of speedy repair after crash damage.

SPECIFICATIONS
Lotus-Climax 18   1960

Engine
Coventry Climax FPF
straight-four
Bore × stroke: 94 mm × 89.9 mm
Capacity: 2496 cc
Magneto ignition
Two Weber sidedraught
carburettors
Maximum power: c 240 bhp at
6750 rpm

Transmission
Lotus, five-speed and reverse

Chassis
Lightweight multi-tubular
spaceframe

Front suspension
Double wishbones, outboard
coil spring/damper units and
anti-roll bar

Rear suspension
Driveshaft as top link, reversed
lower wishbone, twin radius rods,
outboard coil spring/damper
units and anti-roll bar

Brakes
Disc; outboard front and rear

Dimensions
Wheelbase: 90 in (2286 mm)
Front track: 52 in (1321 mm)
Rear track: 53¼ in (1353 mm)
Wheel rim width: 5 in front,
6½ in rear
Formula weight: 980 lb (444 kg)

Tyres
Dunlop

Lotus-Climax 12

This spidery little car was Colin Chapman's first single-seater Lotus, and it was developed in 1956 for the new 1500 cc Formula Two category. Dress rehearsal Formula Two races had been run that season prior to its official introduction in 1957. The Lotus 12 used a very light, multi-tubular chassis with advanced all-independent suspension. This included the so-called Chapman strut at the rear, in which the hub was located by a radius arm and a fixed length half-shaft with a tall coil spring/damper strut rising to a high point on the chassis. This system was later used successfully on the production Lotus Elite GT car, but the little 12 never won a Formula Two race. Versions using 1.9- and 2.2-litre Climax FPF engines gave Team Lotus their Grand Prix debut in 1958.

Lotus-Climax 16

Intended as a much more sophisticated successor to the little Lotus 12, the Type 16 was built around a typically advanced and extremely light Chapman-designed spaceframe chassis and suspension system; the aerodynamic light alloy bodyshell was designed by Frank Costin—a former de Havilland engineer who had styled the Vanwall to match Chapman's highly successful chassis design for that car. The Lotus 16 inevitably became known as the Mini-Vanwall when it was raced in Formula One and Formula Two during 1958 and 1960. But it proved hopelessly fragile, although very fast while it lasted. The adhesion of the Chapman strut rear suspension far exceeded that of the coil-and-wishbone front end, and the 16s became renowned as "prodigal understeerers". Eventually, Colin opted for a completely new mid-engined design, the Type 18.

SPECIFICATIONS
Lotus-Climax 33   1965

Engine
Coventry Climax FWMV
90-degree V-8
Bore × stroke: 72.4 mm × 45.5 mm
Capacity: 1499 cc
Lucas electronic ignition
Lucas fuel injection
Maximum power: c 210 bhp at
10,500 rpm

Transmission
ZF 5DS12, five-speed and reverse

Chassis
Full-length stressed aluminium
sheet "bathtub" monocoque

Front suspension
Top rocker arms, wide-based
bottom wishbones, inboard coil
spring/damper units and anti-
roll bar

Rear suspension
Single top links, reversed lower
wishbones, twin radius rods,
outboard coil spring/damper units
and anti-roll bar

Brakes
Disc; outboard front and rear

Dimensions
Wheelbase: 92 in (2337 mm)
Front track: 56 in (1422 mm)
Rear track: 56 in (142 mm)
Wheel rim width: 6 in front,
7 in rear
Chassis weight: c 75 lb (34 kg)
Formula weight: c 995 lb (451 kg)

Tyres
Dunlop

The Lotus Badge
This geometric design utilizes Lotus's early racing colours of green and yellow. The badge carries the initals of A.C.B. Chapman, the company's founder and long-time chief engineer. For a period following the death of Jim Clark, the great Lotus driver, black badges with silver lettering were carried by the cars.

Anthony Colin Bruce Chapman was born in Richmond, Surrey, on May 19, 1928. He studied at University College, London, learned to fly in the University Air Squadron, and, in the late 1940s, bought and sold some decidedly used cars to supplement his income. He became an enthusiastic member of the 750 Motor Club, building specials to their prewar, Austin 7-based racing formula. He called his first car Lotus, and the name stuck. In 1948, Chapman gained his degree in engineering and went to work for a constructional engineering company. In 750 Motor Club races his Lotus specials were increasingly dominant, and in 1952 he founded the Lotus Engineering Company in the stables at the rear of his father's Railway Hotel in Hornsey, North London. By the mid-1950s Lotus sports cars were the epitome of modern, lightweight, spaceframe chassis design and aerodynamics.

Colin Chapman maintained his dynamism and effort into the 1980s as head of an engineering group producing road cars, Formula One racing cars, luxury motor yachts and power boats, plastics, and undertaking technological research and development for others in the motor industry. Demanding, impetuous, incredibly talented— Colin Chapman has dominated the motor racing scene for twenty years.

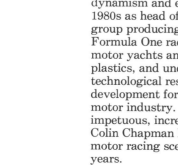

LOTUS

For 1962, Chapman developed a V-8 Coventry-Climax-engined version of the successful spaceframe Type 21. This car, known as the Type 24, was also sold in considerable numbers to private teams. But the Dutch Grand Prix that year saw the debut of Chapman's Type 25 monocoque car, following aviation practice. It set a trend for stressed-skin racing car fuselage construction and, when reliably developed, became one of the all-time classic Grand Prix designs.

The 25 series fathered the uprated Type 33 in 1964-65 as the 1.5-litre formula ran its course. In that period Jimmy Clark won nineteen Grands Prix and numerous minor Formula One events in these wonderful cars. Interim 2-litre Lotus 33 variants raced on into the 3-litre formula in 1966, and Clark won the Tasman Championship with one of these little projectiles in 1967.

At the end of the 1.5-litre formula, Coventry Climax withdrew from Formula One engine production. Lotus, in common with Climax's other former customers, had to look for an alternative 3-litre power unit. For several years Lotus minor formulae production racing cars had been supremely successful, using Ford-based Formula Two and Formula Three engines developed by Keith Duckworth and Mike Costin, both former Lotus employees. Their company, Cosworth Engineering, had established a fantastic reputation for successful racing engines. Colin Chapman asked Keith Duckworth if he could design a Formula One engine for the new 3-litre class. Keith, always uncompromisingly self-confident, was convinced he could do the job for about 100,000 pounds. Chapman raised the money from Ford of Dagenham. In 1967, after a season spent with 2-litre Climax and 3-litre BRM power units, the new Cosworth-Ford DFV engine made its debut in the Lotus 49 at Zandvoort. Clark won easily after team-mate Graham Hill's sister car had qualified on pole position and led the opening race laps.

The Lotus 49 became another new Chapman standard-setter. It achieved victory in twelve World Championship Grands Prix and won the World Championship in 1968. In the initial 1967 season, Clark won the British, United States, Mexican, and non-championship Madrid Grands Prix, in addition to that triumphant Dutch debut.

During the winter of 1967-68 Clark won at Kyalami—his record-breaking twenty-fifth Grand Prix success—and with 2.5-litre DFW Cosworth V-8 engines, he also won the 1967 Tasman Championship. The Tasman Lotus 49Ts were painted in Gold Leaf cigarette sponsorship livery of red, white, and gold. But before the World Championship series recommenced in Europe Jimmy Clark was killed in an insignificant Formula Two race at Hockenheim.

At the wheel of a Lotus 49 variant, Graham Hill picked the team up and put it back on its feet by winning the next two Grands Prix in Spain and in Monaco. When he added first place in the title-deciding Mexican Grand Prix at the end of that season he was World Champion again.

Just like the Types 18, 24, and 25 before it, the 49 was eventually sold to independent teams. Jo Siffert won the British Grand Prix at Brands Hatch in the middle of the 1968 season in a Rob Walker 49B. That season was notable for the development of the strutted aerofoil. This device created aerodynamic downforce on the road wheels, thus greatly increasing tyre grip and cornering, and braking and accelerating traction without adding commensurate extra mass to the car to be braked and accelerated.

In 1969, Jochen Rindt joined Hill in the team. Graham won at Monaco for an extraordinary fifth time, but at the end of the season he crashed badly, severely injuring his legs, in the United States Grand Prix. It was here that Rindt notched his maiden Grand Prix victory. By this time, however, the Lotus 49B was getting old.

Chapman's Lotus design team then toyed with a gas-turbine powered 3-litre Formula One equivalent of their 1968 Indianapolis Type 56 four-wheel drive car. They also tried a DFV-powered derivative of the same thing, known as the Type 63, which failed dismally in 1969.

Lotus-Cosworth 49

When the Cosworth DFV V-8 engine, financed by Ford of Dagenham, was introduced it was intended for the sole use of Team Lotus in their pilot season of 1967. To enable the engine to be developed free of chassis problems, Colin Chapman and Maurice Phillippe, his design engineer, evolved what they regarded as a simple, "basic Grand Prix car" to house the new unit. Since the DFV had a fully stressed crankcase, enabling it to be used as a load-bearing chassis member, the new Type 49 chassis consisted simply of an aluminium monocoque nacelle which terminated in a smooth bulkhead immediately behind the ten-gallon, seat-back fuel tank, (there was also a fifteen gallon tank in each side box). The DFV was bolted rigidly to this bulkhead at four points. The engine carried a ZF gearbox and the complete rear suspension. Releasing the engine mounts and fuel, oil, control, and instrument lines enabled the entire rear half of the car to be removed. The Lotus 49 proved to be incredibly successful, the standard of its day. In uprated 49B form, with strutted wings and Hewland transmission, it continued racing and winning in 1968 and 1969. As the small-wheeled 49C it won into 1970.

Lotus-Cosworth 72

The Type 49 reigned long and regally over Formula One racing, but in 1970 it was evident that another stroke of Chapman genius was required to maintain Lotus's position at the top. With Maurice Phillippe Colin evolved a new aerodynamic machine with super-light suspension and inboard brakes front and rear. Running lighter suspension loads, and with brake heat isolated from the wheels, it was possible to employ the softest, and therefore most sticky, tyre compounds yet devised and to sustain them throughout a Grand Prix distance. Firestone cooperated on the development of these tyres. The Type 72 was evolved using aerodynamics proven in the Type 56 Indianapolis gas-turbine car and with sophisticated torsion-bar rising-rate suspension. In its earliest

outings the wedge-shaped Lotus 72 seemed a disastrous miscalculation. Team Lotus's men worked night and day to correct the initial problems. At the height of the 1970 season, Rindt won repeatedly. He was poised to clinch the World Championship in the Italian Grand Prix when he was killed during practice. In 1971, the Lotus 72s were raced by inexperienced drivers. But one of them, Emerson Fittipaldi, dominated the Championship in 1972, and he and his new team-mate Ronnie Peterson gave Lotus the Constructors' title in 1973, when Goodyear tyres were used. Peterson won three Grands Prix with the continuously updated Type 72s in 1974. By the following year Goodyear no longer made suitable tyres for the wedge-shaped Lotus, and its heyday was over.

Maurice Phillippe, like aerodynamicist Frank Costin, was a former de Havilland aircraft company employee who became involved with Team Lotus and Colin Chapman. Maurice had long been a racing enthusiast and in 1955 built his own monocoque-chassised sports racing car, which he named the MPS or Maurice Phillipe Special. He was an expert in aircraft wing structures and fitted happily into the Lotus scene, working alongside Chapman on the Indianapolis turbine cars, the Formula One Types 49 and 72, and several other projects. In later years, he joined Vel's Parnelli in the United States, and, in 1978, replaced Derek Gardner as Tyrrell's chief engineer.

SPECIFICATIONS
Lotus-Ford 49 1967

Engine
Cosworth-Ford DFV
90-degree V-8
Bore × stroke: 85.7 mm × 64.8 mm
Capacity: 2993 cc
Lucas fuel injection
Lucas electronic ignition
Maximum power: c 410 bhp at 9000 rpm

Transmission
ZF 5DS10, five-speed and reverse

Chassis
Three-quarter monocoque nacelle employing engine as structural member at rear

Front suspension
Top rocker arm, wide-based bottom wishbone, inboard coil spring/damper units and anti-roll bar

Rear suspension
Single top links, reversed bottom wishbones, twin radius rods, outboard coil spring/damper units, and anti-roll bar

Brakes
Disc; outboard front and rear

Dimensions
Wheelbase: 95 in (2413 mm)
Front track: 60 in (1524 mm)
Rear track: 61 in (1549 mm)
Wheel rim width: 12 in front, 16 in rear
Chassis weight: c 80 lb (36 kg)
Formula weight: 1130 lb (513 kg)

Tyres
Firestone

Team Drivers
Cliff Allison • Chris Amon • Mario Andretti • Elio de Angelis • Dick Attwood • Giancarlo Baghetti • Jo Bonnier • Jim Clark • Piers Courage • Jim Crawford • Bob Evans • Emerson Fittipaldi • Wilson Fittipaldi • Dan Gurney • Mike Hailwood • Jim Hall • Walt Hansgen • Paul Hawkins • Graham Hill • Phil Hill • Jacky Ickx • Innes Ireland • Nigel Mansell • John Miles • Stirling Moss • Gunnar Nilsson • Jackie Oliver • Jochen Rindt • Roger Penske • Ronnie Peterson • Hector Rebaque • Brian Redman • Carlos Reutemann • Peter Revson • Pedro Rodriguez • Giacomo Russo • Hap Sharp • Jo Siffert • Moises Solana • Mike Spence • Alan Stacey • John Surtees • Henry Taylor • Trevor Taylor • Tony Trimmer • Dave Walker • Reine Wisell

LOTUS

After the expensive setback of the Type 63, the 1970 Lotus 72 represented a completely new development, virtually starting with a clean sheet of paper. The wedge-shaped Lotus 72 had a prodigiously successful and long Formula One life, which extended from 1970 to 1975. It captured two Drivers' Championships and three Formula One Constructors' World Championships, including no less than twenty individual Grand Prix race wins.

The success of the Lotus 25 in its early outings had led Dan Gurney to introduce Colin Chapman to the Indianapolis 500, at that time the world's most remunerative race. In 1963, the 25-based Lotus 29 was built specifically for Indianapolis, using a 4.2-litre two-cam Ford V-8 engine from Detroit. Clark and Gurney were to drive and the Type 29 monocoque was wider and deeper than the 25's, for enlarged fuel tank capacity and extra structural rigidity. Suspension was similar to that of the Formula One car, while the normally 4260 cc Ford Fairlane V-8 engine was reduced in size by 60 cc to fall within the Indy 4.2-litre capacity limit. Run on gasoline, it produced about 370 bhp at 7000 rpm, as opposed to the opposition's front-engined roadsters, which used four-cylinder Offenhauser engines producing more than 400 bhp on alcohol fuels.

That 1963 Indy 500 passed into history as the event in which the funny green cars from England gave the conservative USAC establishment a terrible fright. Clark finished second, after setting staggering average lap speeds during practice and qualifying.

In 1964, Ford again backed a Lotus team, this time with uprated Type 34 cars which used 500-horsepower, four-cam, Ford V-8 racing engines and ran on specially developed Dunlop tyres, in place of the Firestones used in 1963. A ghastly accident in the opening stages, however, caused a massive fire in which two drivers of mid-engined cars were killed. After the red-flagged race had been restarted the hastily remade Dunlop tyres on Clark's car fell apart while he was leading. He escaped unharmed and, as a safety measure, Gurney's sister car was withdrawn.

Ford's assault on Indy had failed again, too publicly for their taste. In 1965, driven by Clark and Bobby Johns, a NASCAR stock car driver, the glorious Lotus-Ford 38s appeared—running the team's green and yellow colours at Indy for the last time. Dan Gurney was on his own with an independent Lotus 38 painted white and blue and backed by Yamaha. Jimmy won the 500 at an average speed of 150.86 mph and collected more than 150,000 dollars for his day's drive. Parnelli Jones was second in a privately owned Lotus 34, and Al Miller was fourth in an almost vintage Lotus 29. After two years of intensive effort, trial, and deep tribulation, it was a triumph at last for the Anglo-American project.

In 1966, the Lotus Indy effort was backed by Andy Granatelli's STP Corporation. Again they fielded the Lotus 38s after new Type 42 cars intended for the stillborn 4.2-litre BRM H16-cylinder Indy engine failed to appear. Graham Hill won driving a Lola-Ford. Jimmy Clark in an STP Lotus 38 was second.

Lotus's return to Indianapolis in 1967 proved most unhappy. A half-hearted effort gave Clark thirty-first place when his Lotus 38 burned a piston. Graham Hill was thirty-second—also sidelined by a burned piston—in one of the long-wheelbase Type 42 cars, thrown together for the occasion with a Ford V-8 engine.

It was after this debacle that the four-wheel drive gas-turbine-engined Indy programme, which produced the Lotus Type 56, was initiated. They very nearly won the 1968 race after dominating both qualifying and the event itself.

In 1969, Lotus had their final fling at Indianapolis. The always reactionary USAC hierarchy effectively banned gas-turbine power, and the new Type 64 four-wheel drive car fell back on the 2.6-litre turbo-charged Ford V-8 power unit. But after a disastrous practice failure the 64s were withdrawn before the race. Thus the Lotus days at Indianapolis came to an end.

As the Lotus 72 became progressively obsolete in the mid-1970s, Colin Chapman's attention was increasingly concentrated on development problems within his growing production car and boat companies. Formula One racing had subtly changed in recent seasons. The calendar was becoming ever more crowded. Racing was far more competitive and closely matched than ever before. The days when a flash of inspiration could produce success seemed gone. Victory was achieved by delicate adjustment and evolutionary design, rather than by sweeping reforms in concept.

The first attempt to replace the Lotus 72 was made for the 1974

Lotus-Ford 29
Dan Gurney introduced Colin Chapman to the antediluvian world of USAC front-engined roadster racing at the Indianapolis 500 of 1962. Gurney was convinced that a monocoque racing car, like the Lotus 25, but fitted with a big American V-8 engine, would be an easy winner in this the world's richest race. Colin agreed and Ford of America was persuaded to show interest in the project. In 1963 two Lotus 29 cars "Powered by Ford" were driven by Jimmy Clark and Dan Gurney at Indy and nearly won. Clark finished second to Parnelli Jones's Offy-engined roadster after showing shattering pace and manoeuvrability, while Gurney had problems and was sidelined after a similarly strong showing. The monocoque cars used 4.2-litre production-based Ford V-8 engines, and their suspensions were asymmetrical to combat the uneven centrifugal loadings of the rectangular, left-turn-only, American speedway.

season when the company's Type 76 emerged. It was intended to be a "one hundred pounds lighter 72", but failed dismally. The team realized they would do better to fall back on the trusty old Type 72 in updated form. With the brilliant driving skills of Ronnie Peterson they won three Grands Prix at most disparate venues; around the streets of Monaco, on the tight and hilly acrobatic circuit at Dijon, and on the superfast expanse of Monza Autodrome.

When the Type 72 was finally eclipsed during the 1975 season a more major redesign was necessary. Colin Chapman said, "I wanted to find out all over again what made racing cars work."

Lotus-Pratt and Whitney Type 56

Parnelli Jones drove the startling prototype STP Turbocar at Indy in 1967 and dominated the race, only to suffer mechanical failure within six miles of the finish. Andy Granatelli of STP approached Colin Chapman for a new turbine car to attack the 1968 race. He produced the wedge-shaped Type 56 four-wheel drive machines. With relatively modest power output from the Canadian helicopter and power-station gas-turbine engines they dominated the race yet again, driven by Joe Leonard, Art Pollard, and Graham Hill. Unfortunately, conservatism

on the part of the engine manufacturers led to pre-race engine ancillary changes on the two American-driven cars. This sidelined them both when leading and within sight of the finish. The unmodified car of Graham Hill should have been left to win, but it had already suffered a failure of a different kind. It lost a wheel and crashed into the trackside retaining wall early in the race. Andy Granatelli eventually fulfilled his dream of an Indy win the next year when Mario Andretti drove a conventional and ageing Hawk-Ford after the team's complex, four-wheel drive, Ford V-8 turbo-engined Lotus 64 had crashed in practice.

SPECIFICATIONS
Lotus-Ford 38   1965

Engine
Ford 90-degree V-8
Bore × stroke: 96.5 mm × 72.8 mm
Capacity: 255 cu in
Ford-Hilborn fuel injection
Ford-Autolite breakerless ignition
Maximum power: c 500 bhp at 8000 rpm

Transmission
ZF, two-speed

Chassis
Full-length full monocoque stressed-skin nacelle

Front suspension
Top rocker arms, wide-based lower wishbones, inboard coil spring/damper units and sway bar; hull asymmetric with left-side offset

Rear suspension
Single top links, reversed bottom wishbones, twin radius rods, outboard coil spring/damper units and sway bar; hull asymmetric with left-side offset

Brakes
Disc; outboard front and rear

Dimensions
Wheelbase: 96 in (2438 mm)
Front track: 60 in (1524 mm)
Rear track: 60 in (1524 mm)
Hull offset 3 in to left side, at front and rear
Unladen weight: c 1250 lb (570 kg)

Tyres
Firestone

Len Terry, a fine practical engineer, joined Lotus after building his own Terrier sports racing and Formula Junior cars in Britain. As Chapman's design engineer he put Colin's concepts down on paper and made them work, and work reliably. The development of the Lotus 25/33 series was largely his responsibility, and he played the major part in the design of the gorgeous Lotus-Ford 38 which, in 1965, carried Jimmy Clark to a Lotus victory at Indy at their third attempt. Len then moved to Dan Gurney's embryo Eagle concern. In more recent years he has operated quite successfully as a freelance consultant, racing car designer, and engineer.

Constructors' Championship
1963 • 1965 • 1968 • 1970 • 1972 • 1973 • 1978

LOTUS

Two research projects were established; one to keep Team Lotus in racing with the Type 77 and the other to pursue long-term research and development for what became the epochal Lotus 78. The keynote of the first design was adjustability. The Lotus 77 was designed to explore permutations of long and short wheelbases, narrow and wide tracks. Weight distribution front-to-rear could also be changed by shifting its front and rear axle lines in relation to the major chassis and mechanical masses. Unfortunately, the 77 proved itself a flexing, ill-handling, uncompetitive assemblage of nastiness in its first few outings. It lost Team Lotus the services of Ronnie Peterson, who went off early in 1976 to drive for March.

For the Spanish Grand Prix that season Mario Andretti joined the team, and by the time of the Swedish Grand Prix a revised, further developed Type 77 carried Andretti into the race lead before his engine burst. Lotus were clambering back onto that competitive tightrope.

The long-term research and development group headed by Tony Rudd, Lotus Engineering Director, was feeding the racing team with data for the Type 78. By the end of the 1976 season, as the "Adjustacar" 77 was continuously improved, so it became fully competitive. It finally gave Andretti his maiden Lotus Grand Prix victory, in Japan.

Meanwhile, the prototype Lotus 78 had been tested with spectacularly successful results. It was to introduce a whole new era to Grand Prix racing and racing car design—the era of ground-effects vehicles. "Ground effects" in the context of motor racing is the use of aerodynamic suction to create a low-pressure area beneath the chassis of a competition vehicle and so force its tyres down on the road surface to enhance traction. Ground effects had been employed before in sports cars, notably the Chaparral 2J with its auxiliary suction fan which had enlivened CanAm racing briefly before its suction device was banned.

The Lotus research and development team, working under Tony Rudd's direction, had been given a detailed twenty-seven-page concept document dictated by Chapman. In this Chapman suggested research into making use of the air passing beneath the racing car, in addition to that passing over and around it. Rudd worked with Ralph Bellamy, an engineer, Peter Wright, an aerodynamicist, and others in wind-tunnel research. They evolved a system in which a slender monocoque chassis was employed with its fuel centralized between driver and engine bay and with large aerodynamic pods on either side between front and rear wheels. The underside of these pods was smoothly faired, close to the road surface at their forward end and sweeping upwards towards the rear, thus producing a kind of upside-down aerofoil section. Air spillage from the area surrounding the car was controlled by a full-length vertical closing plate on the tip of this

"wing", which protruded about one foot. Spring-loaded skirts were suspended beneath this plate to separate the airflow beneath the wing from the uncontrolled stream alongside the car. The rearward-expanding area enclosed between the wing underside, the road surface, and the end-plate skirt acted like a venturi system; as the airstream met an increasing volume to fill, so its pressure decreased, and this partial vacuum effect heaved the car down onto the road and loaded its suspension and tyres.

Andretti was instrumental in the development of this ground-

SPECIFICATIONS
Lotus-Cosworth 79   1978

Engine
Cosworth-Ford DFV
90-degree V-8
Bore × stroke: 85.7 mm × 64.8 mm
Capacity: 2993 cc
Lucas fuel injection
Lucas electronic ignition
Maximum power: c 480 bhp at
10,800 rpm

Transmission
Hewland FG400, five-speed and
reverse

Chassis
Three-quarter monocoque nacelle
employing engine as load-bearing
member

Front suspension
Top rocker arms, bottom
wishbones, inboard coil spring/
damper units and driver-
adjustable anti-roll bar

Rear suspension
Top rocker arms, bottom
wishbones, inboard coil spring/
damper units and driver-
adjustable anti-roll bar

Brakes
Disc; outboard front and rear

Dimensions
Wheelbase: 108 in (2743 mm)
Front track: 68 in (1730 mm)
Rear track: 64 in (1630 mm)
Wheel rim width: 10 in front,
18½ in rear
Chassis weight: c 86 lb (39 kg)
Formula weight: c 1268 lb (575 kg)

Tyres
Goodyear

effects car, the Lotus 78, and only early disappointments and later mechanical breakages robbed him of the 1977 World Championship title. That season he led more qualifying race laps than any other driver and won four Grands Prix, while his team-mate Gunnar Nilsson—soon to die tragically of cancer—won a fifth in his sister car.

For 1978, Lotus took their new ground-effects concept a stage further with the Type 79, a much improved machine in which Andretti and Peterson, who had returned to the fold, dominated that summer of Formula One racing. Mario won six Grands Prix, while Ronnie won two and took four second places before he suffered fatal injuries in the Italian Grand Prix at Monza—at the wheel of his spare Lotus 78.

During 1979 Team Lotus were expected to maintain their grip with the improved, even smoother Type 80. But it proved a disaster. The Type 81 for 1980 was only marginally more competitive. Colin Chapman seemed unable to bounce back after Ronnie Peterson's tragic death. But for 1981 his team embarked upon another new beginning with a startlingly novel Formula One concept. This Type 88 effectively employed the whole body as a giant aerodynamic surface suspended more or less rigidly on the suspension uprights to exert downforce directly on the wheels. The actual chassis nacelle could meanwhile ride relatively softly sprung upon conventional suspension. Although Lotus described the body as the car's "primary chassis", the car was initially banned and the interim Type 87 with many Type 88 components was introduced. In June the team reverted to its once-familiar black and gold JPS colours on the 87 and 88B.

Peter Wright has been described by Tony Rudd, the Lotus Engineering Director, as a "boffin of the highest order". Wright worked with Tony in 1969 at BRM, when they had a scheme worked out for a side-winged Formula One car, at the time of the revolution within BRM which resulted in Rudd moving to Lotus. Wright left BRM at the same time and ran the wind tunnel for Specialised Mouldings. This Huntingdon company specialized in the design and manufacture of plastic racing-car bodyshells. Wright then joined the Lotus Group to run their plastics company's research programme. In 1979, when their techniques were fully developed and the company was running smoothly, he transferred to Rudd's Formula One research and development section based at Ketteringham Hall, a few miles from the Lotus factory in Norfolk. Peter Wright was the true originator of the modern ground-effects single-seater racing cars.

Lotus-Cosworth 80
After the supreme success of the ground-effects Lotus 79 with its slim hull, wide track, uncluttered suspension, and free-flowing venturi-section aerodynamic side pods, the Lotus team planned in 1979 to run a new car which did everything the 79 could do, and more. Wind-tunnel results from model tests are, however, notoriously difficult to reproduce in the reality of full-size racing cars and racing conditions. The

Lotus 80 was more smoothly fared-in than any earlier Grand Prix car, with its inboard spring/damper units at front and rear tucked away out of the side-pod airstream, and careful attention paid to encouraging air exit from the rear of the sidepods as well as air entry at their leading edge. But the Lotus 80's effect was uncontrollable and in practice it never even looked like becoming a worthy successor to the epochal Types 78 and 79.

McLaren

When Bruce McLaren left Cooper at the end of the 1965 season, he already had a team of his own, well-established and ready to build Formula One cars under his name. It had been founded in 1963 in time to take two special Cooper-Climax cars to New Zealand and Australia for the then important Tasman Championship series of races.

Sadly, by the time the near-legendary McLaren M23 was produced Bruce McLaren, the immensely popular New Zealander, was dead, killed in a CanAm sports car testing accident at Goodwood in 1970. The car which bore his name, however, won two World Championships—for Emerson Fittipaldi in 1974 and for James Hunt in 1976.

Bruce McLaren Motor Racing Limited grew slowly towards the M23. In 1965, while Bruce was completing his Formula One contract with Cooper, they had produced their first Group 7 sports racing cars using large American V-8 engines. First, in 1966, they built a Formule Libre, spaceframe, single-seater, test car for Firestone tyres and then followed it rapidly with a monocoque Formula One chassis, designed by Robin Herd and intended to accept a linered-down version of the successful 4.2-litre Indianapolis Ford V-8 engine. At that time, the problem of finding 3-litre engines to suit the newly introduced Grand

Prix formula was immense, and Bruce's gamble on the American V-8 proved desperately unsuccessful. It was temporarily replaced by an underpowered Italian Serenissima V-8. With this unit behind him, Bruce finished sixth in the British Grand Prix at Brands Hatch to take his first World Championship point in a car bearing his own name. Using a Ford engine McLaren took fifth place and two more points in the United States Grand Prix at Watkins Glen. In the pilot CanAm Championship series of sports car races that year the two McLaren team cars were beaten by John Surtees's privately run Lola.

McLaren Racing attracted many private customers for their sports cars, and a production agreement was reached with Trojan Cars to fulfil private orders. This left Bruce McLaren Motor Racing Ltd., free to pursue their own factory-racing programmes as they saw fit. For 1967, an agreement was made with BRM to use their forthcoming 3-litre V-12 engine in Formula One. This engine took some time to be produced. In the interim Bruce used a Formula Two monocoque, which Robin Herd had just completed for him, and fitted it with a 2-litre BRM V-8 engine developed originally for Tasman series racing. This car brought him a well-deserved third place in the Monaco Grand

SPECIFICATIONS
McLaren-Cosworth M23 1976

Engine
Cosworth-Ford DFV
90-degree V-8
Bore × stroke: 85.7 mm × 64.8 mm
Capacity: 2993 cc
Lucas fuel injection
Lucas electronic ignition
Maximum power: c 465 bhp at 10,500 rpm

Transmission
Hewland-McLaren FG400, six-speed and reverse

Chassis
Stressed-skin three-quarter monocoque employing engine and transmission case as structural members at rear

Front suspension
Top rocker arms and lower wishbones, inboard coil spring/damper units

Rear suspension
Parallel lower links, single top links, twin radius rods, outboard coil spring/damper units

Brakes
Disc; outboard front, inboard rear

Dimensions
Wheelbase: 107 in (2718 mm)
Front track: 64.2 in (1631 mm)
Rear track: 66 in (1676 mm)
Wheel rim width: 10 in front, 18 in rear
Chassis weight: c 115 lb (52 kg)
Formula weight: c 1270 lb (576 kg)

Tyres
Goodyear

Prix, but it later burned out after an accident on the opening lap of the Dutch Grand Prix at Zandvoort.

Still awaiting delivery of his first V-12 engine, Bruce drove as number two in Dan Gurney's Eagle-Weslake team. Finally, in August, the BRM unit arrived and was fitted into a beautiful new McLaren M5A monocoque in time for the Canadian Grand Prix. There, in the rain, Bruce looked set to win, but his car's battery ran flat and forced him into the pits. At Monza, in the Italian Grand Prix, he qualified on the front row, but the engine blew up during the race.

New monocoque-chassised M6A sports cars, driven by Bruce and his team-mate Denny Hulme, dominated the CanAm Championship that autumn. This set the pattern for what became known in succeeding years as the "Bruce and Denny Roadshow", for the McLaren twins continued to dominate CanAm racing in 1968 and 1969. After Bruce's tragic and untimely death, Hulme won the Championship again in 1970. In 1971, it fell to his new team-mate Peter Revson. Only the advent in 1972 of the turbocharged Porsches could break the impeccably organized McLaren team's stranglehold on this lucrative North American racing series.

Team Drivers
Andrea de Adamich •
Mark Donohue •
Emerson Fittipaldi • Peter Gethin •
Bruno Giacomelli • Dan Gurney •
Mike Hailwood • Denny Hulme •
James Hunt • Jacky Ickx •
Brett Lunger • Bruce McLaren •
Jochen Mass • Jackie Oliver •
Alain Prost • Brian Redman •
Peter Revson • Jody Scheckter •
Patrick Tambay •
Gilles Villeneuve • John Watson

The Kiwi
The flightless bird of New Zealand had to form the basis of the Bruce McLaren Motor Racing badge since not only the team founder, but so many of his drivers and personnel were from those islands. It is notable that this sparsely populated country produced three great Formula One drivers—Bruce McLaren, Denny Hulme, and Chris Amon.

Bruce McLaren was born in Auckland, New Zealand, on August 30, 1937, the son of a garage owner. He contracted Perthe's disease, a deformation of the hip, when he was nine, and although he recovered he limped ever after. When he was fourteen, to aid his rehabilitation, his father bought him an ancient Austin 7. One year later Bruce drove it in his first competitive hill climb and took second place. He began to race more seriously, first in a Ford 10, then in an Austin-Healey 100, and ultimately in ex-Brabham Cooper-Climaxes—real racing cars. Bruce won the New Zealand Grand Prix Association scholarship to race in Europe in 1958 and excelled in Formula Two Coopers, which gained him the number two Cooper team seat alongside Brabham for 1959. That December—at twenty-two—he won the United States Grand Prix to become the youngest Grand Prix winner in history. He won the next race, at Buenos Aires. He won again for Cooper at Monaco in 1962. Then, as Cooper's fortunes declined, McLaren established his own team. Always an excellent test driver and engineer he was renowned as a consistent frontrunner rather than always a potential Formula One winner. He was, however, the uncrowned king of CanAm sports car racing until his tragic death on June 2, 1970.

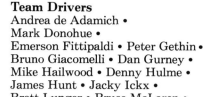

Constructors' Championship
1974

McLAREN

In 1968, McLaren and his partners Teddy Mayer and Phil Kerr decided to use Cosworth V-8 engines. They chose to install these early customer units in new M7-series Formula One chassis which had been designed and developed by Robin Herd before his departure to Cosworth Engineering to build them a four-wheel drive car. The McLaren-Cosworths made an extraordinary racing debut. Bruce won the Brands Hatch Race of Champions first time out in his beautiful papaya-coloured car. Denny Hulme won on their second appearance, at Silverstone, in the International Trophy. Bruce then won the Belgian Grand Prix. Denny went on to win in the Italian and Canadian Grands Prix later in the year and was one of the three drivers who had a chance of winning the World Championship in the final race of the season at Mexico City. The three contenders were Hulme, Graham Hill, and Jackie Stewart. But in the race the suspension of Hulme's M7 collapsed. He spun off, and Stewart's Tyrrell-entered Matra developed an electrical fault. Hill won the Championships for himself and for Lotus.

The M7 cars raced on through 1969 and into 1970, but new M14s were produced that year by the design team now headed by Gordon Coppuck, assisted by Ralph Bellamy, an Australian. Beginning in 1970 with the M15, McLaren also went to Indianapolis. The next year the team emerged with a wedge-shaped multiple-award-winning M16 speedway car which broke all records, but which was defeated in the prestigious 500-mile race itself. In 1972, Roger Penske, one of McLaren's customers, won at Indianapolis with his M16, sponsored by Sunoco Oil and driven by Mark Donohue. Driven by Johnny Rutherford, variants of these Offenhauser four-cylinder cars also won there in factory McLaren colours in 1974 and 1976. In later years, the McLaren USAC cars were more closely derived from the Formula One M23. They used turbocharged 2.6-litre Cosworth engines based on the Formula One DFV, but these M24 variants did not have the success of their predecessors.

Gordon Coppuck had produced his first M16 after close study of the wedge shape of the Formula One championship-winning Lotus 72. He considered the shape ideal for American-style track racing, although he did not wish to adopt it for Grand Prix. In 1972, one of the Indy chassis was tested with a Formula One Cosworth engine and rear end. It proved extremely promising, and the M23 was born. It was this car which at last brought major Grand Prix racing success to the Colnbrook-based team.

In 1973, the M23 was driven to three major victories, one by Denny Hulme in Sweden and two by Peter Revson in the British and Canadian Grands Prix.

In 1974, Emerson Fittipaldi left Lotus and joined the team. After a poor showing in his first race in Argentina—which was won by his team-mate Hulme—he went on to win on his home circuit, Interlagos, in Brazil. He added the Belgian and Canadian Grands Prix to his tally, amassing sufficient points from a series of good finishes elsewhere to steal both World Championship titles by a narrow margin. In 1975, Fittipaldi won twice more for McLaren. His new team-mate Jochen Mass was awarded first place in the Spanish Grand Prix, which had been shortened because of an horrific accident. Fittipaldi was second to Niki Lauda in the World Championship. Then in 1976 Emerson left abruptly to join his brother's Copersucar team. Teddy Mayer immediately began to look for a replacement. Coincidentally, Hesketh Racing had just folded their operation and James Hunt became available. What followed is now part of racing legend. In a sensational season studded with political squabbles and punctuated by a major accident which Niki Lauda, driving a Ferrari, was fortunate to survive, Hunt won seven Grands Prix, was disqualified

from two, and then reinstated in one, and wrested the Drivers' Championship from Lauda in the final race of the season at Japan's Mount Fuji circuit. McLaren were, however, beaten by Ferrari for the Constructors' Championship title.

In 1977, Hunt continued to win for McLaren, and there were hopes for Coppuck's new M26 design. But although Hunt won three races he failed to amass sufficient points to improve upon fifth place in the World Championship table. During 1978, the McLaren team's fortunes went into sharp decline, not only in Formula One, but also in their American USAC track racing operation. Ronnie Peterson had signed on with McLaren for the 1979 season shortly before the Monza accident which claimed his life. John Watson replaced Hunt, but the cars which carried Bruce McLaren's name seemed virtually beyond redemption.

It appeared that the McLaren engineers were unable to adapt their thinking successfully to the new era of ground-effects cars. Although in initial testing Coppuck's latest M28 showed remarkable pace, it would not repeat it once racing began. He had sought increased ground-effect by producing a car with greater side pod area, but this increased the overall weight and frontal area to such a degree that any advantage was more than cancelled out. A replacement car, the McLaren M29, was hastily constructed, but after brief initial promise

McLaren M7
Robin Herd's design for this Cosworth-powered car featured a simple, lightweight, monocoque chassis of the open-topped "bathtub" type in which only the fibreglass nose cone and cockpit surround panelling served to cover the driver. The M7 carried the DFV engine as the rear part of its chassis—like the Lotus 49—and used conventional, outboard coil spring and wishbone suspension. In its long life this design was also produced in a version powered by the Alfa Romeo V-8 sports car derived engine, but this never showed any sign of matching the British DFV.

it proved uncompetitive. It was a mere midfield runner, and this for a team like McLaren was simply not good enough.

When their 1980 M30 flopped, this once great team was on its beam ends. For 1981 Teddy Mayer forged a new team with Ron Dennis's successful Project Four Formula Two operation. And John Barnard, Dennis's designer, set about producing a new Marlboro-sponsored Grand Prix car, an unconventional design using a controversial carbon-fibre-panelled lightweight monocoque chassis.

McLaren M19

Australian Ralph Bellamy, an ex-Brabham engineer, was primarily responsible for the 1971 McLaren M19. This car introduced a Matra-like monocoque shape in its "Coke-bottle" planform. It had rounded, bulbous sides to place the fuel far back and low down around the cockpit, and stressed structural panelling over the driver's shins. Bellamy also devised an ingenious rising-rate suspension geometry, in which the layout of the bell cranks actuating the coil springs forced them to deflect to an accelerating degree the more the road wheels moved. The idea was to provide accurately controlled soft suspension without danger of the car bottoming under heavy fuel loads. In practice the system instead gave the driver misleading messages and it proved impossible for the team to adjust successfully at the circuits. The car was a disappointment.

Gordon Coppuck, a former British National Gas Turbine Establishment aeroengineer, was infatuated with motorcycles until he was invited by his associate NGTE engineer Robin Herd to join McLaren. Gordon became a trusted design draughtsman and, after Herd's departure, McLaren's chief engineer. This quiet, thoughtful man produced brilliantly competitive designs for Formula One, Indianapolis, and CanAm sports car racing. But with the team's fall from competitiveness in 1979 and 1980 his star waned. He left McLaren late in 1980 to join March and to work again with Robin Herd.

SPECIFICATIONS
McLaren M16   1976

Engine
Offenhauser straight-four
Bore × stroke: 111.1 mm × 67.3 mm
Capacity: 159 cu in
Hilborn fuel injection with Garrett AiResearch turbocharger
Maximum power: c 900 bhp at 9000 rpm (dependent on boost pressure)

Transmission
Hewland LG500, three-speed

Chassis
Three-quarter length aluminium monocoque nacelle carrying engine in tubular subframe at rear

Front suspension
Top rocker arms, bottom wishbones, inboard coil spring/damper units and sway bar

Rear suspension
Single top links, reversed bottom wishbones, twin radius rods, outboard coil spring/damper units and sway bar with anti-camber change interconnection between right and left suspensions for banked track racing

Brakes
Disc

Dimensions
Wheelbase: 101 in (2565 mm)
Front track: 58 in (1473 mm)
Rear track: 60 in (1524 mm)
Wheel rim width: 14 in front and rear

Tyres
Goodyear

Teddy Mayer, an American attorney, met Bruce McLaren in 1963 when his brother Timmy Mayer drove Cooper Formula Junior cars. At the end of that season, Teddy helped form Bruce McLaren Motor Racing Ltd., to build special 2.5-litre Cooper-Climax cars to be driven by Bruce and Timmy in the 1964 Tasman Championship. Timmy was killed in a practice accident at Longford. Teddy stayed on to run the McLaren team, and after Bruce's equally tragic death he became its principal.

MARCH

It is neither rare nor unusual for a group of enthusiasts to band together to build a racing car. It is extremely rare and incredibly unusual for that group's cars to be built for Formula One, and actually to win three of their first four Formula One races within their first eight months. Indeed, until March Engineering was formed in 1970, it was unheard of for an absolutely new and unproven group to succeed not only in running a factory Grand Prix team, but also in selling cars to outside teams for drivers who included the reigning World Champion.

The name March itself is an acronym of the initials of the company's founders. They included the financial director Max Mosely, team manager Alan Rees, production manager Graham Coaker, and designer Robin Herd. Each had experience of racing, both Mosely and Rees as drivers of some note, while Herd had designed McLaren and Cosworth Formula One cars and was widely regarded as a brilliant engineer. It was largely upon Robin Herd's reputation that the success of the venture depended. In the high summer of 1969, they began by building a pilot Formula Three car which they called the March 693.

That winter they moved into a factory at Bicester, in Oxfordshire, quite close to the Silverstone circuit. There they established a production line for Formula One, Two, Three, 5000, and sports racing cars. In succeeding years March was to produce cars which dominated all international single-seater formulae, apart from Formula One.

March took on two excellent factory team drivers, Chris Amon and Jo Siffert. Andy Granatelli of STP agreed to sponsor the team. Ken Tyrrell wanted new chassis for his World Champion Jackie Stewart. The American STP Corporation agreed to buy another car for their driver Mario Andretti. In that year Amon won the Silverstone International Trophy while Stewart's Tyrrell-entered Type 701, as the new Grand Prix car was known, won both the Brands Hatch Race of Champions and the Spanish Grand Prix. After that it was all downhill for the hurriedly developed Cosworth-powered 701s.

In 1971, March produced for Formula One the startling 711 with its unique elliptical planform wing mounted on a pylon above the torpedo nose. Both Cosworth and Alfa Romeo V-8 engines were used in this car which, when driven by the fast-rising Swedish star Ronnie Peterson, placed second in no less than six Grands Prix to give him the runner-up position in the Drivers' World Championship.

The 711 was followed briefly in 1972 by the strange Type 721X whose most unconventional feature was the use of an Alfa Romeo-derived gearbox mounted between the engine and rear axle, instead of being overhung behind the axle as was conventional. This feature pushed the engine further forward into the middle of the wheelbase and gave almost even weight distribution. In theory this should have made the car handle extremely well. In practice, it made the car virtually undriveable. Herd quickly admitted the 721X was a mistake. A rushed replacement 721G model was built using the company's successful 722 Formula Two chassis as its basis. The G, jokingly, stood for *Guinness Book of Records* because it had been built in record time. In this new car Peterson immediately became competitive again. But he left March at the end of 1972 to join Lotus for the next season.

The compact, lightweight design of the 721G was actually the basis for a line of Formula-Two-based Formula One March cars. The 731/741/751/761 series which followed in the next four seasons were all Formula-Two-derived, this time from a new basic chassis and running gear originally designed and developed essentially by Harvey Postlethwaite. In 1977, the 761B was a revised 751, but March stole some publicity with an experimental six-wheeled car which employed two sets of driven wheels at the rear. This car, the 2-4-0, was never raced, but in 1979 it was driven successfully by Roy Lane in the British RAC Hill Climb Championship.

In 1973, James Hunt made a meteoric rise in Formula One racing in a private Postlethwaite-developed March 731 entered by Lord Hesketh, but the real success of the March team emerged in Formula

Two and Formula Three racing and in the sale of replica minor formulae cars to private owners. March Engineering became the world's leading manufacturer of single-seater racing cars. Robin Herd's practical, yet highly competitive, designs and his considerable business acumen kept March afloat through seasons marred by mediocrity at Grand Prix level. The decline began in 1973, hardened in 1974, and looked settled in 1975, until Vittorio Brambilla was suddenly successful with an orange-painted car sponsored by the Italian Beta Tools company. Brambilla had the remarkable reputation of crashing possibly more Formula One cars than any other driver in history. Nevertheless, in that year's Austrian Grand Prix at the Osterreichring he scored March's first factory team Grand Prix victory by being in the lead when torrential rain caused the race to be stopped. He was awarded one-half the normal Championship points for his success, and immediately after taking the chequered flag he went off the road!

Ronnie Peterson was lured back to March in mid-1976, to drive the 761. It was his success with that car when he won the Italian Grand Prix at Monza and showed a personal return to competitiveness, which convinced Ken Tyrrell to take him on in 1977 to drive his six-wheeled Grand Prix cars. Thus March were again left without a star driver, but struggled on with diminishing success for another season before selling out their Formula One interests to ATS, a German wheel company.

Despite this departure from Grand Prix racing, March's solvency was always assured by their minor formula production car successes. These included victories in the important European Formula Two

Championship in 1971 (Peterson), 1973 (Jean-Pierre Jarier), 1974 (Patrick Depailler), 1978 (Bruno Giacomelli), and 1979 (Marc Surer).

Of the original four Marchmen, only Robin Herd remained with the company into the 1980s. Max Mosely became deeply involved as legal advisor to the Formula One Constructors' Association, while Alan Rees had long since left to join first Shadow, then Arrows, and Graham Coaker died in 1971, due in part to a club racing accident in a March. During the winter of 1980-81, Gordon Coppuck, formerly McLaren's chief engineer, joined March to strengthen Robin Herd's design team. With his help on the production racing side, Herd was free once more to devote his skills to Formula One, building a new car for the 1981 season—the first Formula One March in three years.

SPECIFICATIONS
March-Cosworth 711   1971

Engine
Cosworth-Ford DFV
90-degree V-8
Bore × stroke: 85.7 mm × 64.8 mm
Capacity: 2993 cc
Lucas fuel injection
Lucas electronic ignition
Maximum power: *c* 440 bhp at
10,000 rpm

Transmission
Hewland FG400, five-speed and
reverse

Chassis
Stressed-skin three-quarter
monocoque employing engine
and transmission case as
structural members at rear

Front suspension
Double wishbones, inboard coil
spring/damper units

Rear suspension
Lower wishbones and links, single
top links, twin radius rods and
outboard coil spring/damper units

Brakes
Disc; outboard front, inboard rear

Dimensions
Wheelbase: 99 in (2514 mm)
Front track: 61 in (1549 mm)
Rear track: 61 in (1549 mm)
Wheel rim width: 10 in front,
15, 16, or 17 in rear
Chassis weight: *c* 100 lb (45 kg)
Formula weight: *c* 1200 lb (544 kg)

Tyres
Firestone

March 721G
This Formula Two-based car set
new standards not only in the speed
with which it was developed and
built, but also in terms of its compact, lightweight design, which combined well with the powerful Cosworth-Ford DFV V-8 engine. The
1972 factory drivers were Ronnie
Peterson and an inexperienced Austrian, Niki Lauda, who proved to
have remarkable development and

testing skills. Peterson gained fifth
place with his 721G on its debut in
the French Grand Prix, was third at
the Nürburgring, and fourth at
Watkins Glen. Because of its compact size and reportedly stiff suspension, the 721G was sometimes
derisively referred to as a "go-kart",
but it was effective and pointed the
way to successful Formula Two
designs and further Formula One
derivatives in later years.

March 751
Following the trend set by the 721G
and its successors, the 1975 March
Grand Prix car featured a narrow
track and a long wheelbase and was
capable of considerable straight-line
speed. It was unfortunate that continuous development and the
strengthening of parts which failed
had destroyed much of the orig-

inal lightweight characteristics, but
the cars were practical and, above
all, paid their way. March operated
them very much on a rent-a-drive
basis for Vittorio Brambilla, the
young German Hans Joachim Stuck,
and the Italian woman driver Lella
Lombardi. The undoubted highlight
of the season was Brambilla's victory in Austria.

Robin Herd left Oxford with a
double first in physics and
engineering. He then spent four
years at the Royal Aircraft
Establishment before joining
Bruce McLaren to design racing
cars. Herd's first designs were the
M1 CanAm sports car and its
derivatives. Then in 1966 he
designed a monocoque for his M2B
Formula One car which employed
a remarkable Mallite sandwich
material in its construction, which
made it the stiffest Grand Prix
chassis ever built. Herd's
subsequent designs for McLaren
resulted in Formula One victories
with the 1968 Cosworth-powered
M7As. Soon after the beginning of
that season, however, Herd moved
to Cosworth to build their four-
wheel drive car for 1969. When this
proved unsuccessful, Robin, who
was at a loose end, met Mosely,
Rees, and Coaker, and March
Engineering was the result.

Team Drivers
Chris Amon • Mario Andretti •
Mike Beuttler • Vittorio Brambilla •
François Cevert • Howden Ganley •
Jean-Pierre Jarier • Niki Lauda •
Lella Lombardi • Brett Lunger •
Patrick Neve • Henri Pescarolo •
Ronnie Peterson • Ian Scheckter •
Johnny Servoz-Gavin • Jo Siffert •
Alex Soler-Roig • Jackie Stewart •
Hans-Joachim Stuck • Reine Wisell •
Roger Williamson

MATRA

In racing it is possible to divide car constructors into those who produce kit cars and those who are "proper manufacturers". The French Matra Sports company fell unmistakably into the category of manufacturers after starting successfully with kit cars. Matra Sports was sired by the enthusiasm of Jean-Luc Lagardère, a young and progressive director of Engins Matra (Mecanique-Aviation-Traction), the mighty French aerospace company whose main products, spearheaded by guided missiles, were high-technology armaments.

Engins Matra also had a plastics division and in the early 1960s this unit supplied competition car bodies to a small kit-car team run by Réné Bonnet. He was building Formula Junior cars around spidery Lotus 25-like monocoque stressed-skin chassis. Since the Lotus borrowed its structural form from aviation practice, the monocoque was well understood by Engins Matra. When Bonnet went bankrupt, in debt to them for their bodyshells, Lagardère was instrumental in forming Matra Sports to carry on where Bonnet had failed.

In 1964, these new Matra cars appeared in Formula Three, using impeccably well-engineered monocoque chassis. During 1965 their reputation grew internationally, for they handled extremely well and their chassis stiffness made them particularly stable under braking—a critical factor in any racing car. In 1966, a liaison was formed with Ken Tyrrell's British team for Formula Two. This agreement brought Matra the services of Jackie Stewart to increase their cross-Channel ties; they had always relied on Cosworth-Ford and BRM engines, since nothing suitably competitive was being produced in France.

The Gaullist Government recognized this deficiency and, fired by Matra's success with foreign motive power, they voted an enormous grant, which was further supplemented by the state-owned Elf fuel company, for Matra to develop their own Formula One engine. While this was being designed, Matra took their first steps into Grand Prix racing with ballasted versions of the 1600 cc Formula Two cars. Then, in 1968, Tyrrell emerged with a Cosworth DFV-powered tailor-made Matra MS10 chassis to be run privately for Jackie Stewart, while the Parisian factory team introduced a completely new MS11 car powered by their own new 3-litre V-12 engine, designed by Georges Martin.

This power unit made the most glorious noise in Grand Prix racing, but it was never to emulate the feats of its English-operated Cosworth-engined sisters. Driven by Jackie Stewart, these cars won the Dutch, German, and United States Grands Prix in 1968. Stewart's MS10 also won the 1969 South African Grand Prix; then using a new MS80 Coke-bottle-shaped chassis for the rest of 1969, he won five more Grands Prix to clinch the World Drivers' and Formula One Constructors' Championship titles.

But from 1970, Matra, whose production car company had been absorbed by Chrysler-Simca, decided to go their own way and concentrate upon the V-12 engine, which they fitted in angular, new MS120 chassis. Apart from their Dunlop, and later Goodyear, tyres, the Matras were considered to be 100 per cent French. With Jean-Pierre Beltoise and Henri Pescarolo driving, they were also quite competitive, taking three third places during the 1970 season. In 1971, Chris Amon replaced Pescarolo in the team to bring truly top-class driving skill back to a Matra cockpit. But after winning the non-championship Argentine Grand Prix at Buenos Aires, Amon had a typical season of misfortune and missed opportunities. One third place and two sixth places were all the team could achieve.

Matra's preoccupation with their sports car programme, and their intense desire to win the Le Mans 24 Hours, was at the expense of their Grand Prix team. Although they scored a hat trick of victories in the classic 24-Hours race they were never to break the jinx on their winning the World Championship with V-12 power. In 1972, only one rounded monocoque MS120D car was produced for Amon, but even Matra's concentration on a single entry could not achieve the desired results. At the end of that season Matra-Simca withdrew from Formula One. Their powerful V-12 engine subsequently appeared briefly in a Shadow chassis in 1975 and then in 1976 in the Ligier, its popular driver Jacques Laffite achieving what Matra's men never could by winning the 1977 Swedish Grand Prix. At the close of 1978, Ligier adopted the Cosworth engine. The wailing Matra V-12 was withdrawn after ten years of hard-fought competition. It seemed to be the end of an era. But during 1980 ties were forged between Ligier, Matra, and Talbot—the Peugeot-controlled former Chrysler-Simca production car company—and plans were laid for a new Matra-engined Formula One Ligier-Talbot 1981-83 programme. The new JS17 cars made their debut at Long Beach in March 1981.

Matra MS84

This remarkable prototype was the most successful of the 1969 crop of four-wheel drive Grand Prix cars which were built to explore the possibilities of this type of transmission at a time when engine power had begun to outstrip the roadholding capabilities of Formula One chassis and tyres. While the British manufacturers confidently, and quite misguidedly, built complex and expensive monocoque cars,

the highly skilled aviation specialists at Matra Sports put together a simple and cheap multi-tubular trial spaceframe to house an about-faced Cosworth V-8 engine. Power was transmitted to a centre differential, behind the driver, from which prop-shafts ran fore and aft to drive all four wheels. This car proved what Matra's men wanted to know—that in the dawning age of wings in Formula One, four-wheel drive was a blind alley.

Matra MS120

Matra-Simca's engineer Bernard Boyer had to produce a new monocoque chassis for 1970 because the World Champion MS80 car of 1969 had its tub divided by bulkheads, which prevented the new regulation flexible bag tanks from being fitted. Boyer produced the wedge-profiled,

flat-surfaced MS120 tub to achieve aerodynamic downthrust from its upper surface, and adopted a wider track and longer wheelbase to improve high-speed and braking stability. The Matra-Simca V-12 engine was mounted in tubular trusses at the rear. Citroën power-assisted steering was tried, but never adopted.

SPECIFICATIONS
Matra-Cosworth MS80
1969

Engine
Cosworth-Ford DFV
90-degree V-8
Bore × stroke: 85.7 mm × 64.8 mm
Capacity: 2993 cc
Lucas fuel injection
Lucas electronic ignition
Maximum power c 415 bhp at 9000 rpm

Transmission
Hewland DG300, five-speed and reverse

Chassis
Stressed-skin three-quarter monocoque employing engine and transmission case as structural members at rear

Front suspension
Top rocker arms, bottom wishbones and outboard coil spring/damper units, bottom wishbones

Rear suspension
Single top links, parallel lower links, twin radius rods, and outboard coil spring/damper units

Brakes
Disc; outboard front, inboard rear

Dimensions
Wheelbase: 94½ in (2400 mm)
Front track: 63 in (1600 mm)
Rear track: 63 in (1600 mm)
Wheel rim width: 9, 10, or 11 in front, 11, 15, or 17 in rear
Chassis weight: 101 lb (46 kg)
Formula weight: 1227 lb (557 kg)

Tyres
Dunlop

The Matra-Simca Badge

Based upon the age-old cockerel symbol, the chanticleer, of France, this badge first appeared on the mediaeval battlefields of Europe. More recently it appeared on the V-12 Matra-Simca Formula One cars.

Jean-Luc Lagardère was the young, enthusiastic, and dynamic Matra executive who conceived and ran Matra Sports. France had not been successful in Grand Prix racing since Amédée Gordini retired in early 1957, but, under the colourful leadership of Lagardère, Matra Sports put France back among the frontrunners of Formula One.

Team Drivers
Chris Amon • Jean-Pierre Beltoise • Henri Pescarolo • Johnny Servoz-Gavin • Jackie Stewart

Constructors' Championship
1969

PENSKE

The success of Penske Racing was, in many ways, an American dream. Roger Penske was a good-looking, young, industrial salesman from Philadelphia who became a racing driver and was one of the first to realize the potential of big-money commercial sponsorship. He drove Cooper specials and, backed by Zerez Anti-Freeze, was extremely successful in the early 1960s. Penske retired from driving in 1965 to concentrate on business—a string of General Motors Chevrolet dealerships and a super-efficient racing team.

The Penske team proved adept at taking manufacturers' cars and developing them into consistently fast and reliable winners, mainly in the hands of Mark Donohue, who was a good engineer as well as a fine driver. The Penske-Donohue partnership achieved remarkable success with vehicles as diverse as big American sedans, a Ferrari 512M, CanAm and USAC track racing Lolas, and CanAm and USAC McLarens. In 1971, Penske hired a Formula One McLaren M19, which Donohue splashed to a promising third place in a rain-soaked Canadian Grand Prix.

Thereafter Penske began to think about Formula One. He bought a disused racing car factory at Poole, in southern England, which gave him a European team facility. He then hired Geoff Ferris, a former Brabham designer, to build a suitable road racing car. Ferris's prototype Penske-Cosworth PC1 was completed in the autumn of 1974. It was tested successfully by Donohue, who had spent several months in retirement, but was sufficiently fired by the car's performance to return to full-time racing as the team's sole Grand Prix driver.

Penske Racing embarked on a full World Championship season in 1975, with sponsorship from the First National City Bank of New York. "Trust Penske to go right where the money is," many observers said. Unfortunately, the team made all the mistakes expected of newcomers to a strange racing scene. Mark consistently qualified sixteenth or eighteenth on the Grand Prix starting grids. Although the car slowly improved it could barely keep pace with improvements in its opposition.

Penske decided to buy a car from an established manufacturer. He chose a March 751 which, in testing at Silverstone, proved to be two seconds per lap faster than the PC1. Still Penske had their problems racing the March. In pre-race testing at Osterreichring, one of Donohue's front tyres exploded and he crashed. He and two trackside marshals were killed in the accident. Penske Racing was rocked to its foundation by the loss of Donohue, their greatest single asset, but they quickly bounced back with John Watson and a new PC3 car, designed by Ferris who drew upon experience with the March.

During 1976, a new car, the Penske PC4, was designed and built at Poole. With this car the team improved steadily and remarkably, culminating in Watson's first, and ironic, Grand Prix victory at Oster-

reichring, where Donohue had been killed just twelve months before. This was to be the zenith of their Formula One fortunes. Internal problems affected Penske's European racing resolve. The team lost its major sponsor and the Formula One programme was halted. Roger Penske retained Geoff Ferris and his British build crew to design USAC track racing cars. They were built in the Poole facility, and reached new heights in USAC competition. The Formula One PC4s were sold to the German ATS wheel company and formed the basis of the ATS Formula One design in 1978.

Penske PC4
When it appeared in 1975, the Formula One Penske-Cosworth PC4 was perhaps the most aesthetically attractive of all contemporary Grand Prix cars. It was a neat, delta-dart-shaped car with hip-mounted, longitudinal radiators, chisel nose, and conventional outboard coil spring suspension front and rear. After his memorable victory in the Austrian Grand Prix, John Watson enlivened the Dutch Grand Prix by battling furiously for second place with Hunt's McLaren until the PC4's gearbox failed. In Italy, the car was handicapped by a fuel problem, and after failing to feature in Canada, Watson placed sixth in the United States Grand Prix at Watkins Glen. In late October 1975, in the PC4's final race—the Japanese Grand Prix—the car's engine failed after Watson ran as high as sixth place. It was sad that during 1977 with ATS the ex-factory PC4s became mere also-rans, but in Formula One the development pace is relentless.

Penske-Cosworth DFX PC9

Geoff Ferris, Penske's chief designer, ventured into the realms of ground-effects chassis form in the interim Penske PC7 car which proved to be very successful in the 1979 USAC Championship, with Rick Mears and Bobby Unser finishing first and second overall. Both had led the prestigious Indianapolis 500 Miles at some stage, but when Unser's fourth gear failed and slowed him up, Mears's sister car went on to victory. These cars were effectively the well-proven PC6 chassis from 1978, modified by the addition of ground-effects side pods. In 1980, Ferris evolved a totally new design which became the Penske PC9—the PC8 having been a stillborn CanAm car project. The PC9 employed inboard suspension springs and outboard brakes all around in order to leave a clear passage to air flowing through the all-important side pods. Four such cars were built. They were driven by Mears, Unser, and Mario Andretti, but they had an indifferent season. Despite all three leading at Indianapolis at some stage, they all encountered trouble and were forced out of top positions.

SPECIFICATIONS
**Penske-Cosworth DFX PC6
1978**

Engine
Cosworth DFX 90-degree V-8
Bore × stroke: 85.7 mm × 57.3 mm
Capacity: 161 cu in
Lucas fuel injection with Garrett
AiResearch turbocharger
Lucas electronic ignition
Maximum power (dependent on
race-tune and boost): c 650 bhp at
10,000 rpm

Transmission
Hewland LG400, four-speed

Chassis
Stressed-skin three-quarter
monocoque employing engine and
transmission case as structural
members at rear

Front suspension
Top rocker arms, wide-based lower
wishbones, inboard coil spring/
damper units

Rear suspension
Parallel lower links, single top
links, twin radius rods, and
outboard coil spring/damper units

Brakes
Disc; outboard front, inboard rear

Dimensions
Wheelbase: 106 in (2692 mm)
Front track: 61 in (1549 mm)
Rear track: 62 in (1575 mm)
Wheel rim width: 10 in front,
14 in rear
Chassis weight: c 110 lb (50 kg)
Unladen weight: c 1530 lb (694 kg)

Tyres
Goodyear

Roger Penske was born in 1937. His father, who was president of a major American warehousing company, told his son, "You can have anything you earn enough money to buy," and Roger took that to heart. He retired as a racing driver at twenty-eight and was a major racing team sponsor at the age of thirty.

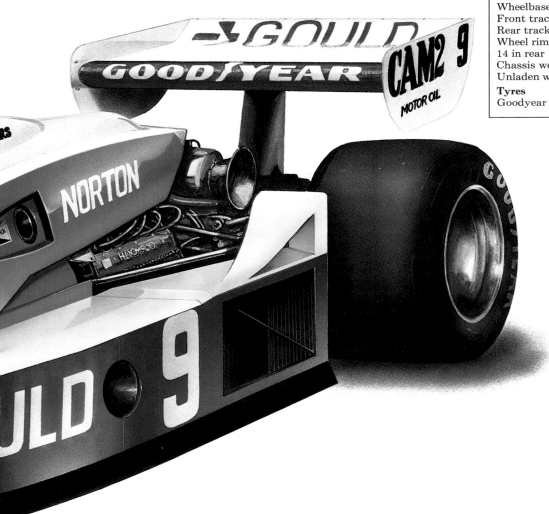

Geoff Ferris established an excellent reputation for himself with his Penske PC4 and his highly successful USAC cars which drew upon the success of the Formula One PC4 and the ground-effects Lotus 79. Quiet, reserved, and thoughtful, he learned his trade with Ron Tauranac and Bernie Ecclestone at Brabham and became another engineer who designed by intuition and achieved major success.

Team Drivers
Mario Andretti • Larry Dixon •
Mark Donohue • Jean-Pierre Jarier •
Rick Mears • Tom Sneva •
Bobby Unser • John Watson

PORSCHE

Since the early 1950s the name of Porsche has always been closely associated with reliable high-speed sports cars for both road and track. Porsche's list of endurance racing successes at all levels is phenomenal, but until the late 1960s they concentrated upon the 2-litre class and did not reach for overall race victories until 1968.

Their earlier ambitions had included Formula Two racing, with 1500 cc air-cooled cars derived from their highly successful sports racers of 1958. By 1960 they were proving competitive in that class. When the 2.5-litre Formula One was discontinued at the close of that season it was replaced by a 1500 cc capacity limit and other restrictions close in detail to the Formula Two regulations of the previous year. This gave Porsche a head start when they entered Grand Prix competition. In 1961-62 their silver-painted cars became an integral part of the World Championship scene.

Porsche hired Dan Gurney and Jo Bonnier, the American and Swedish drivers who had done so well for BRM. During the first season's Formula One racing in 1961 both men proved intensely competitive with the Typ 718. This tubby, squat, little car was directly derived from the sports racing Typ 718RSK and was powered by a horizontally opposed, four-cylinder, air-cooled engine which gave—to quote its often disgruntled drivers—"about as much power as the Volkswagen Beetle on which it's based!" Despite criticism these cars handled well and produced competitive lap times on most of the world's circuits.

In 1962, Porsche introduced a new, jewel-like, air-cooled, flat-8 engine. But that season it was confronted with new V-8 British opposi-

tion from Coventry Climax and BRM, and against those it could not compete. Once again the cars handled well, but the new engine was underpowered, and only rarely could Gurney even approach the performances of Graham Hill and Jim Clark. Bonnier virtually gave up all hope. When Gurney's main competitors had problems in the French Grand Prix at Rouen-les-Essarts, he was victorious. Soon afterwards he scored a popular victory on genuine merit in the non-championship Solitude Grand Prix run outside Stuttgart near the Porsche factory. To add to the Germans' joy that day, Jo Bonnier brought his sister car home in second place.

At the German Grand Prix at the Nürburgring the following weekend, Gurney found his new Typ 804 car handled better than ever, but he was delayed in the early stages when the battery worked loose within the cockpit, bounced around his feet, and caught beneath his pedals. He was mindful of the thirty gallons of fuel contained in alloy fuel tanks on either side of his legs and above his knees, and was terrified that the battery would short and burn a hole in one of them. Understandably, he lost some time while jamming the battery in place, and thereafter, although he caught the leading BRM and Lola driven by Graham Hill and John Surtees, he could not find a way to pass them. He finished a close third, with fastest lap to his credit.

The flat-8 Porsche never again ran so competitively. Although later in the season the drivers were shown a cooling-fan disengagement control which, they were told, would give them twelve extra horsepower for about twenty seconds, they simply never found sufficient power to meet the V-8s on equal terms.

SPECIFICATIONS
Porsche Typ 804   1962

Engine
Porsche air-cooled flat-8
Bore × stroke: 66 mm × 54.5 mm
Capacity: 1492 cc
Four Weber downdraught carburettors
Bosch ignition
Maximum power: c 180 bhp at 9000 rpm

Transmission
Porsche, six-speed and reverse

Chassis
Multi-tubular spaceframe

Front suspension
Top wishbones, lower interlinked near-parallel arms, longitudinal torsion bars and dampers

Rear suspension
Double wishbones, longitudinal torsion bars and dampers

Brakes
Disc; outboard front and rear

Dimensions
Wheelbase: 90½ in (2299 mm)
Front track: 51¼ in (1302 mm)
Rear track: 50¾ in (1289 mm)
Unladen weight: c 1025 lb (465 kg)

Tyres
Dunlop

Porsche realized their limitations. At the end of that 1962 season they announced they would withdraw from Formula One, since its specialized requirements "proved nothing". But for all their Germanic image, the Porsche people were a happy and close-knit family who, above all, raced for enjoyment, while gathering valuable information along the way.

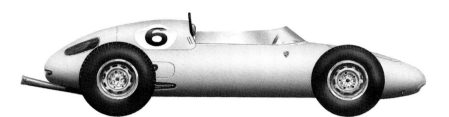

Porsche Typ 718
Porsche always considered that a well-developed, multi-tubular space-frame chassis was the lightest and most competitive structure upon which to base a racing car. The single-seat Typ 718 exemplified that in its spidery latticework frame. But then Porsche's aerodynamicists decided to clothe it with a bulbous bodyshell which gave ample air flow around the engine to cool it and afforded enormous cockpit space, making the car rotund, but popular with larger drivers. The front suspension, consisting of trailing arms and torsion bars, was a faithful copy of that used on the Volkswagen Beetle, while double wishbones and coil springs were employed at the rear. The cars were dumpy, reliable, and fast.

Baron Fritz Huschke von Hanstein was a former motorcyclist and racing driver who virtually grew up with Porsche after World War II and slipped comfortably into directing their racing team operations, sometimes from the cockpit of one of their competing cars. He had won the 1940 Mille Miglia in Italy for BMW, and in 1956 he co-drove with Umberto Maglioli the Porsche Spider that won the Targa Florio. That year he won twelve out of fifteen GT races started. Wherever the Porsche factory raced his cheerful but always coolly dignified figure could be seen, keeping impeccable lap charts, timing all the cars, directing team tactics and strategy with ineffable calm, and speaking crisp German, perfect English, and several other languages as necessary. Von Hanstein retired from Porsche in 1969, but remained in racing as Germany's representative on the international governing body.

Team Drivers
Edgar Barth • Jo Bonnier •
Dan Gurney • Hans Herrmann

103

RENAULT

Grand Prix racing began as a battle between major motor manufacturers, but by the end of the 1950s it had evolved into a confrontation between specialist racing car constructors. Among them only Ferrari and Porsche had any real production road car interests, while Lotus were finding their feet as proper GT and sports car manufacturers. Enzo Ferrari scathingly referred to the English constructors who built chassis to accept stock engines and transmissions from outside suppliers as the *assemblatores*. He was, by contrast, a *grande costruttore*, and it was not until the late 1970s that he was joined in the battle against the specialists by two other *grandi costruttori*, Alfa Romeo and the mighty Regie Renault.

Renault's name had been kept in racing at a modest level during the 1960s, notably by Amédée Gordini's division of the company. Renault-Gordini supported Alpine of Dieppe in building a series of occasionally successful long-distance sports and GT cars with capacities of up to 3 litres, and also Formula Two and Three single-seaters. Alpine-Renault coupés dominated the World Rally Championship in the early 1970s and their handsome sports racing cars swept all before them in the European 2-litre championship. These sports cars used a completely new four-cam V-6 racing engine designed by François Castaing, a young Renault-Gordini engineer. This same unit also dominated the European Formula Two Championship.

When forced induction was permitted by the International Championship of Makes regulations (the World Sports Car Championship), a ridiculously generous equivalency factor was applied to engines so equipped. The overall capacity limit for atmospheric induction engines—that is, those drawing air direct from the atmosphere at ambient pressure—was 3 litres. By applying an equivalency factor of 1.4 (3000 cc divided by 1.4 = 2142 cc), 2-litre turbocharged engines were admitted which were far more powerful than any normally aspirated 3-litre. Alfa Romeo, Porsche, and Renault all took advantage, and the Renault-Gordini turbocharged V-6 showed immense potential in 2.1-litre form. Meanwhile, the governing body had applied an equivalency factor of 2.0 to turbocharged Formula One engines (3000 cc divided by 2.0 = 1500 cc) and this 1.5-litre limit was to prove much fairer. It was relatively simple to reduce the 2.1-litre V-6 turbo sports car engine to 1.5-litres for Formula One, and in December 1976 Renault announced they would be entering the Grands Prix with such an engine in a chassis originated by Alpine.

The new Elf-sponsored Renault RS01 Turbo made its first appearance in May 1977. Jean-Pierre Jabouille drove it in its first race, the British Grand Prix, on July 16th. The car suffered thermal stress and a turbocharger system failure which retired it early in the event. The rest of the season was just as dismally unsuccessful.

Renault's management had been in a dilemma before making their bold decision to re-enter Grand Prix racing. A giant company is vulnerable, for immense prestige is risked by such highly publicized participation. If their new car beat the specialists, like Tyrrell and Brabham, it would not necessarily be news; the mighty is expected to trounce the weak. If, on the other hand, their cars were slaughtered by the specialists that could be sensational. Participation in Formula One might do Renault more harm than good.

In fact in competition 1977 was a bad year for the Regie. Their concentration on a multimillion-franc Le Mans 24-Hours programme yielded only failure, and robbed development effort from the RS01. In 1978 the Grand Prix Renault Turbo continued to prove frustrating, but the 24-Hour team was successful, and funds and personnel were released after Le Mans for proper concentration upon Formula One Turbo development.

A turbocharger system employs a paddle-wheel turbine propelled by the exhaust gases to turn a spindle to which is attached, in a separate chamber, a compressor turbine. This draws in air from the atmosphere, compresses it, and feeds the pressurized charge to the fuel-injected engine. As the driver accelerates there is some so-called "throttle lag" as the exhaust gas flow has to increase before the impeller turbine can accelerate the compressor. Crucial moments pass

before increasing boost pressure is then applied to the induction. This effect demanded a specialized driving technique and meant that under initial acceleration from the startline and away from slow corners the Renault Turbo was effectively a mere 1.5-litre against powerful 3-litre engines. Halfway along most straights the Turbo would reach peak boost and the 500-horsepower of the fully pressurized V-6 was enough to blast it past the 3-litre opposition, even if it would lose out under acceleration again out of the next corner.

Pressure induction made the 1978 RS02 nonground-effects car super competitive in the high-altitude South African Grand Prix at Kyalami where normal 3-litre engines starved for air. Jabouille started from pole position, but his engine failed. The RS10 and RS11 ground-effects cars were introduced at Monaco in 1979. Using smaller twin KKK turbochargers to reduce throttle lag and with properly concentrated development the Renaults became competitive. Happily in the French Grand Prix at Dijon, Jabouille's RS11 dominated throughout to score an historic victory. His team-mate René Arnoux was third after a wheel-banging last laps brawl with Gilles Villeneuve's Ferrari. From then on the Renault Turbo was consistently competitive. In 1980 the RE (standing for Renault-Elf) 20-22 cars brought Arnoux victory after Jabouille retired in both the Brazilian and South African Grands Prix, and the veteran won handsomely in Austria, only to break his legs badly in Canada. In 1981 Jabouille transferred to the Talbot-Ligier-Matra combine and Alain Prost joined Arnoux in the Renault team.

Renault RS01

The RS01 chassis, designed by André de Cortanze, was a neat and compact monocoque machine, and it was as small as its forty-four-gallon (two-hundred-litre) fuel capacity would allow. It used inboard front and outboard rear coil spring/dampers with side-on mounted radiators flanking the extremely compact, almost square planform, V-6 engine. The turbocharger hung low on the exhaust and the car's 98 in (2490 mm) wheelbase made a startling comparison with the 102-108 in (2600-2745 mm) of the opposition, with the exception of Wolf, Surtees, and March.

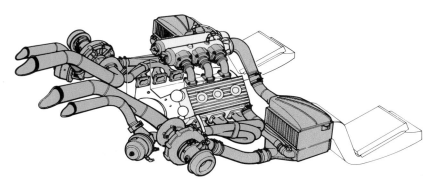

Renault-Elf V-6 Turbo Engine

This schematic cutaway drawing shows how the 1979-80 twin-turbocharged Renault-Gordini V-6 engine carried its turbocharger units low on the trailing exhaust system. Gas flow through the exhausts revolves the impeller turbine wheels which in turn power the compressor turbines in their coupled housings. Each compressor section naturally heats the air as it is compressed. So as to achieve greater efficiency in burning, this compressed charge is then cooled in an intercooler matrix before being introduced to the combustion chambers. After great development problems this power unit brought Grand Prix success to Renault in 1979 and 1980, seventy-three years after the marque's victory in the first Grand Prix of all at Le Mans.

SPECIFICATIONS

Renault-Elf RE-series 1980

Engine
Renault 90-degree V-6
Bore × stroke: 86 mm × 42.8 mm
Capacity: 1492 cc
Bosch Kugelfischer fuel injection and twin turbochargers by Kuhnle, Kopp & Kausch
Marelli Dinoplex electronic ignition
Maximum power: c 500 bhp at 11,000 rpm

Transmission
Hewland FGA400, six-speed and reverse

Chassis
Three-quarter monocoque nacelle employing engine as load-bearing member at rear

Front suspension
Top rocker arms, wide-based lower wishbones, inboard coil spring/damper units and anti-roll bar

Rear suspension
Top rocker arms, lower wishbones, inboard coil spring/damper units and anti-roll bar

Brakes
Disc; outboard front and rear

Dimensions
Wheelbase: 112.6 in (2860 mm)
Front track: 64 in (1626 mm)
Rear track: 67 in (1702 mm)
Wheel rim width: 11 in front, 18 in rear
Chassis weight: c 102 lb (46 kg)
Formula weight: c 1335 lb (605 kg)

Tyres
Michelin

Gerard Larrousse was born in 1940. Twenty-two years later he began rally driving. In 1966 he was racing regularly for the French NSU importers and in 1967 began driving for Renault-Alpine. He won eight events that season and also competed at Le Mans and in the Targa Florio. In 1969 he really came to prominence after a move to Porsche. He had a successful season of racing and rallying, including victories in the Tour de France Automobile, and second place with Hans Herrmann in the Le Mans 24-Hours. In 1970 he was second again on the Sarthe, driving one of the fearsome Porsche 917Ls, and virtually resigned himself to being the eternal second in that classic race. Later, however, driving for Matra-Simca, he partnered Henri Pescarolo in the winning car in both the 1974 and 1975 races whereupon he retired honourably from driving and became director of Renault Sport, a post in which his deep knowledge of racing and rallying and his linguistic ability and diplomacy have been used to the full.

Team Drivers
René Arnoux •
Jean-Pierre Jabouille • Alain Prost

SHADOW

Don Nichols, tall and bearded, first became familiar in international racing circles at the CanAm sports car championship circuits in Canada and the United States in 1968. Nichols's company, Advanced Vehicles Systems Inc., of California, employed Trevor Harris, an engineer, to design a revolutionary AVS Shadow sports racing car. Its design minimized the car's frontal area and therefore, in theory, extracted more speed from its big V-8 engine by extraordinarily low build and the use of tiny, ten-inch diameter front wheels and almost as small twelve-inch rear wheels. Harris calculated a potential straight-line speed in excess of 250 mph, but in practice the tiny flat-iron shaped little car was an uncompetitive oddity. Two drivers, George Follmer, the veteran American sports car ace, and Vic Elford, an Englishman, tried their best to control it, but were unsuccessful. Their "7-litre Go-Kart", as it was called, proved virtually unmanageable.

AVS did not, however, put up its shutters and fade away, as do so many companies whose first racing cars are self-proclaimed revolutionaries. Instead, Nichols hired Peter Bryant, a British-born engineer, and in 1971 a new, more conventional CanAm Shadow sports car appeared. It was driven by Jackie Oliver, a former Lotus Formula One factory team member. It showed more promise than its predecessor. Nichols then persuaded the giant Universal Oil Products Company to sponsor the black-painted car. And so the UOP Shadow team was born.

In 1972, Bryant modified his sports car design, and Oliver began to lead CanAm Championship races. It was early in that season's CanAm Championship that Nichols announced his team's Formula One plans for 1973. To produce the cars and run the team, he took on Tony Southgate, the former Eagle and BRM designer, and Alan Rees, who had managed the March team. The Grand Prix drivers were to be Oliver and Follmer. Meanwhile, Graham Hill had established his own Formula One team, and he was to be supplied with a new Shadow DN1 in kit form for his mechanics to assemble.

With considerable funds available from Universal Oil Products, the Shadow Formula One team was established in Northampton in the English Midlands. Tony Southgate, prior to joining Shadow, had worked with the Eagle-Weslake and BRM V-12 engines, and the new DN1 was to be his first Cosworth-Ford V-8 car. He underestimated the immense vibration of this engine. Consequently, the engine mounts of the prototype Formula One Shadow had to be strengthened immediately after its first run since he had stressed the originals for the silky smoothness of the V-12 engines to which he was accustomed. But Tony was an excellent practical engineer, and his new CanAm Shadow sports car designs, which were also British-built, were operated successfully by the UOP Shadow CanAm team based in Chicago.

During 1973, the Shadow DN1s proved themselves consistent, top-half-of-the-field runners with several points-scoring finishes to their credit, while the CanAm DN2s achieved only two third places. From 1974, Oliver drove solely for the CanAm team and won that year's championship against pitiful opposition. He later raced Formula 5000 Shadow cars until the American operation folded at the end of 1978.

Nichols, meanwhile, had brought Peter Revson into the team for 1974. In Southgate's latest DN3, the New Yorker showed immense promise early that year alongside the very fast young Frenchman Jean-Pierre Jarier. During testing prior to the South African Grand Prix at Kyalami, however, Revson crashed fatally. Brian Redman joined the team briefly before opting out of Formula One. He was replaced by Welshman Tom Pryce. Shadow, with Pryce and Jarier, then had two extremely quick, but very inexperienced, drivers, and their DN3s proved competitive, if unreliable, gaining just one third place. Into 1975 the similarly promising, but again unreliable, DN5 appeared. Pryce drove his car to victory in the Race of Champions at Brands Hatch, but once again Grand Prix results did not emerge. A Matra V-12-engined DN7 prototype was tested, but it was discarded

because development would have been expensive, and UOP had become disgruntled and withdrawn their support.

The team remained severely underfinanced through 1976, literally depending upon good prize money from one race to fund the trip to the next, until Jackie Oliver attracted proper sponsorship from various sources. Tom Pryce drove his heart out in Southgate's still promising, albeit ageing, DN5Bs. The new DN8, introduced late that season, showed tremendous promise, but it was to be hamstrung by lack of finance and by Southgate's temporary defection to Team Lotus.

During 1977 Tabatip cigar sponsorship was boosted by funds from Franco Ambrosio, the Italian financier who brought along his countrymen Renzo Zorzi and Riccardo Patrese as additional drivers. But at Kyalami, for the South African Grand Prix, Shadow again encountered tragedy when the popular and always indefatigable Tom Pryce died in a freakish accident. Alan Jones took his place on the team, and he scored his and Shadow's maiden (and only) Grand Prix victory that August in Austria.

Relations were deeply strained within the team by financial difficulties. Late in 1977, Oliver, Rees, Southgate—who had rejoined the team from Lotus—and Tony's assistant Dave Wass walked out to establish their own Arrows operation, one which was to be under-

Shadow-Cosworth DN1
Tony Southgate's first Shadow design was executed in the garage of his home in Lincolnshire, near the BRM team base where he had formerly been chief chassis engineer. The DN1 was Tony's first Cosworth V-8-powered design, and after early strength problems had been resolved it handled well and was one of the consistent frontrunners in Formula One. The factory team cars for Jackie Oliver and George Follmer were notable for their elegant, completely black livery, while the sister car, operated privately by Graham Hill's own team, was resplendent in white and red Embassy colours.

mined by subsequent accusations that they had stolen the design for their first car from Shadow. They left Nichols with little but an empty Northampton factory and a few obsolete cars. In effect, Shadow had to begin again. Litigation against Arrows's use of a Shadow DN9-type design was successful, however, and Southgate's half-finished designs were completed by John Baldwin, Shadow's new engineer. The cars were driven for the first time in 1978 at Kyalami by Clay Regazzoni and Hans Stuck. But during that season three fifth places were all Shadow could achieve.

Updated DN9B cars—based inevitably on Lotus 79 practice—were raced during 1979 with the youthful Dutch and Italian drivers Jan Lammers and Elio de Angelis, but there was no question of competitive performances. In 1980 Shadow were in a sorry state, and English and Irish drivers Geoff Lees and David Kennedy were usually unable to qualify DN11 ground-effects cars, or the "improved" DN12 which emerged in Belgium early in the summer. After failing to qualify for the French Grand Prix at Ricard-Castellet the team collapsed. For 1981, however, Teddy Yip, the Hong Kong millionaire, persuaded Tony Southgate to build him what was, in effect, a new generation Shadow Formula One car, under the Theodore name, which was driven in 1981 by Patrick Tambay.

SPECIFICATIONS

Shadow-Cosworth DN8 1977-78

Engine
Cosworth-Ford DFV
90-degree V-8
Bore × stroke: 85.7 mm × 64.8 mm
Capacity: 2993 cc
Lucas fuel injection
Lucas electronic ignition
Maximum power: *c* 480 bhp at 10,500 rpm

Transmission
Hewland TL200, six-speed and reverse

Chassis
Three-quarter monocoque nacelle employing engine as load-bearing member at rear

Front suspension
Top rocker arms, bottom wishbones, inboard coil spring/damper units and anti-roll bar

Rear suspension
Parallel lower links, single top links, twin radius rods, outboard coil spring/damper units and anti-roll bar

Brakes
Disc; outboard front, inboard rear

Dimensions
Wheelbase: 107 in (2718 mm)
Front track: 58 in (1473 mm)
Rear track: 60 in (1524 mm)
Wheel rim width: 10 in front, 18 in rear
Chassis weight: 110 lb (50 kg)
Formula weight: *c* 1370 lb (620 kg)

Tyres
Goodyear

Shadow-Cosworth DN9
The 1978 Shadow DN9 provided the team with their first true ground-effects chassis. They used what were to become the conventional, podded suction chambers on either side of a slender, central monocoque. The car was designed by Tony Southgate, but it was to be his last Shadow design before his defection to co-found the new Arrows team. In fact, the Arrows A1 was closely based upon the thinking behind the DN9 and actually appeared before it. The DN9 went on to become the mainstay of Shadow's failing Formula One operation into 1980 in a continually updated DN9B version.

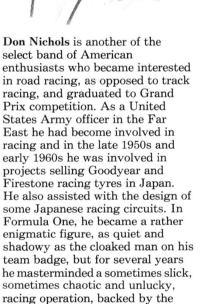

Don Nichols is another of the select band of American enthusiasts who became interested in road racing, as opposed to track racing, and graduated to Grand Prix competition. As a United States Army officer in the Far East he had become involved in racing and in the late 1950s and early 1960s he was involved in projects selling Goodyear and Firestone racing tyres in Japan. He also assisted with the design of some Japanese racing circuits. In Formula One, he became a rather enigmatic figure, as quiet and shadowy as the cloaked man on his team badge, but for several years he masterminded a sometimes slick, sometimes chaotic and unlucky, racing operation, backed by the biggest-money sponsor in the business.

Team Drivers
Elio de Angelis • George Follmer •
Jean-Pierre Jarier • Alan Jones •
David Kennedy • Jan Lammers •
Geoff Lees • Jackie Oliver •
Riccardo Patrese • Tom Pryce •
Brian Redman • Clay Regazzoni •
Peter Revson • Hans-Joachim Stuck •
Renzo Zorzi

SURTEES

John Surtees, the only World Champion motorcyclist to have made a successful transition to racing cars and also become a World Champion Grand Prix driver, established his own sports car team in close liaison with Lola. Team Surtees ran John's CanAm Championship-winning Lola T70 sports racing car in 1966. He was still driving for Ferrari, but abruptly left them in mid-1966 and joined the Cooper-Maserati Formula One team. In 1967 and 1968 he drove for Honda. His team facilities were employed to modify and develop Honda's chassis. In 1969, after an unsuccessful season with BRM, Surtees's team successfully developed and raced a Formula 5000 single-seater, and he decided to build his own Formula One car for 1970. The new Surtees-Cosworth made its debut in the 1970 British Grand Prix at Brands Hatch. The beautiful workmanship of the neat little monocoque car was most impressive. Its Cosworth DFV engine was employed as a load-bearing member and it had delta-form front wings.

During the first half of that season the team's efforts were handicapped by their lowly place on the waiting list for Cosworth engines and maintenance. A string of problems with the DFV minimized Surtees's impact, but nevertheless he ran seventh in the TS7 at Brands Hatch and in Austria before he had to retire. At the non-championship Oulton Park Gold Cup meeting, all Surtees's dedicated and meticulous application to motor racing began to pay off. He won the first heat of the two-part race and was victorious on aggregate with second place in heat two. In the Canadian Grand Prix, the TS7 brought Surtees his first World Championship points in a car of his own manufacture; he finished fifth. The TS7 had few spectacular features. It was essentially a practical, compact, light yet strong, Grand Prix car. It was very much abreast of contemporary Formula One design—short of the Lotus 72 which was enjoying such an outstanding season as the TS7 made its debut.

From the TS7, Team Surtees's small staff, always working under John's close personal supervision, developed the TS9 for 1971. This car was lower, slightly stiffer, and adopted the Hewland FG400 gearbox instead of the heavyweight DG300 used in the TS7. Rolf Stommelen, the German driver, brought sponsorship to the team to run a second car, but neither Surtees nor Stommelen achieved much in World Championship events. John, however, again won the Oulton Park Gold Cup.

In 1972, John retired from full-time driving and concentrated on the design, construction, and running of his cars for the former motorcycle World Champion Mike Hailwood and the Australian driver Tim Schenken. In 1971, Hailwood had made his team debut in the Italian Grand Prix and ran second before his car failed. In 1972, the Formula One Surtees-Cosworths proved quite competitive on occasion, but were never consistent frontrunners.

When the new Formula One regulations specifying deformable structures and extra fuel tank protection came into effect for 1973 Surtees was ready with the TS14 side-radiator design. John drove the car at its debut in the 1972 Italian Grand Prix—his farewell race. Hailwood led the 1973 Race of Champions with a TS14 until it crashed badly after an apparent suspension failure or tyre deflation. For the rest of the season Mike's performances seemed to reflect diminished confidence. Carlos Pace, Hailwood's regular team-mate, drove his TS14 to a fine fourth place in the German Grand Prix and took third place in Austria.

In 1974, Surtees ran updated cars for Jochen Mass and Pace, who left the team soon after, and later for Derek Bell and Jean-Pierre Jabouille, running his flat-tubbed TS16 cars with uncompetitive Firestone tyres, dubious reliability, and sponsorship funds stretched thin. There was little sign of competitiveness, and the Surteeses driven by Bell and José Dolhem failed to qualify for the Italian Grand Prix at Monza. In Canada, the young Austrian Helmuth Koinigg did qualify and finished ninth in the race. Tragically, Koinigg crashed and was killed in the United States Grand Prix at Watkins Glen. It was a terrible end to an awful season.

Still Surtees continued. John Watson drove consistently in mid-

field during 1975, until he moved to the Penske team. Surtees retrenched yet again. For 1976 he rebuilt his team around Alan Jones and somewhat controversial sponsorship from a contraceptive company. That season the triangular-section monocoque TS19 proved much more competitive than its recent predecessors. The TS19 continued to be used in 1977 when the Italian driver Vittorio Brambilla ran one car in the orange livery of Beta Tools alongside the second car sponsored by Durex and driven notably by Vern Schuppan. But the cars never achieved much more than reliable race finishes.

To many observers there was little reason, beyond personal preference, for John Surtees to remain in Formula One, for his cars were doing little to enhance his reputation. In 1978, the Surtees TS20 raced on with aged TS19s in support, all sporting the triangular, Brabham-like hull. At Monza, Brambilla was seriously injured in the multiple crash which claimed Ronnie Peterson's life. A bevy of minor drivers, plus René Arnoux, tried the second TS20. Finally, for the 1979 season, a new ground-effects TS21 car was developed which showed promise, only for the team's prospective sponsor to back out at the eleventh hour. It was then that John Surtees decided to give up motor racing. He was missed . . . but if life is demanding for a Grand Prix driver, it is even harder for a Grand Prix car constructor and entrant.

Surtees-Cosworth TS9

Developed from the TS7, the neat and compact slab shape of the 1971-72 Brooke Bond-Oxo-sponsored Surtees TS9 always represented quality of construction and finish. The cars' results, however, seldom ranked in the front line.

Surtees-Cosworth TS19

The angular Surtees TS19 was introduced for the 1976 season and proved a practical and long-lived Formula One runner, although never a truly competitive contender for outright victory. The cars were continually developed and modified as the seasons passed, but did little more than keep pace sufficiently to qualify on the Grand Prix starting grids. The cars were typically wide-nosed with outboard coil spring-and-wishbone suspension all around.

SPECIFICATIONS
Surtees-Cosworth TS7 1970

Engine
Cosworth-Ford DFV
90-degree V-8
Bore × stroke: 85.7 mm × 64.8 mm
Capacity: 2993 cc
Lucas fuel injection
Lucas electronic ignition
Maximum power: c 430 bhp at
10,000 rpm

Transmission
Hewland DG300, five-speed and reverse

Chassis
Three-quarter monocoque nacelle employing engine as load-bearing member at rear

Front suspension
Top rocker arms, wide-based lower wishbones, inboard coil spring/damper units and anti-roll bar

Rear suspension
Lower wishbones, single top links, twin radius arms, outboard coil spring/damper units and anti-roll bar

Brakes
Disc; outboard front, inboard rear

Dimensions
Wheelbase: 96 in (2438 mm)
Front track: 60 in (1524 mm)
Rear track: 59 in (1498 mm)
Wheel rim width: 10 or 11 in front, 15½ in rear
Chassis weight: 74 lb (34 kg)
Formula weight: c 1225 lb (556 kg)

Tyres
Firestone

John Surtees was born in 1934. Growing up in the midst of his father's motorcycle business gave him an excellent technical grounding. His practical education continued as a test driver for Aston Martin and Vanwall. He then went on to drive minor Formula Coopers for Ken Tyrrell. After this John drove the ultra-modern generation of Formula One cars conceived and built by Colin Chapman and Lotus. In 1963 he joined Ferrari and drove for them until mid-1966. With so much experience in such company John accumulated a remarkable amount of engineering knowledge. He was able to apply his hard-won expertise and engineering instinct when he began to run his own sports car team in conjunction with Eric Broadley and Lola Cars. In 1966 his team won the inaugural CanAm Sports Car Championship. His capabilities were further developed during his years with Honda. Team Surtees then produced pilot Formula 5000 designs in 1969 and John was finally established as a "name" constructor in his own right. He was never a man to delegate responsibility gladly and he kept tight control of every aspect of his team's projects and operations. Sadly, finance was never forthcoming in the lavish quantities necessary for top-line Formula One success and Surtees cars disappeared from the Grand Prix grids.

Team Drivers
Andrea de Adamich • René Arnoux • Derek Bell • Hans Binder • Vittorio Brambilla • José Dolhem • Mike Hailwood • Jean-Pierre Jabouille • Alan Jones • Rupert Keegan • Helmuth Koinigg • Gijs van Lennep • Carlos Pace • Larry Perkins • Henri Pescarolo • Tim Schenken • Vern Schuppan • Rolf Stommelen • John Surtees • John Watson

TYRRELL

It would be difficult to imagine less pretentious headquarters for a leading Formula One team than the wooden planked office of a timber yard in the Surrey countryside. Yet for many years the Tyrrell Racing Organisation operated from such a base at Ockham before opening a purpose-built factory on the site.

In 1951, Ken Tyrrell saw a 500 cc Formula Three race, thought he could drive as well as most of the starters, and bought a car. From 1952 until 1958 he was a leading driver in the class. In 1958, he also managed a pair of Formula Two Coopers. From 1959 he applied his organizational and business talents to team management, convinced that the way to win was with the best cars and drivers—hence his cars were driven by Jack Brabham, Bruce McLaren, and Masten Gregory.

The Tyrrell Racing Team was established in 1960 to run the factory Formula Junior Cooper-BMCs. Their first victory came when Henry Taylor won the Prix Monaco Junior. Tyrrell gave John Surtees his first four-wheeler race in 1960. South Africans Tony Maggs and John Love drove the Formula Junior Coopers in 1961, when the Tyrrell team also ran the successful factory Mini-Cooper saloons.

When John Cooper was injured in a road accident, Ken took on the management of his Formula One team, his introduction to Grand Prix racing. In 1963, he established the Tyrrell Racing Organisation, still contesting Formula Junior with Cooper-BMCs. But when his driver Timmy Mayer was killed in a crash in Tasmania early in 1964, Ken was left without a driver for the new Formula Three, which replaced Formula Junior.

Robin McKay, the Goodwood track manager, suggested Jackie Stewart, a young Scot who had equalled the circuit sports car lap record in a tired old Ecurie Ecosse Cooper Monaco. Ken invited Stewart to Goodwood for a test drive in the new Formula Three Cooper. Bruce McLaren was there to set target times. Jackie equalled them in just three laps and Ken signed him on the spot. During 1964, Jackie won sixteen of his eighteen races in the Tyrrell Racing Organisation's Cooper cars and developed an implicit trust in Ken's abilities. In 1965, Jackie joined the BRM Grand Prix team.

From 1965 until 1967, Ken retained Stewart's services in Formula Two, running Cooper and then French Matra chassis with BRM power units. In 1967, at the Dutch Grand Prix, Ken witnessed the exciting debut of the new Cosworth-Ford DFV engine and immediately placed an order with Cosworth for the 1968 season. He had no idea what chassis he would use, but he was confident that Stewart would join him.

The Matra company came forward to provide Cosworth-powered cars. Ken attracted sponsorship from Dunlop and Elf, the French oil company. In 1968, their team—Equipe Matra International—won three Grandes Epreuves and until the final round Jackie Stewart was in the running for the World Championship.

In 1969, Jackie won six Grands Prix and took the championship easily. At about this time, however, Matra Sports—the racing and road car side of the giant Engins Matra aerospace combine—was taken over by the Simca division of Chrysler. Clearly, Chrysler could not permit the Matra-Ford Formula One relationship to continue and insisted that Stewart use their own Matra V-12 engine. In comparative testing the French V-12 proved inferior to the British V-8. Matra would not build new chassis for 1970 to accept the V-8, and the 1969 chassis could not comply with new 1970 fuel tank regulations.

Ken cast around for a suitable chassis for his reigning World Champion. He bought Type 701s from the new March engineering concern, while secretly hedging his bets by having a car of his own designed by Derek Gardner.

Stewart won the 1970 Spanish Grand Prix in the Tyrrell March, but the car became uncompetitive later in the year. The new Tyrrell 001 made its debut at the end of the season; Stewart led both the Canadian and United States races, but was forced to retire on each

occasion. The car had shown its potential, and more massive Dunlop and Elf sponsorship was forthcoming for 1971.

For that year, Derek built a team of Tyrrell-Cosworth cars, which won eight Formula One races, seven of them Grands Prix. Six fell to Stewart, who clinched his second World Championship, and the seventh to his talented team-mate François Cevert. It was a superb car, exquisitely prepared and piloted by brilliant drivers. The Tyrrell team was on top of the world.

In 1972, Stewart had ulcer problems, and the season yielded only four Grand Prix successes, the last two in Canada and the United States, where the dominant combination of that season—Emerson Fittipaldi and the Lotus 72—was put "in perspective" by Stewart.

Among the original 001-series Tyrrells, the car that numbered 003 became probably the most successful individual chassis in Grand Prix history, winning eight events in Stewart's hands. New short-wheelbase cars, 005 and 006, replaced the original longer-wheelbase, "Coke-bottle" monocoque machines, and although these proved more demanding to drive, they produced faster lap speeds in the hands of drivers of such supreme class as Stewart and Cevert.

In 1973, Jackie Stewart was already planning to retire at the close of that season, but it showed neither in his driving, nor in the

Tyrrell-Cosworth 001
The original Tyrrell Formula One car design was mocked-up in the garage at Derek Gardner's home in Leamington Spa. He had to sell his beloved Bentley to make room for it. Secrecy was such that when Jackie Stewart flew to Coventry to try the mock-up for size, Derek's young daughter—a great Stewart fan—had no idea that Jackie had been in her home. The bulged planform "Coke-bottle" monocoque of Tyrrell 001 was constructed for the team by Gomm Metal Developments. Tyrrell later built their own in the Ockham plant. The design was conventional, but the car was extremely well-made with painstaking attention to safety details and finish. The wide front nose-foil with a shark-mouth radiator air intake below was dropped in 1971 in favour of a full-width nose section. Cars 002-004 were similar in overall design and layout to the prototype, although 002 had a four-inch longer cockpit and a one-and-a-half-inch longer wheelbase to accommodate the lanky François Cevert.

Tyrrell-Cosworth 006
During the summer of 1972, the Tyrrell 005 made its debut in practice for the French Grand Prix at Clermont-Ferrand. Cevert crashed it, and the car was not raced. Derek Gardner had wanted to build a car which was smaller and lighter than the original 001-004 series, one which would be more manoeuvrable. To achieve these aims, 005 was lower and shorter than its predecessors. It had a more centralized mass concentration and inboard brakes at the front and rear to reduce unsprung weight and allow the wheels to react more quickly to road undulations. Stewart had a similar car, numbered 006/2, built for his use in 1973. In it he won the BRDC International Trophy at Silverstone, and the Belgian, Monegasque, Dutch, and German Grands Prix and clinched his world title. This beautiful historic car is today lovingly preserved in the Donington Collection, near Derby in England.

back-up operation mounted by Tyrrell's team. Their 1973 season is a shining example of success in modern Formula One. Stewart won five more Grands Prix, clinched his third world title in an Homeric drive back through the field after a pit stop to finish fourth and set a shattering new lap record in his farewell European Grand Prix at Monza that September. François Cevert excelled in his subsidiary role and finished second no less than six times.

At the close of the season, however, François died in a horrible accident during practice for the United States Grand Prix at Watkins Glen. Stewart withdrew from what would have been his farewell Grand Prix, and his one-hundredth. Lotus stole the World Formula One Constructors' Championship title, which Tyrrell had coveted so much.

Ken had to build a new team for 1974, and Derek Gardner had to design cars which could be driven to their limit by relatively young and inexperienced drivers. Ken took on the South African Jody Scheckter and the somewhat older Patrick Depailler, the French Formula Three king, who had had a couple of team drives in the older Tyrrells. During 1974, Scheckter had a chance of winning the title until the final race, while Gardner's new 007-series cars proved competitively fast and, as expected, very reliable.

SPECIFICATIONS
Tyrrell-Cosworth 003 1971
Engine
Cosworth-Ford DFV
90-degree V-8
Bore × stroke: 85.7 mm × 64.8 mm
Capacity: 2993 cc
Lucas fuel injection
Lucas electronic ignition
Maximum power: c 460 bhp at 10,250 rpm
Transmission
Hewland-Tyrrell, five-speed and reverse
Chassis
Lightweight stressed-skin three-quarter monocoque with engine/gearbox assembly accepting rear suspension loads
Front suspension
Double wishbones with interposed coil spring/damper units and anti-roll bar
Rear suspension
Single top links, parallel lower links and outboard coil spring/damper units
Brakes
Disc; outboard front, inboard rear
Dimensions
Wheelbase: 95.7 in (2430 mm)
Front track: 63 in (1600 mm)
Rear track: 62.9-64.9 in (1598-1648 mm)
Formula weight: c 1200 lb (544 kg)
Tyres
Goodyear

Ken Tyrrell, often known as Chopper Tyrrell, used the woodman's axe as his symbol on the flanks of his own racing car during the 1950s. As the autocratic, and extremely accomplished head of his own racing team during the 1960s and 1970s, his single-minded approach to total team efficiency and his often abrupt and forbidding manner when busy added edge to his nickname. But winning was the name of the game, and nonconstructive niceties were never the Tyrrell way. Off-circuit, Ken is an approachable and sometimes amusing man, but never one to suffer fools gladly. Chopper gives the impression that he enjoys his reputation. Ken's wife Norah and his sons play a vital role in the family racing business, and although the great years now seem long past, more than twenty years' experience and the good fortune of finding another outstanding driver, may make Tyrrell great again.

TYRRELL

Continuing with the same team into 1975, Scheckter won on his home soil at Kyalami and won the British Grand Prix when Niki Lauda's Ferrari punctured a tyre in the closing stages.

The old days of Tyrrell dominance and consistent front running had now passed. Derek Gardner had, however, long thought that a useful way to increase a racing car's lap speed would be to improve its aerodynamic penetration by providing a narrow and low-profile front end and improve its braking and cornering by applying extra rubber to the road at the front by the use of four wheels of small diameter and a narrow overall track width. Thus the Tyrrell Project 34 six-wheeler Formula One cars were born.

Initially the new cars showed ever-increasing promise. They scored a team one-two with Scheckter leading Depailler home in the Swedish Grand Prix on the always freakish Anderstorp circuit (where the Tyrrell 007s had placed first and second the preceding year). From that point on, however, it was all downhill. Scheckter left at the close of the season to join the Wolf Formula One team, and in 1977 rebodied P34s were run for Ronnie Peterson and Depailler. Development of the special front tyres lagged considerably, however, and the cars' excessive weight made them uncompetitive. Both drivers lost interest, and their performances were poor.

Gardner returned to industry, and Ken employed Maurice Phillippe, the former Lotus and Parnelli engineer, to build four-wheeled 008-series cars. Peterson rejoined Lotus, and Didier Pironi joined Depailler in the team. Patrick was barely beaten in South Africa by Ronnie's Lotus. He had been second in no less than eight Grands Prix. It looked as though he would never win. But at Monaco he drove as if inspired, and his 008 survived the pace to bring him and the team a long-awaited victory. The march of ground-effects cars overtook the conventional 008s, however, and they ended the season again outclassed.

For 1979, Phillippe produced the Tyrrell 009 — virtually a replica of the Lotus 79 — and Elf, Tyrrell's long-time major sponsor, opted to concentrate its resources on French teams. Tyrrell pressed on in much reduced circumstances with Jean-Pierre Jarier replacing Depailler alongside Pironi in 009s — eventually backed by Candy, an Italian washing machine manufacturer.

The 1979 Tyrrells, and the 1980 cars, which were again derivative — this time of Williams designs — were no better than good upper midfield runners. But in 1980 the team's best results were fourth and fifth places in the British Grand Prix. Drivers Jean-Pierre Jarier and Derek Daly had a difficult time; component failures contributed to a series of spectacular accidents which befell Daly in particular. At the end of the season both drivers were released. For 1981 Ken Tyrrell signed the American-Italian driver Eddy Cheever and went in search of new sponsors to support his once great team.

SPECIFICATIONS
Tyrrell-Cosworth P34   1976

Engine
Cosworth-Ford DFV
90-degree V-8
Bore × stroke: 85.7 mm × 64.8 mm
Capacity: 2993 cc
Lucas fuel injection
Lucas electronic ignition
Maximum power: c 465 bhp at
10,500 rpm

Transmission
Hewland-Tyrrell, five-speed and
reverse

Chassis
Lightweight stressed-skin three-
quarter monocoque with engine/
gearbox assembly accepting rear
suspension loads

Front suspension
Two sets of double wishbones with
interposed coil spring/damper
units and anti-roll bar

Rear suspension
Single top links, parallel lower
links, interposed coil spring/
damper units and anti-roll bar

Brakes
Disc; outboard front, inboard rear

Dimensions
Wheelbase: 96.5 in (2453 mm) to
1st axle, 78.3 in (1990 mm)
to 2nd axle
Front track: 48 in (1220 mm)
Rear track: 58 in (1475 mm)
Wheel rim width: 9 in front,
18 in rear
Chassis weight: c 72 lb (32.5 kg)
Formula weight: 1267 lb (575 kg)

Tyres
Goodyear

Tyrrell-Cosworth 008

When Maurice Phillippe worked with Colin Chapman to detail the Lotus 49 and 72 designs they became trend setters in Grand Prix engineering. After leaving Lotus, Phillippe built a series of cars similar to the Lotus 72 for the American Vel's Parnelli team. With Tyrrell, his first 008 design for 1978 was not surprisingly a Parnelli development with an extremely shallow monocoque form, hip radiators, and very lightweight construction. The car suffered considerable problems of structural strength early in its career, anathema to Derek Gardner, Phillippe's predecessor. But victory at Monaco, as well as other highly competitive performances, showed the Tyrrell 008 to be one of the best nonground-effects designs.

Tyrrell-Cosworth 010

When Tyrrell produced their first ground-effects car, the 009-series design for 1979, it was embarrassingly similar to the 1978 Lotus 79 in size, shape, and appearance. After the Saudia-Williams performed so well during 1979, the 1980 Tyrrell 010 was to emerge as yet another virtual copy. Such replicating exists at all levels of racing, for few engineers have the time, or the nerve, to follow their own instincts if a well-proven path is open to them. Tyrrell were, after all, in the backwash of their six-wheeler project. The ground-effects Tyrrells all proved reliable midfield runners. They achieved a consistent finishing record in the low points-scoring places—while never threatening the top teams.

Derek Gardner was born in 1931 and was raised in Warwick in the English Midlands. A creative child, with a passion for aviation, when he left school at the age of seventeen he went to work for Constant Speed Airscrews and took an evening course in aerodynamics. In 1949, he switched to mechanical engineering and joined a local engineering firm. His first attempt at motoring design was to produce the folding hood mechanism for the Healey Silverstone. After two years in the RAF he joined Hobbs Transmissions, then Ferguson Research, with whom he became a four-wheel drive engineer working with racing designers from such companies as BRM and Lotus. In 1968, he travelled to Indianapolis with Lotus and "caught the racing bug". When Ken Tyrrell offered him the Formula One car design project he jumped at the opportuniy. A quiet, introverted man, Derek Gardner has a fund of dry but hilarious stories, particularly of aviation and aircraft—his first love. He returned to industry after the 1977 season, his racing ambitions satisfied.

Team Drivers
Eddy Cheever • François Cevert • Derek Daly • Patrick Depailler • Jean-Pierre Jarier • Geoff Lees • Ronnie Peterson • Didier Pironi • Peter Revson • Jody Scheckter • Jackie Stewart

Constructors' Championship
1971

VEL'S PARNELLI

In 1963, Lotus brought the rear-engined revolution in racing car design to the American Indianapolis track racing establishment. In that year's 500-mile sweepstake race only one front-engined roadster of the old school managed to stay ahead of Jim Clark's wailing Lotus-Ford. That winning car was called Ol' Calhoun, and its driver was Rufus Parnelli Jones.

In 1968, this lead-footed track racer from California retired from driving to concentrate upon running the racing team which he had founded with his business partner Vel Miletich. They called the team Vel's Parnelli Jones Racing and it was based in Torrance, California. They ran cars in the USAC Championship Trail, in Formula 5000 road racing, on the dirt tracks, in off-road events, and even in purebred slingshot drag racing. At its height, Vel's Parnelli Jones was probably the largest and most active independent racing team in the world. In the 1976-77 season, they tackled the thorniest racing problem of all—World Championship Formula One.

In every way, they had the pedigree to do it. They had begun building their own advanced Indianapolis cars in 1967, when, with Gene White, they copied a Formula One Brabham tubular chassis. In 1968 track races after Indianapolis they bought and operated an ex-factory Lotus 56 turbine car which was driven by Joe Leonard. In 1969, Jones and Miletich hired Al Unser, the star driver, and George Bignotti, the legendary Indy crew chief. He prepared for them a four-wheel drive Lola T150, and Unser stormed it to second place in the National Championship under their colours.

For 1970 new cars were required, and Bignotti built Lola-like USAC cars which they named "VPJ Colts", since at that time their multiple Ford dealerships were selling Mustang cars, and, of course, the Colts were powered by turbocharged Ford V-8 engines. Miletich won sponsorship for them from the Johnny Lightning toy company, and, in 1970, Al Unser, driving a Colt, raced to victory both at Indianapolis and in the National Championship. In 1971, his team-mate Joe

Leonard—driving a Colt sponsored by Samsonite Luggage—took the Championship while Al won again at Indianapolis in his Johnny Lightning Special.

For 1972 Vel's Parnelli hired the incredible combination of Al Unser, Joe Leonard, and Mario Andretti—all three former National Champions. To produce new cars they hired Maurice Phillippe, the designer of the World Championship-winning Lotus 72. These cars became known as the "Parnellis by Phillippe". Although they had their problems they were far better than their subsequent reputation would suggest.

Vel's Parnelli had always been heavily sponsored by Firestone tyres, as was Mario Andretti, a track driver with considerable Formula One experience. When Jackie Stewart retired at the end of 1973, Goodyear approached Mario for Formula One, but he preferred to stay with Firestone and went to Vel and Parnelli for a Grand Prix

Parnelli VPJ4
This lithe, wedge-shaped beauty impressed all who saw it with its impeccable workmanship and finish. Maurice Phillippe's thinking around the well-established Lotus 72 theme was obvious in every inch. The car used torsion bar suspension, exactly like the 72, instead of the more conventional coil springs, which had also been designed in conjunction with Firestone and, to work at its best, depended very much upon the provision of specially tailored tyres. The water radiators were mounted at a sharp angle on either side. The Cosworth DFV engine, of course, formed a major structural chassis member at the rear, accepting both suspension and gearbox loadings and feeding them forward into a stressed-skin monocoque chassis nacelle.

SPECIFICATIONS
Vel's Parnelli Colt-Ford 1971

Engine
Ford-Foyt 90-degree V-8
Bore × stroke: 91 mm × 48.2 mm
Capacity: 153 cu in
Fuel injection with Garrett AiResearch turbocharger
Maximum power: c 650-900 bhp at c 8000 rpm (dependent upon boost pressure selected)

Transmission
Hewland LG 500, three-speed

Chassis
Full monocoque with rearward horns to support engine/transmission assembly

Front suspension
Single top links, radius rods, bottom wishbones, outboard coil spring/damper units, and sway bar

Rear suspension
Single top links, reversed lower wishbones, twin radius rods, outboard coil spring/damper units, and sway bar

Tyres
Firestone

No dimensions available

car. Phillippe, of course, had enormous experience in designing Grand Prix cars. He brought in other former Lotus personnel and late in 1974 introduced the Cosworth-powered VPJ4 Grand Prix car. Driven by Andretti this beautifully built car made an immediate impression as the "three-inch lower Lotus 72".

During the car's development programme, however, Firestone abruptly decided to close down their racing activities completely. Vel's Parnelli found themselves left with a car tailored to tyres which were no longer to be made. Running in World Championship events as "Team U.S.A." they floundered through 1976 with neither direction nor purpose, and the effort ended in argument and recrimination. After a final twitch of life early in 1976, the VPJ4 Formula One programme died, but the USAC cars raced on, with some success, although in a minor key. The Firestone withdrawal and the American economic recession had hit the Vel's Parnelli Jones empire hard.

Parnelli VPJ6
This remarkably aggressive-looking USAC track racing car was based directly upon the Parnelli VPJ4 design which had proved unsuccessful in Formula One, yet shone brilliantly in developed form on the banked oval tracks of the National Championship Trail series. In 1978, the black VPJ6 version, with a turbocharged Cosworth DFX variant of the familiar Formula One engine, sponsored by Interscope, was run by Ted Field for the Hawaiian driver Danny Ongais. It set many records and proved itself the fastest car in the competition. This car was so effective that by the end of the season even the great A.J. Foyt had been lured out of his own Coyote cars into one, and began his share of record-breaking.

Rufus Parnelli Jones was born in 1933 in Texarkana, Arkansas and was raised in Torrance, California. He rose through jalopy racing to dominate the dirt tracks. In 1961, he was Rookie of the Year at Indianapolis, and he won there in 1963. He would drive anything, anywhere, flat-out all the time. After the disappointment in 1967 of having his STP Turbocar break beneath him while leading at Indianapolis with three laps to go, he began to think of retirement.

Vel Miletich was born to Yugoslavian immigrant parents. He began working in a garage at the age of ten, progressed from engine rebuilder to car salesman, then opened his own business, and never looked back. With Parnelli Jones he won Firestone race tyre distributor rights in eleven states. They owned the Ontario Motor Speedway in California, plus a building division, warehouse concerns, Ford dealerships, their own public relations company, and what was probably the world's most active private racing team.

Team Drivers
Mario Andretti • A.J. Foyt • Joe Leonard • Danny Ongais • Jan Opperman • Al Unser

WILLIAMS

The turn of the decade, from the 1970s to the 1980s, saw a remarkable rise to prominence for Frank Williams's Grand Prix team. It was remarkable because for many years this dynamic former amateur driver and racing car dealer had barely maintained his position as a private Formula One team owner and constructor. His cars sported obsolete bits and pieces bought second-hand from more wealthy teams and his drivers often paid for their rides just for the privilege of driving in Formula One. In short, the Williams team represented virtually the base level of Grand Prix racing, the cannon fodder necessary to fill starting grids to give the aces an active backdrop. They were the extras in the scene. Frank Williams's achievements were emphasised by an old friend when he said, "You can't say Frank started with nothing; he began with less than nothing . . ." and he came to greatness.

Frank developed his passion for racing while still a child. He saved money to buy his first racing car in 1961. It was a humble, tuned Austin A35 saloon. After being damaged in an accident it was replaced by an Austin A40. Frank worked as a mechanic while scraping together enough money for a Formula Three single-seater of his own. At the end of 1966, he retired from the gypsy life of the European Formula Three racing circus to concentrate on buying and selling racing cars, which he did with considerable success.

In 1968, Frank ran a Formula Two Brabham-Cosworth BT23C for his good friend Piers Courage. Piers excelled and for 1969 Williams took the plunge and bought an ex-factory Formula One Brabham BT24 and fitted a Cosworth DFW 2.5-litre engine for the Tasman series in New Zealand and Australia. Piers drove well. Back in England a BT26-Cosworth was built and the Williams team went Grand Prix racing. Both Frank and Piers were twenty-seven years old. With minimal finance, but great enthusiasm and driving talent, these young men stole two lucrative second places in World Championship Grands Prix that season, at Monaco and Watkins Glen.

It was obvious that the team nucleus which Frank had established was an efficient unit. Frank spoke fluent Italian, and was both liked and well-respected by Italian racing personalities. In 1970 he agreed to run new De Tomaso-Cosworth cars built for him by the Modenese company. Tragically, the car was slow to develop and had still not struck form when Piers Courage was killed in it during the Dutch Grand Prix at Zandvoort. Frank was desolated, but saw out the end of the season with stand-in drivers.

This was the beginning of Frank Williams's bad times. In 1971, he tried to survive a Formula One season with a private March and a three-car Formula Two team. He had little success, for his slim resources were spread too thinly. Henri Pescarolo was his prime driver and, in 1972, Frank added Carlos Pace, running Formula One March cars and the first proper Williams car—the Formula One Politoys—produced for him under the sponsoring toy company's name. Pescarolo destroyed the car on its maiden outing, and the Marches were shunted regularly. Then Pace left to join Surtees at the end of the year.

It was only generous sponsorship from Marlboro and promised by Iso cars company which kept Frank in Formula One in 1973. The team struggled on in 1974 with Arturo Merzario and the promising French former racing mechanic Jacques Laffite as drivers. The 1975 season was the thinnest thus far. The old cars were raced under the Williams name and Laffite hit the heights by inheriting a lucrative second place in the German Grand Prix.

Meanwhile, Frank had made contact with Walter Wolf, a wealthy oil businessman, and he financed the Wolf-Williams team for 1976. Early in 1977, however, Frank realized how much he missed active team management and split from Wolf. He took with him Patrick Head, a young design engineer whom he had hired just before Wolf brought in ex-Hesketh cars and their senior designer, Harvey Postlethwaite.

To build a new team from scratch and at the same time stay in Formula One during 1977, Williams and Head ran an ex-factory March-Cosworth 761 for the Belgian driver Patrick Neve. That year yielded little success, but did produce initially modest sponsorship from Saudia (Saudi Arabian Airlines). In 1978, Saudia's sponsorship mushroomed to finance a serious one-car effort, using a new Williams-Cosworth FW06 designed by Patrick Head and driven by the Australian Alan Jones.

The FW06 performed superbly and in a season dominated by ground-effects cars the no-nonsense FW06 was the best conventional Cosworth runner. It brought the team second place in the United States Grand Prix to highlight a promising season. Saudia were delighted and other Saudi Arabian sponsors joined the team for 1979. That season Head produced the FW07 ground-effects design and Clay Regazzoni joined Jones in a two-car programme.

The FW07s were consistent but unlucky frontrunners until mid-season when at the British Grand Prix at Silverstone Jones led at record-breaking pace until a cooling system failure put him out. Here the value of a two-car team was amply demonstrated as Regazzoni's sister car was able to inherit first place and score an emotional maiden Grand Prix success for Frank Williams after so many years of dedicated effort. Better times followed as Jones won the German, Austrian, and Dutch Grands Prix in succession and added a fourth victory in Canada. Alan and Frank were cheated of the World Championships only by a quirk in the scoring system.

Updated FW07B cars appeared for 1980 when Jones, with Carlos Reutemann as his new team-mate, won the Argentine, French, British, Canadian, and United States Grands Prix, plus the subsequently disallowed Spanish event, and became World Champion Driver. Reutemann was first at Monaco and Frank Williams's team became the Constructors' World Champion—the ultimate accolade, never harder won.

Williams FX3

Frank Williams contracted Len Bailey, a freelance design engineer, to produce his first Formula One car in 1971. Len was vastly experienced, having been a member of the Ford GT project team and producing numerous sports, GT, and single-seater designs during the latter part of the 1960s. He based the FX3 upon the then fashionable "Coke bottle" planform. This monocoque nacelle had bulging midships fuel tanks and conventional suspension. After the prototype was spectacularly destroyed by Pescarolo in the opening laps of the British Grand Prix at Brands Hatch, replacements were produced which raced on into 1973 early-season events with updating modifications made by John Clarke, a new Williams engineer.

Wolf-Williams FW05

When Walter Wolf injected massive finance into Williams Racing in 1976 they acquired from the retiring Hesketh team their latest Type 308C Formula One project. They also obtained the services of its designer, Dr. Harvey Postlethwaite. The 308C was a design interesting in its use of a shallow, wide-built monocoque. The car had shown some promise in James Hunt's hands in its initial Hesketh outings late in 1975, but suffered flexibility problems which caused bad handling. Attempts to develop it successfully went astray because Wolf-Williams driver Jacky Ickx and Postlethwaite never established any rapport. When Ickx left, basic levels of comparison were no longer available and the team simply lost its way. The Wolf-Williams FW05 was a disaster, but not wholly because it was a bad car. Failings within the team contributed greatly to its uncompetitiveness.

Team Drivers

Tom Belso • Piers Courage • Nanni Galli • Howden Ganley • Jacky Ickx • Alan Jones • Jacques Laffite • Michel Leclere • Gijs van Lennep • Graham McRae • Arturo Merzario • Patrick Neve • Carlos Pace • Henri Pescarolo • Jacky Pretorious • Brian Redman • Clay Regazzoni • Carlos Reutemann • Tim Schenken

---

SPECIFICATIONS

Williams-Cosworth FW07 1979-80

Engine
Cosworth-Ford DFV
90-degree V-8
Bore × stroke: 85.7 mm × 64.8 mm
Capacity: 2993 cc
Lucas fuel injection
Lucas electronic ignition
Maximum power: c 490 bhp at 10,800 rpm

Transmission
Hewland FGB 400, five-speed and reverse

Chassis
Three-quarter slender monocoque nacelle employing engine as load-bearing member at rear

Front suspension
Top rocker arms, wide-based lower wishbones and inboard coil spring/damper units, anti-roll bar

Rear suspension
Top rocker arms, wide-based lower wishbones and inboard coil spring/damper units, anti-roll bar

Brakes
Disc; outboard front and rear

Dimensions
Wheelbase: 106 in (2692 mm)
Front track: 68 in (1727 mm)
Rear track: 63 in (1600 mm)
Wheel rim width: 11 in front, 18 in rear
Chassis weight: c 80 lb (36 kg)
Formula weight: c 1295 lb (588 kg)

Tyres
Goodyear

Frank Williams has a restless dynamism. He personifies the real racer—a man, hooked by the sport, who professes himself incapable of doing anything else. In 1980, the sport rewarded his single-mindedness. His new and happy team became champions of the world.

Patrick Head is a burly, friendly, talented, and practical man with steely determination. Although his father Colonel Michael Head raced Jaguar sports cars with distinction in the 1950s, Patrick qualified as an engineer the hard way—through a turbulent series of temporary jobs. He found his feet at Lola Cars and after a series of freelance projects he flourished with Williams Grand Prix Engineering.

Constructors' Championship
1980

WOLF

Walter Wolf, an Austrian, arrived in Canada in the early 1950s as a penniless immigrant, and quickly made a fortune in the oil equipment business. He always harboured an enthusiasm for high-performance cars and racing, and in 1975 he appeared at several Grand Prix races with Frank Williams, who headed the Williams team.

Wolf agreed to back Williams Racing in their 1976 season and with Wolf's financial guarantee, a new Formula One car design was about to be laid down. Then Lord Alexander Hesketh announced his own team's abrupt retirement from Grand Prix competition. A new Hesketh 308C, designed by Harvey Postlethwaite, was already built and showing promise, and so Wolf acquired that car, the services of Postlethwaite, and of driver Jacky Ickx.

The result was a tragic and traumatic season. Virtually everything which could go wrong for the team did go wrong. Ickx rapidly decided there was little future in struggling on with an uncompetitive car. Postlethwaite could not establish rapport with Ickx and felt that a sensible development programme—in which the driver must work closely with his designer—was impossible. By the end of the season Walter Wolf had decided upon a complete reorganization of the team. He announced a one-car operation for the 1977-78 seasons in which a completely new car designed by Postlethwaite, to be known as the Wolf-Cosworth, would be driven by Jody Scheckter, the former Tyrrell driver, under the management of Peter Warr, the former Team Lotus manager. Frank Williams did not enjoy the role of sponsorship finder, to which he found himself relegated, and left what had orginally been his team, to start afresh.

When the practical and attractive new Wolf WR1 was unveiled to the press at a London hotel late in 1976, it was obvious that this car, driven by the talented Scheckter, was a potential frontrunner if it could be operated reliably by the reconstituted team. Few people would have dared predict its victory on its debut at Buenos Aires in the 1977 Argentine Grand Prix. Scheckter found himself in an immediate World Championship lead. The Wolf WR1 series proved intensely competitive throughout that season, winning twice more, at Monaco—where both Walter Wolf and Jody Scheckter had homes— and in the Canadian Grand Prix at Mosport Park. This race, in Wolf's adopted country, was an emotional experience for the tough businessman, who found it hard to hide tears of joy. "Canada gave me the opportunity to make something of my life," he said. "This is the happiest moment I have known. . . ."

Jody Scheckter was in contention for the World Championship title until the end of the competition, but he had to be content with second place behind Niki Lauda and Ferrari. His outstanding race, apart from the brilliant drive at Monaco, which netted the Cosworth-Ford engine its one-hundredth Grande Epreuve victory, had been in the United States Grand Prix at Long Beach. There Scheckter's dark blue and gold Wolf-Cosworth led an awe-inspiring tussle with Lauda's Ferrari and Andretti's new ground-effects Lotus 78 until, within sight of the finish, a deflating tyre forced him to fall back to finish third.

In 1978, it was clear that the new generation of ground-effects cars, spawned by the Lotus 78 and 79, was going to outclass the conventional chassis as exemplified by the original series Wolf cars, chassis numbers WR1 to WR4. Consequently, a new ground-effects

WR5 car was designed and constructed by Postlethwaite and his men. It was quite the ugliest and most brutally functional Grand Prix car of its day, but although it enjoyed some degree of competitiveness it did not become a winner. Two second places, in the German and Canadian Grands Prix, were the highlights of a season in which the phenomenal reliability and slick running of the 1977 Wolf team could not be repeated, and Scheckter fell to seventh position in the World Championship. By mid-season Scheckter had decided to leave the team and he signed for Ferrari for 1979.

After Scheckter's departure, the Wolf team took on James Hunt, Harvey Postlethwaite's former Hesketh team colleague. Unfortunately, the sophisticated new WR9-series cars built for the 1979 season were late in appearing and never made up for development time lost. Hunt fell out of love with racing and retired abruptly in mid-season. His disaffection matched that of Walter Wolf, who allowed his team to die at the close of the year. Its plant and leading personnel were absorbed into the Fittipaldi brothers' Formula One operation.

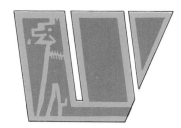

Wolf-Cosworth WR7-9

For the 1979 season the Wolf team replaced Jody Scheckter, who went to Ferrari, with James Hunt, McLaren's former World Champion, who had begun his career in 1974 in Lord Hesketh's cars designed by Harvey Postlethwaite. Now Harvey designed for him a slender-fuselaged, ground-effects car which should have had promise. Hasty preparation for the first race and the subsequent hurly-burly of being locked into a racing calendar without adequate test and development time between events, destroyed the Wolf team's final season. Hunt retired abruptly in mid-season after scoring just one finish. His replacement, Keke Rosberg, took ninth place in the French Grand Prix in his only Championship race finish, and was sixth in the nonchampionship Imola event. WR9 was the last of the Wolf series.

SPECIFICATIONS
Wolf-Cosworth WR1   1977

Engine
Cosworth-Ford DFV
90-degree V-8
Bore × stroke: 85.7 mm × 64.8 mm
Capacity: 2993 cc
Lucas fuel injection
Lucas electronic ignition
Maximum power: c 485 bhp at 10,800 rpm

Transmission
Hewland FGA400, six-speed and reverse

Chassis
Three-quarter monocoque nacelle employing engine as load-bearing member at rear

Front suspension
Double wishbones, outboard coil spring/damper units, and anti-roll bar

Rear suspension
Parallel lower links, single top links, twin radius rods, outboard coil spring/damper units and anti-roll bar

Brakes
Disc; outboard front, inboard rear

Dimensions
Wheelbase: 98 or 103 in (2489 or 2616 mm)
Front track: 55½ in (1410 mm)
Rear track: 60 in (1524 mm)
Wheel rim width: 10 in front, 18 in rear
Chassis weight: c 90 lb (41 kg)
Formula weight: c 1290 lb (585 kg)

Tyres
Goodyear

Harvey Postlethwaite was a brilliant sciences student who, after getting his Ph.D., joined the ICI industrial think-tank at Runcorn, Cheshire, as a research scientist. His personal enthusiasm for cars and racing attracted him to a job offered by March, and he joined them in the early 1970s. Postlethwaite became responsible for the research and development of March's minor formula customer cars.
His 1972 Formula Two and Three designs were highly successful, and in 1973 he joined Hesketh Racing to maintain and develop their private March Formula One car, to be driven by James Hunt. From that project evolved Harvey's own Hesketh Grand Prix car designs. When the Hesketh team folded at the end of 1975, Postlethwaite moved to Wolf-Williams, later Wolf, with mixed results, some brilliant, some ignominious.

Team Drivers
James Hunt • Bobby Rahal •
Keke Rosberg • Jody Scheckter

When looking forward to what the future holds for the Grand Prix car it is necessary first to look back at more than seventy-five years of Grand Prix racing. On close examination, it is quite remarkable just how little has really changed, rather than how much. For years some critics have complained that Grand Prix cars look too little like the cars that are driven on the road. They are too far removed from them technically to be of great use in improving the breed.

That complaint presupposes that the purpose of Grand Prix racing is to improve the breed. If a victorious manufacturer builds road cars for sale to the public, the one indisputable effect of Grand Prix racing is its ability to publicize the breed and promote its sales. Even the earliest Grand Prix cars of 1906-08 were one-off specials, gigantically overpowered, bereft of heavy bodywork and furnishings, and owing little to the road cars which their manufacturers also produced and hoped to sell. The Grand Prix car, indeed, has always been a highly specialized animal and whether Grand Prix racing itself is truly a sport or more a fascinatingly sophisticated and technically advanced publicity stunt is another arguable point. It is certain to continue in this way for as many years as are left to it.

There are two main problems facing Grand Prix racing's future. It has always been dangerous. Drivers and spectators have been killed and undoubtedly there will be accidents in the future. After the Le Mans catastrophe of 1955 the Swiss government banned racing in its country. As yet this remains the only major nation in the world where motor racing is actually illegal. Sweden has come perilously close to calling a halt in recent years and as "civilization" marches on there is no telling what convenient bandwagon some grey band of politicians may jump upon. Grand Prix racing is in the firing line. Its governing body has to make continual sacrifices to the cause of safety to protect its existence, and should the day ever come when safety precautions separate the public from the cars by too great a margin the story will reach its end, unless television can provide vicarious race-spectating thrills for the public.

The second, and far more serious threat, to Grand Prix racing as a competitive business and to the Grand Prix car as an advanced machine is the throttling of its money supply. Grand Prix racing has always been expensive. In 1924, Sunbeam spent the modern equivalent of a million pounds to run three cars in just two Grand Prix races. In 1981, the Saudi-Williams team aimed at a three-million pound budget for a two-car team in many more races. Costs will not diminish, and the Williams team, like so many other modern specialists, is concerned only with chassis developments, buying their Cosworth engines off the shelf for a little more than twenty-two thousand pounds each. The major manufacturers who have the will, the capability, and the funds to develop their own Formula One power units spend much more. In 1966-67 Keith Duckworth produced his brilliantly successful Cosworth DFV engine using one hundred thousand pounds advanced by Ford. It was a bargain price for a superb design. In the 1980s, development of a new engine may cost nearly two million pounds before it begins to race. For most manufacturers there will be no projected return from selling engines into private hands to power competitive chassis. Renault, Fiat (through Ferrari), and Alfa Romeo are in Grand Prix racing to win and to promote their own prestige and that of their money-making production cars. They build and race their own chassis to carry their own engines and only after they are dominant and thoroughly established might they consider providing power for the opposition. This type of support paid Ford enormous dividends with the DFV, but, of course, Ford ran no Grand Prix cars of their own.

It is only the major manufacturers who have a real reason to be in Grand Prix racing. That is the promotion of their commercial products. Specialist teams, including Brabham, Tyrrell, and McLaren, have no interest in anything other than Grand Prix racing. They have exploited its world-wide audience brilliantly to place their sponsors' names before the public and earn quite massive rewards for doing so. If a specialist team's sponsors withdraw their support, and another is not forthcoming the team will collapse because they have no commercial products to fall back on and nothing left but the enthusiasm of their personnel to keep them going.

The economic recession at the beginning of the 1980s made life desperately hard for the specialist teams which were founded in the fat years of big-money sponsorship, before the major manufacturers, led by Renault, stepped back on the Grand Prix stage. This is not to denigrate the achievements of the specialist teams, for they performed wonders in chassis development within the regulations, and generally led the way with Lotus most often at their head. The giants, like Renault, had a difficult time trying to make an impression upon these experienced veterans of the track, and indeed it was no small achievement—no easy victory—when Renault won at last.

But the rise to full competitiveness of the turbocharged Renault engine may come to be regarded as the first nail in the specialists' coffin. Turbo engines are extremely expensive and where results are thin, as they must eventually become when running against such major factory opposition as Renault, Ferrari, and Alfa Romeo, possibly Talbot too, willing sponsors will become hard to find. This augurs badly for Grand Prix racing. The supporting cast has always been important, but with little prospect of a good result and massively expensive engines necessary to qualify for a start, it will probably be thinned out.

Chassis design will become increasingly restricted by the regulations. In the winter of 1980-81 the governing body banned the moveable skirts which had proved so vital in making ground-effect aerodynamic "sucker systems" operate in the previous four seasons. Colin Chapman devised an ingenious new Lotus in which the entire body moved vertically relative to the chassis, the intention being to close off the ground-effect area beneath it. The car became the centre of a lengthy battle for acceptance. One of the great attractions of Grand Prix car design has been the engineers' ability to weave their way around regulations. In the late 1970s, more and more loopholes were plugged, design engineers had less room for manoeuvre, and the chassis—as opposed to the engines in use—became increasingly stereotyped. Winning races became a matter of achieving the best adjustment of one's chassis and engine package. The day of blinding design inspiration seemed to have passed—constant modifications to minor details became the prime road to success.

Future technical innovations not likely to be precluded by regulation changes will involve systems long discussed, and in some cases seen before. "Active" suspension systems are one possibility, in which onboard microchip computers and electro-processers would control hydraulic rams which in turn would adjust suspension settings for the approaching straight or corner. There remains great scope for improvements in transmission because the current "mangle gears" used by all competitors are crude and relatively inefficient, despite their relatively light weight and extreme practicality. Automatic transmissions could make better use of available power outputs if they can be made sufficiently light, reliable, and efficient. Tyre technology has by no means reached its limit, but regulations will probably severely restrict progress.

For enthusiasts, the racing they see in their formative years leaves an indelible impression as "the best there ever was" and, regulations allowing, no doubt the Grand Prix races of the middle and late 1980s will win millions of new followers throughout the world. Technically the double restrictions of blanket regulations governing almost every aspect of a Grand Prix car's design and construction will become extremely limiting and financial restraints may be even more damaging. But one thing remains certain. The Grand Prix car of the 1980s will be the fastest thing on wheels around any road circuit. And that's the name of the game.

THE DRIVERS

NIGEL ROEBUCK

WHEN WRITING ABOUT CARS OR CIRCUITS, evaluations are relatively straightforward, and there is little scope for dissent. That the Lotus 25 was a great car, for example, is beyond dispute, as is the fact that the Nürburgring was a greater test of driving skill than any circuit on the current Grand Prix calendar. The evaluation of drivers, however, is far more difficult, far more open to personal opinion. The introduction of the human element creates problems, for a wide range of qualities, upon which no fixed value can be put, come together to make the great racing driver.

Racing aficionados have argued far into the night about the relative merits of Nuvolari and Caracciola, of Moss and Clark, and much of their opinion stems from their own personalities. The fan who appreciates *bravura*, whose senses are stirred above all by the dramatic, will have pleaded through the years the case of Rosemeyer, Rindt, or Villeneuve. Conversely, the supporter of Fangio and Stewart will be impressed primarily by calm and order and ease.

There follow brief sketches of twenty-five prominent drivers who have raced since the Second World War. There is no attempt to select a "top twenty-five" for such a task would be unending. Some of these men are included for the sheer weight of their achievements, others for what they meant to the worldwide racing public. Most have contributed to motor racing legend, not all to the record books. I have tried to find a balance of craftsman, worker, hero, star—and offbeat. A.J. Foyt, for example, has never raced a Grand Prix car, yet his record in other spheres suggests that he could have done so on equal terms with the best.

You will not find Denny Hulme, the 1967 World Champion, in these pages, yet his fellow New Zealander Chris Amon, who never won a Grand Prix, is included. Carlos Reutemann, as great as any on his day, is not here, yet Clay Regazzoni, beloved by fans the world over, has a place. There is also an attempt to achieve a spread of nationalities. Since the death of Jean-Pierre Wimille in 1948, there has been no French driver of outstanding distinction, but Didier Pironi may be the man to end the drought.

Therefore, look for no particular strain of logic in the selection of these drivers. The choice is a personal one. All these men have made a powerful contribution to the sport, and some will add to it in the future. If it had been possible, included, too, would have been Reutemann, Farina, Musso, Behra, Collins, and Piquet. Some great, some fascinating, like those who follow.

The Grand Prix driver of thirty years ago paid appallingly little heed to his own safety. Picture him on the grid, standing next to his car. He wears soft shoes, lightweight cotton trousers, and short-sleeved shirt. Before climbing aboard he pulls on a tight linen helmet, strings a pair of goggles—with glass lenses—around his neck.

In the deep, roomy cockpit he settles himself. His knees are wide apart, for the throttle pedal and brake are away on the right, the clutch alone on the left. There is no seat belt for him to buckle on, no roll-over bar behind his head. The engine is under that long expanse ahead of him. The exhaust pipe runs by his left elbow. He grips the massive wood-rimmed steering wheel, gets a push start, takes his place on the grid, waits for the starter's flag to fall. He faces a drive of about three hundred miles, and will be working hard for at least three hours. At the end, when he raises his goggles, his oil-smeared face will have a grotesque Mardi Gras appearance. If he has won, he will wear the garland, hold his trophy aloft, stand proudly for his National Anthem. In the evening, there will almost certainly be a formal prize-giving ceremony, which he will attend. After that, there will probably be a party.

Moving ahead thirty years, the scene is rather different. Our modern Grand Prix driver is altogether less casual. If he is particularly fastidious—as Jackie Stewart, for example, used to be—he removes all his jewellery before he gets into his car. Watches, identity bracelets, St. Christopher medals, and rings can tear flesh and break bones in an accident.

All his clothing—his underwear, socks, overalls, and driving boots—is fireproof. Even the stitching is of fireproof thread. Fire is the great dread of the racing driver, and in the close confines of a modern cockpit it is all too easy to be trapped.

As he prepares to get into the car, today's driver puts on a fireproof balaclava with tiny eyeholes. Then comes the helmet. It, too, has a fireproof lining. It is immensely strong and surprisingly light; the flip-up visor is virtually bulletproof. Last of all comes the gauntlet length, fireproof gloves.

His dress complete, our modern Formula One driver climbs in. This in itself is not the work of a moment. So cramped is the cockpit that he must support his weight with his hands on the cockpit sides, sliding his feet up towards the pedals, gradually lowering himself in. That done, he wriggles left and right to get his shoulders in, then joins up the six-point harness—over the shoulders, around the waist, between the thighs—at its quick-release locking point. The shoulder belts are then further tightened by a mechanic, effectively pinning the driver to his seat. Last of all, a member of the team connects a piece of tubing to a nozzle on the driver's helmet; all cars are now fitted with a life support system. In the event of a fire, this triggers automatically to feed clean oxygen to the driver for a maximum of one minute.

Ahead of him the modern Grand Prix driver sees little but road. Cockpit siting has crept forward in recent years to the point that the driver now sits almost between the front wheels. A few inches to the right of the tiny saucer-like steering wheel is the stubby gear lever. The pedals are set close together. Not an inch is wasted.

Grand Prix races are shorter now than in days gone by, with a maximum distance of two hundred miles, a maximum duration of two hours. Today's driver gets on his way when he sees the red light in the overhead gantry change to green. In step with the age, it is more efficient, more clinical, than the fall of a flag. The garlands and trophies follow at race's end. But prize-giving ceremonies are for the archives. By the evening most of the drivers are back home. There are no parties. Prizes arrive later, figures on pieces of paper.

Thirty years ago, the phrase "Grand Prix driver" was a rather more general term than today, implying a level of skill. There were fewer Grands Prix on the schedule in the fifties, and all the leading drivers took part in other types of racing, notably long-distance sports car events. There was far less specialization. Today's Grand Prix driver, however, is precisely that—a specialist. The advent of the big sponsors has meant that success, once merely desirable, is now essential. The drivers are paid a great deal of money. For success constant testing is necessary. There simply is not time to contemplate other forms of racing. And many drivers' contracts specifically preclude it.

To be a naturally fast racing driver is no longer enough. The driver of today must know all about his car. And if that sounds absurdly obvious, bear in mind that there was a time when he was actively discouraged from concerning himself with technicalities. In the fifties, a Ferrari driver had a much easier life if he simply turned up at the circuit, got into his car, and drove. The mechanical side was the business of the engineers and mechanics, who did not appreciate a driver trying to tell them about their jobs.

In some ways, the business has come full circle. In the sixties came the era of the great test driver, who shouldered the task of making the car *au point*, testing endlessly, experimenting with spring rates and roll-bars and wing angles, demanding the changes, making his own decisions. In recent years the racing driver has by necessity reverted somewhat to the role of test pilot, a man who reports the car's behaviour to his team, leaving the changes to the engineer. This became increasingly prevalent in the ground-effects era.

The basic personality of the racing driver has not changed much. There are still the intense and the frivolous, the excitable and the calm. The Grand Prix star of today, however, is infinitely more disciplined than his predecessor. Few touch alcohol, hardly any a cigarette. Parties are strictly for the off-season. There is too much at stake for levity—too much money, too much prestige. Grand Prix is incomparably more competitive than it was, its rewards enormous. Fitness is not optional.

Today's Grand Prix drivers race more intensely than their counterparts of thirty years ago. The practice sessions are no longer relaxed affairs with a few quick laps thrown in. There is more pressure to succeed. But the driver of today earns a fantastic amount of money in a short time, and there is, consequently, an inclination to retire much earlier, to make money and get out. Fangio retired at forty-seven, still World Champion. Niki Lauda left the scene at thirty, and so did Jody Scheckter. James Hunt was thirty-one. The other side of all that coin is pressure. The Formula One star of the eighties carries his helmet in one hand, a briefcase in the other. As in all other sports, increased professionalism has exacted its dues, giving, but also taking away.

CHRIS AMON

To those outside their circle, Grand Prix drivers are not especially pleasant people. It is perhaps unreasonable to expect them to be so, for the qualities within them which have led to their success are not attractive human traits. Many of the great drivers are arrogant, self-centred, ruthlessly ambitious, greedy, narrow-minded, oblivious to the world beyond them. In a racing car these personality flaws work strongly for them; out of a car, they frequently add up to something insufferable. If this is not always completely applicable, it is nevertheless an accurate generalization.

Chris Amon's problem was that he had none of these particular characteristics, but he did have a colossal amount of natural ability to drive racing cars. Amon's personality was altogether too human to be compatible with a career in Grand Prix racing. It was often said that he lacked killer instinct, and this is undeniable; indeed, he has admitted that he took no particular pleasure in being quicker than other drivers. His race was always primarily against himself, his greatest satisfaction the putting together of the perfect lap. It is, therefore, the more remarkable that Jackie Stewart has said that Jim Clark and Chris Amon were the two best against whom he had raced. For Amon never won a World Championship Grand Prix. Countless times he led races and each time the car let him down when victory seemed certain. His misfortunes became motor racing legend. He won the Le Mans 24-Hours, even other Formula One races, but never a Grand Prix. And this remains inexplicable.

He began racing in his native New Zealand when he was sixteen years old, was in Formula One at nineteen, became Ferrari team leader at twenty-three. These, on the face of it, are credentials which should have led to the World Championship, and many were those who forecast exactly that. It was, they said, merely a matter of time. That time should have been 1968. Then into his second season with Ferrari, Chris was living in Italy, working tirelessly on improving the cars. Mauro Forghieri, chief engineer at Maranello for almost twenty years, still maintains that Amon was the best development driver he has known. Together they made the Ferrari 312 the best-handling car in motor racing. It was responsive and forgiving, like a latter-day Maserati 250F, and perfectly suited to Amon's exuberant yet perfectly controlled driving style. Circuit for circuit, Chris and the Ferrari were indubitably the fastest partnership in Formula One that year, although the Italian car's V-12 engine had less horsepower than its British rivals.

After three frustrating seasons Amon decided to leave Ferrari. It was the first of his celebrated bad decisions, and one he was to regret for the rest of his racing career. Soon after Amon left, the Commendatore's team was transformed by an infusion of Fiat money, which allowed the men of Maranello to exploit fully their unsurpassed technical skills. In 1970, Ferrari won race after race, but others reaped the rewards of Amon's development work.

Enzo Ferrari was truly sorry to see Chris go. At the end of 1968 he had taken the unprecedented step of announcing to the press that Amon would have been World Champion that year had the cars not let him down. Chris, too, was sad. He had loved his time in Italy. A traditionalist, he had always wanted to drive for Ferrari, and he would never again enjoy racing so much.

After an unsatisfactory year with March in 1970, Amon spent two years with Matra, and they mirrored precisely his experience with Ferrari. The car handled beautifully, but lacked power. There were more pole positions, more races lost. At the end of 1972 Matra withdrew from Grand Prix racing.

Chris became more and more obsessed by that first elusive Grand Prix victory, and it was an even greater frustration for him when the races were won by drivers with a fraction of his talent. Eventually he came to the conclusion that the only solution was to have his own team and his own car. He had made a great deal of money from racing, and much had been lost in ill-starred business ventures and investments. The remainder was plunged into the Amon Formula One car. It was an unmitigated disaster. At the end of it Chris was broke and in despair.

A year later the familiar red, white, and blue crash helmet was back in Formula One, its owner now driving for the tiny, underfinanced Ensign team. They came amazingly close to success, and with a realistic budget might well have won a Grand Prix. As it was, mechanical failure led to two bad accidents in 1976, and Chris finally decided to call it a day, his reputation for pure driving ability as high as it had ever been.

Chris Amon, this complex man, has left little behind in the record books, but that takes no account of the pleasure his skills gave over the years. His popularity was enormous. All over the world racing aficionados willed his luck to improve. Without a doubt, however, much of his misfortune was of his own making. He was always too trusting, too willing to listen to advice from the wrong people. Much of the time his personal life was chaotic; always he was disorganized about such routine matters as plane tickets and hotel bookings. He hated the commercialization which has overtaken modern Grand Prix racing, often saying that he had been born into the wrong era. Surprisingly, his sense of humour—by no means a universal characteristic of drivers—survived intact. He chain-smoked and chewed his nails, yet was totally relaxed in the cockpit. "Nice guys," Jackie Stewart has clichéd, "don't make it." Chris Amon, consummate skill or not, was proof of those unhappy words.

MARIO ANDRETTI

In terms of versatility, Mario Andretti must be the greatest driver of all time. No other racing driver has ever competed so successfully in so many spheres of the sport. A glance at his triumphs—the Indianapolis 500, the Daytona 500, the Formula One World Championship, encompassing many Grand Prix victories, the Sebring 12 Hours—suggests an almost superhuman talent. Add to that countless wins in midgets, sprints, and Formula 5000 and you have a man who can turn his abilities to anything.

Andretti's career personifies the modern American dream. He was the boy who sailed to the New World in search of fame and fortune—and found it. Born in Italy in 1940, he quickly developed a passionate interest in Grand Prix racing, and was distraught when his parents announced their intention to emigrate. In the aftermath of the Second World War there was little to keep them in Italy, but Mario knew only that there were no Grands Prix in the United States and it was with a heavy heart that he boarded the ship in June of 1955. The family was headed for New York and from there to Nazareth, Pennsylvania, where they had relatives. For a kid who had watched Ascari and Fangio at Monza, it seemed like the end of the world. "Nazareth? I'd only heard of one other guy who came from there, and he'd been gone nearly two thousand years. . . ."

It is said that all Italians love children, opera, and motor racing. Mario's father may have been an unusual Italian, for he didn't love motor racing. He didn't even like it. More than that, he considered racing disreputable. When Mario and his twin, Aldo, began their early forays into local dirt-track racing, it was without the knowledge of their father. Then one night in 1959 Aldo was severely injured in a stock car accident. Fortunately, he recovered, but for months afterwards there was no communication between father and sons.

Andretti's racing indoctrination was tough and ruthless. He learned his craft on the dirt "bull rings" of Pennsylvania and Indiana, where fatalities were everyday facts. Safety facilities were pathetically inadequate. American motor racing was in a transitional state. The greats of Indianapolis were still to be found racing sprint cars three nights a week for absurd purses. It was a rough school, with poor rewards and worse life expectancy. But it was an apprenticeship which had to be served, and Mario revelled in it. He was a thinker, however, and an ambitious one at that. He figured he would give sprint car racing a short, sharp shock, in the hope that someone would recognize his latent talent, pluck him out of there, and take him to Indianapolis.

In 1965, Andretti drove in the Indianapolis 500 for the first time, and finished third behind Jim Clark and Parnelli Jones. Thereafter he dominated USAC Championship racing for years, but his heart, he says, always lay with Formula One, his original passion.

He made his Grand Prix debut at Watkins Glen in 1968, qualifying with a factory Lotus 49 in the pole position. It was a stunning achievement. Jim Clark had been killed earlier in the year and Colin Chapman considered Mario the one man who might be capable of taking his place. But by now Andretti had too much going in America to commit himself wholeheartedly to Grand Prix racing and to Europe. Instead, he agreed to drive for Chapman whenever his USAC schedule permitted.

At that time Andretti was one of the fastest drivers in the world, and his impact as a full-time Grand Prix driver would have been extraordinary. Instead, he chose to concentrate on America, and his Formula One appearances inevitably suffered. Coincidentally, his dominant USAC years were coming to an end. There was less and less to leave behind.

In 1976, his star fading, Mario took the plunge and joined Lotus as team leader. Chapman's team was then in the depths, and it took all the charisma, fight, and determination that Andretti could muster to bring it back to competitiveness. By the end of that first year together, Mario and Lotus were a winning combination. In 1977 they won more races than anyone else, and the following year they took the World Championship.

Andretti is a popular man, yet he is genuinely close to few people. Usually he is charming, but this can be switched off like a light. He is utterly ruthless in pursuit of his ambitions, a characteristic he shares with Chapman. Andretti started with nothing, and does not forget it. His millions are carefully invested, his family the most important aspect of his life. Unfailingly, he returns to Pennsylvania after every race, and in the summer there is a Grand Prix in Europe every second weekend. "I cope with the travel because I set my mind to it." The remark sums up the man perfectly. It also accounts for his success as a racing driver.

"I figure I was put on this earth to drive race cars," is a favourite remark of his, and undoubtedly an accurate one, yet a doubt lingers about Andretti's ultimate status among the great. He does not have the God-given talent of a Moss or a Clark and he is too fallible to be counted among their number. Andretti has "set his mind" to every kind of racing he has tackled. He has evaluated the problems and set about eliminating them. As a test driver his ability to bring a car close to its ultimate performance is phenomenal. In the best car in the race he is near perfection. In less than that, his impatience and still raw aggression have frequently handicapped him. He has had an American passport for many years, but the blood in his veins is Italian. There was never a man who loved motor racing more.

ALBERTO ASCARI

The day they buried him there was silence in the city. Milan had lost her favourite son, Italy her greatest racing driver in a generation. Alberto Ascari had died on home territory, a little way down the road at Monza, and the local populace was in shock. To this day they look in vain for his successor.

He was born into a racing family. His father, a prominent member of the Alfa Romeo Grand Prix team, lost his life in the French Grand Prix of 1925. Alberto was just eight years old at the time, but his fixation on racing had already begun. Despite the pleas and exhortations of his mother, he was always determined to race. His career began with motorcycles, as was usually the way in those days, and he first raced a car — the very first Ferrari — in the Mille Miglia of 1940. In that era of Mussolini, Italy was slow to accept that motor racing would be another casualty of war.

When peace returned, Ascari was twenty-seven. By now he had a wife and children and for a while he contemplated a safer future for himself. But ultimately he allowed Luigi Villoresi, a top Italian driver and his close friend, to persuade him to return to racing. Together they raced Maseratis in 1948, and at the end of that season Enzo Ferrari invited Alberto to join the factory Grand Prix team. It was the beginning of a legendary partnership. The names of Ascari and Ferrari became synonymous.

For five consecutive seasons Alberto led the Maranello team to a staggering number of victories. He was not a driver in the Latin tradition. With his talent there was usually no cause to abuse the car, and the greatest of Ascari was seen on those many occasions when he took the lead from the start and stayed there all afternoon. He was a superb racing machine — calm, precise, unflurried, and simply faster than the rest. Many of their contemporaries actually reckoned Ascari to be quicker than Fangio.

In the seasons of 1952 and 1953 the Ferrari team was supreme, Alberto was indisputably its best driver, and the combination was in a class of its own. There were seven World Championship Grands Prix in 1952: Ascari had a clashing commitment at the Indianapolis 500 and so missed the Swiss race, but he won the other six. The following year was almost as successful, and brought another World Championship. In those two seasons Ascari and Ferrari achieved a level of domination unequalled before or since.

At the end of 1953, Ascari stunned the motor racing world by leaving Ferrari for Lancia, who were coming into Grand Prix racing with a new and unconventional car, the D50. There were many who sadly shook their heads at his decision, and they were proved right. By the time the Lancia was ready to race, most of the 1954 season had gone by. Mercedes-Benz, with Fangio as number one, had made a crushing return, while the Argentine driver's only true rival was on the sidelines for the greater part of the year. Ascari, World Champion in 1952 and 1953, finished 1954 without a championship point to his name.

Ascari was a man of enormous loyalty and integrity. Having committed himself to Lancia, he stayed true to his word and renewed his contract for 1955, convinced that only the Lancia could challenge the Mercedes. By now the Lancia was proving very fast in tests, although its unpredictable handling called upon all of Ascari's genius.

Early in the new season Ascari won two non-championship races at Naples and Turin, and eagerly awaited the European Grandes Epreuves. At Monte Carlo, the first of these, he should have won. The Mercedes of both Fangio and Moss retired, and Ascari was on the point of assuming the lead near the end when he most uncharacteristically made a mistake at the chicane leading to the harbour front. In an instant the dark red Lancia was through the straw bales, flying into space, plunging into the water. After an agonizing interval, the light blue helmet bobbed to the surface. The crowds broke into spontaneous applause as Ascari swam to a rescue launch. He had a broken nose, nothing more.

Four days later came the news which rocked Italy. *Ascari e morto.* After the drama of Monaco, he had returned home to Milan to recover.

Bored by midweek, he had gone out to Monza to watch his protégé Eugenio Castellotti test a new Ferrari sports car. On impulse he had decided to try the car himself. Taking off his jacket, he had borrowed Castellotti's helmet and set off. On the third lap came the fatal accident.

Coincidence — and it can be nothing more — is disquieting. Motor racing has had its share, but none is more eerie than the series of coincidences which connected the deaths of Alberto and his father Antonio. Both were killed on the 26th of the month — one in 1925, the other in 1955. Both were thirty-six years old. Each died four days after a miraculous escape. In neither case was any explanation found for the accident. Both regarded their crash helmets as good luck charms, and each was killed the first time he drove a racing car wearing someone else's helmet. Both were intensely superstitious.

So, a true artist was gone, and the Italians looked forlornly for someone new in whom to invest their affection. Ascari was loved. Like thousands of others, a small and skinny kid named Mario Andretti wept when he heard of his hero's death. Later, he would win at Monza, would take the World Championship, but by then he would be an American. The Italians are still waiting.

JACK BRABHAM

It was a long time before anyone in Europe took Jack Brabham seriously. In his native Australia he had made something of a name for himself, first racing midgets on dirt ovals and then progressing to success in hill climbs and road races. He was almost thirty years old when he arrived in England in 1955, and many of the purists were offended by his untidy, if spectacular, tail-out driving style. It was, they said, a legacy of his dirt track upbringing. He would never amount to anything in serious motor racing.

Brabham stayed in Europe for fifteen years before returning to Australia for good. In that time he founded his own company, became a Formula One constructor, and won the World Championship three times. The purists could only choke on their words.

After leaving school in Sydney, Jack was apprenticed as a motor mechanic, and this gave him an excellent grounding for the career he was to follow. In motor racing history there have always been drivers who liked to tinker with their cars, rather than content themselves with merely driving them. This has frequently been to the detriment of their results. Brabham, however, was always a pragmatic individual, and his contribution was valuable.

In his last season in Australia, Jack had enjoyed considerable success driving a Cooper-Bristol, and when he arrived in England one of his first ports of call was John Cooper's small factory in Surrey. The two men quickly became firm friends, and were to form one of racing's most successful partnerships.

At that time, however, the Cooper Car Company was scarcely ready for the intense competition of Formula One. Grand Prix success was exclusive to the Italians and Germans. When Mercedes-Benz came to Aintree 1955 they scored the most crushing victory of their brief return to racing, finishing first, second, third, and fourth in the British Grand Prix. Pole position had gone to Stirling Moss, and no one took much notice of the man at the other end of the grid, Jack Brabham, whose Cooper-Bristol had lapped twenty-seven seconds slower. Four years later, at the same circuit, the Australian would start from the pole and would win the race.

During those four years Brabham built up a solid reputation, gradually showing himself to be a driver of the front rank, if not a man with World Championship potential. Apart from a brief and disastrous dalliance with a privately entered Maserati 250F in 1956, he remained essentially a Cooper man, but the company was constantly hampered by their underpowered Climax engines. Not until 1959 was the motor available in full 2.5-litre form. Only then did Brabham really emerge.

He scored his first Formula One victory in the International Trophy of that year, and soon after came his first in a Grand Prix. At Monte Carlo he was unable to keep pace with Stirling Moss in Rob Walker's Cooper, but when Stirling's car broke Jack went on to take first place. Later in the year he also won the British Grand Prix, and consistently high placings elsewhere were sufficient to make him World Champion. The Grand Prix world was slightly stunned by Brabham's title, for the pre-season favourites had been Moss, Brooks, and Behra. And Jack himself was well aware that many considered his title to have been "poached".

The following year, however, there were no grounds for complaint. This time Brabham utterly dominated the World Championship, taking five successive victories in Holland, Belgium, France, Britain, and Portugal. Blacksmith driver perhaps, but his record of on-the-trot wins has since been equalled only by Jim Clark. The Australian's second title was decisive.

Then there was a protracted lull. Brabham stayed with Cooper for 1961, the first year of the 1.5-litre Formula One, but the British teams were generally outclassed by the power of the Ferraris. Only the genius of Moss was able to offer a serious—if occasional—challenge. At the end of the season Jack said farewell to John Cooper and went away to build his own Formula One cars. The first of these appeared at the 1962 German Grand Prix.

For the next three seasons, with Dan Gurney as his team-mate, Jack's Brabhams were highly competitive, if less than reliable. The Australian was still driving well, occasionally winning non-championship events, but the team's two Grand Prix wins went to Gurney. Brabham seriously contemplated retirement. His fortieth birthday was approaching. Perhaps it would be better to concentrate on running the team.

After a lot of thought, however, he decided to continue, and history shows that this was a sensible decision. In 1966, with the dawning of the 3-litre formula, Jack Brabham began a lengthy Indian summer. At Reims, in July, he won the French Grand Prix, so becoming the first man ever to win a Grand Prix in a car of his own manufacture. His last Grand Prix triumph had been at Oporto, six years past.

Following the French success, Jack's progress was remarkable. In quick succession he followed it with victories at Brands Hatch, the Nürburgring, and Zandvoort. At the age of forty he was again World Champion.

Brabham was never a man to capture the public imagination. Quiet and undemonstrative, he never used two words where one would do. He had no interest in adulation and social functions, and never became "worldly". Travelling constantly brought its own problems, and he would take vast quantities of steak from England with him, wary of the effects of foreign food. He was one of the pioneers of the now fashionable custom of flying to races in his own light aircraft. He kept himself to himself. Not unfriendly, he was simply an introvert.

On the track, it was a different matter. There was nothing shy about Jack Brabham, racing driver. His grounding, on the dirt ovals of New South Wales, had been rough and ready, and Black Jack knew all the tricks in the business. Time and again one of his rear wheels would flick off the road and into the dirt, giving following drivers a peppering with gravel. He came of a hard school, and accepted the knocks as he gave them. At the end of the race there would inevitably be that innocent half-smile. Who, me?

Brabham was a doughty competitor, a man who truly loved to race. His style was never elegant, with shoulders hunched and head down, but in full cry he was a mighty impressive sight. During 1966, his third World Championship year, he also undertook a full season of Formula Two. He won nine of the races.

His team took the World Championship title again in 1967, but this time the World Champion was Denny Hulme, with Brabham second. There was little success the following year, the cars hampered by their unreliable four-cam Repco engines. For 1969, Jack decided to switch to the ubiquitous Cosworth DFV. Early in the year he won a magnificent victory in appalling conditions in the International Trophy at Silverstone, and looked set for another season of success. But a testing accident at the same circuit left him with a broken ankle, and put him out of racing for nearly half the year. In his absence, Jacky Ickx did the team proud, winning in Germany. The Belgian also triumphed in Canada, where the recovered Brabham finished second.

For 1970, Jack decided to have a final attempt at his fourth World Championship title. He began superbly by winning the South African Grand Prix, but lost in Monaco with a mistake at the last corner and at Brands Hatch when he ran out of fuel a mile from the flag. The title slipped away. After the Mexican Grand Prix in October he confirmed his retirement and returned to Australia. At forty-four, he had been competitive to the last.

TONY BROOKS

He was an artist. In his greatest years, the late 1950s, Tony Brooks was a man ahead of his time. The archetypal racing driver of that era—in the public mind, at least—was a Latin, swarthy and dashing, a man with huge, tanned forearms, with a crooked smile but straight teeth, a cigarette dangling permanently from the corner of his mouth, a woman from each elbow.

Tony Brooks was the antithesis of all that. He was a quiet Englishman, reserved and shy, and his face and physique simply did not seem suited to the cockpit of a Grand Prix car. When first he came on the racing scene, no one could quite believe he had the strength to drive a Formula One car.

The outwardly frail appearance was illusory. Brooks actually possessed extraordinary stamina, and when this was allied to an equal amount of ability he soon began to make his mark. Driving racing cars was entirely natural for him, never forced or uneasy. When you watched him, you began to believe you could do it yourself. And then one of the renowned Latins would come by, struggling for control, and your heart skipped a beat. Suddenly the talent of Tony Brooks was in perspective.

As a young dental student, Tony had begun club racing purely as a means of relaxation, something to free his mind from his books and examinations. It immediately became clear that he was more than an ordinarily competent driver, but he had no real thought of making his hobby a profession. Others saw greatness in him, including John Wyer, then team manager of Aston Martin, who invited him to join the team for the 1955 season. Brooks, still involved in his studies, was flattered by the offer and accepted it.

The turning point came at the end of that year, when Connaught, a struggling and impoverished British Grand Prix team, contacted him. There was a race in Sicily, the Grand Prix of Siracusa. The organizers were offering good appearance money, which the team sorely needed. They also needed a driver. They were aware that Brooks had never even sat in a Formula One car, but they nevertheless invited him to drive. Tony, hard at work at Manchester University, rather absent-mindedly accepted the proposal.

It was disconcerting, when Brooks arrived at Syracuse, to find that the Connaught transporter was nowhere to be seen. With experience of neither car nor circuit, Brooks's position looked impossible. By the time the team arrived in the paddock, the first of the two practice days was lost and Tony was, resourcefully, learning the track on a motor scooter in the dark.

The following day, however, he got into the car and within a dozen laps had set the second fastest time. The Maserati team, expected to dominate before an Italian crowd, glanced nervously at the green car and its novice driver. On race day they were rather more than nervous. Luigi Musso, Maserati's number one driver, led for a while, but Tony Brooks looked menacing behind. He soon passed the Maserati, to howls of Sicilian dismay, and drove away from Musso. It was to be the first Grand Prix victory by a British car for thirty-two years. On the flight back to England, Tony, unmoved if a little bewildered, got back to his books.

That race changed the course of Tony Brooks's life, for there followed offers of full Grand Prix contracts. And Brooks, having now qualified as a dentist, decided to forget teeth for a while. In 1956 he drove for BRM, but it proved to be a calamitous season. In the British Grand Prix at Silverstone a jammed throttle sent his car somersaulting off the road. Tony was fortunate to escape with minor injuries.

That accident brought the beginnings of a change in his racing philosophy, and another, at Le Mans twelve months later, finalized it. Both accidents occurred in cars which had mechanical problems. Brooks, a committed and devout Catholic, vowed that he would never again risk his life in a car that was in less than perfect condition. Life, he said, was a gift from God and suicide was a sin. Risking his life in an unsound car could be equated with attempting suicide.

He was never a man to relish a scrap—indeed, with his talent, there was seldom need for one. In 1957 and 1958 he drove for the Vanwall team, as number two to Stirling Moss. In the second of those seasons each won three Grands Prix, and there was virtually nothing to choose between them.

Brooks was a man ahead of his time because he thought deeply about motor racing, about the best way to win a race, about staying alive. Many of his greatest victories came after he had held back early in a race and swooped in the final stages. Above all, he was a gorgeous driver to watch, immaculate of line, supremely relaxed, a wonderful stylist. Brooks never wasted an inch, never fought with the car, never looked tired after a three-hour Grand Prix.

When Vanwall abandoned racing at the end of 1958, Tony became team leader for Ferrari, whose cars had frequently been beaten by him when he drove for Vanwall. It was a year in which he should have become World Champion. When the teams headed off to Sebring, Florida, for the final round of the World Championship, he was in the running, along with Stirling Moss and Jack Brabham. On the first lap, Brooks's Ferrari was hit by another car. Tony suspected that something might be broken. Against every instinct he possessed as a racing driver, he went into the pits to have the car checked over, and lost two vital minutes in the process. After the delay he fought back to third place. Without it, he would probably have won—and the points would have given him the title. He smiles wryly when he talks of it now. But he still thinks he did the right thing.

After that 1959 season, Brooks drove for two more years, but his thoughts were focused on the future. He was married now, with two children, and had never envisaged a long career in motor racing. At the age of twenty-nine he retired from it, not to become a dentist, but to concentrate on his thriving garage business. He left with no flourish, which was typical of the man, and took away with him one of the greatest talents the sport has known.

JIM CLARK

Hockenheim is a circuit despised by purist and sentimentalist. As a racetrack it is bland and unexciting, but that can be forgiven. It replaced the majestic Nürburgring as the venue for the German Grand Prix, but even that can be excused, if resented. On April 7, 1968, however, it was the place where Jim Clark lost his life. And that damns it.

When Jim Clark died, shock waves rocked motor racing to its core. He was revered everywhere as the world's greatest driver. He was the best of his generation—perhaps of all time. His death frightened many of his colleagues because it confronted them with a simple reality: if it could happen to Jimmy. . . .They regarded him as their leader, inviolate and faultless. It was inconceivable that he had made a mistake. And soon it was clear that he had not. A mechanical failure had put his Formula Two car out of control at 150 mph. In 1968, there were no crash barriers at Hockenheim, and the Lotus pitched into the trees.

In remembering Jim Clark and the life he led, it is easy to believe that the passing of the years has embellished his legend. In truth, however, this is quite impossible. Clark put a stamp on his era, the sixties, in a manner which had never been emulated.

He never intended to become a racing driver. His family farmed in the lowlands of Berwickshire, and that was something Jim never put behind him, not even when he was World Champion. In this lies the key to the man, for in essence Clark was one man who achieved greatness but never changed. He did acquire a little surface confidence and polish, but basically he remained the same quiet person despite all the adoration.

After one or two rallies in Scotland, he drifted into club racing, and initially his aspirations went no further than that. He enjoyed racing, thought it was fun, and he seemed to have an aptitude for it. Colin Chapman of Lotus saw in him rather more, and Jimmy, slightly bewildered, found himself propelled swiftly into the big time. In 1960 he became a member of Chapman's Formula One team. In 1962 he led it—a position he held until the day he died.

Clark and Chapman complemented each other perfectly. Together, both were growing in the sport, although, for a long time, Jim was uncertain of his ambitions. For Chapman there were no such doubts. He had a brilliant and original mind, constantly broke new ground in racing car design, and it was his great good fortune to have Clark develop alongside him.

After Stirling Moss's enforced retirement in 1962, Jim immediately took over as the yardstick by which others were judged. He should have been World Champion that year, but the speed of the Lotus 25 was exceeded only by its unreliability.

In 1963 Clark won seven Grands Prix, a record that stands to this day, and won the championship by a country mile. Everyone had seen it coming. Infinitely more of a surprise was his success in a new Lotus venture. Colin Chapman had built cars for the Indianapolis 500, and these were similar in concept to his Formula One designs. Jim was nominated as one of the drivers.

Indy then was truly the race time forgot. It was still the sacred province of the front-engined roadsters, big, clumsy, and dramatic. When the Lotuses made their first appearance at the track they were greeted with incredulous laughter, which evaporated swiftly when Clark finished second in the race.

The following year, Jim retired from the 500 while leading, but in 1965 everything came together perfectly. He and the Lotus dominated from beginning to end. The hard-nosed men of USAC developed infinite respect for Clark, and there remains an affection for him felt for no other European.

Clark's entire character changed when he got into a racing car. Outside of it, he was a nervous man, never entirely sure of himself even when his face was familiar throughout the world. He chewed his nails constantly, was embarrassed at being pushed through V.I.P. lounges in airports, and positively shrank from making speeches. Usually he was courteous and polite. His love of motor racing was genuine and unstrained. Money was a secondary factor. He would have detested the sport as it is today, with commercialism rampant.

When Jim went into Grand Prix racing, he believed he had his priorities clear in his mind. He would race for three or four years and then return permanently to the farm at Chirnside. Many of his friends believed he would retire at the end of 1965, a year which brought him his second World Championship, as well as that celebrated victory at Indianapolis. They believed he would marry his longtime girl friend, but as it turned out it was that relationship which ended, the racing which was consolidated.

In 1967, because of Britain's punitive tax laws, Clark decided to leave his beloved Scotland for a year, and he moved into an apartment in Paris. He seemed more committed to racing than ever, undertaking a full season of Formula One for Lotus as well as sundry other events which took his fancy. Jimmy had a love of driving—just being in control of a car—which never left him, and often he would take his own Lotus Elan to the continental Grands Prix for the pleasure of the journey.

That 1967 season, his last, saw him at his greatest. Chapman had provided him with the Lotus 49, powered by the then new Cosworth DFV engine. Although the 1.5-litre Formula One days had provided him with his greatest triumphs, Jim revelled in the power and drama of the new 3-litre formula. In initial form the Lotus 49 was a difficult car, but Clark took it to four Grand Prix wins in 1967. He also won the 1968 season opener, in South Africa. That was his last Grand Prix.

Jimmy's sheer superiority was hard to believe. So many times he would finish the first lap two hundred yards clear of the field, leaving others to squabble over second place. Sometimes it seemed that he did not merely win races; rather that the competition surrendered to him in the seconds immediately after the start. And afterwards came what for him was the difficult part—the interviews and press conferences. Today, many years later, motor racing still sorely misses him.

JUAN MANUEL FANGIO

Jackie Stewart put his finger on it when he said, "You can be in a room full of racing personalities, World Champions and so on, and then Fangio comes in. All eyes turn towards him, and everyone else is forgotten."

It is undeniable that this great Argentine has an arresting presence. His steel-blue eyes, in particular, have an hypnotic effect. The sheer charisma of Fangio, however, comes not from an extrovert personality—he is a quiet and gracious man—but from what he has done. Born in 1911, he is motor racing's *grand seigneur*.

Mark Twain's celebrated line about "lies, damned lies, and statistics" has a certain validity in motor racing, as in anything else. But although the record book rarely tells the whole story, Fangio's achievements are so weighty as to be impressive in themselves. Consider this: he won the World Championship five times in eight years; he took part in fifty-one Grands Prix and won twenty-four of them; he started from pole position in twenty-seven. No other driver in history is even close.

Fangio was born in Balcarce. His family was a happy one, but extremely poor. From childhood he wanted to race cars, and after working as a mechanic he began to build makeshift "specials" for local races. These early races were successful, and by the late 1930s Fangio was very much a star of South American racing. Always he dreamed of moving to Europe, but the war years effectively prevented that.

It was 1949 before he was able to go abroad and begin his Grand Prix career, and he was already thirty-eight years old. But Fangio's intrinsic genius in a racing car soon attracted attention, and by 1950 he was a member, the fastest member, of the Alfa Romeo factory team.

Fangio finished that season as a close runner-up in the World Championship to his team-mate Giuseppe Farina, but the following year he won the title after a fierce battle with Alberto Ascari of the Ferrari team. At the end of 1951, however, Alfa Romeo made a sudden and unexpected decision to quit Grand Prix racing, and Fangio was left without a regular ride for 1952.

Throughout that season, the Argentine—the reigning World Champion—failed to score a single championship point. Worse than that, he finished it in hospital, his neck broken in an appalling accident at the Italian Grand Prix. But he recovered, and his skills were clearly unimpaired. Driving for Maserati throughout 1953, he was second in the championship to the redoubtable Ascari. And he could be certain that better times lay ahead. Mercedes-Benz were to make a return in 1954 and Fangio had been asked to lead the team. He would win ten of the next thirteen Grands Prix.

Those two years with Mercedes added up to the most complete domination of Grand Prix racing imaginable. The W196 cars enjoyed an undeniable technical superiority, and that, allied to the skills of the world's greatest driver, gave the races a farcical quality, each result a foregone conclusion. But the Germans, pragmatic to the end, withdrew at the end of 1955. Sales of the road cars, waning before the Grand Prix comeback, now flourished again. The Mercedes image had been rejuvenated.

Fangio went to Ferrari for the first and only time in his life. The 1956 season was not one he enjoyed, but it brought a fourth World title. He hated the politics endemic in the Scuderia Ferrari, and gave no thought to staying with the team for 1957. Instead, he accepted an offer from Maserati, and the scene was set for his greatest, most memorable year.

At Fangio's disposal was that most elegant of all racing cars, the lightweight 250F. That car was made for an artist. It matched itself to Fangio's greatness, as the Lancia-Ferrari of 1956 had stubbornly refused to do. It had not the power of the Vanwalls, the sheer straight-line speed, but through the corners Fangio could bend it precisely to his will. Winning with it was sometimes so easy that opposite-lock power slides replaced the classic drift as the maestro indulged himself.

Having dominated the first half of the 1957 Grand Prix season, Fangio was obviously heading for his fifth World Championship, but the speed of the Vanwalls was beginning to assert itself. In August,

the British cars were off form at the Nürburgring, but Ferrari, during a lacklustre period, made something of a comeback, with Mike Hawthorn and Peter Collins running second and third, behind "the old man". When Fangio came in for fuel the two Englishmen moved ahead and the result seemed settled.

The closing laps of that race defy description. Fangio constantly broke the lap record as he moved in to menace the Ferraris. There was no denying him. In the dying minutes he took back the lead, winning finally by three seconds. No one had ever seen a drive like that. He had set the fastest time during practice, yet he put in a lap near the end of the race eleven seconds faster! It was his greatest victory and proved to be his last. Vanwall took the remaining races of 1957, but Fangio's points total was unapproachable. By now he was forty-six years old, yet unquestionably still the best. And that, he decided, was the perfect time to stop. After a handful of events in 1958, he announced that he would race no more.

As a racing driver, Fangio was a proud man, but never arrogant. With a superiority as blatant as his, there was no need to shout. His

manners were as refined as his driving. As a competitor he was necessarily ruthless, but he was never callous. He was revered by his contemporaries, none of whom ever presumed to question his place on the pedestal.

Fangio's greatest strength lay in his freakish concentration. At Monaco, in 1950, his Alfa Romeo led the first lap. Behind him, at the blind Virage Tabac, there was a multiple accident, the track was blocked by wrecked cars. Driving at the limit on his second lap, Fangio came out of the chicane and on down to Tabac, scene of the carnage, all of it out of his sight. Disaster seemed imminent, yet, unaccountably, the Alfa slowed to a crawl, and threaded its way through the devastation. What sixth sense had made him ease off? "No sixth sense," he said. "I came out of the chicane, and there was something different in the colour of the crowd. I was leading the race, but they weren't watching me. Instead of seeing their faces, I was seeing the backs of their heads. Obviously, something had happened down the road to hold their attention. . . ."

Juan Manuel Fangio was one of a kind.

EMERSON FITTIPALDI

Emerson Fittipaldi was still a few months away from his twenty-eighth birthday when he clinched his second World Championship in 1974. It was the first year of his contract with the McLaren team. The following season belonged to Niki Lauda and Ferrari, but Emerson, still with McLaren, took a comfortable second place. His record was phenomenal. In his first five Grand Prix seasons his positions in the World Championship standings had been sixth, first, second, first, second. And then he threw it all away, sparking off one of the great unheralded tragedies of modern motor racing. Since the beginning of 1976, Emerson Fittipaldi, with all his wondrous talent, has been a bit player.

He was born in São Paulo, that sprawling, unlovely, Brazilian city which has the magnificent Interlagos circuit at its outskirts. Fittipaldi did not, however, come from the shanty town areas, but from a prosperous quarter. His father was—and still is—a prominent motor racing journalist and broadcaster, and there was a certain inevitability that Emerson would drift in the direction of the sport. As a young teenager he raced karts with great success, and early outings in local club races indicated an unusual ability. By the time he came to England, in 1969, he was already a highly accomplished driver.

In a short time Fittipaldi was the dominant force in Formula Ford, that most cutthroat of junior formulae, and he swiftly progressed to Formula Three, and then Formula Two. The string of his success was unbroken. Grand Prix team managers took note.

Eighteen months after leaving Brazil, Emerson entered Formula One, making his debut at the British Grand Prix in 1970, at the wheel of a factory Lotus 49. In his second race, in Germany, he finished fourth. All the team managers—other than Colin Chapman—cursed and wished they had acted sooner.

Chapman's regular drivers at that time were Jochen Rindt and John Miles. The magnificent Austrian was into his greatest season, winning race upon race, but Miles's first season of Formula One was proving a disappointment. Rindt and Fittipaldi looked like a strong pairing for 1971.

At Monza, in September, everything changed. Emerson had his first big accident there, during practice. Unhurt but shaken, he was preparing to go out again when silence descended on Monza Parco. Soon word filtered back to the pits that Rindt had crashed, and later it became known that he had died soon after being taken from the wreckage. The entire Lotus team was withdrawn from the race, and Miles, shattered by Jochen's death, did not drive for Chapman again. Emerson Fittipaldi, after only three Grands Prix, was suddenly the Lotus number one.

One month later, at Watkins Glen, after a consistent and canny race, Fittipaldi assumed the lead in the American Grand Prix when Pedro Rodriguez pitted for fuel with ten laps to go. It was Emerson's fifth Grand Prix and it brought him victory. From the depths of their lingering despair, Lotus team members were revitalized. Great things were forecast for 1971.

As so often happens in racing, however, the wine took a little longer to mature than expected. The basic quality was indisputably there, but it needed another year or so to come to greatness. There were flashes of brilliance from Fittipaldi in 1971, but no victories. A bad road accident, in which his wife, Maria Helena, was severely injured, took its toll of his confidence.

By the beginning of 1972, however, Emerson was ready. He drove a completely revamped Lotus 72 and during that year Jackie Stewart proved to be his only competition. With five wins and many other places, his World Championship points total proved unbeatable. Hardened, cynical observers began to talk of him in terms of Jimmy Clark. Lotus took the Constructors' Championship, and every one of their points was earned by Fittipaldi.

Ronnie Peterson joined Emerson in the Lotus team for 1973, and soon it became clear that the Swede, while less reliable than Fittipaldi, was indisputably quicker. Emerson finished the year with three more points than his team-mate, but Ronnie was obviously the man in favour at the season's end. And so Fittipaldi moved on to McLaren.

His relationship with the people at McLaren was always excellent, and they could have asked little more of him during his two years with them. Therefore, they—along with everyone else in motor racing—were almost incredulous when, at the end of 1975, Emerson announced that he was on the move again. Throughout that season there had been on the starting grids a Brazilian-built Grand Prix car, driven by Emerson's older brother, Wilson. The project had been a disaster, for the car was totally uncompetitive and Wilson was a driver of no real consequence. There had been rumours from the outset of the Copersucar-Fittipaldi venture that ultimately Emerson would take over as driver, but no one expected it yet.

It was the end of Fittipaldi as a serious contender. Each succeeding season brought a new car, each as relatively uncompetitive as the last. Those who remembered Emerson's great years looked on sorrowfully as this immense talent went to waste, squandered on machinery unworthy of his name and his abilities.

Fittipaldi's greatness as a driver was clearly defined in his years with Lotus and McLaren. He was always a popular man, gracious, courteous, and modest, but the true stature of Fittipaldi the man has become yet more evident during his years of adversity. Being beaten regularly by drivers with a fraction of his ability would have made a lesser man angry and bitter, quick to blame the inadequacies of his car for a series of lamentable results. But Emerson is a gentleman, preferring to leave those things unsaid. Unknown are the things he might have achieved had he put patriotism and family loyalty behind his personal ambitions.

A. J. FOYT

As far as anyone knows, A.J. Foyt has never so much as sat in a Grand Prix car, but the sheer weight of this man's achievements dictates that he be an automatic choice for inclusion in any list of great postwar drivers.

He is a bullish man, with a huge chest and broad shoulders, and his personality matches his build. There is nothing reticent about A.J. Foyt. In every era of every type of motor racing, there is just one person who has that intangible something to which the public—sometimes in spite of itself—clings. Stirling Moss has it; NASCAR driver Richard Petty has it. In USAC oval racing, Foyt has it. He can be quite devastatingly rude and loud-mouthed one day, positively awash with charm the next. He is The Man, and quite early in his long career he realized that. Over the years he has unashamedly used it.

There have been a great many years. Eisenhower was in the White House when Foyt first raced in the Indianapolis 500. It was 1958, Foyt was twenty-three and had been running in the minor leagues for some time. A month after Indy, he drove in a five-hundred-mile race at Monza. Also in the programme that day was Juan Fangio. A.J.'s pedigree, you see, is there. Men like that deserve respect, and Anthony Joseph makes sure he gets it.

When Foyt started, American championship racing was rough. Most of the races were run on dirt ovals. Car owners tended to be self-made men who hired and fired drivers with alacrity. You had to be good to keep your ride. It was a time of plenty—for some—in the United States, but the racing drivers of the time were not rich, pampered kids who had bought their way in. They had come from the bush leagues, from midgets and sprint cars. There were no sway bars on the cars, no trick fuel tanks. When a car hit a wall, it tended to explode. And fireproof clothing was in the future. Racing was a real macho business in those days.

The great drivers of the time had clawed their way up the tree and were not about to let go. Few earned a living from racing. In the winter months many worked as truck drivers or garage mechanics. The signs of a racing driver then were oil under the fingernails and peppery language rather than the Gucci loafers and public relations clichés of today.

Foyt has never forgotten those beginnings. There may be alligator shoes on his feet and an expensive hair-weave under his helmet, but when A.J. is dissatisfied with his crew or in battle with officialdom the whole pit lane knows about it. Foyt in full spate is a fearsome sight and the atmosphere is suddenly redolent of a sprint car night in Salem or Williams Grove twenty years earlier. And, likely as not, his clenched fists will be oil-stained, for Foyt is a man who pitches in with his mechanics, and probably knows more about engines than most of them.

Everything Foyt has he has earned. And he has a lot. He comes, appropriately perhaps, from Texas, and Houston carries frequent reminders of his success: real-estate businesses here, Chevrolet dealerships there, a stud farm out of town. Yet now, with all his original colleagues long retired or dead, he races still. Through all the fights, injuries, rages, and triumphs, his love for the sheer business of driving racing cars remains as pure as ever. Why else would he continue? His record looks unassailable, his future is financially secure.

Above all, Foyt's name is wedded to the Indianapolis Motor Speedway. He had driven in the 500 more than twenty times, the only man in history with four Indy wins to his credit. It is something to finish at the Brickyard, but Foyt has placed in the first ten on thirteen occasions. Statistically, his championship record stands alone.

Oval racing has changed enormously in twenty years. Colin Chapman and Jimmy Clark revolutionized it when they took their Lotus to Indianapolis in 1963. Their intrusion was resented by many of the old guard, but Foyt soon realized that, like it or not, the roadsters were now a thing of the past. He did not pretend to like the little rear-engined cars at first, but recognized that he had to have one. Many roadster drivers could not unlearn the habits of a racing lifetime and retired in bitterness. A talent like Foyt's, however, coped with it easily. In 1965, the first year he ran "one of them funny cars" at

Indianapolis, he placed in pole position. Two years later, in one of his own cars, a Coyote, he scored his third win.

Ten days after that 1967 victory, A.J. was in France for the Le Mans 24 Hours. Ford were committed to beating Ferrari and to this end had entered a great many cars, crewed by a goodly selection of the world's best drivers. It was a classic piece of Detroit overkill. Hardly subtle, but ultimately the policy prevailed.

Foyt was paired with Dan Gurney, and their red, 7-litre, Ford Mk IV led virtually the whole way. It was Foyt's only drive at the Sarthe, and it gave him immense satisfaction. Europe had plundered the hinterland of Indianapolis, but he had done something to redress the balance.

It is nothing less than tragic that Foyt never got into a Formula One car. He now acknowledges this himself. A talent like his would have come through anywhere, although it is doubtful that his personality could have tolerated the constraints of the European public relations machine.

Foyt's versatility in a race car is remarkable. Although he gave up running the sprinters long ago, many consider him to be the greatest driver on dirt there has ever been. In NASCAR stock car racing, too, his success has been remarkable. He has won the prestigious Daytona 500, and is deeply respected by the men of the South.

When you speak of Foyt, you speak of an institution in American automobile racing. He is a man who says what he thinks without necessarily thinking before he says it. He is a man whose mere presence can put thousands on the gate, and who inspires fanatical loyalty from his fans. His temper, ferocious off the track, is unfailingly in check when he drives. Rivals say he is hard, but strictly fair. Some like him, others do not. But no one quarrels about his stature as a racing driver.

THE DRIVERS
DAN GURNEY

In April 1968 most of the world's Grand Prix drivers made a sorrowful journey to Chirnside, in Berwickshire, to attend the funeral of the great Jimmy Clark. Among their number was Dan Gurney, who had travelled from California. Like so many of his contemporaries, Gurney had revered Clark, as a driver and as a man.

After the funeral Dan talked with Jim's parents. "You know, Dan," said Mrs. Clark, "you were the only one Jim ever worried about." In its way, this was the ultimate accolade. And Gurney, a man of great sensibility and compassion, almost broke down.

Those few words put this lanky American's status into perspective more clearly than anything else ever said or written about him. The stark facts of history will not substantiate them, for Dan Gurney's career—in terms only of results—has been eclipsed by many men with but a fraction of his talent. History books pay no heed to a racing driver's sheer class, and Gurney had ability to throw away.

His arrival in the upper strata of motor racing was nothing less then meteoric. The beginnings of a lifelong obsession began when his father, an opera singer, retired and moved the family from New York to California. Here was the heart of America's sporty car set, and the Gurney family moved to the Los Angeles suburb of Riverside, which later became famous as the site of a great road circuit.

Dan raced for the first time in 1955 with a Triumph TR2, which he later traded in for a Porsche. By 1957 he was racing Ferraris for wealthy American sportsmen, and two years later he was a member of the Ferrari factory team, living in Europe, driving both sports and Grand Prix cars for the Commendatore. His Formula One debut, at the 1959 French Grand Prix, came less than four years after his first race. Short on experience, Gurney nonetheless had a splendid opening season, finishing second, third, and fourth in three of his four Ferrari Grand Prix drives, and retiring in the other.

Enzo Ferrari was eager that Dan should stay on for 1960, but a Maranello contract excluded driving for anyone else, and Gurney was reluctant to accept such restrictions. Instead, he moved to BRM—and disaster. The 1960 season brought not a single championship point, although Dan was quick enough to put the recalcitrant car on the pole at the demanding street circuit of Oporto. Worse by far, however, than the lack of success was an accident in the Dutch Grand Prix. Gurney's brakes failed at the end of the pit straight and the BRM went off the road, killing one spectator and injuring others.

Dan's only success in a desperate season was a victory, with Stirling Moss, in the Nürburgring 1000-kilometre sports car race. For 1961, the first year of the 1.5-litre Formula One, he moved to Porsche. Reims should have brought his first Grand Prix victory, but the German car was beaten on the line by the sheer power of Baghetti's Ferrari. He was also second at Monza and Watkins Glen, and finished third in the World Championship.

The elusive win finally came for Gurney at Rouen the following year, but it was to be Porsche's only Grand Prix victory. At the end of the season they withdrew from Formula One, and Dan went off to drive for Jack Brabham's new team. He remained with Brabham for three years, during which his ill-luck became legendary. There were a couple of wins—at Rouen and Mexico in 1964—but there should have been many more. Gurney was the main competition for Jimmy Clark and Lotus, but the American was let down constantly by his car's unreliability. The 1964 Belgian Grand Prix, for example, was totally dominated by Gurney. In the pole position by two full seconds, he led from the start, left the others behind to fight over second place. Right at the end, however, the Brabham spluttered to a halt out on the circuit. The fuel tank was dry.

By 1965 Dan had decided to take the big step: he would become a constructor himself. Throughout his career Gurney had always been an active racing driver, eager to drive all kinds of car as often as his schedule permitted. Every year he drove a NASCAR stock car in the season opener at Riverside, and usually he won. It was Dan who persuaded Colin Chapman to build cars for Indianapolis, where he had again proved himself as quick as any. He was prominent, too, as a sports car driver.

Then, as 1966 approached, he made up his mind to build his own cars, for Grand Prix racing and for Indianapolis. It was an ambitious programme, and his friends questioned the wisdom of it. If Gurney had a fault, it was that he tended to meddle too much. Like Stirling Moss and John Surtees, he had a compulsion to make modifications to his cars in the search for that extra tenth. Quite often this inability to leave well alone cost these men dear. None of them was able to accept that his own ability was enough to give him that tenth—and more. Now, Gurney believed, running his own team, he would have a free hand in this area.

The 1966 season was a total disaster for Dan and his Eagles. At Indianapolis he was eliminated in a multiple accident at the start.

And his Grand Prix season was blighted because the new Weslake V-12 engine was a long time coming. The Eagle ran with an old Climax engine, by then hopelessly underpowered. But Gurney was encouraged by the car's excellent handling, and was confident that all would be well when the new engine was developed.

At first it seemed that he had been right all along. The Eagle-Weslake won its first race of 1967, the Race of Champions at Brands Hatch, and later scored a superb victory in the Belgian Grand Prix at Spa. Gurney always excelled on the classic circuits, where driver ability is all. At the Nürburgring he led most of the way, but the car failed. And that was really the story of the season. Spa apart, Dan's only other championship points came from a third place in Canada. Everywhere else the Eagle retired—after a few swift laps. But there was some consolation in an all-consuming win at Le Mans—the race which requires more luck than any other. Gurney and A.J. Foyt pounded their 7-litre Ford around the Sarthe for twenty-four hours, averaging over 135 mph, a record which may stand forever.

The Eagle was far less competitive in 1968, to the point that Gurney bought a McLaren for use late in the season. At the end of it he gave up the unequal struggle of trying to run teams on both sides of the Atlantic. The European operation was closed, and Dan decided to concentrate on America. At the end of 1970, now a successful builder of Indy cars, he announced his retirement as a driver.

Today Gurney is still in the business, still building racing cars. He has been through good and bad times—several of each—but his famous boyish grin is never far away. His sense of humour remains. He is one of the greatest men the sport has known and is much loved.

Dan Gurney was a racing driver who had a feel for the roots of motor racing. He truly loved it for its own sake and never looked upon it as a means to make a quick buck. To see his face as he watched a demonstration by Fangio was to look at an adoring schoolboy lost in admiration for his hero.

Early in 1980, at the age of forty-eight, Dan made a one-race return to motor racing, taking part once more in the NASCAR race at Riverside which he had so often dominated. After an absence of nearly ten years, he nevertheless ran in the first three—until he retired. He was a consummate racing driver, perhaps the greatest Grand Prix driver America has yet produced.

MIKE HAWTHORN

Mike Hawthorn was the crystallization of a type, the English sportsman of the fifties. Had he been born a few years earlier, he might have flown a smoky, battered Lancaster—struggling back to base after a night raid, landing it with crippled undercarriage, heading for the bar, ordering a beer, modestly shrugging off the whole experience.

As it was, Hawthorn missed World War II. Motor racing became his stage. He began in 1950 when he was twenty-one. It was a hobby, nothing more, and indeed it remained so for the duration of a splendid career. After only a couple of seasons in club racing, Mike got the opportunity to drive a new Formula Two Cooper-Bristol, and his performances led to the offer of a Ferrari contract for 1953.

In some ways Hawthorn's career was inevitably overshadowed by that of Stirling Moss. Contemporaries, they got along well enough, but were utterly dissimilar. Stirling, after all, was the first of the dedicated professionals, serious and committed. Motor racing was a passion for both, but for Mike it was never a profession, never something which mattered above all else. He drove racing cars because he was very good at it, enjoyed it, and revelled in the life style of the Grand Prix driver. In any generation, a Stirling Moss would tread the same path, but a Mike Hawthorn would have had no interest in the ascetic existence of the modern Formula One stars.

By the same token, a current Formula One team would never contemplate hiring a man like Hawthorn, a man who looked upon motor racing as just one of the good things of life. His attitude would be considered dangerously light-hearted and frivolous. Even in his day, allowances had to be made, for if he felt no enthusiasm for racing on a given day, he made no particular effort to hide the fact. Conversely, when his mood was right he was capable of performances quite beyond the scope of most men in the sport's history. On his day, he was the fastest driver in the world.

One of the many ironies of Hawthorn's racing life is that his name should be forever associated with Ferrari, for he was a patriot of the purest kind. But force of circumstance took him to Italy, since there was no viable British team in the early fifties. To be competitive, you needed a Ferrari. Better, Mike reasoned, to be at the front in a red car than at the back in a green one. . . .

Hawthorn's first season in the Commendatore's team also produced his first Grand Prix victory, and it came at the end of what many consider to be the most exciting race of all time. In the French Grand Prix, at Reims, a battle of incredible intensity developed between Mike's Ferrari and Juan Manuel Fangio's Maserati. Hawthorn was into a sudden-death play-off with the best there was, and he beat the great man by a few feet. *God Save the Queen* rang out across the champagne country; this was just a matter of days after the coronation of Queen Elizabeth II and the triumphant ascent of Everest. Optimism was alive and well. England had another new hero.

But perhaps the early days went just a little too well. For 1954 Mike stayed with Ferrari, and it was a year when everything went wrong for him. Mercedes-Benz returned to Grand Prix racing after an absence of twenty-five years, and all other cars were suddenly obsolete and outpaced. Early in the season Hawthorn was seriously burned in an accident at Syracuse, which put him out of racing for several weeks. Later he was the butt of a particularly vicious Fleet Street campaign, which accused him of evading his National Service, then compulsory in Britain. Hawthorn had actually been granted indefinite deferment because of a kidney ailment, but this was overlooked. In the midst of the drama, his father, always his most loyal supporter, was killed in a road accident. For Mike these were dark days, relieved in some degree by a late-season victory in the Spanish Grand Prix.

It would have been easy, understandable, to have felt nothing but contempt for a country which had treated him so shabbily, yet Hawthorn chose this moment to quit Ferrari for Vanwall, the British team then in its infancy. His patriotism was ill-rewarded, the car unreliable and slow. Moss, now with Mercedes, was raking up the successes, very much the man of the hour.

Hawthorn's solitary major triumph of 1955 came at Le Mans, where he won for Jaguar, but even this victory was clouded. There occurred at the Sarthe that year the most appalling disaster motor racing has known: Pierre Levegh's Mercedes flew into a spectator area and killed more than eighty people. Hawthorn was openly blamed for triggering the catastrophe, and there was more press vilification. Months later, an official enquiry completely exonerated him.

By 1956, a third English star was emerging to join Hawthorn and Moss. Peter Collins was a happy-go-lucky character whose motor racing motives squared precisely with those of Hawthorn, and the two men became close friends. But while Peter joined Ferrari, and Moss Maserati, Mike decided to keep the faith with the British and signed for BRM. Patriotism was costing him a great deal.

After yet another season in the wilderness, Hawthorn returned to Ferrari for 1957, but the cars were usually uncompetitive, and his season was memorable only for a wonderful drive at the Nürburgring where he was eventually beaten by an inspired Fangio.

He gave serious thought to retirement at the season's end, but eventually decided to renew his Ferrari contract. Throughout 1958 he scored only one victory—a dominant flag-to-flag affair at Reims—but constantly finished high in the points. The World Championship developed into a straight fight between Moss and himself, and was resolved only at the final race of the year, at Casablanca. Stirling won, but Mike finished second, and that was enough to give him the title by a single point. He was the first Englishman to win it.

And then he decided to stop. It was a good time. He had achieved his ambition, and the fun was ebbing. In August, at the Nürburgring, Peter Collins had crashed fatally a few yards in front of him. The month before, another Ferrari team-mate, Luigi Musso, had been killed at Reims. Casablanca had taken the life of Vanwall driver Stewart Lewis-Evans.

Mike had in mind to devote himself to the family garage business in Surrey, perhaps to get married, spend time with his friends, enjoy his beer and pipe, walks with his dog. Without any doubt he would have remained part of the motor racing scene, if not as a driver.

Only three months after clinching his World Championship, however, Hawthorn was killed in a road accident near Guildford. Driving the beloved 3.4 Jaguar which he had so often raced, he hit ice, went off the road and into a tree. He was twenty-nine years old.

Today Mike Hawthorn is remembered with great affection by all who knew him. And the countless thousands of his fans recall that handsome face, the blond hair, peaked cap, sports jacket, and the bow tie—which he always wore when racing.

THE DRIVERS
GRAHAM HILL

On a shivering morning, early in December of 1975, the small city of St. Albans was unusually crowded. Police directed traffic into emergency parking areas. Celebrities of every kind were among those there. Up the road, in the cathedral, all was in readiness for the funeral of Graham Hill.

He had died with several members of his team, including the brilliant young driver Tony Brise. Hill had been at the controls of his own light aircraft, returning on a freezing, foggy night from a test session in the winter sun at Paul Ricard. After a faulty approach to the small airfield at Elstree, the plane crashed in dreadful visibility on a nearby golf course—and was totally burned out.

It should have been no surprise that so many, famous or not, would wish to pay their final respects, for Graham Hill, racing driver, had always been enormously popular. His personality, however, had taken him beyond his own immediate sphere. He was held in affection by people who had never been near a race circuit. He was among the best-known British sportsmen of his time.

For a man with a highly dangerous job to die violently in some other way is always ironic, but it was particularly so in the case of Graham Hill. Four months earlier, at the age of forty-six, he had finally called a halt to his career as a Grand Prix driver. Years past his best, he had continued to race, to the great anxiety of his friends, who were fearful not only for his safety, but also for his reputation. Here, after all, had been one of the great drivers of all time, and it was with sadness that his supporters watched him struggling to qualify, running near the back of the field.

Hill himself never saw it that way. Driving racing cars, he argued, was reward in itself, his main passion in life. He had always enjoyed it for its own sake, and winning, while desirable, was not essential.

It had not always been so. For most of Graham Hill's racing life he was a potential winner. He had succeeded as a Grand Prix driver through relentless effort and determination. With no family wealth to support his early endeavours, he had to work his passage into motor racing, offering his services as a mechanic in return for the chance of a drive. And this he did to good effect with Colin Chapman's newly born Lotus team in the mid-fifties. Eventually, in 1958, Chapman went into Formula One and Graham went with him, making his Grand Prix debut at Monte Carlo.

After two desultory seasons with unreliable and uncompetitive cars, Hill snapped up an offer to join BRM for 1960. It was the beginning of an association which would last for seven years.

If Jimmy Clark stood head and shoulders clear of the rest in the early sixties, Graham was invariably his closest rival. Time after time, these two finished first and second in Grands Prix across the world, but Hill's party piece was always the Monaco Grand Prix, a race which Clark was never able to win. Graham came close in 1962—the year of his first World Championship—but retired a few laps from the end when he was leading comfortably. Thereafter he reeled off a hat trick in the principality, and the last of these wins, in 1965, was especially remarkable.

From the pole Hill led the first twenty-four laps before being forced down the escape road by a back marker. The BRM's engine stalled, but Graham leaped out, pushed the car back up the road, jumped in again and rejoined the race, now far back in fifth place. At his magnificent best, he shattered the lap record repeatedly to catch and pass those ahead. It was a famous victory, devalued only slightly by the absence of Clark, who was away winning the Indianapolis 500. The following year it was Hill's turn to win at the Brickyard.

During 1966 Graham remained with BRM, but in that first year of the 3-litre Formula One the cars were uncompetitive. As well as that, he felt a need to change teams "for the sake of it". It was an astonished racing world, therefore, which awoke one morning to the news that Hill was returning to Lotus, as team-mate to Clark.

In 1967, Colin Chapman's new 49 had a colossal power advantage over its rivals, for Lotus alone had the use of the new Cosworth DFV engine. Clark took the car to four wins, but Hill's season was a chapter of retirements.

The following year, every aspect of Hill's strong character was called into play. In April 1968 Clark was killed at Hockenheim, leaving Lotus personnel distraught and bewildered. Two weeks later, in the midst of the tragedy, Graham won the Spanish Grand Prix. Days later, Mike Spence lost his life in a factory Lotus at Indianapolis, and soon afterwards Hill took another victory at Monte Carlo. In talking of those dark days, Colin Chapman has frequently paid tribute to Graham's courage and incalculable contribution to team morale.

Together they went on to the World Championship that year, Hill clinching it—as he had in 1962—by winning the final, deciding race. Everyone rejoiced.

In 1969, there was another Monaco win—the fifth—but this time it was lucky. During the season Hill was generally outpaced by his new team-mate Jochen Rindt, but far more serious was a dreadful accident at Watkins Glen, in which he badly broke both his legs. He was forty now, and it might have been a good time to stop. But he gritted his teeth once more, recovered, and returned to drive for Rob Walker's private team, finishing fifth in his comeback race at Kyalami.

The following year Graham drove for the Brabham team, and briefly enjoyed an Indian summer, winning the International Trophy at Silverstone and running quite competitively elsewhere. But he was no longer quite on the pace, and when the team dropped him at the end of 1972 many people thought—and hoped—that he would quit. That season he had added to his record victory in the Le Mans 24 Hours, driving a Matra. The World Championship, Indianapolis, Le Mans. No one else has ever put together those three.

Instead of retiring, however, Hill formed his own team, the Embassy-Hill Racing Team. The last two seasons of his career were something of a sad embarrassment to all who had seen him at his peak. Especially poignant was the sight of him climbing from the car after practice at Monaco in 1975, having failed to qualify in this, his race. He never drove again, formally announcing his retirement at the British Grand Prix. Everyone was glad to see it, glad that he had survived, glad that he would remain in the sport running a car for young Brise. One phase of his motor racing career was over, another just beginning. And then came the tragedy.

After his death, perhaps the eulogies were a little too bland. Certainly he had been a superb racing driver, brave and resilient and determined; certainly he had been a wonderful ambassador for his sport and his country; certainly he had worked strenuously for a variety of charities, had a great sense of humour, could be patient and kind. But his charm could be switched on and off. He could be crushingly rude.

Graham always knew what he wanted, and he had to fight harder than most to get it. The perpetual myth that he charmed his way to the World Championship sells him short. If his stubbornness was sometimes unattractive, it was also precisely what made him the driver he was.

PHIL HILL

He was a racing driver in spite of himself. Outside a car, Phil Hill was an introspective, nervous man. Before a Grand Prix he would pace up and down, chain-smoking, like a man on death row. But put him in a racing car, and the nerves disappeared, his style became easy and composed and confident. He was one of those who excelled at the un-yielding circuits—Spa and the Nürburgring, places like that. And he was exceptional, too, in poor conditions. Give him rain and murk and he would conquer it.

Hill never really understood the motivation for his racing career. After a prosperous, if unsettled, childhood in California he developed a true love of cars (a trait by no means universal among racing drivers). He was fascinated by cars, learned about them. And then he began to drive them—fast.

Early outings in amateur sports car races revealed a diamond talent, but it was rough and heedless and needed polishing. Soon Phil became smoother, and he then rapidly became the best road racing driver in America. A Jaguar XK120 gave way to a succession of Ferraris, owned by various wealthy sportsmen.

Phil Hill came to Europe in 1955, invited by Enzo Ferrari to drive for the Ferrari factory sports car team. The first race on his schedule was the tragic Le Mans 24 Hours, in which eighty people, the majority spectators, lost their lives. Witnessing that catastrophe was almost enough to send him back to the United States, to forget the whole thing. But he stayed, and won many long-distance races for the Scuderia.

At Le Mans, in 1958, he scored a memorable victory in atrocious weather, driving for most of the night when the rain was at its most pitiless. Hill, faultless, threaded the Ferrari Testa Rossa through the floods and accidents. His co-driver on that occasion was Olivier Gendebien. It was the beginning of the most successful sports car partnership in racing history.

For Hill, however, the goal was Formula One. For some time he had tried to persuade Ferrari to give him a Grand Prix drive, but the Commendatore had Mike Hawthorn, Peter Collins, and Luigi Musso for his three-car team. Phil, in desperation, accepted a ride for the French Grand Prix in an old Maserati. That day, at Reims, Musso was killed and Hill was the logical replacement for the number three Ferrari car, but it went instead to Wolfgang von Trips. A month later, in the German Grand Prix, Collins lost his life, and in those dreadful circumstances Hill was finally promoted.

Hill's debut for the Formula One team, at Monza, was sensational. For much of the way he led, a pit stop dropping him to third. In the last race of the year, at Casablanca he selflessly handed over second place to Hawthorn, thereby allowing the Englishman to win the World Championship.

Throughout 1959, Hill was a permanent member of Ferrari's Formula One Team. There were no wins, but he was usually well in contention, and in 1960 he was *numero uno* at Maranello. By now, the front-engined cars were outclassed on all but the very quick circuits. Phil nonetheless put in some phenomenal drives, winning the Italian Grand Prix at the end of the year.

The victory at Monza, however, was not altogether satisfactory, for the race had been boycotted by the British teams on safety grounds. But Hill's time came in 1961, the first year on the 1.5-litre Formula One. Ferrari were the top of the field with only Phil and his team-mate, von Trips, in serious contention for the World Championship.

Hill clinched the title on a most sorrowful day. The crucial race was Monza, and again he won. But von Trips was killed early in the race. There began for the American a period of self-examination. He had, after all, fulfilled his dream. And all around him there was pressure from friends that now was the time to quit.

Phil, however, was firmly wedded to his way of life—willingly or not. He had grown accustomed to the ways of Italy, where he could indulge his passion for music and could frequently go to La Scala in Milan. While he had wanted that title for itself, he heartily detested all the attendant trappings of glory and would run from formal functions and parties. But he was not through with racing.

For 1962 he remained with Ferrari, the team complacent after the triumphs of the previous season. It was a dismal year, and at the end of it Hill finally severed his ties with the team. For a long time the internal politics had gnawed at him and when he was blamed for the deficiencies of the machinery he knew that it was time to move. Rarely, however, do a driver's fortunes take an upward turn when he forsakes Ferrari for another team. And so it was with Hill. Two desultory years, with ATS and Cooper, followed, but he gave up Formula One at the end of 1964 to concentrate once more on sports car racing with Ford and Chaparral.

After winning the BOAC 500 in 1967, Hill returned to the United States for good. There was no formal announcement of retirement. He slipped comfortably back into California life, devoting himself to the restoration of old cars. He got married, relaxed, enjoyed himself. Today, in his fifties, he can still drive as fast as most when the mood takes him. He is a man with lots of things in his life. He is gentle, yet acutely perceptive. It is doubtful that anyone more intelligent has ever sat in a racing car.

Hill says that, given his time over again, he would never be a racing driver, and it is stretching credibility too far to suggest that a career second time around could be as satisfactory. In nearly twenty years of racing, he won a World Championship, the Le Mans 24 Hours three times, and countless other races—and he was never once hurt. No one can reasonably ask more than that.

JAMES HUNT

James Hunt was the *enfant terrible* of the seventies. He arrived in Grand Prix racing when the sport was undergoing a transformation. The reign of Jackie Stewart was coming to a triumphant close and there was no heir apparent. Hunt never assumed the Scot's position as a racing driver, but for a time his public appeal was enormous.

He is a complex individual, a man of surprises. Capable of consummate charm, he was nevertheless occasionally incredibly boorish during his racing career. Truth to tell, he did not deal well with pressure—although it rarely showed in his driving.

Hunt is an intelligent man, well aware of the dangers of driving racing cars. And he was brave enough to admit sometimes to being scared. Frequently, as the race drew near, he was physically sick. Often, he frankly acknowledged, he was loath to climb into the car. And his ability to conquer himself had to be admired, too, for there is no merit in apparent courage when it is actually an unawareness of risk.

Once aboard, however, all the doubts were past. James was among the best starters in the business, the type who always gains places in the first mile of the race. In a battle he was a hard man, occasionally quite ruthless, a committed racing driver with no sign of nerves.

The early part of Hunt's career was patchy, and he gained a reputation as one of the quickest men on the track—while he was on it. He won a lot of races and had a lot of accidents. And while many of his contemporaries in Formula Three moved on to higher things, it seemed that James would miss the big break so vital to those without bulging wallets. His public school background was very comfortable, but when it came to motor racing he was on his own.

The big break finally materialized in the portly shape of Lord Alexander Hesketh, an improbable young man with a great deal of money, an almost obsessive belief in Queen and Country, and a newly discovered passion for motor racing. James and His Lordship got along famously from the start, and when Alexander decided to go Grand Prix racing, first as an entrant then as a constructor, there was only one driver in his mind.

This new Formula One partnership came to fruition in 1973, making its debut at the Race of Champions with a rented Surtees, James finishing a worthy third. Thereafter, Alexander bought a new March, which the team progressively modified during the season. By midsummer it was clear that, despite the rather contrived hail-fellow-well-met atmosphere—which all the members of the team tried desperately to create and maintain—James Hunt and Hesketh Racing were becoming a real force. Sixth in France, they progressed to fourth in Britain, third in Holland, second in the United States. There were no wins in that first season, but it had been an impressive beginning.

Now Hesketh decided to go the whole route, to have his own cars built. In 1974, Hunt won the International Trophy at Silverstone in the Hesketh 308, but once again a Grand Prix victory eluded him. For that he had to wait another year. In the 1975 Dutch Grand Prix, James finally triumphed after a fierce challenge late in the race from Niki Lauda's Ferrari. Hunt and Lauda . . . their rivalry would later make headlines across the world.

At the end of 1975, Lord Alexander came to the conclusion that enough of the family fortune had been invested in motor racing. For three years the champagne had flowed unceasingly, but now Hunt had to find another employer. He went to work for Teddy Mayer, the diminutive American lawyer who had controlled McLaren Racing since Bruce's death in 1970.

The association was an immediate success. The 1976 season quickly shaped into a straight fight between Hunt and Lauda. The early races were dominated by the Austrian, but Hunt came into the picture more and more, his every move apparently dogged by controversy. In Spain he beat Lauda, but was afterwards disqualified because of a tiny technical infringement. At Brands Hatch, James once more finished ahead, but there was further drama. He had been

involved in an accident at the first corner, after which the race was stopped. Previously, in these circumstances drivers with damaged cars were out for the day, but the public was screaming for its hero, and James—with the others involved—was allowed into the restart. After winning superbly, he was disqualified once more.

The complexion of the 1976 season changed utterly at the Nürburgring, where Lauda had his terrible accident. Hunt won that race and then took the Dutch Grand Prix. And later, in its wisdom, the sport's governing body reinstated his victory in Spain.

Niki was back, incredibly, for Monza. He finished fourth, while James had an unnecessary accident with Tom Pryce. Three races remained, and Lauda had a fourteen-point lead in the championship.

It was then that the true courage and resilience of James Hunt was seen. He won magnificently in Canada and America, and dominated in Japan, finally finishing third after a tyre change. An unforgettable season was over. And Hunt—by a single point—was World Champion.

The following year brought three Grand Prix victories, but the McLaren team's brief spell at the top had come to an end. James stayed on for 1978, but there were no wins in sight, and he left at the end of the year to join Walter Wolf. The 1979 season, he said, would be his last, and so it proved. The car was uncompetitive, and Hunt, ever more mindful of the risks, abruptly retired after the Monaco Grand Prix, rich and safe.

Around the circuits his spirited, often inspired, driving is missed, but not so his occasional tantrums and self-important hangers-on. James himself brought a lot to the party.

march

Winners
Indy & World
Championship
1974 & 1976
McLAREN
RACING

Marlboro
11
GOOD YEAR

JACKY ICKX

One of motor racing's many clichés—and myths—is that Grand Prix drivers are all individualists. Since the early days of the sport, writers have advanced pretentious theories about why men race cars, delving into their life stories, pointing out their "significant" dislike of team games, their history of rebelliousness at school, their desire to stand on their own feet. Hemingway country, this, with the racing driver standing in for the matador.

Most of this theorizing is palpable nonsense. Far from being individualists, most racing drivers are essentially similar. Some cope better than others with the various problems of success and failure. Some are pleasant and some are not. Nearly all are obsessed by their profession, largely unaware of a wider world beyond Kyalami and Monza and Silverstone, the stages upon which they play. They could not be called, in general, a well-rounded bunch of people. Therefore, when a racing driver emerges who is truly different from his fellows, he is a man of unusual interest. And it is as such that the sport will remember Jacky Ickx.

Perhaps Ickx's background goes some way towards explaining the man. He was born in 1945, the son of a celebrated Belgian motoring journalist who appears to have had a most civilized attitude towards his family. Although motor racing was inevitably a part of Jacky's early upbringing, it had no particular attraction for him. When, at thirteen, he was taken by his father to Spa for the Belgian Grand Prix, he found it all a great bore, and begged to be taken home. Ten years later he was back at Spa, this time on the front row of the grid.

There was never any pressure on Ickx either to take up racing or to leave it alone, but because it had for so long been a part of his life, it was of no particular excitement or interest to him. When, having shown no enthusiasm for school work, he began to drift into motor racing, it seemed a natural thing to do. By the time he was twenty, it was clear that he had an extraordinary natural talent for it, allied to apparent fearlessness. And so it was that he emerged from the shadows of club racing and into the big time, with a shrug of the shoulders and an amused expression.

Ickx really shook the Grand Prix world in August of 1967 with a shattering performance at the Nürburgring. Short of Formula One entries, the German Grand Prix organizers accepted a few Formula Two cars to run concurrently, but in a separate class. Jacky therefore appeared with Ken Tyrrell's Matra, and qualified third overall with half the horsepower of a Grand Prix car. In the race itself, he ran fourth before retiring. Minutes earlier, Jackie Stewart, himself out of the running, had been down to the Tyrrell pit, begging Ken to slow Jacky down before he hurt himself.

A month later, Ickx made his Grand Prix debut at Monza in a Cooper-Maserati. And soon it was announced that he had signed a Ferrari contract for 1968. The year brought his first Grand Prix victory, in treacherous rain at Rouen. To the end of his career he maintained a reputation for being a stupendous wet weather driver.

By now Jacky was also establishing himself as perhaps the best sports car driver in the world, winning many races in 1968 with one of John Wyer's Ford GT40s. It was an association he was keen to continue, but a problem arose when Enzo Ferrari announced his intention to return to sports car racing for 1969. Ickx could not drive for the Commendatore in Formula One and against him in sports car races. So he left, signing a Grand Prix contract with Brabham.

Ickx was formidable in 1969, winning superbly the German and Canadian Grands Prix. But it is his drive at Le Mans that year for which he will always be remembered. In Wyer's GT40 he fought a running battle with Hans Herrmann's faster Porsche for two hours, finally taking the lead on the last lap to score the closest victory imaginable. In later years, he would win the 24-Hour Race three times more.

In 1970, he returned to Ferrari, winning in Austria, Canada, and Mexico. Jochen Rindt, his World Championship apparently secure, died at Monza, and there appeared, in the last three races, the

possibility that Ickx would snatch the title. It was, after all, his job to win races. After retiring at Watkins Glen, thereby losing his chance, Ickx wrote to Rindt's widow. By no means had the two men been friends, but Jacky said that he was glad not to have taken Jochen's title. Not a sentiment which would have come to all Grand Prix drivers.

After that season Ickx was never again a consistent winner in Formula One. He triumphed superbly against Pedro Rodriguez at Zandvoort in 1971, and was utterly in his own class at the Nürburgring the following year, but Ferrari could not consistently provide him with a competitive car. At the end of 1973, he left them to spend a desultory couple of seasons with Lotus, thereafter sliding into Formula One obscurity with Wolf, Ensign, and Ligier.

In a sports car, however, he remained the very best. After the Le Mans 24 Hours in 1980, however, he formally announced his retirement from motor racing, his dream of being the first man to win the event five times unfulfilled. But, twelve months later, Jacky was tempted back to Le Mans by Porsche—"only a fool never changes his mind"—and he led virtually throughout to take an emotional victory. Ickx left wonderful memories for all who saw him race. He was at his best on the classic "driver's circuits" like Spa and the Nürburgring, where his fluent, effortless style could be seen to advantage. He was an artist, a true individualist. The unsubtle technique required by ground-effects cars did not suit him. He loved the traditions of motor racing, despite his early lack of interest, and insisted on taking part in the last Targa Florio, in 1973.

Ickx was a racing driver, in the literal sense. Merely testing racing cars bored him. Between races, he preferred to stay at home, ride his horses, read, immerse himself in his collection of modern art. His gravelly voice and old-fashioned charm are much missed at the Grand Prix circuits of the world. "I don't want competition, actually," he once said. "I just drive as if I were alone on the track, and hope that it is faster than the others. For me, it is a real pleasure—but without excitement."

ALAN JONES

Alan Jones is the hard man of modern Grand Prix racing. Stockily built, he looks the part and drives the part. He can also act it with conviction. In 1980, he achieved his life's ambition and won the World Championship, due reward for years of sacrifice and struggle. Getting there was hard and he likes people to remember that.

At the root of Alan's motivation lies a genuine passion for motor racing. His father was a star of Australian racing in the fifties, a successful businessman and farmer who went to the circuits for sport. But Alan's aspirations went higher than that. He wanted to go all the way, move to Europe, eventually get into Formula One. By the time he was seventeen he had won the Australian National Kart Championship, and early club racing successes indicated that he had a lot of talent.

Stan Jones was an enthusiastic supporter of his son's career and would doubtless have smoothed his path with financial backing, but unhappily a credit squeeze in Australia put him out of business in the mid-sixties. If Alan were to make it, he would have to do it alone. And today Jones believes that this served only to sharpen his ambition. Indeed, his only sadness is that his father, whom he revered, did not live to share his success.

In 1970, Alan came to England, virtually penniless, resolved to break into Formula Three, and this he somehow financed by constant wheeling and dealing in secondhand cars. But there was no overnight glory on the track. Jones gained a reputation for being steady and reliable. There were no signs of a World Champion in the making. Money was so tight that Alan simply could not take chances. And those days have instilled in him a healthy appreciation of his own worth. Team owners will tell you that Jones always goes for top dollar—and they will add that he gives back 100 per cent in effort and commitment.

The big break came in 1975 when Harry Stiller, for whom Alan had driven a Formula Atlantic car, decided to buy a Formula One Hesketh. He chose the gritty young Aussie to drive it. Suddenly Jones was where he wanted to be. His Grand Prix debut came at Barcelona, and a few weeks later he was invited to join Graham Hill's team.

His career was progressing well now, but still along familiar lines. He did not shake the Formula One world in the way of his Hill team-mate, Tony Brise (who died with Graham at the end of the year in the light aircraft disaster). He was "useful".

A flash of Jones's true potential was seen at Brands Hatch in 1976. Driving for John Surtees, he led the Race of Champions convincingly for a while, and eventually finished a good second to James Hunt. As the season progressed, however, his relationship with Surtees deteriorated, and the two men parted company at the end of it. That left Alan out on the street for 1977.

He picked up a ride, finally, in tragic circumstances. After the death of Tom Pryce at Kyalami, the Shadow team asked Jones to take his place. Their car of the time, the DN8, was hardly a front-runner, but Alan finished seventh in the championship with it, along the way scoring a superb first Grand Prix victory, a wet-dry affair at the Osterreichring where he beat Niki Lauda's Ferrari fair and square.

At the end of that season, it seemed that he would go to Ferrari for 1978, but the Italian team changed their minds and Jones signed instead with Frank Williams. It was the beginning of one of racing's great partnerships, although neither man anticipated it at the time.

Their first season together, 1978, was competitive but unreliable. Thereafter, the pieces fell into place, so that Alan Jones and the Williams FW07 became natural pacesetters, the usual favourites. Man and team had absolute faith in each other, and the circumstances produced victory upon victory. In 1980 they took the World Championship. Moreover, they did it in the best way, simply by winning more races than anyone else.

The hallmarks of Jones's driving are enormous aggression and supreme perspicacity. He runs hard all the time, freely admitting that he finds it difficult to throttle back even when the pressure is off. The strongest card in his hand, however, is unquestionably his stamina, an ability to sustain a daunting pace. On occasion it has enabled him to beat faster cars. Lap after lap he has sat there behind them, nibbling away at their advantage, wearing them down.

Success has brought great wealth. There are houses in California and Switzerland, a huge farm in Australia. Alan collects exotic road cars by the shoal, and he still enjoys dealing—now for its own sake. He is an unashamed materialist. But his father was a big spender who went broke, and Alan is determined that the same thing will not happen to him.

Like so many top drivers through the years, Jones can be truculent. Sometimes rude and offhand, he is nevertheless incredibly sensitive to criticism in the press. On another day, with the pressure off, he can be kind, helpful, extremely amusing. In a racing car, however, he is never moody. When the green light flashes, his is invariably the first car to move. In the initial dash from the line Jones's car can be seen darting through tiny gaps, firmly squeezing out those behind.

In the fight game they talk about "boxers" and "fighters". Jones is from the second group, a Marciano of the tracks. And Rocky, remember, retired undefeated.

Niki Lauda was never a sentimentalist. In the history of Grand Prix racing no man seemed to be more uncomplicated. When he answered questions or discussed his car his voice was clipped, brusque, utterly Germanic, unnerving, his comments sprinkled devastatingly with English swear words. The minute the conversation was over he was gone.

To the world in general, Lauda's name became news on the night of Sunday, August 1, 1976. Already he was champion of the world, but that meant little to the daily press. Now he lay in a German hospital, and he was not expected to live. Thirty-six hours later, a visiting priest gave him the last rites. Five weeks after that Niki Lauda was back in the cockpit of his Ferrari, practising for the Italian Grand Prix at Monza, trying to cling to his dwindling World Championship lead.

Racing drivers regularly astonish the medical world with their speedy recuperative powers, but Lauda's performance in Italy that weekend bordered on the unbelievable. In the inferno of his Nürburgring accident he had suffered horrifying burns to his face, but the major problem had been the inhalation of poisonous fumes. Once his lungs had started to recover, there remained only the healing of his burns, for which skin grafts were required. Lauda ignored his doctors' advice, and, wearing a helmet large enough to accommodate his bandages, he raced at Monza. He finished fourth. By the end of the race, his scars had opened, soaking the bandages with blood.

The season did not have a fairy-tale ending for Niki, for he lost the World Championship by a single point, to James Hunt. Now, however, Lauda's name was known everywhere. People without the slightest interest in motor racing equated it with courage of a stupefying order.

Not only had Lauda returned to the profession which had so nearly killed him, he had gone back to a familiar world with dreadful scars, inevitably to face camera-bearing ghouls eager to capitalize on his disfigurement. Here Lauda's rigidly unsentimental approach to his life and job worked for him. He faced the problem of disfigurement because, he reasoned predictably, there was no alternative. Having resolved that in his own mind, he promptly forgot about it. If it made other people uncomfortable, well, that was their problem.

Before his accident, Niki Lauda had held sway in Grand Prix racing for almost two years. His arrival in the top echelons had been unconventional. He had bought his way in — and had done it successfully. He had never seriously doubted his ability to be a top Formula One driver, but chose the bankroll route to save time, borrowing the money from an Austrian bank, whose security was his life insurance policy. After two seasons of little success but ample promise with March and BRM, Lauda joined Ferrari for 1974.

Niki and the B3 should have won the title that year, but his comparative lack of experience — and a liberal dose of bad luck — cost him dear. Methodical and calculating, however, Lauda filed away his mistakes, and they were not repeated. The following year he displayed an overall superiority which made the World Championship almost a formality. He tested constantly at the team's Fiorano test track, improved the car all the time, and displayed no weaknesses at the races. It made a change when somebody else won.

History shows that back-to-back titles are virtually unknown in Grand Prix racing, particularly when the driver stays with the same team. Yet Lauda remained with Ferrari, and the pattern of victory continued unstemmed far into 1976. When he went to the Nürburgring for the ninth round of the championship, his results read: first, first, second, second, first, first, retired, first. He had sixty-one points at that stage; his nearest challenger, Jody Scheckter, had thirty.

The accident — inexplicable to this day — robbed him of the title that year, and also brought about a major change in his relationship with the Ferrari team. In truth, they had not expected Lauda to return so quickly, if ever, and took the precaution of hiring Carlos Reutemann to replace him. When Niki did come back, six weeks after the 'Ring, it caused great embarrassment. When he told them he wanted to stay for 1977, they were obliged, having signed Reutemann, to wave Clay Regazzoni, Lauda's longtime team-mate and friend, towards the door. And when Niki voluntarily quit the Japanese Grand Prix at the end of the year on safety grounds, he was roundly condemned in Italy for throwing away the championship, for being "a coward".

At the beginning of the following season, it was clear that Ferrari personnel were looking upon Reutemann, whom Lauda frankly detested, as *numero uno*. He was given the best of everything and started the year with better results than Lauda. Clearly the Austrian would have to play all the cards in his hand. When he was asked by an Italian journalist, "Do you regard Reutemann as a team-mate or rival this year?" his reply, accompanied by a withering expression, was, "Neither. . . ."

Lauda reasserted himself on the track, winning superbly in South Africa, and usually running well ahead of Reutemann thereafter. His goal for 1977 was to win back that World Championship, as much as anything to prove Ferrari wrong. He did that — and then left. It was a cold and clinical decision, Lauda at his purest. It might have been a logical time to retire, but Lauda went instead to Bernie Ecclestone's Brabham team. There he scored two controversial victories in 1978 and none at all in 1979. After the first practice session in the 1979 Canadian Grand Prix at Montreal, he stepped from his car and told Ecclestone he had decided to stop. There and then. The decision was entirely in character. Simply, he had no further use for racing. That compartment of his life was closed. From then on he would devote himself to building up his airline, to becoming, in his own words, "Austria's Freddie Laker".

Lauda's wicked sense of humour and usually overwhelming honesty are recalled with affection by the few who came to know him well, but mainly he is remembered with respect, for his silk-smooth driving style, his sheer efficiency in the environment of motor racing. He would work with a Grand Prix car, bring it up to its best, then match it with his own ability.

Those who disliked him did so probably because they were baffled by him. Who could understand the motivation of a man who, by his own admission, had no love of racing cars or their folklore, had made himself more than enough money for a lifetime, very nearly gave his life to the business, returned to it once again with raw wounds to win more prizes, more trophies, all of which he then gave away, dismissing them as "useless"? Lauda seemed to work hard at his anti-hero image, loved to deflate the *macho* concept of his job. Which is why, when you saw him privately struggle to remove helmet and bloody face-mask at Monza, you could only stand back and be awed by him.

STIRLING MOSS

Many of his fans were sad when Stirling Moss made a motor racing comeback in 1980. Until then, they had their memories of Moss, indisputably the greatest driver of the late fifties and early sixties, and believed by many to be the best of all time. At his peak—and that was a long plateau—his driving was virtually without flaw and always he was plainly quicker than the rest. It was that way until Easter Monday, 1962, when a crash at Goodwood ended his Grand Prix career. When he returned, eighteen years later, it was at the wheel of a saloon car, and for the purists that was akin to Margot Fonteyn dancing in a village hall.

For Stirling, however, it meant fun and a good deal of money. During his time at the top he always had the financial side of his career well under control, but there had been little time for the light-hearted existence enjoyed by most of his colleagues. While Mike Hawthorn and Peter Collins were at the bar, Stirling was asleep. He enjoyed a party as much as anyone, but there was a time and place for it. And if driving a racing car figured in his immediate plans, that came first. Moss was a dedicated professional. That was one of the reasons for his superiority.

He took up racing in 1948, won a number of Formula Three races, and immediately attracted attention. In a Jaguar he scored his first major victory, the Tourist Trophy, in 1950. He was still only twenty years old and clearly something of a prodigy.

In the world of today, major sponsors and teams would have been clamouring for his services, but in the early postwar years, England had no Grand Prix teams worthy of the name. Ferrari considered the young man with the thinning hair, even entered a car for him in the Bari Grand Prix one year, but when Stirling arrived he was told that the car had been assigned to someone else. Justifiably furious, Moss was never to race a Formula One Ferrari thereafter, and Enzo Ferrari would look back on his decision to change drivers as "my biggest mistake".

For Stirling, racing was a serious business, a career which he wanted to pursue indefinitely. While the carefree Hawthorn went off to Ferrari, Moss laboured gamely with a succession of uncompetitive British Grand Prix cars. In 1954, however, increasingly frustrated, his strong patriotism weakened. Stirling purchased a new Maserati 250F, to be run by his own team and mechanics.

The 1954 season brought Moss onto the world stage and his qualities were seen in a Formula One context for the first time. In the Maserati he was a consistent frontrunner, far superior to any of the Italian company's factory drivers. By midseason they had themselves recognized this, offering Stirling "factory assistance" to an extent which made him virtually a member of the team. At Monza, towards the end of the year, he led conclusively until the 250F's oil tank split with only a few laps left.

Moss's first serious Grand Prix season had coincided with the return of Mercedes-Benz, with whom Juan Manuel Fangio had won the World Championship. In 1955, they chose Stirling Moss to partner the Argentine. In terms of hard competition, it was to prove the least arduous Formula One season of Stirling's career, for the Mercedes-Benz W196 was markedly superior to all its rivals in performance and reliability. From the head of the field Fangio dictated the pace and Moss's instructions were to sit behind the

master. As they cruised to victory, Stirling watched Fangio, followed his example, and learned a tremendous amount about technique and racecraft. He revered Juan Manuel.

At Aintree, Moss was allowed to win the British Grand Prix, his first, and in the 1955 World Championship he finished a comfortable second to Fangio. In a sports car, however, he was already better than his mentor and his legendary victory in the Mille Miglia of that year stands as one of the greatest drives in the sport's history.

At the end of 1955, Mercedes-Benz withdrew from racing, leaving Fangio to go to Ferrari and Moss to renew his association with Maserati, now as official team leader. Stirling won superbly at Monte Carlo and Monza, but his most significant victory was perhaps that in the International Trophy at Silverstone. Maserati were not represented and he was free to drive a Vanwall. The English team was just beginning to come good, and Moss agreed to drive full time for them in 1957.

This was the dawn of British supremacy in Grand Prix racing. Little went right in the first half of the season, but thereafter Stirling was virtually unbeatable. The good times began at Aintree, in July. His own Vanwall an early retirement, Moss took over Tony Brooks's car, climbed through the field, and won. Further victories followed at Pescara and Monza. But, as in the two previous years, Fangio took the title and Stirling was second.

He was second once more in 1958, this time to Mike Hawthorn. It was an absurdity. With Fangio retired at half-season, no one could contest Moss's right to the crown. He won four Grands Prix in 1958, to Hawthorn's one, yet the fatuous World Championship scoring system denied him. It was the last race of the season, at Casablanca, which all would remember, and perhaps it painted as good a portrait of Moss as any he ever drove. To take the title he had to win the race and set the fastest lap (for which there was then a point), with Hawthorn finishing lower than second. Stirling led all the way, won, and got the fastest lap. Mike, a minute and a half behind, was second. Moss lost the Championship by a single point.

Tony Vandervell retired his team from racing at the end of 1958 and thereafter, until the end of his career, Stirling drove for Rob Walker's private team. Taking the title in 1959 and 1960 should have been straightforward, for there was no other driver of his class. But Stirling's inability to "leave well enough alone" was given comparatively free reign with the Walker team. He would insist on searching out that tiny mechanical advantage over his rivals. He began 1959 with a Cooper-Climax, played briefly with a Cooper-BRM, raced a BRM at midseason, then reverted to the Cooper-Climax again, winning brilliantly in Portugal and Italy. In the meantime, Jack Brabham, by no means his equal as a driver, had been racking up points in his Cooper-Climax, finishing the year as World Champion.

In 1960, Walker ran a Lotus 18 for Moss, who dominated the Monaco Grand Prix but then had a dreadful accident at Spa when the suspension broke. Stirling, taken from the wreckage with broken legs and damaged spine, returned to racing six weeks later—and won.

Moss's last full season was in 1961, and his pair of victories at Monte Carlo and the Nürburgring, where he alone took on and beat the dominant Ferraris, rank with any the sport has known. At thirty-two he was better than ever. And then, early the following year, came Goodwood.

No racing driver has ever captured the public imagination like Stirling Moss. When his life hung in the balance, millions across the world waited for news. Eventually, he recovered, but his own dissatisfaction with his reflexes brought the decision to quit. He had been the best of his time, in any kind of car. He brought to racing a commitment seen neither before nor since, but his Grand Prix career was finished. Those who watched his greatness, winced in 1980 at the sight of Stirling Moss, just another driver in a sea of anonymous saloon cars.

RONNIE PETERSON

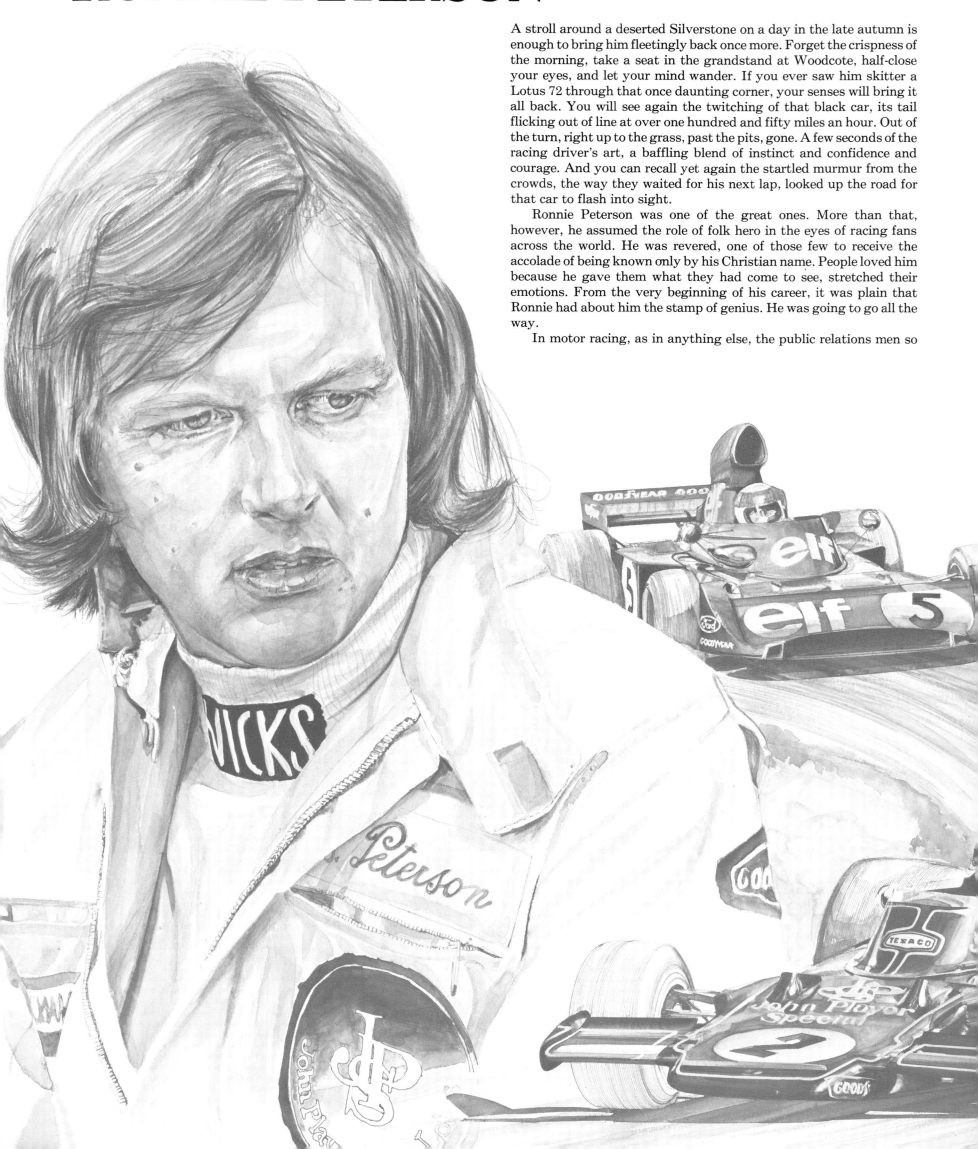

A stroll around a deserted Silverstone on a day in the late autumn is enough to bring him fleetingly back once more. Forget the crispness of the morning, take a seat in the grandstand at Woodcote, half-close your eyes, and let your mind wander. If you ever saw him skitter a Lotus 72 through that once daunting corner, your senses will bring it all back. You will see again the twitching of that black car, its tail flicking out of line at over one hundred and fifty miles an hour. Out of the turn, right up to the grass, past the pits, gone. A few seconds of the racing driver's art, a baffling blend of instinct and confidence and courage. And you can recall yet again the startled murmur from the crowds, the way they waited for his next lap, looked up the road for that car to flash into sight.

Ronnie Peterson was one of the great ones. More than that, however, he assumed the role of folk hero in the eyes of racing fans across the world. He was revered, one of those few to receive the accolade of being known only by his Christian name. People loved him because he gave them what they had come to see, stretched their emotions. From the very beginning of his career, it was plain that Ronnie had about him the stamp of genius. He was going to go all the way.

In motor racing, as in anything else, the public relations men so often get it wrong. To win the love of the populace, a driver's personality is built up, layer by glamorous layer, loud and brash and unsubtle, to a point where absence from the gossip columns is a cause for panic. Sometimes this approach enjoys temporary success, but usually the public recoils from cardboard heroes. True idols rise into place, and so it was with Ronnie Peterson.

Truth to tell, Ronnie was beyond the scope of the PR world. They could do nothing with him. He was quiet and shy, with a baby face. He hated making public appearances. After nine years of living in England his mastery of the language was something less than total. Outside a racing car he was a simple, docile man, a true child of Sweden. The fans liked that about him, and the metamorphosis he underwent at the churning of a starter motor.

After emerging as the dominant figure of Formula Three racing, Peterson went into Grand Prix racing in 1970, when he was twenty-six. After a season of driving a privately entered March, he joined the factory team the following year, finishing it as World Championship runner-up (to Jackie Stewart), despite not winning any of the races. But the next season was a complete disaster, the March was uncompetitive, and Ronnie left at the end of it to join Lotus, the team with whom his name became synonymous.

It was in 1973, his first year with Colin Chapman's team, that he took over the role of the natural pacesetter. At no stage of his career was he as well-rounded a Grand Prix driver as Jackie Stewart, nor the "technician" which Niki Lauda would become. But, day for day, he was quite simply the fastest driver in the business, a man who could make the impossible happen. He won a lot of races for Chapman.

For all his stupefying car control, however, there were chinks in Peterson's armour. After a season of considerable success with the Lotus 72, he went into 1974 with an all-new car, the 76. After brief flashes of promise at Silverstone and Jarama, the car—and Ronnie—slipped from contention. His testing abilities were never of the best, and weeks of frustration ended with the decision to revert to the faithful 72. In the short term this was the answer. The car was getting a little old, but Peterson was comfortable with it, and his ability was sufficient to bring it three more victories.

By 1975, however, the car was simply off the pace, and no replacement appeared throughout the season. An also-ran, Ronnie held his tongue and signed another contract for the following year. Now there was a new Lotus, the 77, and its initial form brought despair to Peterson. The parting less than cordial, he left the team after the opening race and returned to March, who provided him with a car of reasonable competitiveness and appalling unreliability. Still, it was good enough to take him to victory in the Italian Grand Prix, his third win at Monza in four years.

After a desolate year with Ken Tyrrell's six-wheelers, Ronnie's stock was at its lowest, but his fans kept the faith, and so, too, did many team managers. Nevertheless, the racing world was sceptical when rumours of Peterson's return to Lotus began to circulate; it was incredulous when the rumours became fact.

By this time, Chapman and Mario Andretti had worked the team back to a position of supremacy, and Andretti was less than overjoyed when he was advised of Ronnie's return. The terms of the Swede's contract seemed harsh, dictating as they did that Andretti was the unquestioned team leader, and that Peterson should not try to beat him. Ronnie accepted with equanimity; what he wanted was the car that would let him be competitive again.

In 1978 the true measure of the man was seen. Winter testing had rekindled the old enthusiasm. By the beginning of the season he was leaner and fitter than he had been for a long time. He was happy to be at the front once more. As the year progressed he established himself once more as indubitably the fastest in the world. And, more remarkably, his reputation for integrity remained without blemish. He stuck religiously to the terms of the contract, never trying to beat Mario, sitting obediently behind, at the same time clearly conveying the message that he could go quicker if he wanted to.

The hard-boiled brigade predictably considered him an idiot for keeping his word, but it seemed to bother Ronnie less than they. "This is Mario's year," he would say. "He brought Lotus back, and he deserves it." He had rebuilt his reputation, and he was content. He had won two Grands Prix, the second a brilliant, top-drawer drive in the rains of Zeltweg, and dutifully followed Andretti in others. He had signed a contract with McLaren for the 1979 season. There were no team orders, except to get out there and win. At last it seemed that the cards had fallen for him.

And then came Monza. Within a quarter of a mile of the start, there was a multiple accident. Peterson's Lotus was pitched into the guard rail, and he was taken from the wreckage with dreadful injuries to his legs. Early medical reports said he would recover in time, but that night complications developed during surgery, and he died in the early morning. Mario Andretti was distraught when he was told of his friend's death. Across the world countless thousands shared his grief.

DIDIER PIRONI

Since the Second World War, France's participation in Grand Prix racing has been patchy and erratic. Occasionally there was a flash of success from the cars of Amédée Gordini, but usually the small, sadly underfinanced company was embarrassingly off the pace. The little blue cars disappeared for good at the end of 1957, and there followed a long interlude. The year before, in the French Grand Prix at Reims, the name of Bugatti had briefly resurfaced, but the new rear-engined car's pace brought tears to the eyes of all who remembered Ettore Bugatti's past glories.

In 1968, the blue of France returned to the Grand Prix circuits carried by Matra, a company which had already enjoyed success in Formulae Two and Three. It, too, quit the sport at the end of 1972, but Matra's mellifluous V-12 engine lives on in the cars of Guy Ligier, whose Formula One team made its debut in 1976. The following year, of course, Renault arrived, complete with turbocharged engines. The French were back in force.

A continuing sadness to Gallic enthusiasts, however, had been the lack of great French drivers, the last of whom was Jean-Pierre Wimille, who lost his life at Buenos Aires in 1948. Since then, France has produced a great many excellent *pilotes*—Sommer, Behra, Trintignant, Beltoise, Depailler, Laffite—but none has had the spark of real genius which marks a Fangio or a Clark. All of them have shown greatness on a given day, none consistently.

By 1980, though, there was cause to believe that the drought was over. In Didier Pironi, France now had a driver of consummate talent, a man capable of winning regularly on merit. In terms of sheer speed the young man was being rated with Gilles Villeneuve, and spoken of as a future World Champion.

Pironi arrived in Formula One in 1978. For some years his successes in Formule Renault had drawn favourable comment, and 1977, his first season in Formula Two, had been highly promising. Almost from the beginning of his career he had received backing from Elf Petroleum, and when Ken Tyrrell's Elf-sponsored Grand Prix team needed a replacement for Ronnie Peterson, Didier was an obvious choice.

He stayed with the Tyrrell team for two seasons, and they were what Mario Andretti would call "character-building". After the years of glory with Jackie Stewart, the team was in sharp decline, its cars rarely competitive. During his time with Tyrrell, Pironi had numerous accidents, most of them through no fault of his own. He was unhurt each time, but a lesser man might have become unnerved.

For 1980, Pironi joined Ligier as team-mate to Jacques Laffite, and at last he had a car worthy of his talents. From the very beginning of the season he was undeniably quicker than Laffite, and soon, at Zolder, he scored his first Grand Prix victory. It was a faultless drive. Although Alan Jones's Williams had been fractionally faster in qualifying, Pironi made a better start and confidently squeezed out the Australian at the entry to the first turn. From there the Ligier eased away into the distance, and there was nothing that Jones could do about it.

That win seemed to lift Pironi to yet greater heights. At Monte Carlo, the next race on the schedule, his form was brilliant. From pole position he led away, unmoved by the pressure of leading on a tight street circuit where the tiniest mistake puts you into the barriers and out of the race.

The blue car ran easily at the front until twenty laps from the end. By then rain was falling, and the track was greasy, but more of a problem to Pironi was the fact that third gear was jumping out, and he had to hold the lever in place. After fifty-four laps in the lead, Didier—one-handed—fractionally overcorrected a slide at Casino Square, and the Ligier nudged the barriers. It is the race everyone loves to win, yet the Frenchman stepped from the car with no exhibition of temper, no sign of emotion, hardly a backward glance.

Pironi is almost eerily in control of his feelings, and perhaps this contributed in part to his alienation from the very Gallic, sometimes overemotional, Ligier personnel. As the season wore on, it became clear that Didier and some members of his team were at odds. He is not a typical Frenchman, does not conform to a system. He goes motor racing for Didier Pironi. By the time of the French Grand Prix, in July, Guy Ligier and team manager Gerard Ducarouge were treating him almost like a naughty schoolboy. He was showing dangerous signs of independence, and Ligier was heard to say that he would not be renewing Didier's contract for 1981.

The young man seemed totally unmoved, apparently oblivious to the hostility. He finished second to Jones in the French race, then moved on to Brands Hatch and another tremendous performance. On pole position by a huge margin he easily led the first quarter of the race until a cracked wheel brought him into the pits. Then began a staggering drive in which he brought the Ligier through the field from twenty-first place to fourth, breaking the lap record time and again, travelling at a completely different pace from every other car in the race.

Towards the end he suddenly pulled off and stopped out on the circuit. Another wheel had cracked, and a tyre was flat. All that work and inspiration had brought no reward. And yet again there was that cold control.

As season's end approached, the men of Ligier, recognizing Pironi's natural gift, had decided that they would keep him, after all. But Didier had other ideas. He was not tied to the blue of France, and he had never felt truly comfortable at Ligier. Therefore he signed instead for Ferrari, and brought the wrath of Velizy down on himself. He was leaving France for Italy. . . . Why, it was the act of a traitor! The news broke the weekend of the Italian Grand Prix, and the Ligier pit at Imola was very tense indeed.

Pironi is intensely professional in everything he does, and he is a racing driver who genuinely loves cars. His first winter with Ferrari was one of hard work, with constant testing. He is ideally equipped to handle the political in-fighting intrinsic in the Maranello team. There is an apparent aloofness about him, but this is illusory. On the track he is a man who gives his all—the end of a race or practice session will find him sweating and dishevelled. A few minutes later, however, after a shower and a change of clothes, Pironi is his normal, relaxed self, watching the razzmatazz around him with a faintly mocking smile.

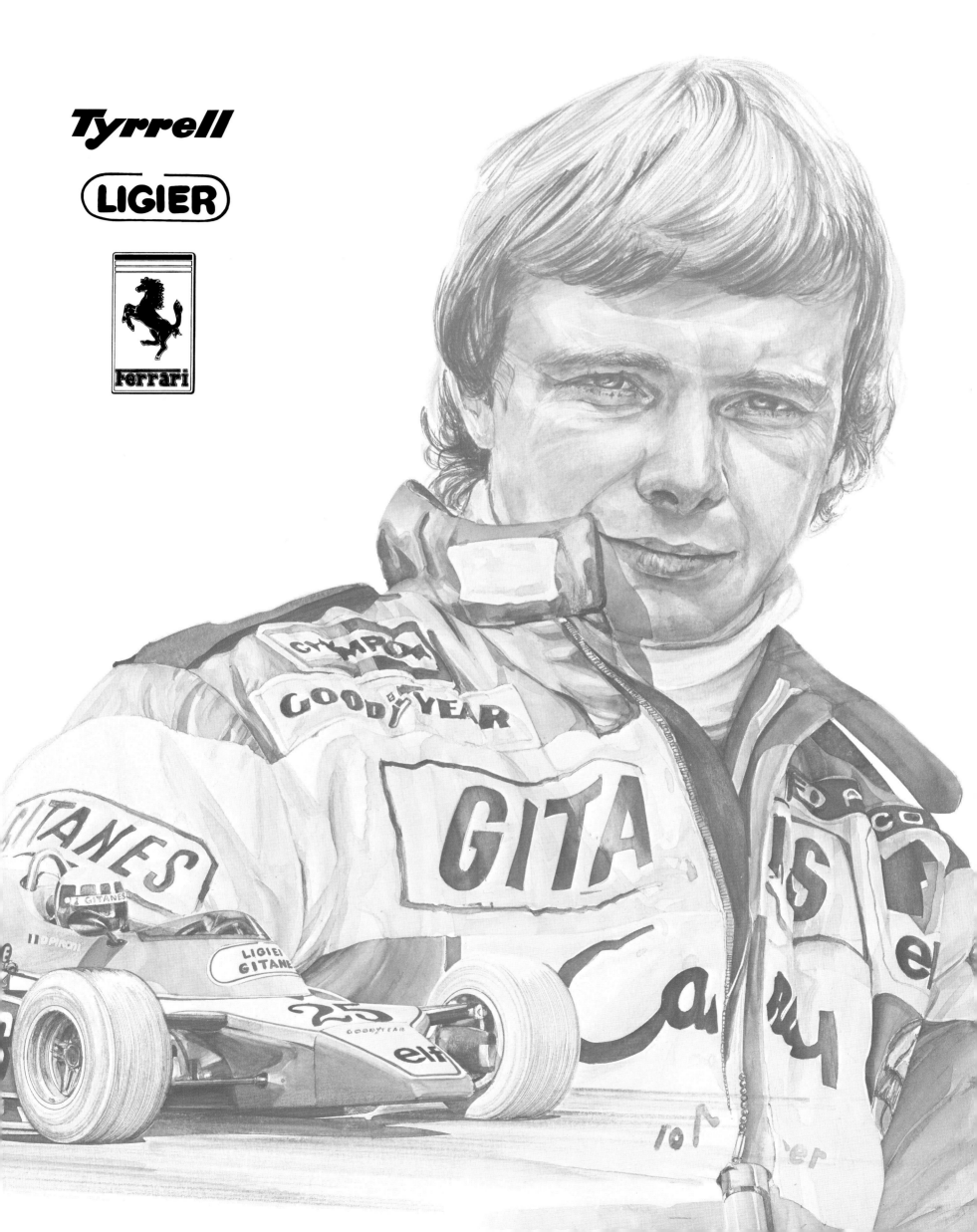

CLAY REGAZZONI

Clay Regazzoni once said that he had been born fifteen years too late. Indeed, he would have been in his element in the fifties and early sixties, before the metamorphosis of Grand Prix racing took it away from the classic circuits, when chassis tuning was a primitive art, when more depended upon the bravura of the driver. There are few drivers of the modern era one can comfortably envisage in a front-engined Ferrari, perched up high, working away at a huge wood-rimmed steering wheel. But Regazzoni presented no problem to the imagination. He was every schoolboy's idea of a racing driver. There is a famous photograph of Clay, a passionate fan at the Italian Grand Prix in 1961, gazing wistfully at a Formula One Ferrari. Nine years later one of the red cars won at Monza—and Regazzoni was the driver.

He was always a difficult man to categorize. During his early career, in Formula Three and then Formula Two, he showed himself clearly to be a very quick driver, but equally he soon gained a reputation for having major accidents. In 1968, his Formula Three Tecno went clean under the guard rail at Monaco, and to this day no one quite understands how he emerged unhurt from the wreckage. His life seemed to be charmed.

Regazzoni was a natural Ferrari driver, everything about him, his looks, manner, driving style, was curiously appropriate for Maranello. And was there ever a more suitable name for a Grand Prix driver?

In 1970, Enzo Ferrari had only Jacky Ickx on contract for the Formula One team, but there were plans to give other drivers a run as soon as the new flat-12 312B proved reliable. At Spa, Ignazio Giunti made his debut and finished fourth. At Zandvoort, the next race on the schedule, it was Regazzoni's turn, and he, too, finished fourth. There was not a little surprise when Clay was nominated for the drive in Holland, for few saw him as a future Grand Prix star. He was wild, they said, and crashed too often.

Occasionally, however, a driver comes along without much reputation in the lower leagues—and he confounds everyone with his performances in the top echelon. Regazzoni was such a driver, and his day of days came at Monza less than three months after his Grand Prix debut. The Formula One world was still shocked by the death of Jochen Rindt in practice when Clay took a perfectly judged victory. That September afternoon Regazzoni became a national hero in Italy, although he was from over the border, a native Swiss. Lugano, his home town, was nearby, and his first language was Italian. He looked Italian. For the Monza *tifosi* his references were close to impeccable.

The adulation in which Clay was held was by no means confined to Italy. In every kind of sport there are those, small in number, who are the happy possessors of charisma. Like style, it cannot be achieved or acquired. It simply is. And Regazzoni had charisma to spare. Spectators loved his driving for its flamboyance and derring-do. Off the track, signing autographs in the paddock, they found him quiet, humorous, content, gentle. Marry all that to his swarthy bandit face and ready smile, and you had a folk hero. Everybody liked Clay Regazzoni—even those fellow drivers who occasionally muttered about his sometimes excessive zeal in the cockpit.

It is doubtful that any racing driver ever enjoyed his career more than Clay, and his pleasure came from a charmingly simple love of driving racing cars. As many of the people involved in Grand Prix racing became increasingly cynical through the seventies, with some drivers arriving, making their fortunes, and clearing out before their fragile egos were shattered, Regazzoni remained blissfully immune. Success he enjoyed, of course, but it was the striving rather than the winning which was important. A really sensational drive through the field after a pit stop would give him more pleasure than an easy victory, and he would not hesitate to say so.

Clay had six seasons with Ferrari, but at no stage was he the official team leader. It never ruffled him. He was happy simply to be a Ferrari driver. And it was doubly unfortunate, therefore, that he should have been treated so shabbily at the end of his time at Maranello. Nobody at Ferrari would tell him straight that he had been dropped in favour of Carlos Reutemann. The fact of his dismissal he could accept; the manner of it he could not. He was a straightforward and honourable man, unable to comprehend deviousness after years of loyalty to his employers.

Regazzoni was not a great racing driver of the Moss and Clark idiom, but there were days in his racing life when he was very great indeed. That first victory at Monza was outstanding, particularly for a man in only his fifth Formula One race. He repeated the win in 1975, having led from flag to flag at the Nürburgring a year earlier. At the inaugural Long Beach Grand Prix, in 1976, he simply pulverized everyone—including his team-mate Niki Lauda—with a majestic, faultless performance, in front all the way.

After leaving Ferrari, Clay was stuck for a couple of years with poor cars, and many observers were quick to write him off as a has-been. Not so. In 1979, Frank Williams signed him as number two to Alan Jones, and Regazzoni did a wonderful job, winning the British Grand Prix and consistently finishing in the points. At the end of the season he was replaced—by Reutemann again—and perhaps it was a logical time to retire. He was forty years old, with little chance of ever racing a truly competitive car again. But he decided against retirement, and rejoined the Ensign team, for which he had driven in 1977. "You must understand," he said, "that, for me, being a part of Formula One is important. Winning is not essential. I love to drive."

At Long Beach, the scene four years earlier of perhaps his greatest victory, Clay and the Ensign were running fourth in the late stages. At the end of Shoreline Drive, the fastest part of the circuit, he found himself without brakes. The car hit a barrier head on at over 150 mph. Miraculously he was alive, even conscious, as they worked to free him, but he had suffered appalling injuries. After one hundred and thirty-two Grands Prix, his career was over.

During the following months in hospital, Clay had to face the possibility that he might never walk again. This required more than the merely fleeting courage of a racing driver. He reacted with determination and fierce pride, undergoing repeated surgery over a long period of time, facing months of pain with raw gallantry. A year after the accident, another major operation brought grounds for genuine optimism, and the racing world rejoiced for him. Few men in the sport have been so universally loved.

JOCHEN RINDT

Here was a true folk hero, a man from that select band whose public appeal knows no boundary. In the course of his brief time at the top, Jochen Rindt captivated racing fans everywhere. It is easy to admire the skills of a great racing driver, but Rindt drew more than admiration from the people who watched him. He had their affection, certainly, but mainly they loved him for what he did to their senses. When Jochen was making his pitch, particularly during one of his legendary charges through the field, there was a crackle of excitement in the air, a sense of impending drama. As with Ronnie Peterson, there was the feeling that the impossible might just happen. Jochen made people catch their breath.

His early career gave no hint of greatness to come. As a Formula Junior driver in the early sixties he was remarkable only for flamboyant dress and a loud mouth. Not until 1964 did the racing world take note of Jochen Rindt. In Formula Two then, his arrival in the big time was spectacular. Early in the season, at Crystal Palace, he took his first major win after a hectic battle with Graham Hill. Three months later he was given his first Formula One drive, appropriately in front of a home crowd at the Austrian Grand Prix, and later he signed a contract with Cooper for the 1965 season.

In terms of results, Jochen's first year of Grands Prix produced little. He had a great deal to learn and the Cooper was not competitive in this, the last season of the 1.5-litre Formula One. But there were compensations, and his victory in the Le Mans 24-Hour race that year is part of the Sarthe folklore.

Rindt, sharing a Ferrari 250LM with Masten Gregory, had lost a lot of time with mechanical problems early in the race and seemed completely out of the reckoning. The two drivers therefore came to a private agreement: they would drive absolutely flat out. This, they figured, would either take them right up the leader board—for people do not drive on the limit in a twenty-four-hour race—or the Ferrari would expire, and they could go home. Somehow the car took all that abuse, and a famous victory was won.

Success in Grand Prix racing, however, was a long time coming. Rindt dominated Formula Two through the sixties and was usually well to the fore in the Grands Prix, but here success eluded him. He finished third in the 1966 World Championship after a wonderful year with the underpowered and heavy Cooper-Maserati, but his points came from consistent places. There was little chance of victory with this car, but he put in a sensational drive at Spa in the rain, surviving a massive spin on the first lap to pass Surtees for the lead on lap four. The first win seemed a real possibility for he led conclusively for a long time, Surtees taking the Ferrari by with only four laps left. Jochen's showing, however, deeply impressed everybody with its raw aggression and phenomenal car control.

The Cooper team was completely outpaced in 1967, and Rindt accepted an offer from Jack Brabham for the following year. It was a season which promised much, but unfortunately the cars, while competitive, were woefully unreliable. Jochen enjoyed his time with the Brabham team, but now Colin Chapman was beckoning. In a Lotus, Rindt was sure he could win the World Championship, so he signed to partner Graham Hill in 1969.

It was a year of highs and lows. Quickly Jochen asserted himself

as the fastest man in the business. At the beginning a combination of the Austrian's natural pace and Chapman's Lotus 49 looked irresistible. But the fates seemed to conspire against Rindt. In the Spanish Grand Prix he led the early stages comfortably, until the Lotus's high rear wing collapsed, pitching the car out of control and into the guard rail. It then hit Hill's sister car, which had crashed earlier for the same reason. Jochen's car was totally destroyed and he was more than fortunate to get away with light injuries.

The accident marked the beginning of a sour relationship between Rindt and Chapman. Jochen was not one of the world's diplomats, and he spoke freely of his fears and doubts about driving for Lotus. In the races, however, he put such worries behind him, being Jackie Stewart's only serious rival. But by midseason he had virtually made up his mind to switch teams again for 1970.

At the German Grand Prix, Chapman, fearful of losing his star, was persuasive. He spoke of the new car he had planned for 1970, promised him absolute priority within the team. Jochen wavered, then agreed tentatively. Thereafter his fortunes took an upward swing. At Monza he finished second—a yard, no more, behind Stewart—and at Watkins Glen he finally won his first Grand Prix. It was no different from any other drive that season, he said afterwards. For once the car had stayed together.

Less than twelve months later Jochen Rindt was dead, the sport's first posthumous World Champion. The new Lotus 72 had been as competitive as Chapman had promised, indeed it made obsolete every other chassis in the business. Rindt won with it in consecutive races in Holland, France, Britain, and Germany.

Jochen's greatest victory, however, was his first of the year. With the 72 not yet race-ready, he drove the then ageing Lotus 49 at Monte Carlo, and was displeased at having to do so. In practice he was far from inspired, and in the race he made no real impression for the first hour, running most of the time in sixth place. As those ahead retired, however, Rindt found himself elevated to second place, behind Brabham. A whiff of victory was all Jochen ever needed, and the way he drove that Lotus in the closing laps will never be forgotten. It was pure inspiration, wildly spectacular, totally under control. At the last corner of the last lap the pressure told on Brabham, whose car slid into the barrier, allowing Rindt to score an extraordinary win. His last lap was exactly two and a half seconds quicker than his fastest practice lap.

That race at Monaco in 1970 summed up perfectly the reasons for Jochen Rindt's place in the public's affection. He had made the impossible happen, along the way frightening the spectators, and entrancing them. He had shown them genius.

Throughout his final season Rindt became ever more aware of the risks of racing. In the month of June, Bruce McLaren and Piers Courage both lost their lives. When asked to drive a Porsche in the 1000-kilometre sports car race at his native Osterreichring, Jochen refused, on the theory that if you go to the Gates often enough they will eventually open.

He was an arrogant man in many ways, intolerant of fools, yet there was about him a vulnerability. He worried during the summer of 1970 that everything was suddenly going almost too well for him. The others were having the bad luck. The World Championship was virtually won.

On September 5th, the day before the Italian Grand Prix, Jochen's Lotus 72 went off the road during the final practice session. The accident occurred on the approach to the Parabolica, where driver error was inconceivable. Taken from the wreckage with appalling injuries, Rindt died almost immediately. He never knew that history would record him as World Champion.

People recall his staggering control, his clipped voice, tousled hair, and boxer's nose. A great deal went out of racing when Jochen died. Later, Ronnie Peterson would stir the same emotions in those who watched, and later he, too, would die at Monza in a Lotus. Like Ronnie, Jochen Rindt was a *racing* driver.

JODY SCHECKTER

In 1972 they were saying that Jody Scheckter was going to be one of the great ones. He had arrived in Europe a year before, a little raw and unpolished, as the Formula Ford champion of South Africa. People remarked on his husky build and thick, tight accent. And they noticed, too, his extraordinary car control and apparent fearlessness. His driving in those days was much like his manner, a little rough, but it was clear that his potential was enormous. Eighteen months after stepping off that plane from Johannesburg, Jody was on the grid for his first Grand Prix.

Scheckter was given his big breaks, first in Formula Two, then in Formula One, by McLaren Racing. Having two established drivers, Denny Hulme and Peter Revson, already in the team, McLaren could not give Jody a regular ride, but occasionally fielded a third car for him. When that happened, the team got into the headlines.

In the French Grand Prix of 1973, Scheckter rattled the establishment by taking the lead at the start and holding it for most of the race. Eventually, an almost desperate Emerson Fittipaldi, then at the height of his powers, clouted Jody's McLaren M23 and both men were out.

The pressures on Scheckter at this time were extreme. Still short of experience, he was nevertheless a natural pacesetter. After his sensational showing at Paul Ricard, McLaren once more entered him to run with Hulme and Revson, this time in the British Grand Prix at Silverstone. And thus was occasioned the most massive—and most frequently televised—accident in the history of Grand Prix racing.

Silverstone's Woodcote Corner was majestic then, not yet humbled by a chicane. It was a daunting corner, open yet bumpy, taken at 150 mph. It called for judgment and great courage.

Scheckter had qualified sixth, and a strong getaway saw him in fourth place as they came up to complete the opening lap—and into Woodcote. And there Jody got it all wrong, running wide on to the grass, where the McLaren spun chaotically back into the middle of the pack. For endless seconds there was complete mayhem, with cars in the air, breaking up, finally settling back under a pall of smoke and steam. The race was stopped, and, to their astonishment, marshals discovered that only one driver, Andrea de Adamich, was hurt, and he not seriously. But eight cars, including Scheckter's McLaren, had been completely destroyed. Jody instantly became the outcast of Formula One. Up went the cry "Ban him!"

Chastened, but certainly not cowed, Jody was then "rested" by McLaren for a while. He made his return in the Canadian Grand Prix, and that race also ended for him with an accident, this time with François Cevert of the Tyrrell team. A fortnight later, the news broke that the two were to be team-mates. Jackie Stewart was about to retire, and Ken Tyrrell had signed Scheckter to partner Cevert in 1974. The alliance, however, never came to be, for the Frenchman was killed during practice at Watkins Glen. Jody, in preparation for his last race for McLaren, was the first man on the scene. That experience, he has admitted, had a profound effect upon him.

Scheckter, therefore, went into 1974 as a number one driver and Ken Tyrrell bent himself to the task of taming his new team leader. Over a period of time he was successful in this—indeed, perhaps a little too successful. Certainly Jody became more consistent, but Tyrrell's influence also served to remove some of his confidence and aggression. He was finishing more, leading less, although it must be said that his first Grand Prix wins, in Sweden and Britain, came in that year.

The following year he won perhaps his greatest victory, at home in South Africa, after fighting off the Brabham team all the way, but there were no more wins in 1975. Jody stayed with Tyrrell for 1976, however, but this was the first season of the P34 six-wheeler, a car he never liked. It brought him another win, in Sweden, but at the end of the year he moved away to join Walter Wolf Racing.

The new partnership began spectacularly, if fortunately, with a first-time victory in Argentina, and Scheckter followed this with a sensational win at Monaco, by now his place of residence. And later there was a third triumph, in Canada. Jody finished second in the World Championship to Niki Lauda. But the following season, 1978, brought frustration, disappointment, and no wins. As early as August, Scheckter announced that he had accepted an invitation to go to Ferrari for 1979.

There followed all manner of gloomy predictions for the liaison. The Italians are proud and excitable, and Jody can be quite dramatically blunt and tactless. Oil and water, people said. It would never work. Remarkably, however, it did work. In 1979 Jody Scheckter won three Grands Prix and finished well in many others. And he finished the year as World Champion, his eternal goal finally realized.

From the early days of the South African's career in Europe, his success had had a certain inevitability about it. Ironically, however, Jody's title came from canniness, playing a waiting game, and not from the frantic aggression and pace of his beginnings.

The championship won, there was nothing to keep Scheckter in the cockpit of a Grand Prix car. For some time the business of motor racing had bored him, and thoughts of his own safety weighed increasingly on his mind. Ferrari had a dreadful season in 1980, but Jody, already committed to retirement at the end of the year, kept on to the end of his contract, unlike some. He is an honourable man, quite sentimental in his way, and much misunderstood, with a nice, world-weary, and cynical sense of humour. And on his day he was a quite remarkable racing driver.

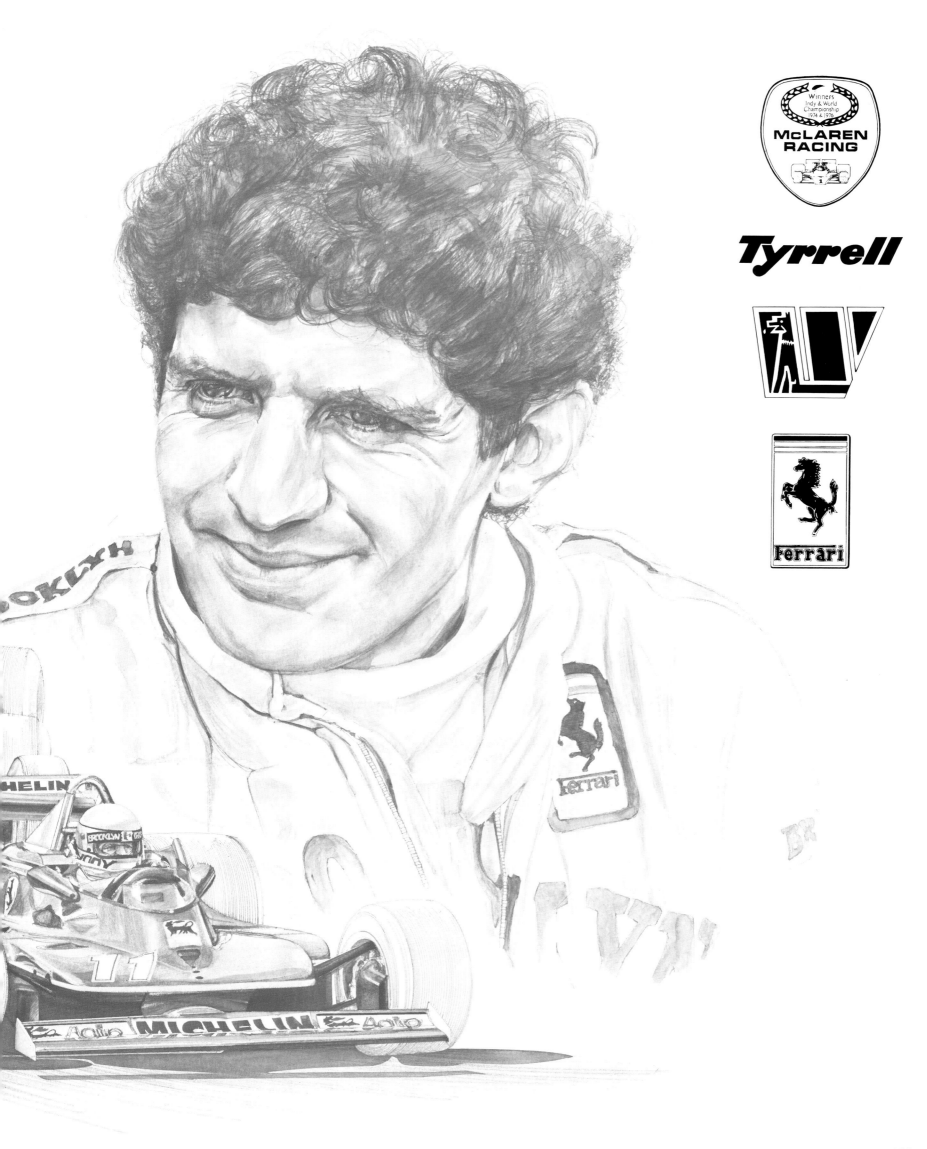

JACKIE STEWART

From the very start it was evident that Jackie Stewart was a winner. Not only was he instantly successful in terms of results—there have been many like that who have faded from view—but there was something about him, his whole being, which radiated confidence and strength. Like most of history's great racing drivers, he is a small man. And his walk, that jaunty step, immediately brings Stirling Moss to mind. Both men would walk through the paddocks of the world's circuits as if they owned them. In a way they did. Moss's position, in Grand Prix protocol, after the retirement of Fangio, was mirrored precisely by Stewart's standing, following the death of Jim Clark. In sum, they were indisputably the best of their respective eras. They knew it, and everyone else knew it.

Like most of the great ones, Stewart reached his elevated position quickly. A talent as natural and flowing as his soon comes to the surface. After a couple of seasons in club racing, he drove for Ken Tyrrell's Formula Three team in 1964, and was completely dominant. There was about him at that time a curious innocence, that of the small-town boy in a world of bright lights, but it was already apparent that he was a true son of Scotland. He was certainly canny. At the end of that year the Grand Prix teams were clamouring for him. Of particular interest were the two blue ribband rides of the time—Lotus, as Clark's number two, and BRM, as partner to Graham Hill. The obvious choice was to go to Lotus because they built the fastest cars, but Stewart was wiser than that.

The second Lotus drive, most attractive on paper, had a variety of pitfalls attached. First, Colin Chapman and his men devoted most of their attention and energies to Clark's needs. This was quite understandable, but inevitably attention to the second car suffered and affected its reliability. Second, Chapman is a man who demands results—and quickly. Stewart reasoned, sensibly, that he could do without that kind of pressure in his first Grand Prix season. BRM offered a good, competitive car, and the chance to play himself in. He settled for that.

Jackie's sheer class soon made itself obvious. After only a few races in 1965 he proved consistently faster than Graham Hill, emerging as the natural rival to Clark. At the end of the year he won the Italian Grand Prix at Monza, and he finished third in the World Championship, behind Clark and Hill.

The rise and rise of Jackie Stewart faltered, however, in June of 1966. He had recently won the Monaco Grand Prix, and lost his first—and only—Indianapolis 500 when his car expired near the end. The future could scarcely have been brighter, but it was almost snuffed out in the rains of Spa.

Stewart's BRM was one of several cars to crash on the opening laps of the Belgian Grand Prix. Although his most serious injury was a broken collarbone, he was trapped in the wreckage for some time, during which the risk of fire was enormous. That day went a long way towards reshaping Jackie's attitude towards motor racing safety, and was to have a profound effect upon the future of the sport. It also had a temporary effect upon Stewart's career.

He was soon back in the cockpit, but for a while the edge was gone from his driving. It came back. Twelve months after his accident, Jackie returned to Spa with the difficult and cumbersome BRM H16. And, despite having to steer the thing with only his left hand (the right being used to hold the lever in gear), he led much of the race and finally took second place.

Stewart's great years began in 1968. In April, Clark was killed at Hockenheim, and the Formula One dynasty was temporarily without a leader. By his actions—on the track and off—over the next few months, Stewart laid claim to the mantle. Ken Tyrrell had made the decision to go into Grand Prix racing, and Jackie left BRM to join him. One of the sport's most illustrious partnerships was on its way. In Tyrrell's Matra MS10, Stewart won three Grands Prix in 1968, including a quite extraordinary victory in the gloom and drear of a foggy, sodden Nürburgring, where he triumphed by four minutes. . . .

For the next five Grand Prix seasons Jackie was the dominant

force in Formula One, winning the World Championship three times. When he retired, at the end of 1973, his Grand Prix tally was twenty-seven victories from ninety-nine starts. Not all statistics, perhaps, are damned lies. Stewart's superiority was beyond dispute.

Away from the cockpit, too, his influence was felt. He campaigned unceasingly for improvements in racing safety, and to good effect. By so doing he incurred the wrath of traditionalists who felt that a man had to take his chances if he drove racing cars. Certainly there were times when Stewart imposed his ideas without a great deal of subtlety, but he felt that if a matter was urgent, kid gloves were useless in a fist fight with the establishment.

In addition, the sport's elder statesmen—and others, too—resented the enormous wealth which Jackie amassed over the years. He was only too aware of his market value, and he unfailingly went for top dollar. In return, none of the companies with whom he became associated will say that it ever received less than its money's worth. To his product endorsement jobs, his television work, his PR appearances, Stewart brought exactly the same relaxed professionalism which characterized his driving. In truth, a lot of people disliked him for no other reason than that he was so capable in so many ways—and that he dared to grow his hair long.

Many drivers have won the championship since Stewart, but none has equalled his driving skill and class, nor his willingness to put back into the sport something in return for his considerable rewards from it. It has become the vogue, sadly, to treat sponsors and the public with contempt. Jackie Stewart would see that as both rude and stupid, and neither adjective is applicable to him.

He remains one of the sport's great figures, as well-known now as in his racing days. His sense of humour is as sharp as ever, and he has a great talent for using few words to put something in clear perspective. In the late sixties he moved from Scotland to Switzerland, immediately attracting the criticism of the press. How could he be so unpatriotic? "Because," he explained, "it suddenly occurred to me that, nine weekends out of ten, I was risking my life for the Chancellor of the Exchequer. . . ."

And you remember, too, the sublime confidence of a man who clearly knew his position in his own world. You think of Paul Ricard, scene of the French Grand Prix in 1971. Stewart had set the fastest practise time, and is standing around in the pits, chatting with a few friends. Over the PA system comes the news that Jacky Ickx's Ferrari has set a quicker time. "Christ," says Jackie, reaching for his helmet, "that means I'll have to go out again. . . ."

JOHN SURTEES

John Surtees was a star before he ever sat in a racing car. In the late fifties he was incomparably the greatest motorcyclist of the era, the winner of many World Championships. To the Italian *tifosi* his motorcycle exploits made him *Il Grande John*, John the Great, which the British press mistranslated as Big John. History shows that rarely is success on two wheels a guarantee of further glories on four, but from the earliest days of John's career in cars it was apparent that he was again going to be a champion.

Surtees began to make the switch in 1960, during that summer driving for the Lotus Formula One team as and when his commitment to the MV Agusta motorcycle outfit permitted. At one extraordinary stage he won the Isle of Man Senior TT for MV, and within a month finished second in the British Grand Prix—only his second Formula One race—for Team Lotus. The next Grand Prix on his schedule was in Portugal and only mechanical problems prevented his winning. As it was, he started from pole position, led and set fastest lap, thereby embarassing the aces of the day, including Stirling Moss who was driving an identical Lotus.

John abandoned motorcycles at the end of 1960, preferring to concentrate entirely on cars. The 1961 season belonged almost exclusively to Ferrari and life for the British teams was hard. But Surtees, driving a Cooper for the Yeoman Credit team, had a good win in the non-championship Formula One race at Goodwood, and drove impressively throughout the year. At the end of it, indeed, he turned down an offer to go to Ferrari for 1962, deeming himself "not quite ready for that". Instead, he stayed put, running a Lola, and finished fourth in the World Championship. The Ferrari contract was waved once more and this time it was signed.

The Italian team had been through a dreadful season in 1962. At the end of it the Commendatore swept clean, bringing in new engineers and designers as well as his new number one driver. Together they made excellent progress, building their competitiveness to a point where Surtees won his first Grand Prix, at the Nürburgring in August. Throughout his career Surtees would star at the difficult classic circuits. His other great favourite was Spa-Francorchamps.

In 1964, John became the first—and still the only—man to win a World Championship for both motorcycles and cars. His was a late-season charge, the title seemingly destined either for Jimmy Clark or Graham Hill. But conclusive victories at the Nürburgring and Monza brought Surtees into the reckoning, and all three men went to the grid for the final race, in Mexico, with the chance of becoming World Champion. While both his rivals retired, John finished second, the title his by a single point.

Surtees by no means confined his activities to Grand Prix racing. During his years with Ferrari he was highly successful in the sports car team, and also began a small outfit of his own, running Lola

CanAm cars. It was in one of these that he nearly lost his life at the end of 1965, when suspension failure flipped the car off the track at Mosport. Critically injured, John fought back to fitness, rejoining Ferrari for 1966. It was typical of the man that he should break the lap record at Modena, Ferrari's test track, on the day of his return. After so many years of working with sceptical Italians, he felt it necessary to squash their doubts about his physical health. He then proceeded to win his first two races of the season.

One man, however, remained to be convinced—or refused to be convinced. The team manager, Eugenio Dragoni, had never got along well with Surtees, primarily because John completely over-shadowed Lorenzo Bandini, whom Dragoni regarded as his protégé. Although John and Lorenzo were good friends, their team manager went out of his way to cause friction and discord.

For a while, Surtees lived with it. Early in the 1966 season, it was apparent that he was going to walk the World Championship. In this, the first year of the 3-litre formula, Ferrari were in better shape than any other team. John led at Monte Carlo until retirement, and then scored a memorable victory in the rain at Spa. At Le Mans, however, came the parting of the ways. Once more casting aspersions on his fitness, Dragoni snapped Surtees's patience. The Englishman left before the race and terminated his contract. He went to the Cooper team and by the end of the year, in Mexico, he had trans-formed the heavy Maserati-powered car into a winner. He also won the first CanAm Championship.

In 1967 and 1968, John drove for Honda, giving the team all the commitment and hard work he had devoted to Ferrari. It was a difficult struggle, with a heavy car and temperamental, if powerful,

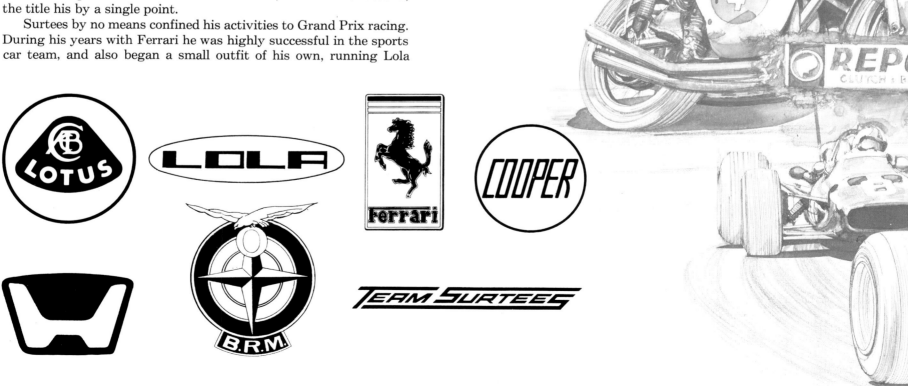

engines. Once more, however, he made it a winner, beating Jack Brabham to the line at Monza, after a dramatic battle in the late stages of the race. The following season brought no more victories— although Surtees came close more than once—and at the end of it Honda retired from Formula One, leaving John to embark upon his most disagreeable season, with BRM.

Throughout his career, Surtees's biggest problem was that he never learned diplomacy. He always spoke his mind, a quality hardly universal in Grand Prix racing, and was never afraid to be a lonely voice in the wilderness. Old-fashioned qualities like truth and honesty and adherence to principle mattered to John Surtees. Less laudable, perhaps, were his incredible stubbornness and his unwillingness to delegate. Although far more knowledgeable about the workings of racing cars than most drivers, he was not an engineer. Yet he tried to act like one. This inevitably affected his driving.

After the year with BRM, Surtees decided to go it alone. He had already become a constructor, building competitive Formula 5000 cars. Now he started work on a Surtees Formula One machine. It appeared in mid-1970 and was clearly on the pace. At the Oulton Park Gold Cup John won in the car, a feat he repeated the following year. But there were no Grand Prix victories.

At the end of 1971, Surtees went into semi-retirement as a driver, to concentrate on running the team. Several times that breakthrough seemed close, but gradually the team faded from competitiveness, most of its drivers leaving disillusioned, bitter because Surtees usually believed he knew more about the cars' behaviour than they did. In truth, it is probably a tragedy that John never had in his team a driver of his own class, a man who had his respect.

Perhaps the heart of Surtees's problems lay in having spent so many years in motorcycle racing. He never became truly acclimatized to the comparative lack of camaraderie in Grand Prix racing, to its many pretensions. Essentially a friendly, straightforward individual, he was repelled by many of the changes which the sport underwent in the seventies, by its increasing commercialism, its obsession with safety, its callous disregard for its own heritage. At the end of 1978, John decided that enough was enough, and the Surtees Formula One team was wound up. The loner went his own way once more.

The great sadness is that many will have known John Surtees only as the failed constructor, having never seen him as the truly great racing driver he was.

Nobody knew quite what to make of Gilles Villeneuve when he came to Silverstone to make his Formula One debut in 1977. To some extent, his reputation had preceded him. His domination of the Canadian Formula Atlantic scene was beyond dispute, but how good were his rivals? He was said to be incredibly quick, with remarkable reflexes, great courage, and spectacular style. Perhaps he was a little braver than was good for him.

As Villeneuve, a small, compact man, strolled arm-in-arm with his wife around the paddock, he looked too young to be allowed anywhere near a Grand Prix car. Once in it, however, he gave a foretaste of the dramatic touch which would become his hallmark. His progress in the McLaren was intoxicating. As you watched, you were staggered by his natural pace, yet also a little scared for him. He drove very close to the edge, setting fast times, yet spinning frequently. Was he unaware of his limits? Significantly, he did not make a mistake in the race itself, and made a considerable impression before jetting back to Quebec.

There should have been further drives for McLaren that summer, but for various reasons these did not come about. The team had an option on Gilles's services for 1978, but, finally, this was not taken up. In their wisdom, the McLaren management decided instead to hire Patrick Tambay, who had also made his Formula One debut at Silverstone, in an Ensign, and continued with the car throughout the season with excellent results. In racing, as in everything else, you are only as good as your last performance, and when the time came for decisions, Villeneuve's one and only Grand Prix appearance was some months in the past.

It was a considerable surprise when Enzo Ferrari announced that Gilles would be replacing Niki Lauda in his team for 1978. The Commendatore traditionally waits for young drivers to win their spurs elsewhere before inviting them to Maranello. After a single Formula One appearance, Villeneuve was a Ferrari driver.

The association began disastrously. Gilles was seconded into the team at short notice for the last two races of 1977. Lauda, his title clinched, had no further use for Ferrari, whose cars had slipped, in late season, into appalling handling problems. In Canada Gilles spun and hit things. In Japan he had an almighty accident, launching the Ferrari over Ronnie Peterson's Tyrrell and beginning a sequence of wild flips which ended with inexplicable escape for Villeneuve, but death for several spectators in a prohibited area.

In the aftermath of this frantic baptism there were suggestions that Ferrari should reconsider his decision, even that Gilles should be banned. But the storm finally abated, and Villeneuve settled down to a winter of testing in Italy, learning all about Ferrari.

After more accidents in the early part of 1978, the true measure of the man began to emerge. By season's end he could run with anyone. At Monza he fought a pitched battle with Mario Andretti's ruling Lotus 79, losing only in the late stages. At home in Montreal, he won his first Grand Prix. Desperation to triumph in twelve months.

Since the beginning of the 1979 season, Villeneuve has been acknowledged as the fastest of all Grand Prix drivers, his sheer ability frequently compared with that of a Clark or a Stewart. His driving appears to be without weaknesses, his enthusiasm without equal. Ferrari, of course, go through highs and lows, like any other team. When you see Villeneuve's car at the end of a race, be it first or tenth on the results sheet, you can say with absolute confidence that it could have been driven no harder. He will fight for either place with equal zest, a quality reminiscent of Stirling Moss. "Stroking," he has observed, "is a bad habit to get into. . . ."

Villeneuve is a calm man. Behind the bubbling eagerness is an unruffled mind. He should have won the World Championship in 1979, would have done, too, with a little more percentage driving and an eye on the points. Instead he tried to win all the races, a policy which endears him to fans the world over. He doesn't have off-days. Yes, of course he would like the title, he admits, but life can still be worth something without it. Winning races is far more important.

This approach to the job has inevitably brought him the kind of adulation accorded to just one man in every racing generation. The public identifies with him, just as it did previously with Ronnie Peterson and Jochen Rindt. When they see him step into a racing car, they expect drama, the unexpected, the raising of their senses. They remember the French Grand Prix at Dijon in 1979, when Arnoux's Renault went past Gilles's Ferrari near the end. Tyres shot, Villeneuve's position looked hopeless, but back he came, somehow retaking his second place. The intensity of those laps brought condemnation from some, plaudits from others. That kind of aggression had been absent from Grand Prix racing for a long time.

Not being schooled in European motor racing, Gilles lives by his own rules, eschewing all elements of the jet-set life. At the races he usually avoids the ritzy hotels, preferring to live with his family in a huge motor home, brought over from Quebec. His reasoning makes sense. He knows what he likes to eat, and he prefers to sleep in his own bed. Also, the camper is parked close to the Ferrari area in the paddock, and he likes to keep in touch with the mechanics. Late at night he is often to be found with them as they work on his car. Not surprisingly, their loyalty to him is devout.

The biggest test of a racing driver's character, however, is the way he reacts when good results are rare. And in 1980 Gilles was faced with just such a plight. Ferrari were totally uncompetitive. Significantly, his efforts never wavered as he constantly taxed his own abilities to compensate for the shortcomings of the car. Nor did his sense of humour suffer. What did become clear as the season progressed, however, was an increasing disillusionment with the path of Formula One. He hated the emphasis on downforce, the impotence of the driver to overcome shortcomings of the car. Any technical development which minimizes the driver's contribution is, after all, to his detriment.

For all that, he has won several Grands Prix, and there will be many more. He makes very few mistakes, far fewer than many of his supposedly more sanguine rivals, and works constantly to develop his talent. Villeneuve is one of those who really do make Grand Prix driving look easy, and his stamina matches his skill. At the end of a race he is fresh and cool, having needed to exert far less energy than most. In time, he must assuredly win the World Championship—and spectators everywhere must hope that he keeps faith with them, getting there by winning the races. The signs are that he will.

In the two decades between 1960 and 1980, racing car design accelerated at an unprecedented pace. In 1960, Ferrari—invariably the most conservative of racing car builders—were still campaigning front-engined cars. Only a year or so before that had they gone to disc brakes.

It was in the season of 1960 that Colin Chapman's Formula One cars were first taken seriously. The Lotus chief has always had the reputation of being the great innovator, but actually his true genius had always lain in his ability to sift through other people's ideas, ignoring the blind alleys, and adopting, refining, and perfecting the remainder.

Chapman has, of course, had a most profound effect upon the course of motor racing history, but the man who really changed its basic direction was John Cooper. In the late fifties, Cooper's apparently flimsy, lightweight, and underpowered mid-engined cars seemed ill-equipped to cope with the might of Ferrari, Maserati, and Vanwall, who were still building cars to the classical formula. But by 1958 it was becoming clear that at any circuit where handling was of paramount importance the small Cooper cars were pointing the way. In 1959 and 1960, the Cooper team won the World Championship, and the following year they went to the unknown territory of Indianapolis.

Cooper were never to capitalize on their early successes. It was left to Chapman and his Lotus team to do that—in both Formula One and the Indy 500. But Cooper had changed the direction of motor racing thought. From then on, the engine went behind the driver, and the accent was on lightness, nimble handling, and aerodynamic efficiency, features largely ignored in the preceding years.

Changes to the cars necessarily required changes by the drivers. There is something in the theory that a great artist can adapt his talent to changing times. But new techniques bring problems. There was evidence of this during the era of the Auto Union, in the years leading up to the Second World War. Unwieldy and unforgiving, the massive rear-engined cars were totally different from any other cars of their time. Luigi Fagioli, Achille Varzi, Tazio Nuvolari—great drivers all—took the wheel of an Auto Union after years of success in such "conventional" machinery as Bugatti, Alfa Romeo, and Mercedes-Benz. With ability like theirs, none disgraced himself, but no one ever handled an Auto Union with the authority, confidence, dash, and sheer pace of Bernd Rosemeyer.

There are those, even today, who claim that during his brief Grand Prix career—a little more than two seasons—Rosemeyer displayed a natural ability unequalled before or since. But, as a driver of Auto Unions, the brilliant German had one major advantage over his team-mates: the Auto Union was the only Grand Prix car he ever knew. He came straight into Grand Prix racing with them after a successful career on motorcycles. He had nothing to unlearn.

When the revolution came to Grand Prix racing, at the end of the fifties, the sport's two greatest protagonists were Stirling Moss and Tony Brooks. It may be argued that Brooks's commitment to Grand Prix racing was already waning by this time, whereas Moss, with ambition to go on for another fifteen years, was as enthusiastic as ever. Whatever the circumstances, the fact remains that Tony, virtually Stirling's equal in a "conventional", front-engined Formula One car, was never able to adapt so readily to the new breed. Moss continued without breaking his stride, pitting himself against a new genius, Jimmy Clark—who, like Rosemeyer, had known nothing else.

On the other side of the Atlantic, the story was much the same. After Jack Brabham's pioneering Cooper drive in 1961, and

particularly after Clark's barnstorming debut two years later, it became clear to the Indianapolis establishment that they had to follow suit, to copy the English cars. The truly great drivers among their number, such as A.J. Foyt and Parnelli Jones, were able to make the transition without difficulty, but a man like Rodger Ward, twice the winner of the 500 and the equal of almost anyone in a traditional "roadster", found himself off the pace, out of the headlines, in the new "funny cars".

The evolution of the Grand Prix car has, in the last twenty years, made classification of the drivers much more difficult. There remain, of course, the poor, the mediocre, the good, and the great, and by the nature of things that will never change. But it is unquestionably far less simple today to categorize them. The visible difference between, say, the mediocre and the good is not as apparent as used to be the case. It is a comforting time for the average driver of a good car, a frustrating one for the great artist in a bad one.

Time was when a Grand Prix car amplified a driver's ability. The front-engined cars, with narrow tyres and a low adhesion breakaway point, lent themselves more to the free expression of the driver. A Fangio was breathtaking to watch, a lesser mortal pathetic by comparison. And, to a decreasing extent, the same was true of the first decade of mid-engined Grand Prix racing—until there came the leap in tyre widths and, more particularly, the arrival of the "slick".

Slick tyres are the despair of the great driver. Coupled with increasingly sophisticated chassis, wings, and, later, the downforce born of ground-effects technology, they have reduced the "art" of cornering. Add to that the safety crusade of recent years which has led to a plethora of artificial chicanes and a consequent reduction in the number of genuinely fast corners, and there exists a situation which reduces the opportunity for the great driver to show his class. The call for delicacy, the need for precision, has been reduced. Too many corners are "flat" for everyone, instead of being the province of the truly gifted.

In 1935, Nuvolari's brilliance, in an outdated and underpowered Alfa Romeo, was enough to defeat the might of Mercedes-Benz and Auto Union at the Nürburgring. And Moss's Lotus humbled the Ferraris at the same circuit twenty-six years later.

Today, however, such feats are inconceivable. In 1980, even the mammoth talent of Villeneuve was suffocated by the inadequacies of his car. All his brilliance and unflagging effort was impotent in the face of brute "downforce and grip", as those with a fraction of his ability drove by him. It is a sad state of affairs. Grands Prix are increasingly won on the drawing board rather than in the cockpit, which is unfortunate for the hapless driver landed in the wrong team at the wrong time. Inevitably, it is the results which linger in the minds of those who watch.

Today's Grand Prix driver will enter corners at speeds unimaginable even five years ago. Braking distances have been more than halved. The g-forces endured through fast corners are staggering. The driver of the eighties needs tremendous physical stamina, but he needs it for less time than his predecessors because the races are considerably shorter. He also requires an infinitely greater appreciation of things mechanical than the driver of twenty years ago. In his cockpit he has such niceties as levers for adjusting the front and rear roll-bars and the brake balance.

By 1980, though, the Grand Prix driver, necessarily something of a free spirit, had started to rebel against his restrictions—particularly if he were driving a second-rate car. "We're just chauffeurs these days, almost passengers," was a frequently heard complaint. "There's no room these days for the driver to express himself. You can only hope you're in a team where the designer has got his sums right...."

THE CIRCUITS

NIGEL ROEBUCK

THE INTERNATIONAL GRAND PRIX CALENDAR achieved a certain stability in the late seventies, with a fairly certain schedule. In the preceding decade, Formula One had undergone a massive metamorphosis as increasingly safety-conscious drivers repeatedly expressed dissatisfaction with certain circuits and demanded that alternative venues be found. The majority, with safety facelifts, survived, but a great many of the classic tracks are gone for all time.

In a normal year, the Grand Prix Championship begins in January in South America, with a pair of races in Buenos Aires, close to the centre of the city, and Interlagos, on the outskirts of São Paulo. Thereafter, the circus moves on to Kyalami, a few miles from Johannesburg. Long Beach, a Monaco-style race, is a recent and most unlikely addition to the calendar. After a shaky start, in 1976, its popularity has blossomed, its place has become secure.

Next begins the long haul through the European summer. The month of May has no fixed racing pattern. Sometimes the European season gets underway at Zolder, sometimes at Monte Carlo, sometimes at Jarama. In 1981 it began at Imola with a fixture which may become permanent. Zolder, in wooded countryside near Liege, is not a popular place, and enthusiasts yearn for the day the Belgian Grand Prix returns to Spa-Francorchamps—albeit on the new, shorter track. The Monaco Grand Prix is, of course, the Race of Clichés, the place to be seen. It is no longer a race, but still affords an unparalleled opportunity to view the art of the racing driver at close quarters. Jarama, close to the dingy tenements of Madrid's outskirts, is no one's favourite race circuit. Now that Sweden no longer hosts a Grand Prix, June is a comparatively still month, a time for testing. The Formula One brigade arrives in France at the beginning of July, when the weather is perfect. Dijon, in the heart of Romanee-Conti country, must compete with Paul Ricard, whose greatest asset is the beach at nearby Bandol. In England the choice is between Silverstone, where legend increasingly lives, and Brands Hatch, a fun fair with racing cars in the middle of it. Rain, of course, is a threat at either. . . . August traditionally begins with the German Grand Prix, and these days that means Hockenheim, fast and unloved successor to the Nürburgring. Next on the agenda is the magnificent, swirling Osterreichring, in the foothills of Styria. From Austria we move to Holland, to Zandvoort. A Grand Prix circuit for more than twenty-five years, Zandvoort now begins to assume the aura of history, but the atmosphere is not comparable with that at Monza, scene of triumph and tragedy for fifty years and more. The Milanese track marks the end of the European campaign.

The season closes with the bright skies and bitter cold of Montreal, followed by the freezing winds and habitual rain of Watkins Glen, an undistinguished village in upstate New York, which comes alive briefly in early October.

One of the sadnesses of modern Grand Prix racing is that increased speeds—and corresponding safety demands—have robbed the sport of many of the circuits on which its history was laid. The strands of continuity have, one by one, been broken. Eight of the tracks used in the 1980 World Championship came into Grand Prix use only in the 1970s. Most of the modern, purpose-built tracks are as safe as such places can reasonably be, but inevitably many lack the atmosphere which comes only with fable and legend, and none is as challenging as some of those put out to pasture.

The French racing fan, for example, must close his mind to thoughts of Clermont-Ferrand and Rouen-Les-Essarts, two great theatres of battle now considered fit places only for local saloon car races. And Reims, five flat-out miles through the champagne country, has lost all links with its distinguished past, now merely a series of public roads, increasingly anonymous as the pits and grandstands crumble, and the landmarks are torn down. The paddock area is a local football pitch. In the seventies, therefore, the focal point of French motor racing became increasingly the Circuit Paul Ricard, near Marseille, which is civilized, but unexciting.

In 1976, the Formula One transporters pulled out of the Nürburgring for the last time. In the afternoon, Niki Lauda—for long a fierce critic of the circuit—had crashed his Ferrari. When the teams arrived back at base early the following day, the World Champion's life hung in the balance. He survived, of course, but the 'Ring did not. In the welter of adverse comment which followed, there was no chance for it. Hockenheim, which had itself taken the life of the great Jim Clark, took its place. It is bland and monotonous—but safer.

Hockenheim has no subtleties. It consists of a pair of long straights, linked at one end by a tight "stadium" section of slow corners, at the other by the one testing spot in its entire distance, a flat-in-fifth right-hand corner. Compare that with those fourteen miles in the Eifel mountains, looping through every type of curve and gradient, making call on every bit of a racing driver's ability.

For show business purposes, of course, the Nürburgring was a dead loss; the cars came by only every seven minutes or so, out of step with the "instant" entertainment of today. Yet anyone who ventured out into the country, watched a true artist in the last moments of practise straining sinew at such places as Fuchsröhre, Bergwerk, or the Adenau Bridge, has seen every romantic justification for Grand Prix racing. It left you trembling slightly, searching for your cigarettes.

Some of the drivers, looking over their shoulders, were sad and a little resentful at leaving the Nürburgring for all time. Many had been drawn to the life of Grand Prix racing by reading of such circuits during their formative years, and relished the prospect of pitting themselves against them.

On the eve of the 1977 German Grand Prix, however, John Watson said, "I'd rather race at the Nürburgring, but I'd rather survive at Hockenheim."

In terms of logistics, of course, the 'Ring had been obsolete from the day of its opening. To marshal adequately a circuit of such length amounts to near impossibility. If there is an accident, the layout is such that speedy rescue of the injured is difficult to achieve. When Lauda crashed, it was left to fellow drivers to free him from the burning wreckage, and it was this rather than the

Signals and Flags

Traditionally, Grand Prix starts were signalled with a national flag, but the modern starting signal is a green light which comes on ten seconds after the red light. (This should be shown when all drivers are in position and stationary after their warm-up lap.) Once a race is underway flags are used to convey information and warnings to the drivers. These flags are of different colours and designs and have proved to be the most efficient and effective way of communicating with drivers who are travelling at high speeds. The flags are all approximately 23 by 31 inches (60 by 80 cm). A flag is displayed motionless unless it is in close proximity to the cause for its use, when it is waved to give emphasis to its message. When flags are doubled it is an indication that there is an extremely serious emergency. Sets of flags are kept at each marshal's post and are the responsibility of the chief of the post and his assistant. In a few cases flags have been replaced by coloured lights.

The blue flag held steady indicates that "another car is following closely". When the flag is waved it means that "another car is trying to overtake".

The white flag signifies that there is a slow moving car or service vehicle on the track. It is displayed at all marshals' posts at the same time and the flag immediately preceding this temporary, mobile hazard is waved.

The red flag is the sign for "a complete and immediate stop for all cars". Unless the track is blocked this effectively means that the driver must continue to the pits.

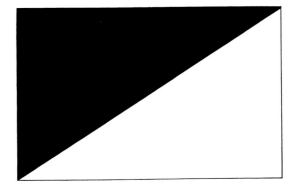

The black and white flag is a warning to the driver whose number is displayed with it to cease unsportsmanlike behaviour before the black flag is displayed which will oblige him to stop at the pits immediately.

dangers inherent in the circuit itself which turned many of them against the Nürburgring. For all that, however, there were several who felt that the satisfaction justified the risk.

The Nürburgring was only one of many casualties of the seventies, and there is no doubt that much of the grandeur of Grand Prix racing has been lost with their passing. Spa-Francorchamps—perhaps the most dramatic of all circuits—underwent sustained attacks in the sixties, finally succumbing in 1970. At Spa the problem was one of sheer pace, eight miles of fast, sweeping curves, calling for enormous courage and precision. So quickly were the cars travelling at virtually every point of the circuit that an error of judgement invariably had serious consequences. A purist, of course, will argue that there lies the challenge: the object of the exercise is not to make mistakes.

Unfortunately, though, the story does not end there. In the sixties and seventies, mechanical failures leading to accidents became much more prevalent. Jim Clark, Jo Schlesser, Bruce McLaren, Jochen Rindt, Jo Siffert, Roger Williamson, and Peter Revson all died in circumstances indicative of car failure. As speeds increased dramatically, so, too, did the demands for improved circuit safety.

In itself, this is only reasonable. Perhaps the popular press is correct in its constant assertion that there are ghouls who like to see accidents, but no one wants to witness unnecessary injury or death. "If the danger factor remains the same as it always was," Mario Andretti has said, "then that is acceptable. But as speeds go up, it is fair for us to expect that safety precautions will keep pace."

The pity of it is that sufficient money has rarely been available to make major safety changes to the classic circuits. Of their number, only Monza, Monaco, and Silverstone survive. Newer circuits, built with modern safety facilities, have tended to sweep the classic tracks aside. Aesthetically, they are a disaster, with miles of crash barrier and catch fencing jarring to an eye which appreciates trees and parkland. It is, however, easy to understand why beautiful scenery rates low on a driver's list of priorities.

Many feel that much of the responsibility for the loss of Grand Prix racing's heritage lies with the Great God Progress. The safety crusaders maintain that certain tracks have become unsuitable for the modern Grand Prix car. Former World Champion Phil Hill has suggested that this could be a case of the tail wagging the dog, and that view has a sizeable lobby of support. If we toss Grand Prix history lightly aside, do we not run the risk of turning a sport into little more than an impressive design exercise? There are many who would agree with Stirling Moss's contention that "It's no fun playing cards for matches."

In the last few years we have lost—in addition to the Nürburgring and Spa-Francorchamps—Clermont-Ferrand, Reims, Rouen-les-Essarts, St. Jovite, Mosport Park, and Barcelona, all of them either classic "driver's circuits" or places which crackled with drama and legend. In their stead, we have gained Paul Ricard, Dijon, Zolder, Jarama, Hockenheim, Long Beach, and the Osterreichring. With the exception of the last two, that seems like a poor rate of exchange.

The modern, purpose-built, autodrome abounds in telex machines and smoked glass, in elaborate pits and sumptuous hospitality suites. The sun-dimmed glass keeps out the glare—and also the romance and mystique.

The yellow flag is a forewarning that there is danger on the track and it signals to drivers not to overtake and to reduce speed.

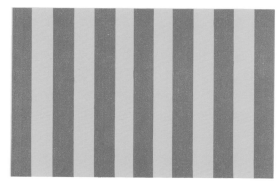

The red and yellow striped flag indicates that "the road surface is slippery". It is usually referred to as the oil flag and is of great help to drivers for it warns them of oil on the track, one of the worst hazards a driver can encounter.

The green flag informs drivers that "a previously notified danger has been cleared". When this flag replaces the red and yellow flag, for example, it means that the oil has been removed.

The black flag is accompanied by a white number and signals that the driver whose car number is displayed must stop at the pit on the next lap.

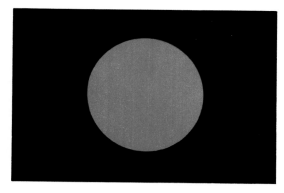

The black flag with a central orange disc warns a driver that his car has a mechanical problem or is on fire, and that he must stop.

The black and white chequered flag, which has come to symbolize Grand Prix racing, signifies the end of the race.

BUENOS AIRES

Grand Prix racing at Buenos Aires has had a chequered history. It began with a chaotic race in 1953. At the first Argentine Grand Prix there was an immense crowd, fiery and exuberant, all of them concentrating squarely on their national hero, Juan Manuel Fangio. They wanted to see him, touch him, be close to the action. Unwillingly, they stayed behind insubstantial fences, restrained only by hordes of soldiers and police.

Then President Perón arrived, and the National Anthem followed. While the troops stood to attention, the spectators, clearly less affected by protocol, broke down the barriers, rushed past the uniforms, and stationed themselves by the trackside. All attempts to move them back proved fruitless. Eventually the organizers decided to start the race on a circuit literally lined with people.

Ascari took the lead, and there he stayed for the duration of the race. But the event is remembered chiefly for an accident which was perhaps inevitable. A foolhardy spectator attempted to cross the track in front of Farina's Ferrari. The Italian swerved to avoid him, lost control of his car, and ploughed into the crowd. Nine people were killed, forty injured.

Fangio retired from the race that day, leaving his passionate supporters disappointed. But thereafter he dominated the Buenos Aires race until the end of his career, winning the Argentine Grand Prix for the next four years. And his victory in the 1955 race stands as one of his greatest ever, a triumph of dogged courage.

As the cars went to the grid for the start of the three-hour race, the temperature was exactly one hundred degrees in the shade. Throughout the event drivers came into the pits with heat exhaustion, rested a while, then took over as their team-mates stopped for relief. Even Froilan Gonzalez, a local man accustomed to high temperatures, had to surrender to blurring vision.

On and on went Fangio, apparently with mercury in his veins. He finished a clear winner from a Ferrari driven successively by Gonzalez, Farina, Trintignant, Gonzalez, and Farina.

In 1958, the great man made his final appearance in front of his home crowd, but in the Argentine Grand Prix his car failed, and victory eventually went to Stirling Moss in Rob Walker's tiny Cooper. Conceding a tremendous amount of power to Maserati and Ferrari, the Cooper was nevertheless nimble, and Stirling was able to last the distance with the same set of tyres. In the final laps, with his Dunlops almost worn down to the canvas, Moss was reeled in by Musso's Ferrari, but he made it to the flag by just over two seconds. For the Argentine crowds, however, there was consolation in

Fangio's victory in the non-championship Buenos Aires Grand Prix which followed.

After 1960 Argentine disappeared from the World Championship calendar for more than a decade, but in 1971 a race, albeit not a Grande Epreuve, was organized. This race was won by Chris Amon in a Matra. It was watched by a huge crowd, and plans were made for a championship race the following year. It coincided precisely with the beginning of Carlos Reutemann's full-time Grand Prix career, and the organizers could have asked for nothing more.

Reutemann had finished third in the 1971 event with an old McLaren, but now he was a fully fledged member of the Brabham team. And the citizens of Buenos Aires became positively light-headed with delight when he qualified his new car on the pole. It was, by any standards, a remarkable achievement, proof positive of the wonders of adrenalin.

Race day, however, went wrong for Carlos, and the pattern has persisted. Nowhere in the world is a single Grand Prix so much the province of one man. "Lole! Lole!" is the dominant sound, the crowd chanting his nickname. He is a hero beyond compare since the days of Fangio. They applaud his every move, will him to victory. And yet this man who has won so many races elsewhere always has

something go wrong at Buenos Aires. Many times he has led here, even dominated, but the Fates conspire without pity.

Often it is not the swiftest who wins the Argentine Grand Prix. The last win of Denny Hulme's career came in the 1974 race after Reutemann's Brabham failed late in the day. In 1977, Jody Scheckter's outpaced new Wolf outlasted the rest. In 1980 Alan Jones made several mistakes, spun more than once, yet got to the flag first.

The atmosphere in the autodromo is always highly charged. Inevitably the weather is extremely hot, the crowd volatile, its eyes on Reutemann, the most phlegmatic Argentine in the place. Fire trucks spray the spectators in the grandstands, offering temporary relief, but within minutes soaked shirts are bone dry once more.

And everywhere there are soldiers and police, all heavily armed, trained to anticipate—even expect—revolution. They are perhaps somewhat overzealous. A few years ago, the fire extinguisher in Mario Andretti's Lotus exploded in the heat. The immediate supposition was that a bomb had gone off, and for a few minutes there was bedlam, the sound of boots moving quickly over concrete, the sight of guns at the ready, safety catches off. Buenos Aires is not for the faint of heart.

BUENOS AIRES

Avda Roca X Avda Gral Paz
Buenos Aires
Argentina

Circuit Length
3.71 miles/5.97 km

Automovil Club Argentino

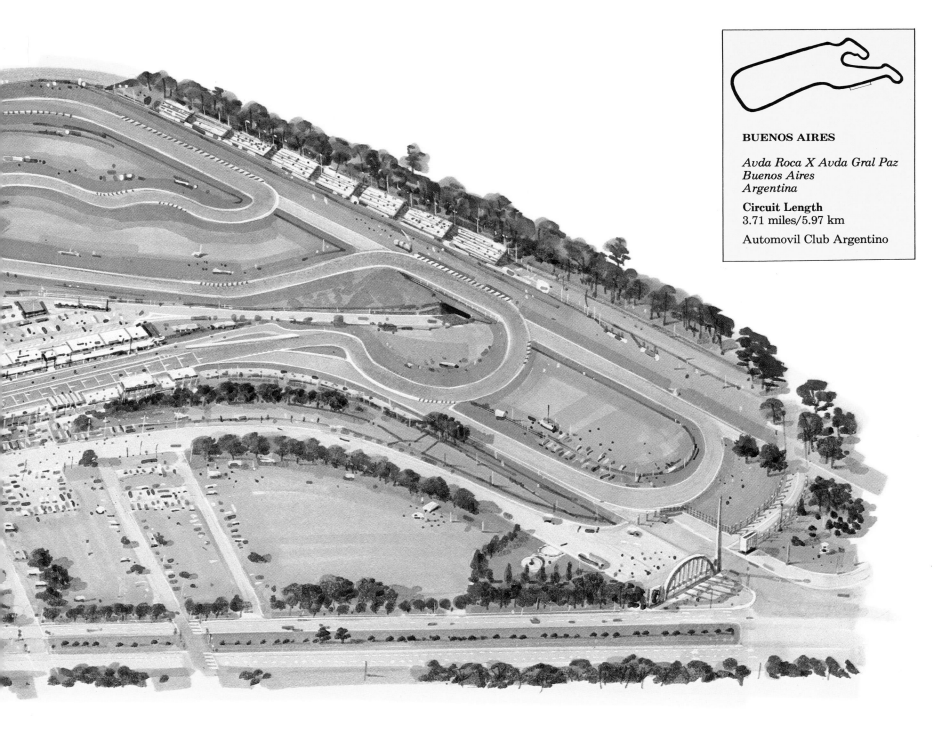

INTERLAGOS

Grand Prix drivers tend to have strong feelings about Interlagos. In recent times there has been considerable disquiet from some quarters about the safety facilities of the track. The very bumpy surface comes in for particular criticism.

Then again, there are those who dislike it because, privately, it is too good for them, too much a test of real driving ability for them to feel happy. Just as at Spa, where the distant sound of an exhaust note in the clear morning air was enough to distinguish between the ace and the also-ran, so Interlagos amplifies skill—or the lack of it. The first two corners, treated as a single ultra-fast arc, will show you why they are that side of the guard rail, you on this side.

In comparision with most World Championship venues, Interlagos

is very old. The first race meeting there was held in May of 1940, although Formula One cars did not set wheel in the place until 1972, when a non-championship event was run.

The television camera lies about Interlagos, giving an impression of rolling countryside and a land of plenty. True enough, the track itself is set in a natural, hilly amphitheatre, like the Osterreichring, but close by is the ugly, urban sprawl of São Paulo, with its belching, acrid chimneys, vulgar wealth, and appalling poverty. And the approach to the track, with its horrifying shanty towns and hovels, is enough to make uneasy the most committed capitalist as he surveys the profligacy of motor racing's public relations machine in the paddock nearby. On the face of it, then, Interlagos is an

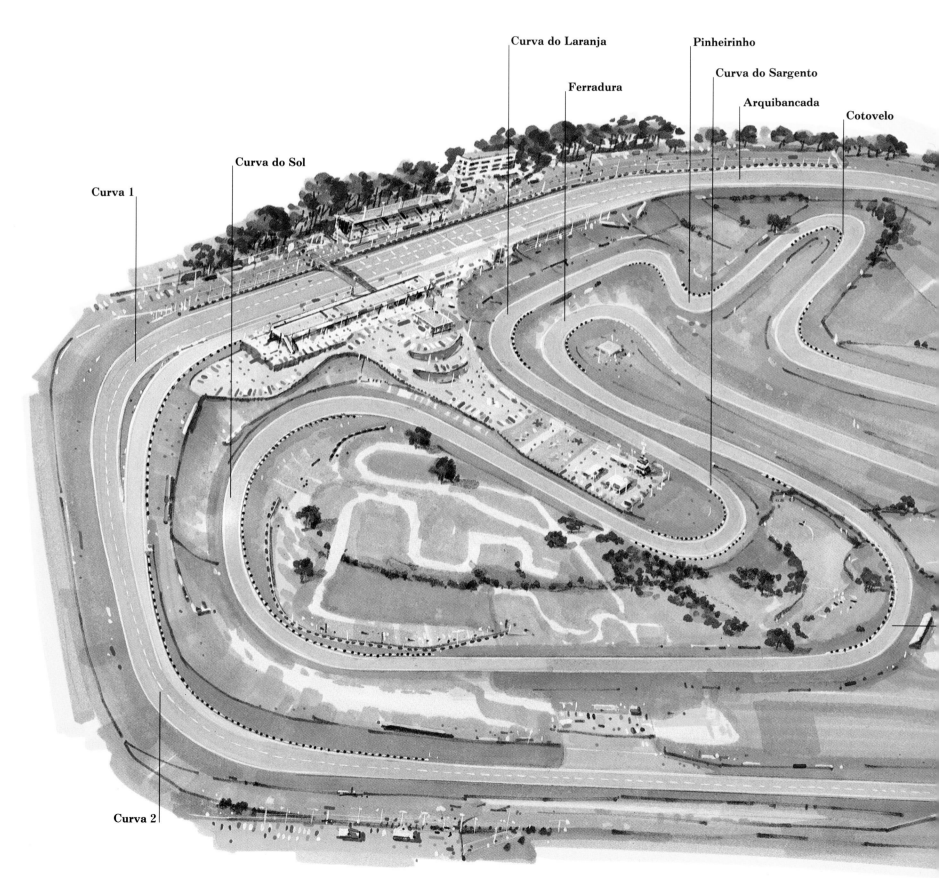

uncomfortable spot for jetsetters, more at their ease when enjoying the vacuous charms of Monte Carlo or Rio de Janeiro.

Every so often, the Beautiful People get their way, however, for Rio now has its own circuit, supposedly an alternative to Interlagos, to be used for every other Brazilian Grand Prix. It is as bland as Interlagos is exciting, although there is always Copacobana.

The construction and layout of Interlagos is unusual in several respects. Although—at almost five miles—a long circuit by the standards of today, the track was designed by an ingenious man, for it fits into an area normally required for a circuit only half that length. Again, it runs anticlockwise, a feature shared only with Imola.

For all the destitution of the surrounding area, there is an absolute fanaticism for racing here. Interlagos's late baptism as a Grand Prix circuit coincided precisely with the coming to power of Emerson Fittipaldi, a national hero in Brazil to the end of his career and beyond. Emerson dominated that first non-championship race at Interlagos, although he did not win it. But when the teams assembled for Brazil's first Championship Grand Prix, in 1973, Fittipaldi was the reigning World Champion, and had recently starred in a civic parade through São Paulo, watched by millions.

The entire country was therefore in the grip of racing fever when the Grand Prix circus rolled into Interlagos. This reached heights of delirium when Emerson proceeded to lead all the way in a Lotus 72. In 1974, now with McLaren, Fittipaldi did it again, laying the trail for his second World Championship.

The following year, however, Fittipaldi had to settle for second place in a race notable for other reasons: first, it was won by Carlos Pace, a brilliant Brazilian who was never to score another Grand Prix victory, and who died nearby in a light aircraft accident two years later; second, it was dominated, if not won, by Jean-Pierre Jarier's Shadow for reasons not apparent to this day; and third, it marked the first appearance before a home crowd of Brazil's first Formula One car, the Fittipaldi, driven by Emerson's elder brother, Wilson.

The next two races at Interlagos belonged to Ferrari. Niki Lauda's victory in 1976 came in the middle of a period when the Austrian and his 312T were all but unbeatable. Twelve months later Carlos Reutemann, winner of that first non-championship race in 1972, took the spoils.

The Argentine Ferrari driver was also triumphant in 1978 when the race was run at Rio, but there was some joy for the Brazilians when Fittipaldi, in the backwaters since leaving McLaren to drive for "the family firm", took second place.

Interlagos faced severe criticism in 1979 when the ground-effects generation arrived. The phenomenally hard springs necessarily used with ground-effects cars served to multiply variations in the track surface. In modern racing, circuits are expected to suit cars, rather than the other way round, and suddenly Interlagos went from bumpy to unacceptable. Later in the year similar complaints would be made about Watkins Glen.

The Grand Prix fell to the Ligiers of Jacques Laffite and Patrick Depailler simply because the French team had their chassis working better than any others. The day when driving ability counted for more than anything else at Interlagos had passed—temporarily, it is hoped. In 1980, victory for the French was even more conclusive, this time for the Renault team by the simple expedient of having a great deal more power than the rest.

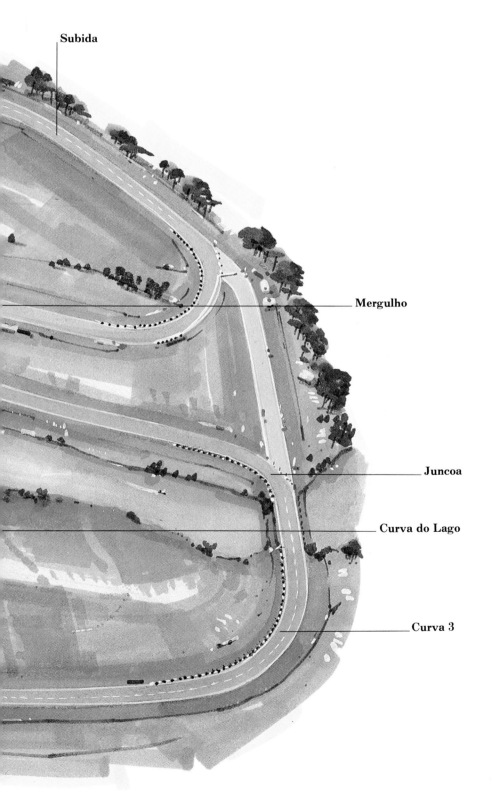

Subida

Mergulho

Juncoa

Curva do Lago

Curva 3

INTERLAGOS

Estrada Parelheiros No 15
São Paulo
Brazil

Circuit Length
4.95 miles/7.97 km

Confederacao Brasiliera
de Automobilismo

KYALAMI

Kyalami invariably provides drama, and not all of it comes from the motor racing. The place seems to suffer from constant financial problems, and every year the wire services carry panic stories from Johannesburg: unless major sponsorship can be found, it seems unlikely that there will be a South African Grand Prix next year. . . . And somehow, miraculously, the money always materializes from somewhere. Kyalami's place in the Grand Prix world is fully established.

The track itself, incomparably South Africa's best, opened late in 1961. Its first major event, a non-championship Formula One race, the Rand Grand Prix, was won by Jimmy Clark. But when, the following year, the country was granted a championship race for the first time, the East London circuit was chosen and there the South African Grand Prix stayed until 1967. That year, on January 2nd, it came to Kyalami, and a colossal crowd came out to watch. For them, the day almost had a storybook ending.

Most of the race was dominated by Denny Hulme's Brabham, but the New Zealander was increasingly beset by brake problems and these brought him into the pits with only twenty laps to go. And in the lead, remarkably, was John Love, a veteran Rhodesian with an old but superbly prepared Cooper and a vast experience of Kyalami. This was his one Grand Prix of the year, and he was going to beat all the stars. With only seven laps left, there were groans from the grandstand as the little car stammered into the pits, out of fuel. Eventually Love rejoined, but by now his lead was gone, and at the flag he took second place to Pedro Rodriguez in a factory Cooper-Maserati. All in all, however, Kyalami's first Grand Prix was a huge critical success, and the track's future as a World Championship venue was assured.

Kyalami is a peculiar circuit in several respects. Like Zandvoort, it has "fast days and slow days." No one has ever quite understood why this should be so, although the South African track's situation—almost six thousand feet above sea level—has been put forward as a possible reason. Then again, Zandvoort is precisely at sea level, the North Sea breakers crashing in only a couple of hundred yards from the circuit. . . . It is beyond dispute, however, that drivers at both places sometimes find themselves unaccountably incapable of approaching lap times they had previously achieved. "No point in staying out there today," a pragmatist like Niki Lauda would say. "It's a slow day. . . ."

Because of the high altitude, it is always a relatively slow day at Kyalami. In the thin air, racing engines lose about 20 per cent of their normal horsepower. "It's not a difficult circuit, anyway," Jackie Stewart has said, "and with only about four hundred horsepower available, the cars are obviously easier to drive than usual."

All animals were equal at Kyalami until Renault brought turbocharged engines into Formula One. Because turbos create their own air pressure, they are immunized against the altitude and produce their usual horsepower—in normal circumstances superior to conventionally aspirated engines. For the French team, therefore, Kyalami was a cakewalk and the yellow cars would pass their rivals on the straight with even more than their usual ease. In practice for the 1980 race, Jean-Pierre Jabouille was almost two full seconds quicker than all but his Renault team-mate, René Arnoux, and that in Formula One terms is a lifetime.

Over the years, Kyalami has known its share of racing legend. Jimmy Clark scored his last Grand Prix victory here in 1968, as did Jack Brabham two years later. It was the scene of Mario Andretti's first win, back in 1971 when he was a Ferrari driver, and of Carlos Reutemann's, in a Brabham in 1974. It has witnessed a brilliantly aggressive victory by its hometown hero Jody Scheckter, in 1975, and a superb pair of back-to-back wins by Niki Lauda in the two years following. For the record, the Austrian's race times—each over a distance of 199 miles—differed by only three seconds.

Contrasting vividly with the feverish excitement of Ronnie Peterson's last-lap overhaul of Patrick Depailler in 1978 was

Arnoux's boring, effortless horsepower triumph two years later. And in 1981 there was the sad spectacle of a decimated field, the South African Grand Prix a victim of FISA-FOCA political machinations.

There have been dark days at Kyalami, especially for the now defunct Shadow team, which lost two team leaders here. Peter Revson was killed instantly during testing in 1974, when a front suspension breakage pitched him into the guard rail at the ultra-fast Barbeque Bend. And in 1977 there occurred perhaps the most bizarre accident in racing history. Tom Pryce, passing the pits at 170 mph, hit a marshal who was stupidly running across the road with a heavy fire extinguisher in his arms. Pryce was struck in the face by the extinguisher, and the Shadow continued on down the straight towards Crowthorne Corner, its driver already dead, his foot jammed hard against the throttle pedal. In its mindless course the car overtook several other drivers braking for Crowthorne, and hit Jacques Laffite's Ligier before finally coming to rest against the outside crash wall.

In other than freak circumstances, however, Kyalami's safety record is excellent, and the South African Grand Prix is a race enjoyed by the drivers, who relish a few days of heat and relaxation before the long haul of the European season.

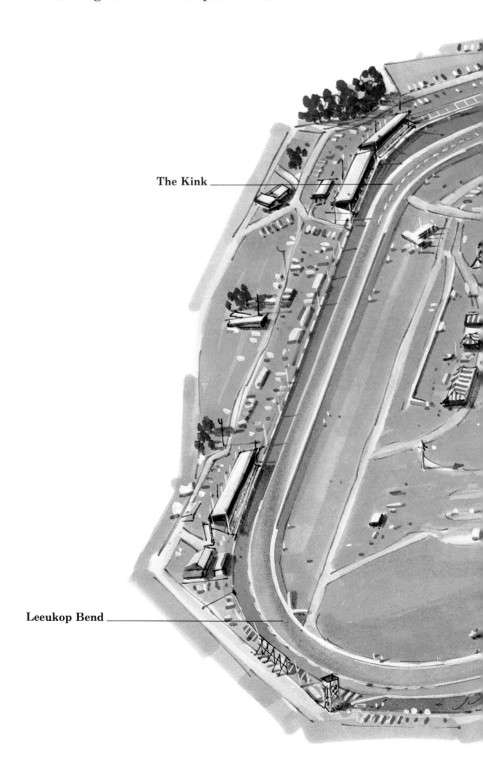

The Kink

Leeukop Bend

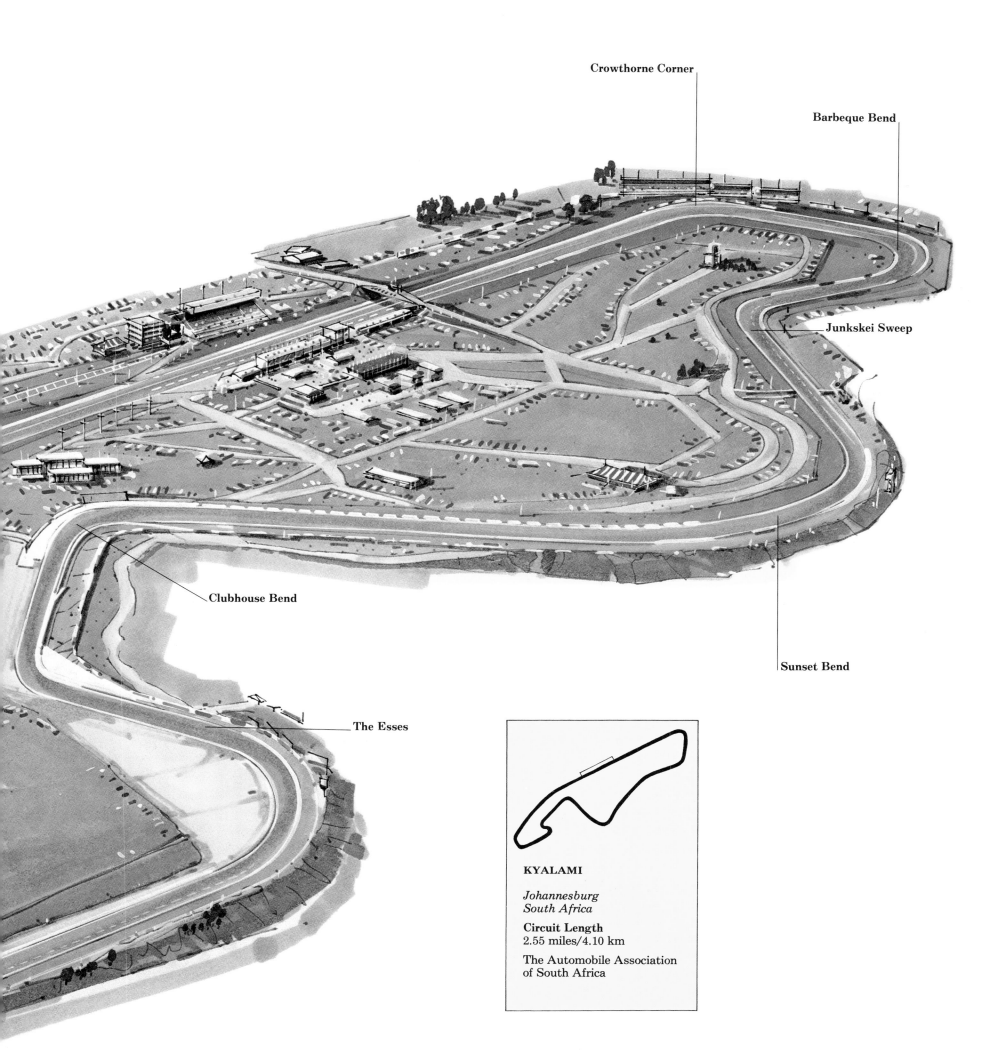

Crowthorne Corner

Barbeque Bend

Junkskei Sweep

Clubhouse Bend

Sunset Bend

The Esses

KYALAMI

Johannesburg
South Africa

Circuit Length
2.55 miles/4.10 km

The Automobile Association
of South Africa

LONG BEACH

When Christopher Robin Pook first conceived the notion of running a Grand Prix through the streets of Long Beach, his idea was taken seriously by very few. Despite a fair sprinkling of massage parlours and porno movies, Long Beach is not predominantly a place of the youthful and most of the locals did not care to contemplate the taking over of their town by a bunch of noisy racing cars.

Pook, however, is a determined man, and he set about the task of realizing his dream. A longtime racing fan, the expatriate Englishman ultimately managed to persuade City Hall that a Monaco-style Formula One race in California would bring a lot of publicity to Long Beach, that it would be good for the place. Permission granted, he and his colleagues buckled down to organizing the first race in 1975.

The inaugural event, though, could not be a Grand Prix, for motor racing's governing body decreed long ago that any new circuit wishing to host a Grand Prix must first prove itself capable of doing the job by organizing a prior meeting for another type of car. Pook opted for a Formula 5000 event, assembling the greatest field of such cars ever seen, along with many top drivers.

That first Long Beach race was a huge success. Most of the drivers thoroughly enjoyed the new street track, with a series of tight turns through the town and a long, curving blast down Shoreline Drive, past the laid-to-rest *Queen Mary*. The race was won by Formula 5000's most successful driver, Brian Redman, but on this day the Lancastrian was lucky. The talk of the town was the sensational drive of England's young Tony Brise, who coolly dealt with both Mario Andretti and Al Unser and looked set for victory until his car failed. When motor racing returned to Long Beach, six months later, the brilliant Brise was gone, one of the victims of Graham Hill's air crash.

The first United States Grand Prix West (later to be called the Long Beach Grand Prix) took place on March 28, 1976, and—novelty value apart—was remarkable chiefly for the manner in which Clay Regazzoni annihilated his rivals. Starting from pole position, Gianclaudio led from first to last, setting fastest lap along the way. It was perhaps the most perfect drive of his career.

It was not an exciting race, however, in no way comparable with the Formula 5000 race of the previous autumn. And it lost a lot of money for its organizers, although the name of Long Beach was seen in headline stories across the world; James Hunt, having collided

with Patrick Depailler, stood in the road for a while, angrily shaking his fist at the Frenchman every time he passed. Cameras recorded it everywhere.

Despite financial problems, Pook and his organization were determined to press on, and in this they were backed by the Long Beach City Council. What was needed was a hard, close race, preferably with an American winner. In 1977 it worked out precisely that way, with Jody Scheckter, Mario Andretti, and Niki Lauda circulating in close tandem for the entire eighty laps. Finally, Mario took the victory when Jody was slowed by a deflating tyre late in the race.

After that, the Long Beach Grand Prix never looked back. In

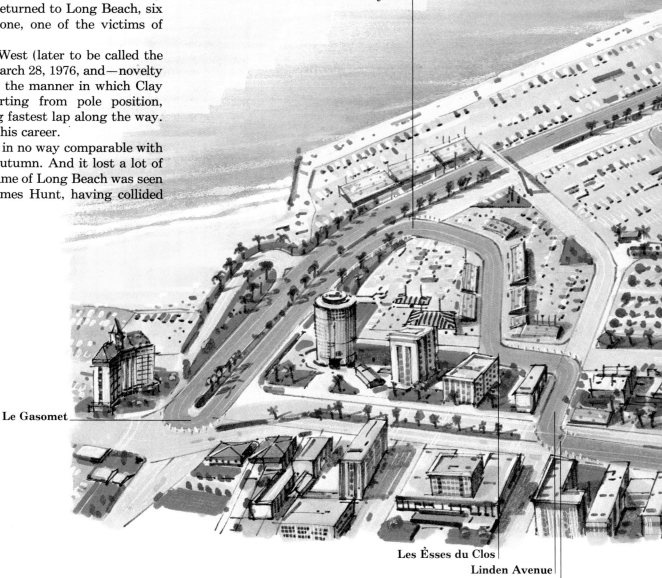

Indy Left

Le Gasomet

Les Ésses du Clos

Linden Avenue

Cook's Corner

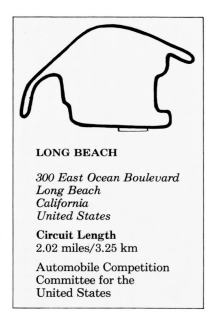

LONG BEACH

300 East Ocean Boulevard
Long Beach
California
United States

Circuit Length
2.02 miles/3.25 km

Automobile Competition
Committee for the
United States

1978, the pace and exuberance of Gilles Villeneuve seemed certain to win the day, but his relative inexperience told when he clouted a slower car, leaving the win to his Ferrari team-mate, Carlos Reutemann.

Twelve months later, Villeneuve was back to try again, and this time there was no mistake. The Ferrari led all the way, with a frantic battle for second place behind.

In 1980, there was an equally conclusive win, this time for Nelson Piquet and his Brabham. But the joy of the Brazilian's first Grand Prix victory was muted. Late in the race, Regazzoni, running fourth in the Ensign, arrived at the end of Shoreline Drive with complete brake failure. (At this point the cars are travelling at close to 180

mph before braking hard for the Queen's Hairpin.) Unchecked, the Swiss's car shot down the escape road, struck a car abandoned earlier, and cannoned into the tyre-faced wall beyond. Dreadfully injured, Regazzoni faced months in hospital and the possibility that he would never walk again. It was Long Beach's first serious accident, and the end of a great career.

The place of the Long Beach race on the Grand Prix calendar is now established and secure. Indeed, it is quickly acquiring the kudos of a classic event, refreshingly different from any other. Old men in wheelchairs, young men in racing cars, blue rinses everywhere, and rhinestone-studded glasses amplifying the spring sun. Long Beach in March.

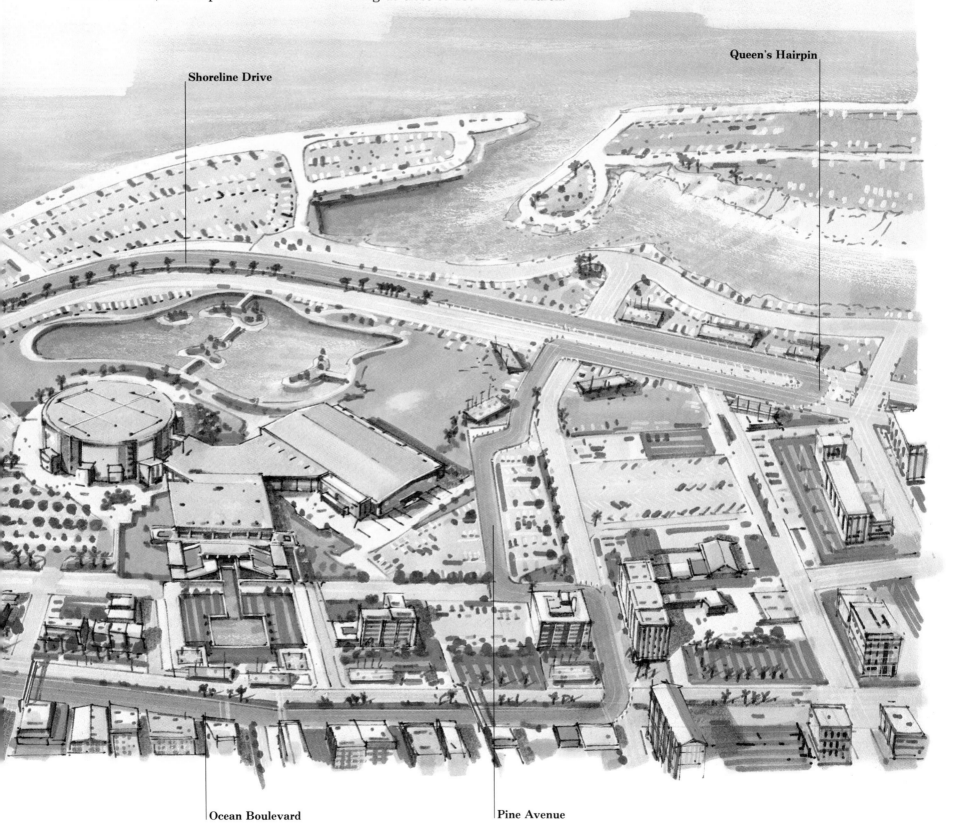

Shoreline Drive

Queen's Hairpin

Ocean Boulevard

Pine Avenue

ZOLDER

Zolder's lot is an unhappy one. Just as Hockenheim's status as a Grand Prix venue suffers inevitably in comparison with its predecessor, the Nürburgring, so Zolder lives in the shadow of Spa-Francorchamps, perhaps the most daunting and spectacular of all Grand Prix circuits.

Spa was dramatic and dangerous, a downhill ski race of a circuit, the fastest road course in existence, which made demands of a racing driver's every quality, in particular his precision and courage. It was nearly nine miles of public road, now climbing steeply, now plunging through a series of fast, open bends. It had the Masta Kink, a left and right blink of the eye, between houses, at close to 200 mph. And it had history, the authentic "feel" of a theatre of battle long established. And over the years, of course, it exacted its dues.

The last Belgian Grand Prix at Spa was run in 1970, a fraught affair which involved a race-long fight between Pedro Rodriguez and Chris Amon, who finished a second apart with an average a mite shy of 150 mph. With that, a whole chapter of Grand Prix racing came to a close. Spa, proclaimed some of the drivers (who did not include the stars of the final race), was too quick, too dangerous. It had to go.

Belgian motor racing was then faced with a choice of alternative sites. While the authorities pondered the problem, 1971 came and went without a Belgian Grand Prix. The Walloons (from French-speaking Belgium) and the Flemish both wanted the race for their own area. Finally, an unwilling compromise was negotiated: the Belgian Grand Prix would henceforth be held alternately at Nivelles, a new circuit close to Brussels, and at Zolder, near Liège.

For 1972 Nivelles was chosen. It was a modern "racing facility" with no character whatever, and a pit and paddock area with all the charm of a motorway services parking area. After a second race in 1974—won, like the first, by Emerson Fittipaldi—the circuit was beset by money problems and sank without trace. So Zolder became the home of the Belgian Grand Prix.

The circuit's situation is pleasant indeed, with thickly wooded countryside all around, and the track itself has several interesting corners. What Zolder lacks, however, is a pleasant ambience. Too often, a visit means clashing with officious policemen, who ride understandably timid horses through banks of traffic, and truculent officials with harsh faces and bad breath. Muzzled dogs abound. The paddock has a concentration camp atmosphere.

The track itself is very, very hard on cars, particularly on their tyres and brakes. Frequently, victory here goes to the man whose car lasts best, as was the case with Jody Scheckter's Ferrari in 1979. In the early stages, the South African was left behind, running most of the race in fourth place, but he went the full seventy laps faster than anyone else, which is what decides the points and the money.

Zolder's entry into the world of Grand Prix racing, in 1973, was extremely controversial. Extensive safety modifications, demanded by the Grand Prix Drivers Association, were started late in the day and track resurfacing was carried out only the week before the race. Consequently, the fresh surface had insufficient time to harden and settle, and broke up badly as soon as qualifying began. More work was done, but bodywork and crash helmets were peppered with stones throughout the weekend, and there was considerable doubt that the race would take place.

Jackie Stewart and François Cevert took first and second for Ken Tyrrell in that first race, but Zolder's next pair of Grands Prix were dominated by Niki Lauda and Ferrari. The Austrian was then at the height of his powers, and looked set to make it three in a row when he led the 1977 race for much of the way. It was a dreadful day, black and cold and wet. The pre-race favourites, Mario Andretti and John Watson, had crashed on the opening lap. Lauda's hat trick, however, was prevented by a remarkable drive by the Lotus number two driver, Gunnar Nilsson, who caught and passed the Ferrari to score the only win of his Grand Prix career. Within eighteen months, the popular Swede had died from cancer. Andretti, victorious the next year in the remarkable Lotus 79, dedicated the win to his friend.

Scheckter's somewhat fortunate victory in 1979 was overshadowed by a fantastic drive from his team-mate Gilles Villeneuve. After a pit-stop early in the race, the French-Canadian stormed back from twenty-third position to third, only for his Ferrari to expire, out of fuel, a couple of hundred yards from the chequered flag. Another pint of fuel would have given him four World Championship points . . . and the title.

The 1980 race was a clear-cut affair, however, a conclusive first Grand Prix win for Didier Pironi, whose Ligier led from the start and was never threatened.

Zolder's hold on the Belgian Grand Prix will cease when the Formula One circus returns to Spa-Francorchamps, where a revised circuit, using part of the original course, has been built. Belgium will then have a truly great Grand Prix circuit once more.

Lucien Bianchibocht

Sterrewachtbocht

Kanaalbocht

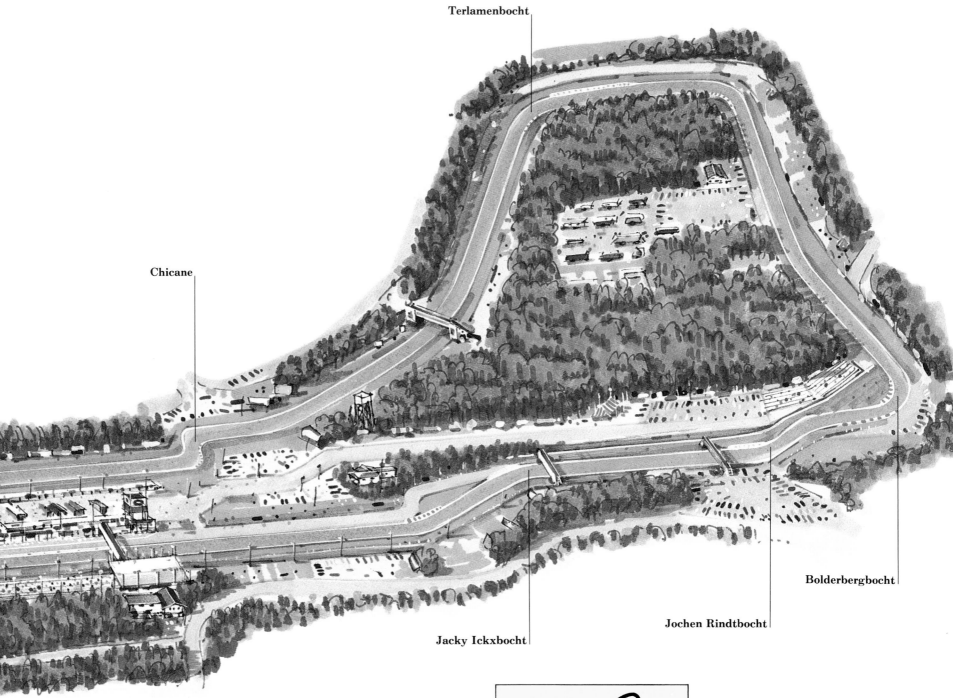

Terlamenbocht

Chicane

Bolderbergbocht

Jochen Rindtbocht

Jacky Ickxbocht

ZOLDER

Kontroletoren
B-3540 Zolder
Belgium

Circuit Length
2.65 miles/4.26 km

Royal Automobile Club
de Belgique

MONACO

Monte Carlo in May. The annual encounter between Grand Prix racing and the jet set, Bay of Plenty for the gossip columnists, a time of sweaty overalls, monokinis, tinsel, tyre marks through the town.

There was a time when the Monaco Grand Prix was really a race, when cars used to overtake each other. It was never easy, of course, in the tight confines of the principality's streets, but it was possible, given the right amounts of skill, wit, and judgement. But diverse elements of the last decade have come together to make it merely a high-speed parade. As an opportunity to view the art of the Grand Prix driver at close quarters it remains without equal. As a race it is a joke.

Progress in racing car design has killed the Monaco Grand Prix—that and the financial voracity of the organizers. Formula One cars have grown wider, laying claim to ever more of the limited space available, and their cornering and braking powers are now such that passing opportunities have been decimated. The track itself, inviolate for more than forty years, changed fundamentally in the 1970s. Simply to cram in more paying spectators, the wonderful curving chute down to the old hairpin at Gazomètres was eliminated and replaced by a twisting ribbon of road around the harbour-front swimming pool and down to Rascasse, a new and fatuously confined hairpin. To watch a Grand Prix car being driven through here in the rain is to feel embarrassed for it. It is like a beached whale, bellowing and thrashing to no avail. In one move the essential character of the circuit—and its prime overtaking spot—was lost.

After this, there remained only the end of the pit straight, into Sainte-Dévote, for the brave to get by. But some of the drivers felt the corner was becoming uncomfortably fast, hemmed in by guard rails. Unless you start knocking down buildings, there is no provision for run-off areas in Monte Carlo. So a quite ludicrous chicane was installed before Sainte-Dévote, and overtaking became virtually a memory. The new chicane has probably caused many more accidents than it has prevented.

But you do not go to Monte Carlo in May to see a race. You go there to watch the sublime skills of the five or six men who, in any era, find the secret of going quickly there. They leave you stunned with their deftness and precision and courage.

Or, you are there to pose, to "profile", to show off your possessions, from Lamborghini, Gucci, Cartier, Balenciaga. Materialism is all in Monaco during race week. Finished a few days before is the Cannes Film Festival, and many of the stars stay on—and many of the starlets, too, who find a happy home and rich pickings on the arms of ageing roués "down for the races". It is not pretty, being in Monaco during race week.

What it is, however, is dramatic when the drivers are out there, doing their work. And the enthusiast can revel in it, and in the sense of history around him. The Monaco Grand Prix was run for the first time in 1929, and most of the track—the actual piece of road in front of you—is exactly as it was. Achille Varzi drove over it, and won. And so did Chiron and Farina and Moss and Rindt and Stewart. Monaco, like Monza, has about it a feeling of continuity. Both survived the changes foisted upon them by time.

Most of the drivers love Monaco, simply as an exercise in the art of guiding a Grand Prix car, harnessing five hundred horsepower through the streets of a small town. Flair counts for a lot, precision with the wheel, delicacy with the throttle. Here the driver's ability counts for more than it does anywhere else; his car counts for less. A tiny mistake probably means contact with the barriers.

There is no opportunity to relax, no straight worthy of the name where you can loosen for a few seconds. There is even a tunnel to strain your eyes—blinding sun, comparative darkness turning right at 130 mph, blinding sun again. Luigi Fagioli died in there, in 1952.

And there is the chicane, very fast, leading on to the harbour front. On its exit, just the other side of the guard rail, is the Mediterranean. In 1955, Alberto Ascari, leading in the last laps of the race, lost his Lancia's brakes, went through the barrier—straw bales in those days—and into the sea. He was rescued by frogmen, and suffered only a broken nose.

In 1967, however, there occurred at the Monaco chicane an accident which was to have a profound effect on safety thinking. Lorenzo Bandini, nearing the race's end, was in second place and trying to catch the leader. Exhausted, he made a mistake, putting the Ferrari perhaps six inches off line. The car clipped the chicane wall, was pushed out wide and hit the straw bales at the exit. After somersaulting, it came to rest upside down and on fire. While futile attempts by ill-equipped marshals were made to rescue him, Bandini was hideously burned. He died three days later.

Courbe des Gazomètres

Virage de la Rascasse

The Italian had been an expert at Monte Carlo, but he never won here. Nor, for that matter, did Jimmy Clark. Yet Graham Hill put together five victories, Stirling Moss and Jackie Stewart three each.

Today, the highlight of the Monaco weekend is the final qualifying session, run the day before the race. No starting grid in the world carries so much importance. You must start at the front—or close to it—to be in with a chance on race day. In consequence, you will see some very desperate driving against the stopwatch in that last hour.

The Grand Prix, now? Awe-inspiring still. But an exhibition match, an annual cavalcade for the Beautiful People. It packs them in, but it is not a race.

MONACO

AC de Monaco
23 blvd Albert 1er
Monaco

Circuit Length
2.06 miles/3.32 km

Automobile Club de Monaco

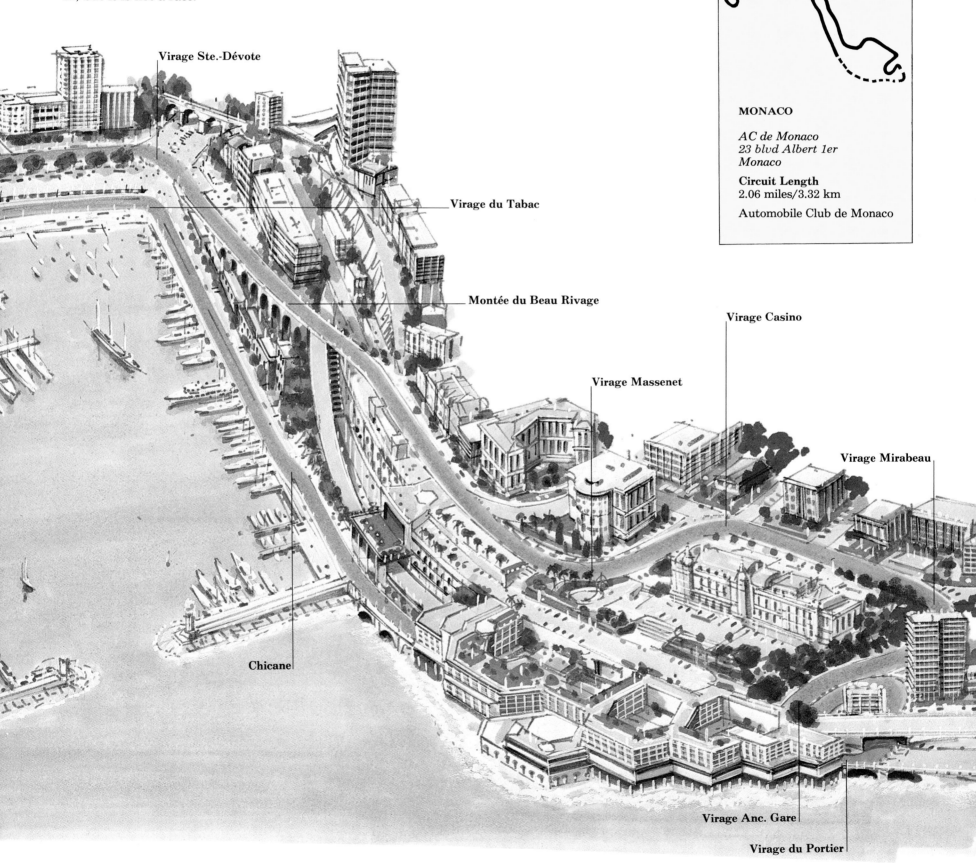

Virage Ste.-Dévote

Virage du Tabac

Montée du Beau Rivage

Virage Casino

Virage Massenet

Virage Mirabeau

Chicane

Virage Anc. Gare

Virage du Portier

JARAMA

Jarama, on the outskirts of Madrid, is known primarily as the site of one of the bloodiest battles of the Spanish Civil War. By curious coincidence, it was the scene, more than forty years later, of the first major skirmish in Grand Prix racing's civil war—the fight between the FOCA, the Formula One Constructors Association, representing most of the teams, and the FISA, the governing body of Grand Prix racing.

The track at Jarama was designed by John Hugenholtz, who also designed the Zandvoort circuit, and was opened in July of 1967. As a Grand Prix circuit it is unremarkable, a typically bland late-model autodrome with a long pit straight and a multitude of tight corners. Jackie Stewart has called it "the most physically tiring of all the tracks on the World Championship calendar."

Before Jarama was built, Spain's motor racing history was patchy. Prior to the Second World War, a street circuit at San Sebastian was used. After the war, Grands Prix were staged irregularly at Pedralbes, another track which consisted of public roads, just outside Barcelona. Until the coming of Jarama, Spain had been without a Grande Epreuve since 1954.

The first international race on the new circuit was a Formula Two event in 1967, won by Jimmy Clark, who was also triumphant later

the same year in the Madrid Grand Prix, a non-championship race for Formula One and Two cars. In a Lotus 49, he trounced the opposition.

Six months later the transporters were back at Jarama, this time for the Spanish Grand Prix, a full-blown World Championship event. The atmosphere in the paddock was sad, however, for Clark had died at Hockenheim shortly before, and this was the first gathering of the teams without him. There were only thirteen starters on that hot May afternoon and spectators were relatively few. Amon's Ferrari dominated, but retired as usual, and the race was left to Graham Hill, his victory precisely what Team Lotus needed at that time.

From most points of view, Jarama's first Grand Prix was not a success. Drivers complained that the track was boring and featureless, and they were not happy with the safety arrangements. In their efforts to do the thing right, the circuit owners had installed liberal quantities of fashionable guard rail, but it was of the single-layer "motorway" type, mounted a couple of feet from the ground and potentially lethal for single-seaters, which could easily slide underneath.

That, however, could be modified. Far more worrying for the organizers were the almost empty grandstands. With Madrid only a

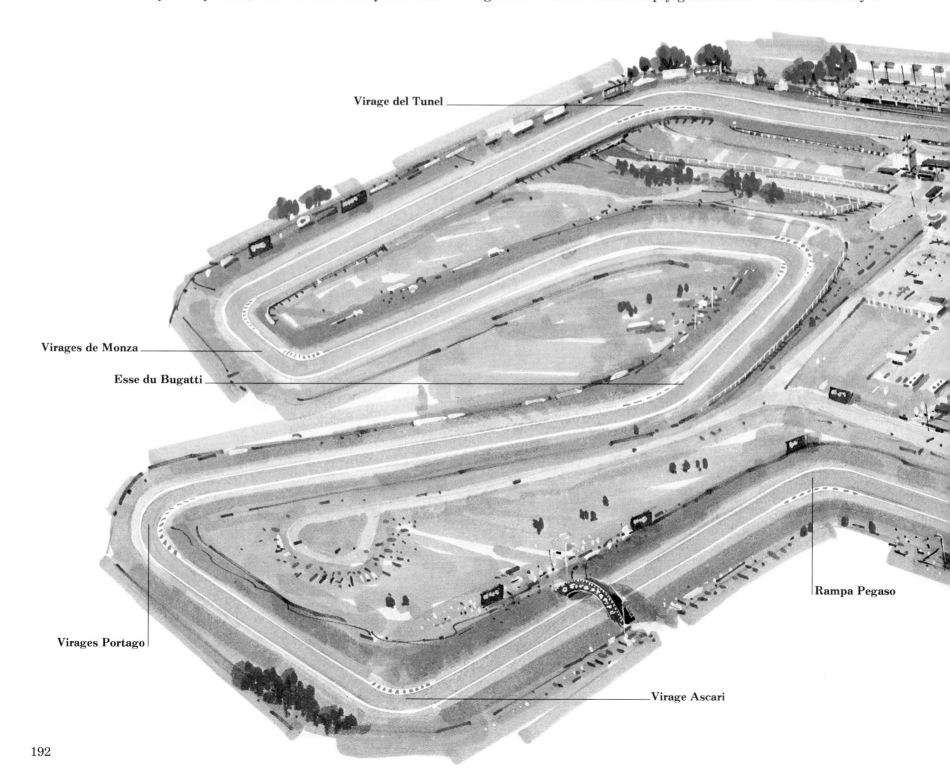

Virage del Tunel

Virages de Monza

Esse du Bugatti

Rampa Pegaso

Virages Portago

Virage Ascari

few miles away, they had been hoping for a huge crowd. They had reckoned without the rival attractions of the football stadium and the bullring—both packed to capacity that Sunday.

In 1969, there seemed to be every sign that Jarama was a white elephant, for the Spanish Grand Prix was run at Montjuich, in parkland above Barcelona. Here was a true road circuit, a fast street track, a driver's challenge. Everyone loved it and hoped that Spain's major race had found a permanent home. Local politics decided otherwise, however, and it was agreed that in the future Jarama and Montjuich would share the event, hosting it in alternate years.

The pattern, once established, continued until 1975, with the Barcelona race providing joyous, uninhibited road racing in a pleasant atmosphere and splendid setting, while the Madrid race, dour and colourless, added nothing to the Grand Prix tapestry. Sadly, however, the Montjuich organizers' attention to detail did not equal their enthusiasm. When the circus came to town in 1975, many of the drivers were dissatisfied with the assembly of the guard rails, fearing that they could burst open if hit by a car. Some, including then World Champion Emerson Fittipaldi, all but boycotted the event. The race was finally stopped after half an hour when Rolf Stommelen's car, leading Hill, suffered a mechanical failure, cleared the guard rail and killed several onlookers. The accident was in no way connected with the earlier guard rail problem, but the damage was done. As a Grand Prix circuit, Montjuich Park was finished.

Since then, the unremarkable Jarama has been the only possible venue for the Spanish Grand Prix. The crowds have improved, but for Madrid motor racing clearly remains a minority interest. This is a humourless place, with the officious *Guardia Civil* much in evidence. The theme music from the movie *Grand Prix* is played endlessly and loudly.

In recent years, the race has been graced by the presence of King Juan Carlos, a popular figure with racing people and a genuine aficionado. But the arrival of His Majesty sends everyone in the paddock scuttling for cover as the helicopter whips up a storm of the sand which proliferates. Simultaneously, the *Guardia Civil* become dramatically overzealous, and the whole scene is best avoided.

Jarama was the venue of Niki Lauda's first Grand Prix victory and of Patrick Depailler's last. In the final analysis, however, its most significant claim to fame may prove to be that here civil war raised its foul head again, albeit a less bloody civil war, between Grand Prix factions. In 1980, Jarama was a place of disgrace— through no fault of its own.

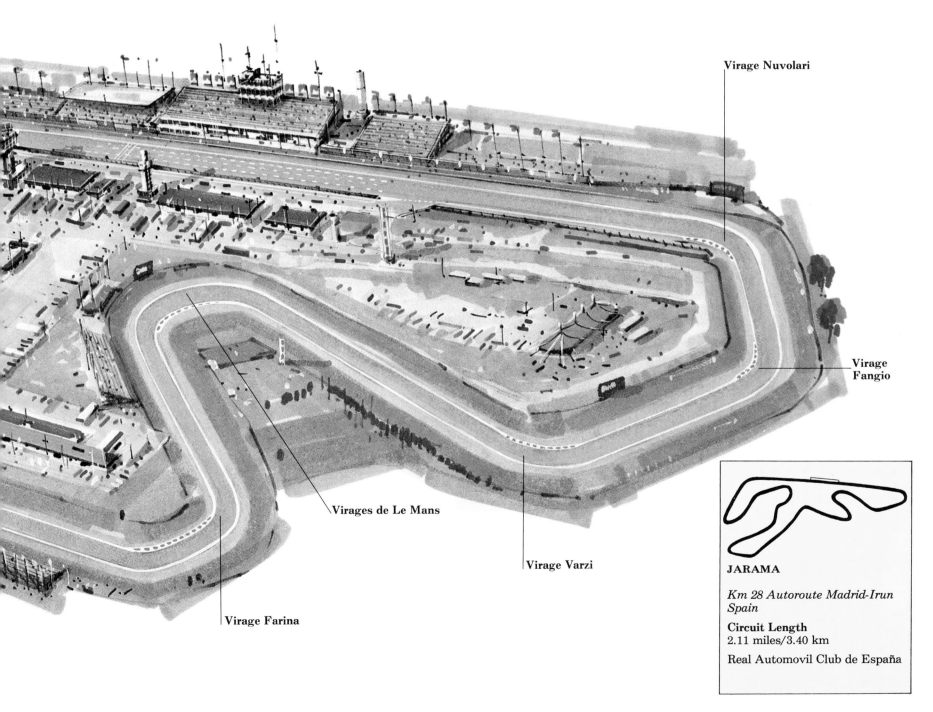

Virage Nuvolari

Virage Fangio

Virages de Le Mans

Virage Varzi

Virage Farina

JARAMA

Km 28 Autoroute Madrid-Irun Spain

Circuit Length
2.11 miles/3.40 km

Real Automovil Club de España

PAUL RICARD

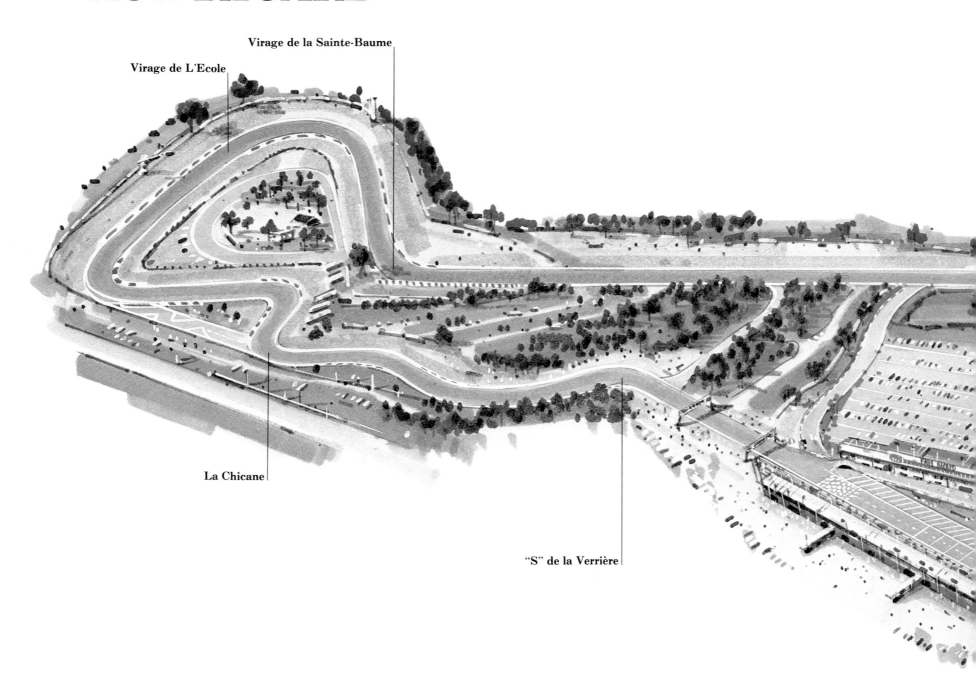

Virage de la Sainte-Baume

Virage de L'Ecole

La Chicane

"S" de la Verrière

When M. Ricard, of pastis fame, built his Circuit Paul Ricard near Marseilles in the late sixties, most people considered it a white elephant. At the time, the French Grand Prix alternated between two great circuits, Clermont-Ferrand and Rouen. Reims, five flat-out miles through champagne country, was well into its death throes, and the Bugatti circuit at Le Mans, used for the race in 1967, had been considered a poorly attended joke. Now came this new circuit, chosen as the venue for the 1971 French Grand Prix.

As a track, pure and simple, Circuit Paul Ricard had little to commend it, although most people approved of its location, close to the coast. The drivers found it bland, with few testing corners and a ludicrously long straight of more than a mile. And no one could quite understand how or why M. Ricard had selected the only piece of flat land in the area on which to build his autodrome. In sum, it was seen as a useless venture, an impression given strength by its first Grand Prix, a tedious race in stifling heat, watched by very few.

The making of the Circuit Paul Ricard, however, was in the changing times. It was indisputably a safe racetrack, and that, with Grand Prix racing's safety crusade in full spate, was its strong suit. In 1972, the French Grand Prix was held for the last time at the classic Charade circuit, in the hills above Clermont-Ferrand. It provided a memorable race, but some of the drivers reacted

vigorously against it. The track, they said, was too narrow (or the cars too wide), and, unfortunately, there was insufficient money available to move back the mountains.

In many respects Ricard is a civilized circuit, complete with air-conditioned, smoked-glassed rooms above the pits for race control staff and the press, as well as for the myriad hangers-on who always congregate here. It abounds in beautiful women.

Its place on the Grand Prix schedule seems secure, although few of the drivers have any enthusiasm for it as a test of their skills. It is a circuit, first of all, of compromise, a matter of adjusting the wing setting so that the car has good downforce for the corners without jeopardizing its speed down that seemingly endless straight—almost a third of the lap.

After Jackie Stewart's cantering victory in 1971, the French Grand Prix returned here two years later, and was dominated by Jody Scheckter in only his third Grand Prix. Shortly before the end, the South African was unceremoniously pushed out of the race by an increasingly desperate Emerson Fittipaldi. Both were eliminated, and the afternoon was left to Ronnie Peterson. That was his first Grand Prix win.

The race was run at the new Dijon circuit in 1974, but reverted to Ricard the following year. Victory went to Niki Lauda and Ferrari,

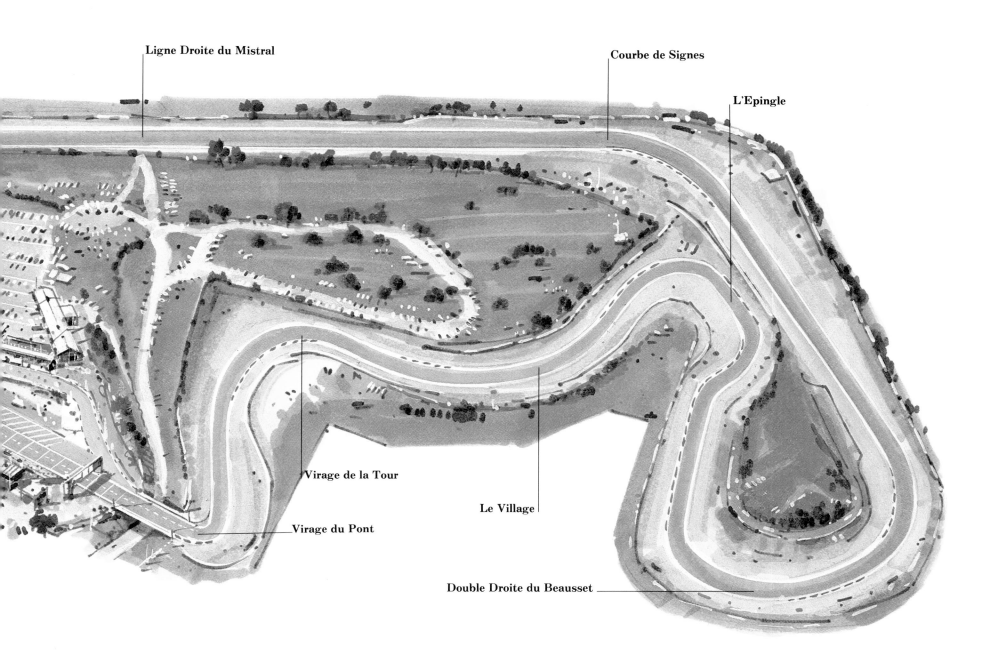

Ligne Droite du Mistral

Courbe de Signes

L'Epingle

Virage de la Tour

Le Village

Virage du Pont

Double Droite du Beausset

then into their runaway first World Championship together. The Austrian looked set to repeat his triumph in 1976, but the flat-12 engine most uncharacteristically blew up on the Mistral straight. James Hunt was first past the flag. He featured strongly again in the 1978 race, giving furious—if hopeless—chase throughout to the Lotuses of Mario Andretti and Ronnie Peterson.

Hopes of a French victory were high in 1980, with the Ligiers and Renaults up at the front of the grid. But the day belonged to Alan Jones, who drove his Williams to the limit from start to finish, forcing the Ligier drivers to destroy their tyres.

Through the years, however, the downbeat atmosphere prevails. Some tracks amplify excitement in the race. Others dispel it; Paul Ricard is one of these. With its lovely climate, the place is ideal for winter testing. For the staging of Grands Prix, its pleasant ambience needs a shot of adrenalin.

PAUL RICARD

Route National 8
F-83.330 Le Beausset
France

Circuit Length
3.61 miles/5.81 km

Fédération Française
du Sport Automobile

DIJON-PRENOIS

People arrive at the little circuit of Dijon-en-Prenois in the right frame of mind, expecting to like the place. How else could it be when they have driven through the gorgeous Burgundy countryside, eaten superbly in the gastronomic centre of the universe, passed through villages with names like Vosne-Romanée and Gevrey-Chambertin, evocative words for lovers of great wines?

The circuit was built on an undulating slice of land in the early 1970s, and was first used for the French Grand Prix in 1974. The Formula One world had mixed feelings. It was agreed, on the one hand, that the new track contained some excellent and testing high-speed corners, that the setting was extremely pleasant, and that it was a supremely good circuit for spectators. On the other hand, there was no doubting that, at a fraction over two miles, it was too short—bearing in mind its high lap speeds—for serious consideration as a Grand Prix venue.

Niki Lauda's pole position lap required just over fifty-eight seconds, and the entire race, won by Ronnie Peterson's Lotus, lasted little more than one hour and twenty minutes. Basically enthusiastic at the thought that an alternative to Paul Ricard had been found, most people agreed that Dijon-en-Prenois needed revision before hosting another Grand Prix.

The French Grand Prix returned to Ricard for the next two summers, but a curious non-championship race, calling itself the Swiss Grand Prix (motor racing is, of course, banned in Switzerland) was run at Dijon in 1975, and the original course was used once more. The race was won, appropriately, by Clay Regazzoni's Ferrari, but was never repeated.

There were no Formula One races at Dijon in 1976, but the French Grand Prix was scheduled to return the following year, and work began on a new circuit extension. This interrupted the sequence of flowing swerves along the back stretch, plunging sharply downhill to the left after the "S" de Sablières, after which a short straight led into a right-hand hairpin with a steeply uphill exit. Another brief straight then took the cars back to rejoin the original track at the Courbe des Gorgeolles. This loop added about six hundred yards to the total length, and reduced lap speeds by seven miles per hour.

In 1977, Dijon-en-Prenois produced an exceptionally exciting race between John Watson's Brabham-Alfa Romeo and Mario Andretti's Lotus 78; the Brabham had the edge on the straights and the Lotus was better through the turns. Although Andretti had been conspicuously faster in practice, he could find no way past Watson

during the race, dogging the Ulsterman and looking set to go by, but never making it.

For lap after endless lap the black car stalked the red in the heat of the afternoon, but as they disappeared from sight to begin their eightieth and last tour, it seemed that John had done enough. But no. Just a mile from the chequered flag—on the steep climb from the new hairpin—the Alfa flat-12 faltered momentarily. In an instant, Andretti had ducked out from behind and gone by. At the flag Watson was a second behind.

DIJON-PRENOIS

F-21 Dijon
France

Circuit Length
2.36 miles/3.94 km

Fédération Française
du Sport Automobile

Ligne Droite de la Fouine

Courbe de Pouas

It had been a memorable day, and everyone clinked their glasses of Bourgogne, overlooked the decidedly overzealous actions of some of the paddock officials, and anticipated the next Grand Prix at Dijon with pleasure.

Two years later, the scene was even more frantic. In the immediate aftermath of the 1979 French Grand Prix there was great celebration, for Jean-Pierre Jabouille had trounced the field. It was his first victory, and Renault's—and it had happened in France. *Jour de gloire!*

The perfect result was denied the French, however, by the actions of Gilles Villeneuve. The Ferrari star had led much of the race, but tyre wear meant that he could do little to resist Jabouille. Late in the day, René Arnoux's Renault began to close in on Villeneuve's second place, passing him with three laps to go. This was the most uninhibited combat seen in Grand Prix racing in a decade, and the final laps were terrifying in their intensity, the cars touching every few seconds, going off the road, rejoining, repassing. At the end it was Villeneuve, Arnoux!

At the 1979 race many of the drivers had unkind words for Dijon, for the nature of the circuit makes it extremely tiring. The criticism should have been directed not at the track, but at the designers of their cars. Ground-effects technology had raised cornering speeds to a point where, in the swoops and turns of Dijon, the drivers were experiencing g-forces they found frankly uncomfortable and a little daunting. For all that, though, the day had been a resounding success, witnessed by a huge crowd. And while France's great circuits languish and crumble, this one in Burgundy lays claim to being the best available for the eighties.

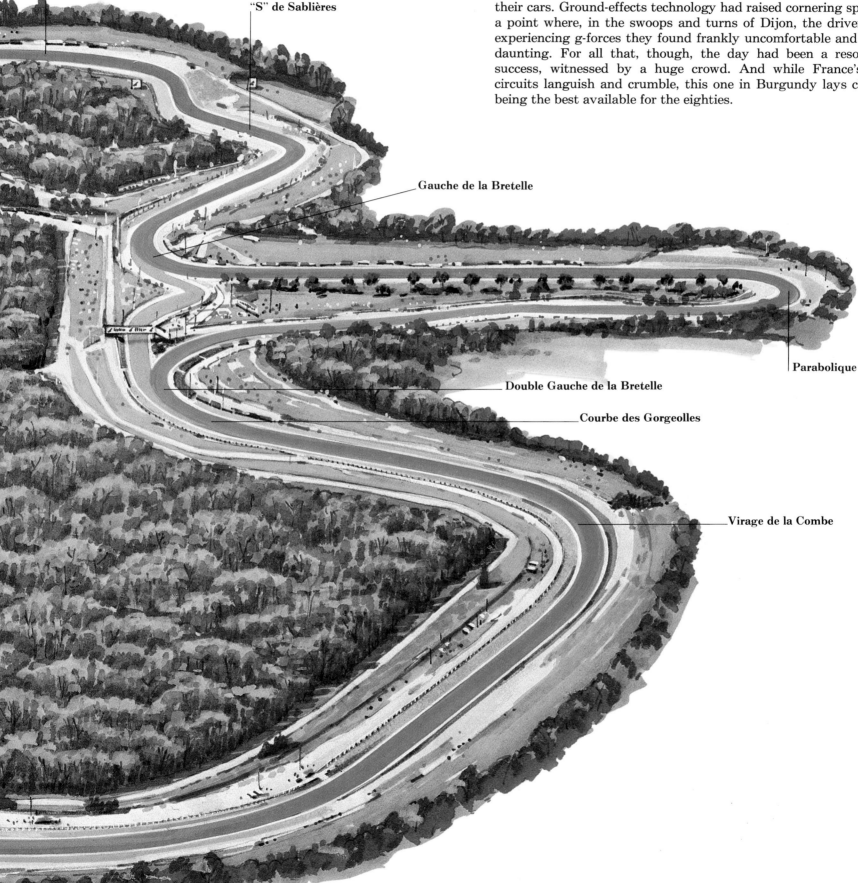

Double Droite de Villeroy

"S" de Sablières

Gauche de la Bretelle

Parabolique

Double Gauche de la Bretelle

Courbe des Gorgeolles

Virage de la Combe

BRANDS HATCH

Opinions of Brands Hatch tend to be vehement. Mario Andretti loves it; Jackie Stewart detested it. Those who go and watch there are equally divided.

The Kentish circuit originally took shape in the thirties as a rough and ready motorcycle grass track. A few years after the end of the Second World War it was revived, and later asphalted. And over the years it achieved a certain prominence in British racing circles, largely as a venue for club events. At 1.24 miles, it was too short for any serious motor racing. But gradually it moved up the scale, and by the late fifties Formula Two events were scheduled there.

Brands Hatch came of age, however, in 1960, when an extension was built, bringing it out to 2.61 miles. For the first time it was suitable for major international events. Formula One cars were raced there in August of that year, the scars of the facelift still unhealed.

Since 1955 it had been traditional for the British Grand Prix to alternate between Aintree, home of the Grand National, and Silverstone, but by 1964 the Liverpool circuit—as a venue for motor racing—was in serious decline. The Brands Hatch management, never backward in coming forward, secured Britain's premier event. It has been shared with Silverstone ever since.

Brands Hatch is a mixture of pros and cons for competitor and spectator alike. As a test of a driver's ability, its status is unquestioned, for there is every type of corner, camber, and gradient, and most drivers admit to a sense of satisfaction after a really quick lap there. Against that, the surface is bumpy, and many have come close to despair in their search for an acceptable compromise in setting up their cars. And Brands is most definitely not the place to have an accident, with an abundance of unforgiving banks and a relative absence of run-off areas. By 1980 it had become a 130-mph circuit, and the bulk of the world's Grand Prix stars, while still relishing its challenge, were distinctly edgy as they spoke of the possible consequences of an accident. Safety measures have been improved over the years, but the problems of constructing run-off areas in the wooded countryside were immense. And no one could have foreseen the staggering increase in cornering speeds which came in the late seventies with the introduction of skirts and ground-effects.

Spectating at Brands Hatch—particularly in the original "stadium" area—is unrivalled at any Grand Prix circuit in the world; the natural amphitheatre in which nearly half the track sits allows a clear view of almost one and a half miles. The fans like that. They are less enthusiastic, however, about the rather artificial showbiz atmosphere of the place, the muddy car parks, and the diabolical traffic jams.

For all that, spectators can be fairly sure when they go to Brands for the British Grand Prix that it will be a good race. This circuit has a way of providing them; the 1980 event was a curious exception. Over the years, there have been some epic Grands Prix there. In 1964, for example, Jimmy Clark and Graham Hill qualified first and second, ran first and second all the way and finished less than three seconds apart after eighty laps. Four years later there was a race of incredible tension between Jo Siffert and Chris Amon, and two years after that Jochen Rindt won when Jack Brabham ran out of fuel on the last lap.

The chief protagonists in the 1972 race were Emerson Fittipaldi and Jackie Stewart. They were together virtually all the way. And then in 1974 Niki Lauda's Ferrari dominated until a punctured tyre brought him in and handed the race to Jody Scheckter.

Perhaps, however, Brands Hatch's most dramatic day came in July of 1976, when the Lauda-Hunt confrontation was at its height. There they were, making up the front row of the grid, on a hot afternoon. . . .

At the first corner there was a multiple accident, with no one hurt but several cars damaged—including Hunt's McLaren. The race was halted. Then came the dramatic announcement that the restart would take place shortly, without those with bent cars. No spare cars would be used. Hunt would be excluded.

Up in the stands the phlegmatic Brits forgot themselves, baying at the organizers for the return of their hero. It was all decidedly ugly.

Finally there was a *volte-face* from those in charge. Spare cars might be allowed, after all. The delay in reaching a decision permitted James's mechanics to repair his original chassis. All was well, and the fans screamed feverishly as Hunt took the McLaren past Lauda's Ferrari at half-distance and held on to win. Months later, a CSI court decided to disqualify him after all.

A couple of years later, Lauda again figured in the drama of the day, this time losing the race late in the afternoon to an inspired Carlos Reutemann.

Yes, there have been memorable days at Brands Hatch. It is perhaps unfortunate that a magnificent track should be bordered by a fairground atmosphere. Inevitably this detracts from the sense of great occasion which should predominate on British Grand Prix day.

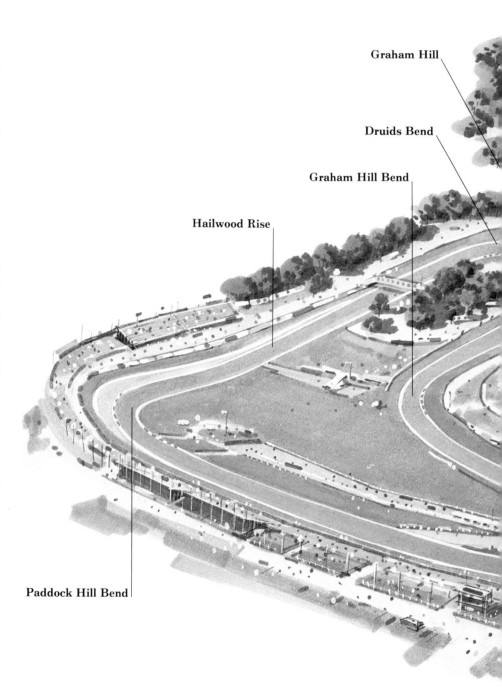

Graham Hill

Druids Bend

Graham Hill Bend

Hailwood Rise

Paddock Hill Bend

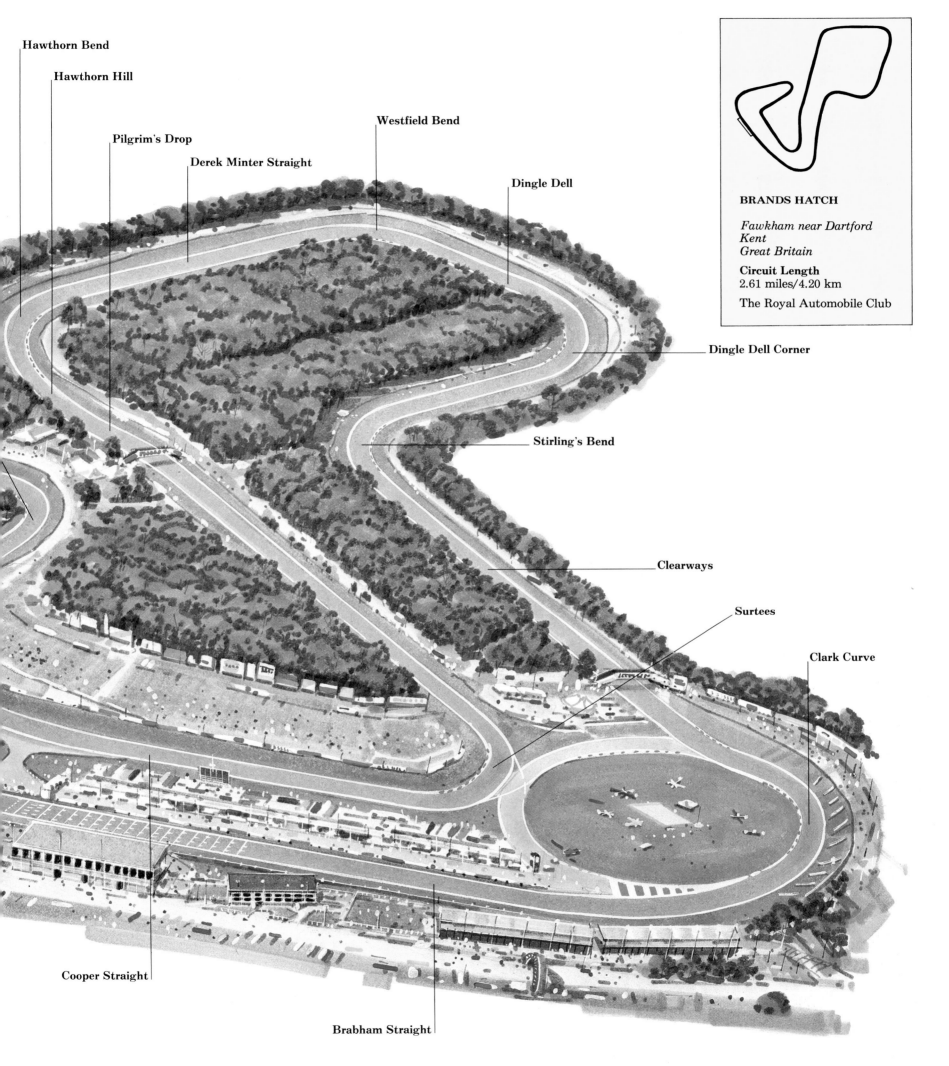

Hawthorn Bend

Hawthorn Hill

Pilgrim's Drop

Derek Minter Straight

Westfield Bend

Dingle Dell

BRANDS HATCH

Fawkham near Dartford
Kent
Great Britain

Circuit Length
2.61 miles/4.20 km

The Royal Automobile Club

Dingle Dell Corner

Stirling's Bend

Clearways

Surtees

Clark Curve

Cooper Straight

Brabham Straight

SILVERSTONE

Silverstone's great strength is its heritage. It hosted the first true British Grand Prix, in 1948, and although required later to share the event, first with Aintree and later with Brands Hatch, it has always maintained its status. Its rather stuffy claim to being "the home of British motor racing" is not an altogether idle boast. Anyone with a soul rejoices in the odd years on the Formula One calendar, when the British Grand Prix is held here.

As a circuit pure and simple, there is nothing remarkable about Silverstone, save that it is immensely fast, with a lap speed nudging 150 mph. During the years of the Second World War it was the site of an airfield, and the original track was made up of runways and sections of a perimeter road—hence the abundance of straights. In the centre of the circuit there is still a landing strip, now rough and pockmarked, but used for the private aircraft of the racing rich.

Through all the razzmatazz of modern Grand Prix racing, the essential dignity of Silverstone remains. There lingers the wisp of a gentler, more optimistic, time. When the place was making its name, a war-torn Britain was rebuilding, its people looking for diversion after years of austerity. Among other things, they went to Silverstone to watch motor racing. In their tens of thousands they went. Even Royalty turned up. Now, more than thirty years later, there is still

something of the feel of those times. Cosmetic changes have updated Silverstone, but have not cheapened it.

Then again, there is the Silverstone Type. In the paddock of the Northamptonshire track you will see the regimental blazer, the duffle coat, the wicker picnic basket. The ST talks of Brands Hatch as "that place in Kent or somewhere" and wouldn't be seen dead there. For him, the British Grand Prix is a biennial affair. He parks his Lagonda, adjusts his cap, heads for the clubhouse for a noggin. He carries a shooting stick and has binoculars over his shoulder. He invariably wears suede shoes.

Once at the bar, he reminisces with his friends. They have been coming here for years, and there is ample scope for anecdote, embellished inevitably as the day wears on. Beneath all the layers of Glenfiddich and Beefeater, however, there is a solid core of truth become legend. In thirty years Silverstone has been witness to many remarkable happenings.

Almost certainly there will be talk at the bar of Froilan Gonzalez, the huge Argentine who won only two Grands Prix in his career, in 1951 and 1954, both of them at Silverstone, both of them lone battles for Ferrari against considerable odds. They will remember the intervening races, both dominated by Alberto Ascari, also in the Ferrari

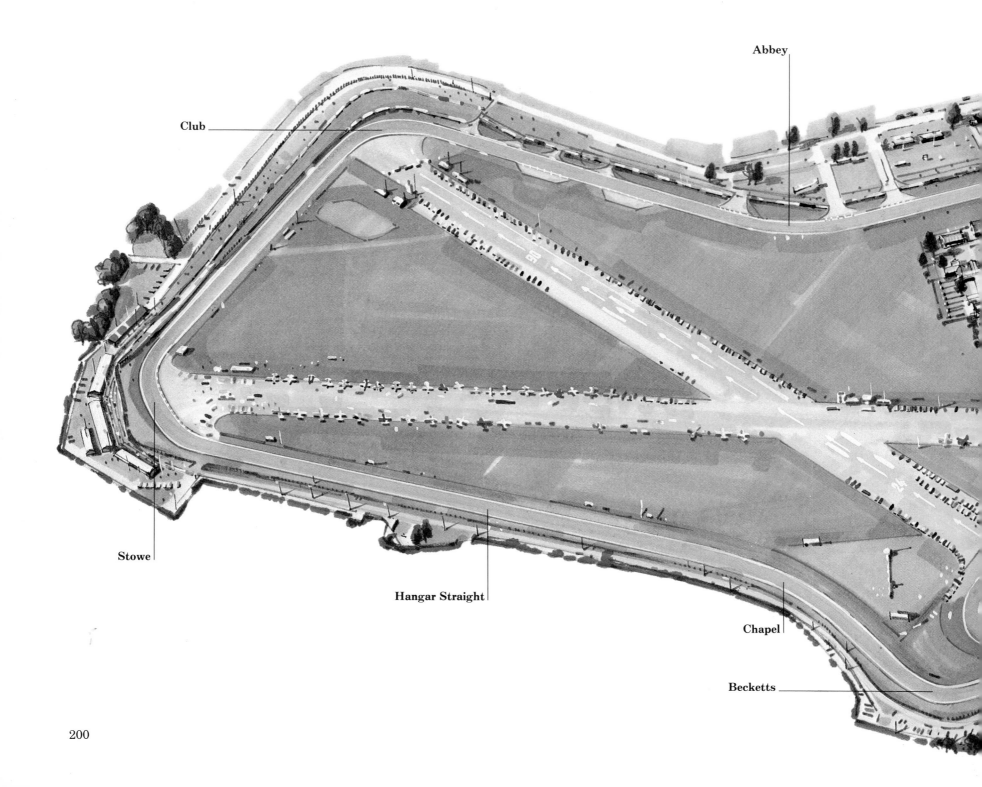

Abbey

Club

Stowe

Hangar Straight

Chapel

Becketts

team, of course. Wistfully, they will recall the great days of the International Trophy—a Grand Prix meeting in all but name—which was held traditionally in the spring. How about the 1951 race, old boy, when the rain was so bad that they had to stop it after six laps, with Reg Parnell miles ahead of all the foreigners? And then there was May 5, 1956, when Stirling Moss raced a Vanwall for the first time and trounced the Italians.

Remarkably, Juan Manuel Fangio won only once in England, and it was among the most fortunate victories of his career. In the British Grand Prix of 1956, Stirling's Maserati retired from the lead a few laps from the end, leaving it to Fangio and Ferrari. At 101 laps—300 miles—it was a long race in those days.

Remember, the ST goes on, that International Trophy of 1957 when Jean Behra led a one-two-three for BRM? Or the Grand Prix the next year when Peter Collins outdrove the rest to win with his Ferrari, only to die in it a fortnight later at the Nürburgring?

Other days, other memories. . . . Harry Schell's fatal accident on Friday the thirteenth in May of 1960, Graham Hill's unbelievable last-corner defeat of Jimmy Clark in the International Trophy of 1962, and the Scotsman's narrow defeat of Hill in the Grand Prix three years later. Silverstone is renowned for its close finishes and intense battles. Who can ever forget the *mano a mano* combat of Jackie Stewart and Jochen Rindt in the Grand Prix of 1969?

The seventies began with a first-ever Formula One win for Chris Amon, in the International Trophy. Second in that race, Stewart was an effortless winner of possibly the most boring Formula One event in Silverstone's history, the British Grand Prix of 1971. Two years later, the race had to be stopped when Jody Scheckter's McLaren caused a multiple accident at the end of the first lap. The 1975 race was also halted prematurely, this time because of heavy rain.

That 1975 race was the first in the history of the revised circuit, the first to be run with the notorious Woodcote chicane in place. In the opinions of some, Woodcote Corner, taken on the limit only by the very brave and highly skilled, had become a little too fast. To howls of protest from spectators, it was therefore diluted by a chicane. By the end of the decade, dramatic strides in the cars' cornering ability meant that their exit speed from the corner was almost as high as in the old days—with none of the spectacle.

Silverstone nevertheless remains a wonderful place for a day of motor racing, and there remain spots—Stowe, in particular—so fast as to cause a sharp intake of breath. Anyone in the clubhouse would agree with that.

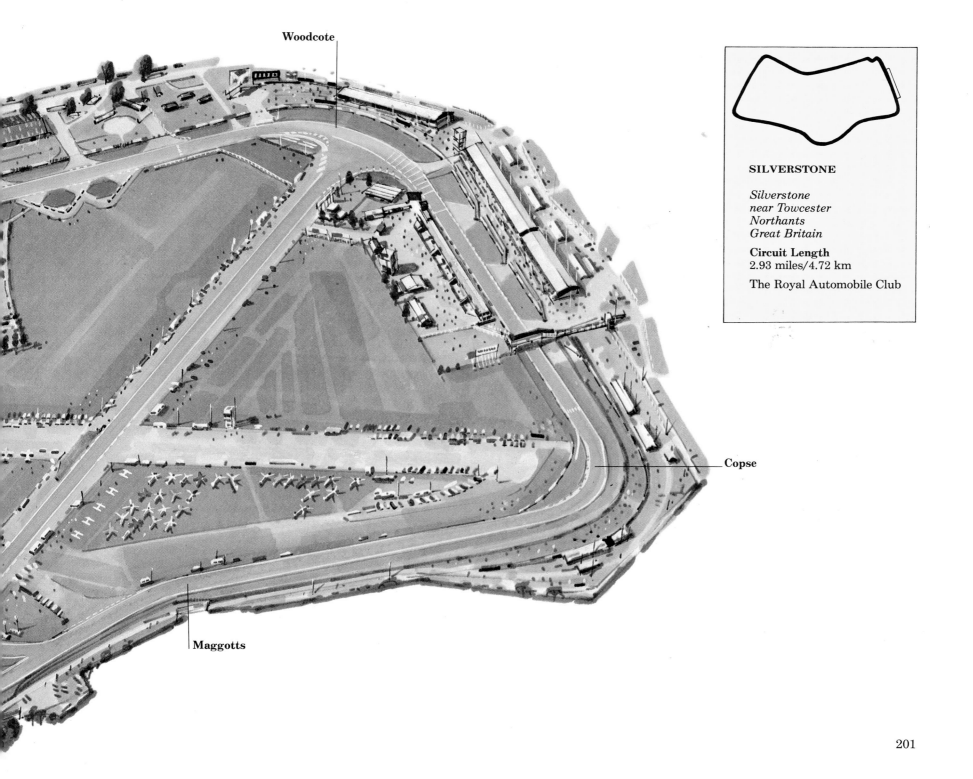

Woodcote

Copse

Maggotts

SILVERSTONE

Silverstone near Towcester Northants Great Britain

Circuit Length
2.93 miles/4.72 km

The Royal Automobile Club

HOCKENHEIM

Nobody likes Hockenheim very much, least of all the men who have to drive around it. There is little premium placed on a driver's ability here. What he needs is a lot of horsepower from an engine which will run flat out for a long time. Everything else can be fudged over.

The original circuit was opened in 1939 and Mercedes-Benz were quick to make use of it. They had constructed new 1.5-litre cars specifically for a single event, the Tripoli Grand Prix, and Hockenheim, essentially two lengthy straights with a corner at each end, made an ideal test track for the ultra-high speeds of Tripoli.

After the Second World War, racing at Hockenheim was restarted, but no major international events were run. The track was inevitably in the shadow of the Nürburgring, legendary and traditional home of German motor racing. How could four miles of mindless straight compete with more than fourteen of devilish challenge through the mountains? Hockenheim stayed firmly in its place, acceptable as a site for small national meetings, but not worthy of consideration for serious racing.

In the early sixties the track was closed for some time to permit the building of a new *autobahn* to nearby Karlsruhe, and this bisected the circuit. Amply compensated, presumably, the track owners went to work on a revised, shorter layout. The straights, still absurdly long, were nevertheless reduced considerably, and a new, twisty section was built in the stadium area. Racing began once more in 1966.

The name of Hockenheim became known across the world on April 7, 1968, a damp and dreary Sunday. Two races of consequence were scheduled for that day—a major sports car race at Brands Hatch and a Formula Two event at Hockenheim. Jimmy Clark, indisputably the greatest driver in the world, had originally intended to run in England, but a late change of plan took him instead to Hockenheim with a factory Lotus 48. For reasons which have never been clear, the car went out of control on the slippery outward straight and flew off the road. There were no protective barriers at that time, and the Lotus shattered against the trees. Since then Hockenheim has remained in everyone's mind as "the place that killed Jimmy Clark".

For all that, there is no denying its pulling power. The forest-lined circuit is in the middle of a densely populated region and race

Sachskurve

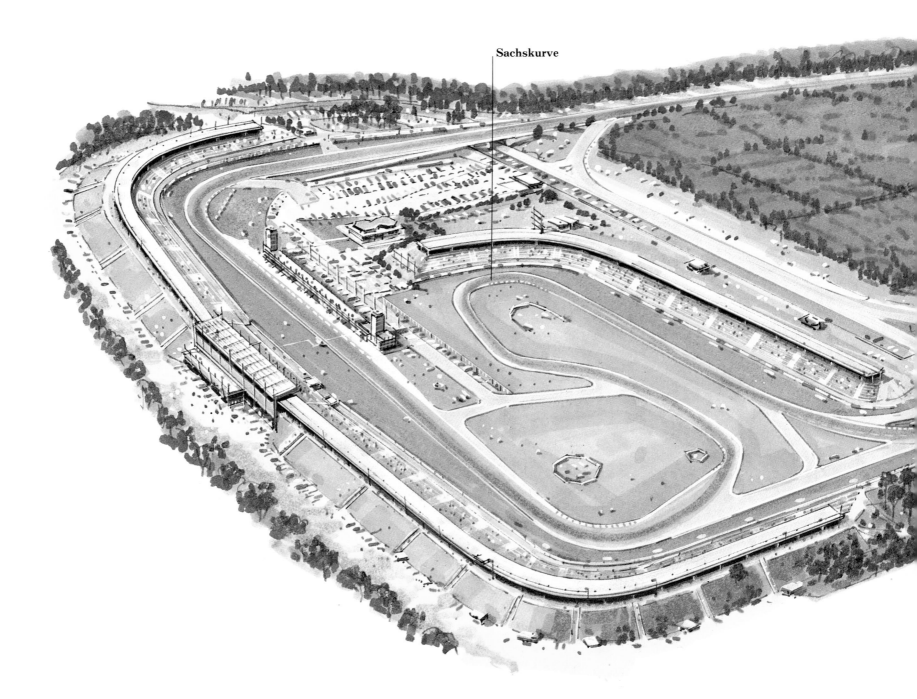

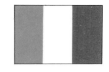

hometown skirmish, with Fangio and Moss the respective team leaders. The Argentine retired his own Ferrari, but then took over the car of Peter Collins, the selfless Englishman. There was a lot to make up, but then Moss ran out of fuel. All seemed lost until Luigi Piotti, a nondescript Italian also in a Maserati, gently nudged Moss's car to the pits where it took on a few gallons and resumed, winning the race by six seconds.

In 1970, Regazzoni, driving a Ferrari, broke away from the pack late in the race, and scored his first Grand Prix victory. And in 1971 Peter Gethin's BRM took first place by a couple of feet from Peterson's March. Only three-fifths of a second separated the first and the fifth cars. All that came to an end when they put in the chicanes.

But the atmosphere survives. To compare Monza with, say, Paul Ricard is to compare the city of São Paulo with Brasilia. Monza is stained with the passing of time. Its undeniable eeriness, the undercurrent of tension, is heightened by the most fanatical racing fans anywhere. The Italian Grand Prix at Monza is more than a day out for the *tifosi*. They are informed and knowledgeable, if obsessively biased towards Ferrari.

Monza has claimed many celebrated lives. Alberto Ascari died here, at the curve now named after him, while testing in May 1955. Wolfgang von Trips, World Champion elect in 1961, was killed when his Ferrari crashed at the Parabolica on the second lap of the race.

Nine years later, Jochen Rindt lost his life at the same spot when his Lotus went out of control during final practice. He was the sport's first posthumous World Champion. And in 1978, within three hundred yards of the start of the race, Ronnie Peterson's Lotus was pitched into a guard rail which blocked off the disused banking. The great Swede died the following morning.

If Monza has given racing some delicious moments of drama and triumph, it has also exacted its dues. And you feel it as soon as you walk through the gates.

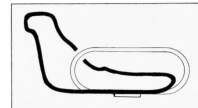

MONZA

Autodromo Nazionale di Monza
20052 Monza Parco
Italy

Circuit Length
3.60 miles/5.79 km

ACI/Commissione Sportiva
Automobilistica Italiana

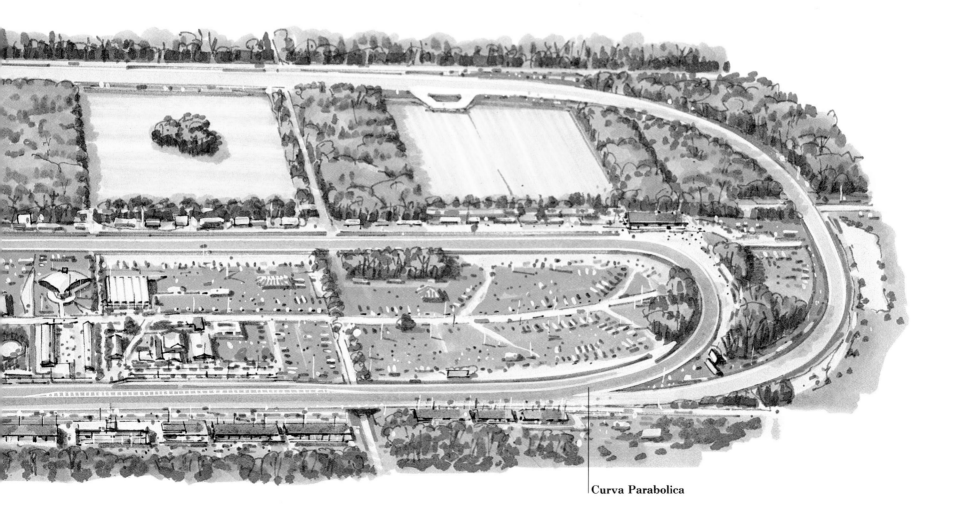

Curva Parabolica

MONTREAL

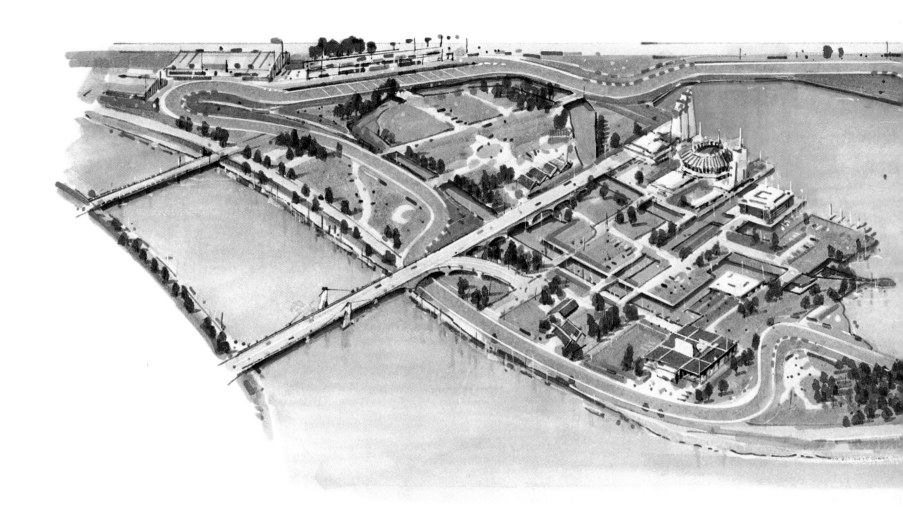

It was not until 1967 that Canada figured in Grand Prix racing, although major sports car races had been held there for many years before. When the Formula One circus finally ventured into Canada, it was to Mosport Park, near Toronto, for a race absurdly scheduled in mid-August, so that the whole entourage crossed the Atlantic, returned to Europe for the Italian Grand Prix, then went Stateside for the race at Watkins Glen.

In the early years of the Canadian Grand Prix, the race was run alternately at Mosport and St. Jovite, both truly excellent drivers' circuits. After staging the 1970 event, however, St. Jovite was criticized on safety grounds, and the funds necessary to make it satisfactory to the Grand Prix Drivers Association were not available. After that the Canadian Grand Prix was the exclusive province of Mosport. Racing enthusiasts in French Canada were understandably disappointed.

Time passed, and speeds increased. By the mid-seventies, Mosport Park was incurring the drivers' wrath on the same grounds as St. Jovite had. Certainly, it had not kept pace with most of the Grand Prix circuits of Europe. In addition, there were financial disagreements between the Formula One Constructors Association and the race organizers. In 1975, indeed, the event did not take place, and there was a great deal of acrimony by the time of the 1977 race. It was to be Mosport's last.

For years the French-Canadians had dreamed of once again staging the Canadian Grand Prix, but there remained the problem of a suitable circuit. When plans were announced for a track in Montreal, few in Europe took the news seriously.

Even more fantastic was the projected site—weaving around the futuristic buildings of Expo 67 on the man-made Ile de Notre-Dame in the St. Lawrence Seaway. It all sounded a little unreal, but the organizers confidently predicted that the Canadian Grand Prix would be staged there in October 1978. Still doubts remained, amplified by the news in mid-July that work on the circuit had not yet started in earnest. The track did not yet exist.

Nevertheless, in the cold Canadian autumn there were the familiar faces and cars. The track was completed, and only heavy rain on that first day of qualifying blighted an altogether remarkable achievement. The drivers' reaction to the circuit itself was not all favourable. There were many complaints that it was too narrow and contained too many slow chicanes. But the ambience was pleasant, the attitude of the organizers helpful, and everyone felt that an important new venue had come to Formula One.

Race day could have produced nothing better for the local populace, for Gilles Villeneuve, in his first full Grand Prix season, scored his maiden win in the Ferrari. The freezing temperature was forgotten as Quebec celebrated the triumph of a new hero. After that, the Montreal race revolved around Villeneuve as the Argentine Grand Prix revolved around Carlos Reutemann—prophets not without honour in their own countries. They are worshipped, and much of the success of their races rides with them.

True to their word, the organizers listened to criticism and they acted upon it. By the time of the 1979 race, the first chicane had been

eased considerably, to the point that it was now a pair of very fast corners, left and right. It was through these that Villeneuve led the field on the first lap, the spectators screaming with delight. He drove a hero's race that day, holding off Alan Jones's faster Williams for fifty of the seventy-two laps, but finally had to settle for second place.

The Australian won again in 1980, thereby clinching the World Championship. But it was a contentious victory, coming only after the penalization of Didier Pironi, whose Ligier won "on the road".

The atmosphere at the Montreal track is quite unlike that of any other on the World Championship circuit. From a distance, the eccentric shapes of the pavilions and exhibition halls of Expo 67 are impressive and unearthly, but closer inspection reveals that they were built for a specific purpose—and not to last. Many are already crumbling. Behind the pits and paddock are rows of grandstand seats, all of them facing away from the track. They were constructed for spectators at the rowing events in the 1976 Olympic Games, which were staged on a stretch of water beyond, between the race circuit and the St. Lawrence Seaway.

Race day at Montreal invariably means bright autumn sun, chilling temperatures, tyres consequently giving less grip than usual, thick gloves, breath clouds in the air. The future of the circuit for Grand Prix racing seems assured, and traffic problems may be avoided by the canny. To get back into town, you merely board a subway train.

MONTREAL

1415 est, rue Jarry
Montreal
Quebec
Canada

Circuit Length
2.80 miles/4.51 km

Canadian Automobile
Sports Club

WATKINS GLEN

Once in a while the weather is good at Watkins Glen. It is nearly always cold in upstate New York at the beginning of October, but when there are clear skies and a pale, wintry sun the Glen is a pleasant place to be. Its location, in the hills above the town, is glorious in the fall, with burnished forest all around. But usually it rains. And when that happens, Watkins Glen has a nightmarish quality, freezing and muddy and dark, perhaps the most cheerless place in the world of Formula One.

Racing began at Watkins Glen in 1948. The early events were run over a six-mile course through the streets of the town. It was all very primitive. The course at one point crossed railway tracks, but from the start it was clear that local enthusiasts had their priorities right. During racing it was the trains, not the cars, which were flagged to a stop. After four years of rather chaotic race meetings, the track was transferred to public roads above the town. This location became the site of the permanent circuit, which was opened in 1956, before the United States had a Grand Prix.

The first two Grands Prix in America were held at Sebring, Florida, and Riverside, California. Both were dismal failures. In 1961, therefore, the race was transferred to Watkins Glen, where it has remained ever since. Locals remember that first race because Enzo Ferrari refused to send any cars over, thereby robbing the American racing fraternity of the opportunity to pay homage to Phil Hill, who had clinched the World Championship a month earlier. The

1961 event was also notable because it provided a first Grand Prix victory for Innes Ireland and Team Lotus. Then, a few weeks later, Colin Chapman fired his team leader. Ireland, bitter to this day, would win no more Grands Prix; for Lotus it was the beginning of a legend.

The man who replaced Innes, Jimmy Clark, annihilated the rest in 1962, after which there came a remarkable trio of wins for Graham Hill and BRM. Clark came back in 1966, however, to score a fluke win with the Lotus 43, remarkable in that the car was powered by the BRM H16 engine, which for once went the distance. The following year Jimmy did it again, this time in the Lotus 49, and it was a demonstration of Clark virtuosity. In the closing laps, the offside rear suspension broke. Any other driver would have come into the pits. Somehow, however, Clark nursed it around the remaining miles and took the flag, the car's left rear wheel drunkenly canted.

Tragically, this was to be Clark's final appearance in America. When the teams next assembled at the Glen, Jimmy was dead and his fellow countryman Jackie Stewart looked set to take over the mantle. Stewart won the race, a landmark in Grand Prix history because it also marked the first Formula One appearance of Mario Andretti—who started from the pole.

The 1969 race brought a first Grand Prix victory for Jochen Rindt, but his Lotus team-mate, Graham Hill, suffered dreadful leg

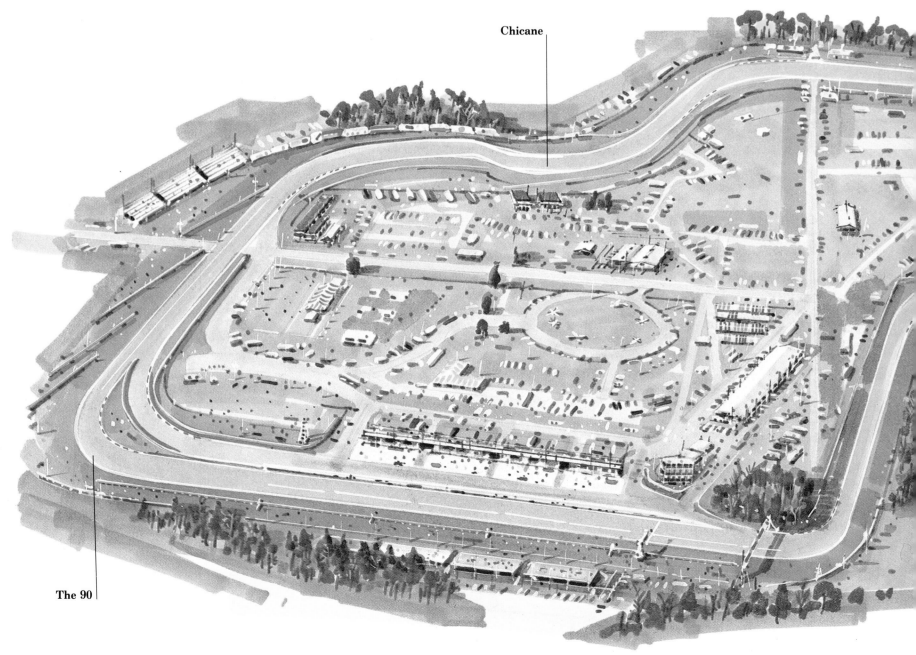

Chicane

The 90

214

injuries in an accident late in the afternoon. Twelve months later, Graham was back at the Glen and the Lotus team was still shell-shocked from the recent death of Rindt at Monza. They fielded two novices, Emerson Fittipaldi and Reine Wisell, who finished, astonishingly, first and third.

In 1971, the year the track was extended to its present 3.4 miles, François Cevert scored his only Grand Prix win at the Glen. Throughout his career the Frenchman was an obedient and content number two to his mentor Jackie Stewart and was waiting eagerly to assume the Tyrrell team leadership after Jackie's retirement. Their last race together was to be the American Grand Prix of 1973. In the event, no Tyrrells appeared on race day, for Cevert died instantly in an horrific practice accident and the other team cars were withdrawn.

After the Frenchman's death, a chicane was installed to slow down the swerves after the pits, but sadly there was another fatality in 1974 when the Austrian Helmuth Koinigg was decapitated as his Surtees split open the guard rail. Intense speculation had centred on the race, which would settle the outcome of the World Championship, but the anticipated battle between Regazzoni and Fittipaldi never came about, for Clay was in trouble from the start, and Emerson stroked home to fourth place and the title. From flag to flag the day had belonged to Carlos Reutemann, who also triumphed for Ferrari in 1978.

By 1980 there were grave doubts about Watkins Glen's future as a Grand Prix circuit. During the sixties, the United States Grand Prix had been the one everyone wanted to win, for the prize money was considerably higher than for any European race. But the Glen did not keep pace with the changing image of Formula One, and the rumours of financial problems were confirmed by the end of the seventies. The big sponsors, and attendant hangers-on, were not impressed by the primitive facilities at the track, the muddy, unpaved acres through which they had to wade to reach their motor homes, and the lack of decent hotels in the area.

The Glen's image is to some extent permanently hampered by a very special kind of "fan," a creature who emerges once each year, daubs obscenities on his ancient Chevy camper, dons checked lumberjacket and hunting cap and sets off for the Glen. The back of the camper is given over entirely to cans of beer, and these he works through steadily as the weekend progresses, pausing occasionally to fall over in the mud and shout at nobody in particular. His greatest pleasure, however, would come on Saturday evening when he made his way to the notorious "Bog". Here he met more of his own kind and they playfully stabbed each other and chanted hysterically as they pushed cars into the swamp and set fire to them. . . .

Mercifully, the Bog has now been concreted over, the rusting pale blue guard rail repainted, the track partly resurfaced. But all that may have come too late to save a first-rate circuit, on a nice day a delight.

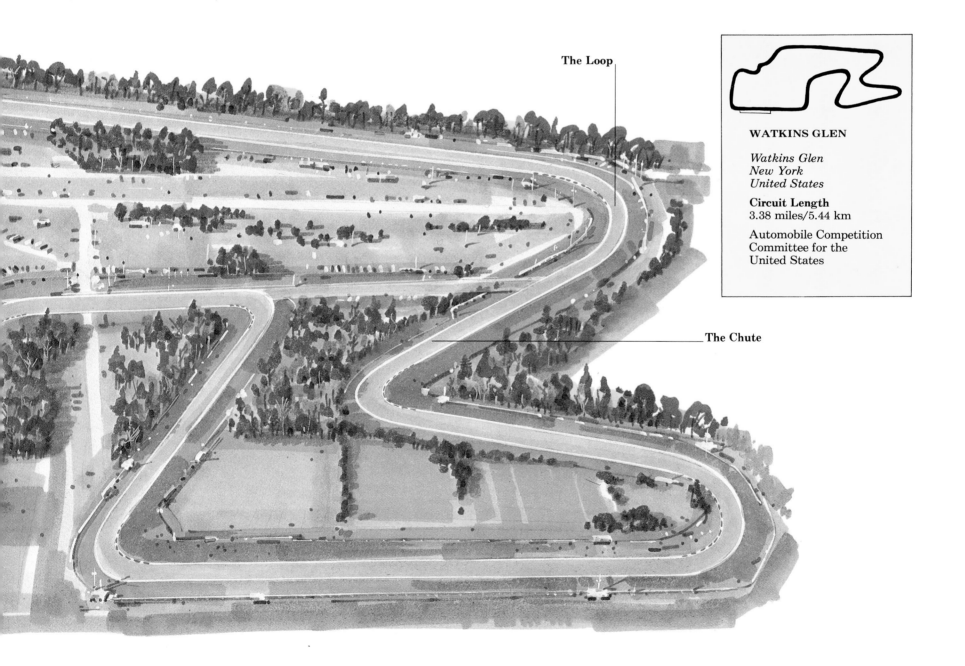

The Loop

The Chute

WATKINS GLEN

Watkins Glen
New York
United States

Circuit Length
3.38 miles/5.44 km

Automobile Competition
Committee for the
United States

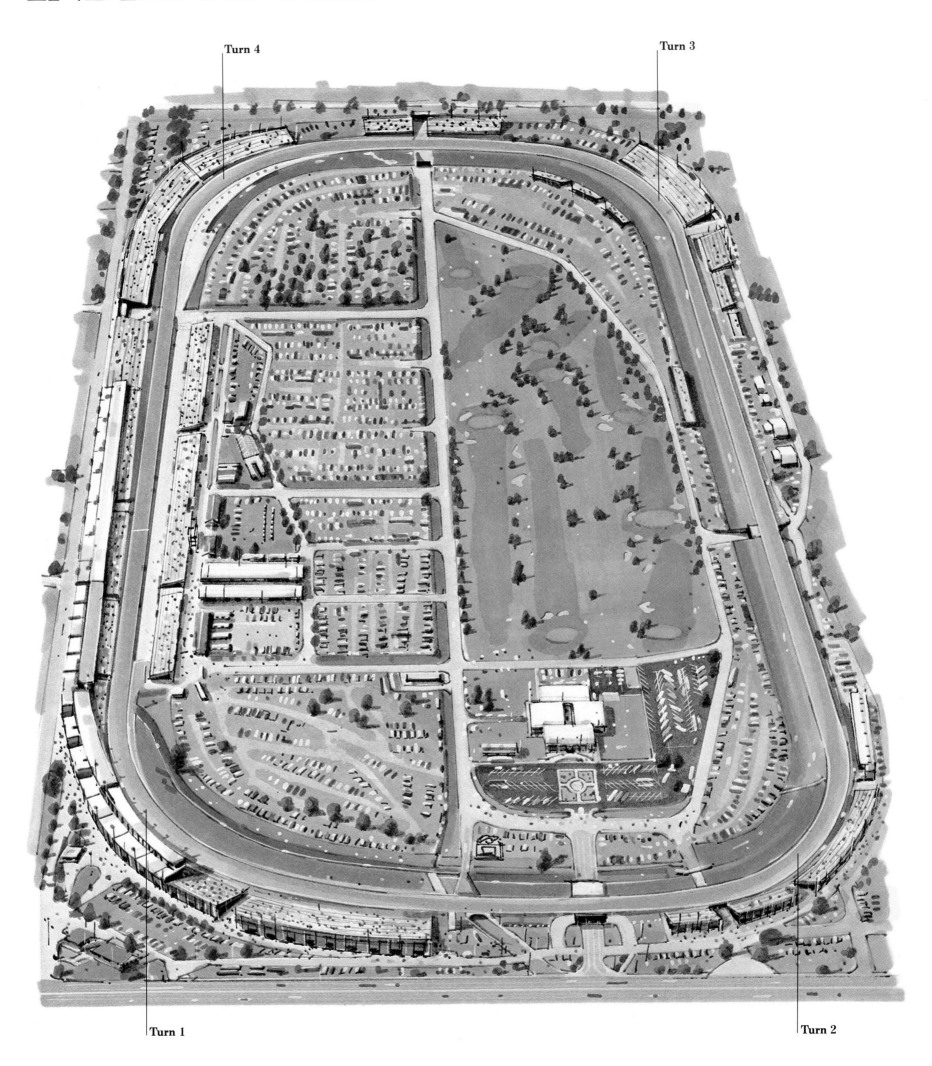

Turn 4

Turn 3

Turn 1

Turn 2

For reasons which have never been entirely clear, the Indianapolis 500 used to be a round of the World Championship. Until the end of 1960, names like Jimmy Bryan, Rodger Ward, and Jim Rathmann would appear regularly in the point standings, names which had nothing whatever to do with Grand Prix racing. Indy took its place on the schedule because of its prestigious name. It remains the most famous automobile race in the world.

For eleven months of the year, that celebrated two-and-a-half mile oval in dozy Indiana sits like a hallowed, antique chair—unused, fiercely protected, endlessly tended. Occasionally a race car might flit around on a tyre-testing session, while the paddock garage area—legendary Gasoline Alley—is the permanent home of many American championship teams. But for racing the Indianapolis Motor Speedway is used only once each year. The whole of the month of May is given over to practice, qualifying, and running the 500. And after each race there are many who swear they will never be back. And always they return. The pulling power of the place becomes irresistible for driver and spectator alike.

First and foremost, Indianapolis is marinated in folklore. The inaugural 500 was run in 1911, the site precisely the one used today. For most of its seventy-year history the track was surfaced in brick, hence its nickname, the Brickyard. It was paved in 1956, but a ribbon of the original brick remains on the start-finish line. Americans are unashamedly sentimental in matters such as this, fiercely guarding their traditions, and that, in large part, accounts for the continuing success of the Indianapolis 500. History lives there, as it does at few Grand Prix circuits in competitive use today.

At a glance, the oval shape of the track seems absurdly simple and straightforward in comparison with Grand Prix venues. Jochen Rindt, who hated the place with a passion, dismissed it thus: "No problem so long as you remember to turn left every fifteen seconds. . . ." Actually, the four apparently similar left-hand turns all have their own quirks, and each requires a different technique.

And Indianapolis is fast! Blazingly so. A reduction in the turbocharger boost pressure rules has lately reduced speeds a little, but in 1978 Tom Sneva took the pole with a four-lap average of better than 202 mph. At that time, championship car engines were producing more than 800 bhp, a daunting prospect within the tight confines of the Brickyard, where run-off areas do not exist. Any mistake—or mechanical failure—will lead you straight into the concrete wall which borders the entire circuit. As the great A.J. Foyt has so succinctly put it: "If you're running two hundred miles per hour, and somebody screws up in front of you, baby, school's out!"

Much of Indy's modern legend hangs on this man, and the race will lose a lot when he finally brings down the curtain on his driving career. He has won the 500 four times—in 1961, 1964, 1967, and 1977—and his record stands alone. Foyt's presence brings a lot of people to Indianapolis in the month of May.

If A.J. remains the all-time favourite hero, however, there are others who run him close, who have earned their places in Brickyard folklore. There was Bill Vukovich, determined to vanquish the superstition that "nobody wins the 500 three times in a row". Vuky nearly took it in 1952, won it in '53 and '54 and died in '55 while leading. There are the Unser brothers, Bobby and Al, with five victories between them, and Jerry, who was burned to death in 1959. There was 1965, when Jimmy Clark conclusively ended the era of the front-engined roadsters, winning decisively in Colin Chapman's Lotus. And, further back in time, there are names like Wilbur Shaw, Mauri Rose, Ted Horn, and Tony Bettenhausen, men who never even thought about Grand Prix racing.

The Indianapolis 500 is a pageant. What other sporting event in the world has a month-long build-up merely to decide the contestants? Race day is packed tight not only with people, but also with schmaltz, much of which borders on the maudlin. An appalling would-be baritone voice tear-jerks out the words of God Bless America. Priests say prayers for a safe race. Drum majorettes abound. Commentators reach fever pitch. And the drivers pace about, look at their watches, try to shut it all out, will the time on to eleven o'clock so that all this can be drowned by earplugs and helmets and engines, and they can get out there and race.

Finally they step aboard, their cars formed into qualifying order. Engines are fired up and the pace car leads them away, gradually picking up speed before pulling off into the pit lane after two or three laps, the race cars holding station, cruising. If their formation is perfect, the green light goes on and the thirty-three drivers begin the first of two hundred laps. . . .

The Indianapolis 500 is, inevitably, a dangerous race, particularly in the early laps when the pack is tightly bunched. There are not thirty-three great drivers in the race. Ability and experience vary enormously. At the front are the Rutherfords and Foyts and Unsers in superbly prepared machines, but down the field you find a collection of ageing cars and rookie drivers. Mingle these ingredients and you have something very volatile. The 500's safety record used to be appalling, but track facilities are now at least as good as anywhere in the world, and fatalities have become mercifully rare.

It is a long way to race, 500 miles, and the man who makes it to Victory Lane each year has been through it. But Indy remains the dream of every man who ever stepped into a sprint car at a bullring in Pennsylvania, Ohio, or wherever. It was like that for Mario Andretti, who won the 500 in 1969. "From a career standpoint," he says, "winning Indy is really important, something that's always going to be there in your record. In some ways, the race is very over-rated, but there is a certain mystique about the place. You'd go a long way in a single day to achieve more satisfaction then when you win there, whether you take the lead on the first lap or the last. It's a milestone, and gives you more prestige than any other single event in racing.

"But winning it—the driving part of it—is out of all proportion to the fame and fortune. It's just a matter of everything hanging together on a particular day. If it happens to be *that* day at the Brickyard, you're made."

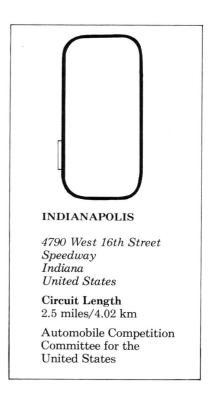

INDIANAPOLIS

4790 West 16th Street
Speedway
Indiana
United States

Circuit Length
2.5 miles/4.02 km

Automobile Competition
Committee for the
United States

CHAMPIONSHIP RESULTS

ARGENTINE GRAND PRIX

Year	Driver	Car	Speed mph	km/h
Buenos Aires				
1953	Ascari	Ferrari 500	78.14	125.75
1954	Fangio	Maserati 250F	70.14	112.88
1955	Fangio	Mercedes W196	77.52	124.75
1956	Musso/Fangio	Lancia-Ferrari D50	79.39	127.76
1957	Fangio	Maserati 250F	80.62	129.74
1958	Moss	Cooper T43	83.61	134.55
1960	McLaren	Cooper T51	84.66	136.24
1971*	Amon	Matra-Simca MS120	99.18	159.61
1972	Stewart	Tyrrell 003	100.43	161.62
1973	Fittipaldi	Lotus 72	102.95	165.68
1974	Hulme	McLaren M23	116.72	187.84
1975	Fittipaldi	McLaren M23	118.60	190.86
1977	Scheckter	Wolf WR1	117.71	189.43
1978	Andretti	Lotus 78	119.19	191.82
1979	Laffite	Ligier JS11	122.77	197.57
1980	Jones	Williams FW07	113.98	183.43

*non-championship race

BRAZILIAN GRAND PRIX

Year	Driver	Car	Speed mph	km/h
Interlagos				
1972*	Reutemann	Brabham BT34	112.89	181.68
1973	Fittipaldi	Lotus 72	114.23	183.83
1974	Fittipaldi	McLaren M23	112.23	180.61
1975	Pace	Brabham BT44B	113.40	182.50
1976	Lauda	Ferrari 312T	112.76	181.47
1977	Reutemann	Ferrari 312T	112.92	181.72
Jacarepagua				
1978	Reutemann	Ferrari 312T	107.43	172.89
Interlagos				
1979	Laffite	Ligier JS11	117.23	188.66
1980	Arnoux	Renault RE20	117.40	188.93

*non-championship race

SOUTH AFRICAN GRAND PRIX

Year	Driver	Car	Speed mph	km/h
East London				
1960*	Frere	Cooper T45	84.88	136.60
1960*	Moss	Porsche 718	89.24	143.62
1961*	Clark	Lotus 21	92.20	148.38
1962	G. Hill	BRM P57	93.57	150.58
1963	Clark	Lotus 25	95.10	153.05
1965	Clark	Lotus 25	97.97	157.66
1966*	Spence	Lotus 33	97.75	157.31
Kyalami				
1967	P. Rodriguez	Cooper T81	97.09	156.25
1968	Clark	Lotus 49	107.42	172.87
1969	Stewart	Matra MS10	110.62	178.02
1970	Brabham	Brabham BT33	111.70	179.76
1971	Andretti	Ferrari 312B-1	112.36	180.83
1972	Hulme	McLaren M19A	114.23	183.83
1973	Stewart	Tyrrell 006	117.14	188.51
1974	Reutemann	Brabham BT44	116.22	187.03
1975	Scheckter	Tyrrell 007	115.55	185.95
1976	Lauda	Ferrari 312T	116.65	187.72
1977	Lauda	Ferrari 312T-2	116.59	187.63
1978	Peterson	Lotus 78	116.70	187.81
1979	Villeneuve	Ferrari 312T-4	117.19	188.59
1980	Arnoux	Renault RE21	123.19	198.25

*non-championship race

U. S. GRAND PRIX (WEST)

Year	Driver	Car	Speed mph	km/h
Long Beach				
1976	Regazzoni	Ferrari 312T	85.57	137.71
1977	Andretti	Lotus 78	86.89	139.83
1978	Reutemann	Ferrari 312T	87.10	140.20
1979	Villeneuve	Ferrari 312T-4	87.81	141.31
1980	Piquet	Brabham BT49	92.90	149.50
1981	Jones	Williams FW07	87.60	140.00

BELGIAN GRAND PRIX

Year	Driver	Car	Speed mph	km/h
Spa-Francorchamps				
1950	Fangio	Alfa Romeo 158	110.04	177.09
1951	Farina	Alfa Romeo 159	114.32	183.98
1952	Ascari	Ferrari 500	103.13	165.97
1953	Ascari	Ferrari 500	112.47	181.00
1954	Fangio	Maserati 250F	115.06	185.17
1955	Fangio	Mercedes-Benz W196	118.83	191.23
1956	Collins	Lancia-Ferrari D50	118.44	190.61
1958	Brooks	Vanwall	129.92	209.09
1960	Brabham	Cooper T53	133.63	215.10
1961	P. Hill	Ferrari Dino 156	128.15	206.23
1962	Clark	Lotus 25	131.90	212.27
1963	Clark	Lotus 25	114.10	183.62
1964	Clark	Lotus 25	132.79	213.70
1965	Clark	Lotus 33	117.16	188.55
1966	Surtees	Ferrari 312	113.93	183.35
1967	Gurney	Eagle T1G	145.99	234.94
1968	McLaren	McLaren M7A	147.14	236.79
1970	P. Rodriguez	BRM P153	149.94	241.30
1972	Fittipaldi	Lotus 72	113.35	182.42
Zolder				
1973	Stewart	Tyrrell 006	107.74	173.38
Nivelles-Baulers				
1974	Fittipaldi	McLaren M23	113.10	182.01
Zolder				
1975	Lauda	Ferrari 312T	107.05	172.30
1976	Lauda	Ferrari 312T	108.11	173.98
1977	Nilsson	Lotus 78	96.64	155.52
1978	Andretti	Lotus 79	111.38	179.24
1979	Scheckter	Ferrari 312T-4	111.24	179.02
1980	Pironi	Ligier JS11/15	115.83	186.41

MONACO GRAND PRIX

Year	Driver	Car	Speed mph	km/h
1950	Fangio	Alfa Romeo 158	61.33	98.70
1955	Trintignant	Ferrari 625	65.81	105.91
1956	Moss	Maserati 250F	64.94	104.51
1957	Fangio	Maserati 250F	64.72	104.15
1958	Trintignant	Cooper T45	67.99	109.42
1959	Brabham	Cooper T51	66.71	107.36
1960	Moss	Lotus 18	67.46	108.56
1961	Moss	Lotus 18	70.70	113.78
1962	McLaren	Cooper T60	70.46	113.39
1963	G. Hill	BRM P57	72.42	116.55
1964	G. Hill	BRM P261	72.64	116.90
1965	G. Hill	BRM P261	74.34	119.64
1966	Stewart	BRM P261	76.51	123.13
1967	Hulme	Brabham BT20	75.90	122.15
1968	G. Hill	Lotus 49B	77.82	125.24
1969	G. Hill	Lotus 49B	80.18	129.03
1970	Rindt	Lotus 49C	81.85	131.72
1971	Stewart	Tyrrell 003	83.49	134.36
1972	Beltoise	BRM P160B	63.85	102.75
1973	Stewart	Tyrrell 006	80.96	130.29
1974	Peterson	Lotus 72	80.74	129.93
1975	Lauda	Ferrari 312T	75.53	121.55
1976	Lauda	Ferrari 312T-2	80.36	129.32
1977	Scheckter	Wolf WR1	79.61	128.12
1978	Depailler	Tyrrell 008	80.36	129.32
1979	Scheckter	Ferrari 312T-4	81.34	130.90
1980	Reutemann	Williams FW07B	81.20	130.68

SPANISH GRAND PRIX

Year	Driver	Car	Speed mph	km/h
Pedralbes				
1951	Fangio	Alfa Romeo 159M	98.79	158.98
1954	Hawthorn	Ferrari 553	97.05	156.18
Jarama				
1967	Clark	Lotus 49	83.59	134.53
1968	G. Hill	Lotus 49	84.41	135.84
Montjuich				
1969	Stewart	Matra MS80	92.91	149.52
Jarama				
1970	Stewart	March 701B	87.22	140.36
Montjuich				
1971	Stewart	Tyrrell 003	97.19	156.41
Jarama				
1972	Fittipaldi	Lotus 72	92.35	148.62
Montjuich				
1973	Fittipaldi	Lotus 72	97.86	157.49
Jarama				
1974	Lauda	Ferrari 312B-3	88.48	142.40
Montjuich				
1975	Mass	McLaren M23	95.54	153.75
Jarama				
1976	Hunt	McLaren M23	93.01	149.68
1977	Andretti	Lotus 78	92.53	148.91
1978	Andretti	Lotus 79	93.52	150.50
1979	Depailler	Ligier JS11	95.97	154.44
1980	Jones	Williams FW07B	95.69	154.00

FRENCH GRAND PRIX

Year	Driver	Car	Speed mph	km/h
Reims				
1950	Fangio	Alfa Romeo 158	104.84	168.72
1951	Fagiola/Fangio	Alfa Romeo 159	110.97	178.58
Rouen				
1952	Ascari	Ferrari 500	80.13	128.95
Reims				
1953	Hawthorn	Ferrari 500	113.64	182.88
1954	Fangio	Mercedes-Benz W196	115.97	186.63
1956	Collins	Lancia-Ferrari D50	122.29	196.80
Rouen				
1957	Fangio	Maserati 250F	100.02	160.96
Reims				
1958	Hawthorn	Ferrari Dino 246	125.45	201.89
1959	Brooks	Ferrari Dino 246	127.43	205.07
1960	Brabham	Cooper T53	131.80	212.11
1961	Baghetti	Ferrari Dino 156	119.85	192.87
Rouen				
1962	Gurney	Porsche 804	101.84	163.89
Reims				
1963	Clark	Lotus 25	125.31	201.66
Rouen				
1964	Gurney	Brabham BT7	108.77	175.04
Clermont-Ferrand				
1965	Clark	Lotus 25	89.22	143.58
Reims				
1966	Brabham	Brabham BT19	136.90	220.31
Bugatti au Mans				
1967	Brabham	Brabham BT24	98.90	159.16
Rouen				
1968	Ickx	Ferrari 312	100.45	161.65
Clermont-Ferrand				
1969	Stewart	Matra MS80	97.71	157.24
1970	Rindt	Lotus 72	98.42	158.39
Paul Ricard				
1971	Stewart	Tyrrell 003	111.66	179.69
Clermont-Ferrand				
1972	Stewart	Tyrrell 003	101.56	163.44
Paul Ricard				
1973	Peterson	Lotus 72	115.12	185.26
Dijon-Prenois				
1974	Peterson	Lotus 72	119.75	192.71
Paul Ricard				
1975	Lauda	Ferrari 312	116.60	187.64
1976	Hunt	McLaren M23	115.84	186.42
Dijon-Prenois				
1977	Andretti	Lotus 78	113.71	182.99
Paul Ricard				
1978	Andretti	Lotus 79	118.31	190.40
Dijon-Prenois				
1979	Jabouille	Renault RS	118.88	191.31
Paul Ricard				
1980	Jones	Williams FW07B	126.15	203.02

BRITISH GRAND PRIX

Year	Driver	Car	Speed mph	km/h
Silverstone				
1950	Farina	Alfa Romeo 158	90.96	146.38
1951	Gonzalez	Ferrari 375	96.11	154.67
1952	Ascari	Ferrari 500	90.92	146.32
1953	Ascari	Ferrari 500	92.97	149.62
1954	Gonzalez	Ferrari 625	89.69	144.34
Aintree				
1955	Moss	Mercedes-Benz W196	86.47	139.16
Silverstone				
1956	Fangio	Lancia-Ferrari D50	98.65	158.76
1957	Brooks/Moss	Vanwall	86.80	139.69
1958	Collins	Ferrari Dino 246	102.05	164.23
Aintree				
1959	Brabham	Cooper T51	98.88	159.13
Silverstone				
1960	Brabham	Cooper T53	108.69	174.91
Aintree				
1961	von Trips	Ferrari Dino 156	83.19	135.04
1962	Clark	Lotus 25	92.25	148.46
Silverstone				
1963	Clark	Lotus 25	107.75	173.40
Brands Hatch				
1964	Clark	Lotus 25	94.14	151.50
Silverstone				
1965	Clark	Lotus 33	112.02	180.27
Brands Hatch				
1966	Brabham	Brabham BT19	95.48	153.66
Silverstone				
1967	Clark	Lotus 49	117.64	189.32
Brands Hatch				
1968	Siffert	Lotus 49B	104.83	168.70
Silverstone				
1969	Stewart	Matra MS80	127.25	204.78
Brands Hatch				
1970	Rindt	Lotus 72	108.69	174.91
Silverstone				
1971	Stewart	Tyrrell 003	130.48	209.99
Brands Hatch				
1972	Fittipaldi	Lotus 72	112.06	180.34
Silverstone				
1973	Revson	McLaren M23	131.75	212.03
Brands Hatch				
1974	Scheckter	Tyrrell 007	115.74	186.26
Silverstone				
1975	Fittipaldi	McLaren M23	120.02	193.15
Brands Hatch				
1976	Lauda	Ferrari 312T-2	114.24	183.85
Silverstone				
1977	Hunt	McLaren M26	130.36	209.79
Brands Hatch				
1978	Reutemann	Ferrari 312T-3	116.61	187.66
Silverstone				
1979	Regazzoni	Williams FW07	138.80	223.37
Brands Hatch				
1980	Jones	Williams FW07B	125.69	202.28

GERMAN GRAND PRIX

Year	Driver	Car	Speed mph	km/h
Nürburgring				
1951	Ascari	Ferrari 375	83.76	134.79
1952	Ascari	Ferrari 500	82.20	132.28
1953	Farina	Ferrari 500	83.91	135.04
1954	Fangio	Mercedes-Benz W196	82.87	133.36
1956	Fangio	Lancia-Ferrari D50	85.45	137.51
1957	Fangio	Maserati 250F	88.82	142.94
1958	Brooks	Vanwall	90.31	145.36
Avus				
1959	Brooks	Ferrari Dino 256	145.35	233.91
Nürburgring				
1961	Moss	Lotus 18/21	92.30	148.54
1962	G. Hill	BRM P57	80.35	129.31
1963	Surtees	Ferrari 156	95.83	154.22
1964	Surtees	Ferrari 158	96.58	155.43
1965	Clark	Lotus 33	99.76	160.54
1966	Brabham	Brabham BT19	86.75	139.61
1967	Hulme	Brabham BT24	101.41	163.20
1968	Stewart	Matra MS10	85.71	137.93
1969	Ickx	Brabham BT26A	108.43	174.50
Hockenheim				
1970	Rindt	Lotus 72	124.07	199.67
Nürburgring				
1971	Stewart	Tyrrell 003	114.45	184.18
1972	Ickx	Ferrari 312B-2	116.62	187.68
1973	Stewart	Tyrrell 006	116.79	187.95
1974	Regazzoni	Ferrari 312B-3	117.33	188.82
1975	Reutemann	Brabham BT44B	117.73	189.46
1976	Hunt	McLaren M23	117.18	188.58
Hockenheim				
1977	Lauda	Ferrari 312T-2	129.57	208.52
1978	Andretti	Lotus 79	129.41	208.26
1979	Jones	Williams FW07	134.27	216.08
1980	Laffite	Ligier JS11	137.22	220.83

DUTCH GRAND PRIX

Year	Driver	Car	Speed mph	km/h
Zandvoort				
1950	Rosier	Lago-Talbot	76.65	123.32
1951	Rosier	Lago-Talbot	78.45	126.26
1952	Ascari	Ferrari 500	81.13	130.56
1953	Ascari	Ferrari 500	81.05	130.43
1955	Fangio	Mercedes-Benz W196	89.65	144.27
1958	Moss	Vanwall	93.93	151.16
1959	Bonnier	BRM P25	93.46	150.41
1960	Brabham	Cooper T53	96.27	154.93
1961	von Trips	Ferrari Dino 156	96.23	154.86
1962	G. Hill	BRM P57	95.40	153.53
1963	Clark	Lotus 25	97.53	156.96
1964	Clark	Lotus 25	98.02	157.74
1965	Clark	Lotus 33	100.87	162.33
1966	Brabham	Brabham BT19	100.10	161.10
1967	Clark	Lotus 49	104.45	168.09
1968	Stewart	Matra MS10	84.66	136.24
1969	Stewart	Matra MS80	111.04	178.70
1970	Rindt	Lotus 72	112.96	181.79
1971	Ickx	Ferrari 312B-2	94.06	151.37
1973	Stewart	Tyrrell 006	114.35	184.02
1974	Lauda	Ferrari 312B-3	114.72	184.62
1975	Hunt	Hesketh 308	100.48	161.70
1976	Hunt	McLaren M23	112.68	181.33
1977	Lauda	Ferrari 312T-2	116.12	186.87
1978	Andretti	Lotus 79	116.91	188.14
1979	Jones	Williams FW07	116.62	187.68
1980	Piquet	Brabham BT49	116.19	186.99

AUSTRIAN GRAND PRIX

Year	Driver	Car	Speed mph	km/h
Zeltweg				
1963	Brabham	Brabham BT7	96.34	115.04
1964	Bandini	Ferrari 156	99.20	159.64
Osterreichring				
1970	Ickx	Ferrari 312B-1	129.27	208.03
1971	Siffert	BRM P160	131.64	211.85
1972	Fittipaldi	Lotus 72	133.29	214.50
1973	Peterson	Lotus 72	133.99	215.63
1974	Reutemann	Brabham BT44	134.09	215.79
1975	Brambilla	March 751	110.30	177.51
1976	Watson	Penske PC4	132.00	212.43
1977	Jones	Shadow DN8	122.98	197.91
1978	Peterson	Lotus 79	118.03	189.95
1979	Jones	Williams FW07	136.52	219.70
1980	Jabouille	Renault RE23	138.69	223.20

ITALIAN GRAND PRIX

Year	Driver	Car	Speed mph	km/h
Monza				
1950	Farina	Alfa Romeo 158	109.70	176.54
1951	Ascari	Ferrari 375	115.52	185.91
1952	Ascari	Ferrari 500	110.04	177.09
1953	Fangio	Maserati A6SSG	110.68	178.12
1954	Fangio	Mercedes-Benz W196	111.98	180.21
1955	Fangio	Mercedes-Benz W196	128.49	206.79
1956	Moss	Maserati 250F	129.73	208.77
1957	Moss	Vanwall	129.72	208.76
1958	Brooks	Vanwall	121.21	195.06
1959	Moss	Cooper T45	124.38	200.16
1960	G. Hill	Ferrari Dino 246	132.06	212.52
1961	P. Hill	Ferrari Dino 156	130.11	209.39
1962	G. Hill	BRM P57	123.62	198.94
1963	Clark	Lotus 25	127.74	205.57
1964	Surtees	Ferrari 158	127.77	205.62
1965	Stewart	BRM P261	130.46	209.95
1966	Scarfiotti	Ferrari 312/66	135.92	218.74
1967	Surtees	Honda RA300	140.50	226.12
1968	Hulme	McLaren M7A	145.41	234.01
1969	Stewart	Matra MS80	146.97	236.52
1970	Regazzoni	Ferrari 312B-1	147.08	236.70
1971	Gethin	BRM P160	150.75	242.60
1972	Fittipaldi	Lotus 72	131.61	211.80
1973	Peterson	Lotus 72	132.63	213.44
1974	Peterson	Lotus 72	135.10	217.42
1975	Regazzoni	Ferrari 312T	135.48	218.03
1976	Peterson	March 761	124.12	199.75
1977	Andretti	Lotus 78	128.01	206.01
1978	Lauda	Brabham BT46	128.95	207.52
1979	Scheckter	Ferrari 312T-4	131.85	212.19
Imola				
1980	Piquet	Brabham BT49	113.98	183.43

CANADIAN GRAND PRIX

Year	Driver	Car	Speed mph	km/h
Mosport Park				
1967	Brabham	Brabham BT24	82.99	133.56
St. Jovite				
1968	Hulme	McLaren M7A	97.22	156.46
Mosport Park				
1969	Ickx	Brabham BT26A	111.19	178.94
St. Jovite				
1970	Ickx	Ferrari 312B	101.27	162.97
Mosport Park				
1971	Stewart	Tyrrell 003	81.96	131.90
1972	Stewart	Tyrrell 005	114.28	183.92
1973	Revson	McLaren M23	99.13	159.53
1974	Fittipaldi	McLaren M23	117.52	189.12
1976	Hunt	McLaren M23	117.84	189.64
1977	Scheckter	Wolf WR1	118.03	189.96
Ile Notre-Dame				
1978	Villeneuve	Ferrari 312T-3	99.67	160.40
1979	Jones	Williams FW07	105.36	169.56
1980	Jones	Williams FW07B	110.00	177.02

U.S. GRAND PRIX

Year	Driver	Car	Speed mph	km/h
Sebring				
1959	McLaren	Cooper T51	98.83	159.05
Riverside				
1960	Moss	Lotus 18	99.00	159.32
Watkins Glen				
1961	Ireland	Lotus 21	103.17	166.03
1962	Clark	Lotus 25	108.61	174.79
1963	G. Hill	BRM P57	109.31	175.91
1964	G. Hill	BRM P261	111.10	178.80
1965	G. Hill	BRM P261	107.98	173.77
1966	Clark	Lotus 43	114.90	184.91
1967	Clark	Lotus 49	120.95	194.64
1968	Stewart	Matra MS10	124.89	200.99
1969	Rindt	Lotus 49B	126.36	203.35
1970	Fittipaldi	Lotus 72C	126.79	204.04
1971	Cevert	Tyrrell 002	115.09	185.21
1972	Stewart	Tyrrell 005	117.48	189.06
1973	Peterson	Lotus 72	118.05	189.98
1974	Reutemann	Brabham BT44	119.12	191.70
1975	Lauda	Ferrari 312T	116.70	187.81

U. S. GRAND PRIX (EAST)

Year	Driver	Car	Speed mph	km/h
Watkins Glen				
1976	Hunt	McLaren M23	116.43	187.37
1977	Hunt	McLaren M23	100.98	162.51
1978	Reutemann	Ferrari 312T-3	118.58	190.83
1979	Villeneuve	Ferrari 312T-4	106.46	171.33
1980	Jones	Williams FW07B	126.37	203.37

JAPANESE GRAND PRIX

Year	Driver	Car	Speed mph	km/h
Fuji				
1976	Andretti	Lotus 77	114.09	183.61
1977	Hunt	McLaren M23	129.14	207.84

MEXICAN GRAND PRIX

Year	Driver	Car	Speed mph	km/h
Mexico City				
1963	Clark	Lotus 25	93.30	150.12
1964	Gurney	Brabham BT7	93.32	150.15
1965	Ginther	Honda RA272	94.26	151.66
1966	Surtees	Cooper T81	95.72	154.01
1967	Clark	Lotus 49	101.42	163.18
1968	G. Hill	Lotus 49B	103.81	167.02
1969	Hulme	McLaren M7A	106.15	170.79
1970	Ickx	Ferrari 312B	106.78	171.81

MOROCCAN GRAND PRIX

Year	Driver	Car	Speed mph	km/h
Ain Diab, Casablanca				
1958	Moss	Vanwall	116.20	186.96

PESCARA GRAND PRIX

Year	Driver	Car	Speed mph	km/h
1957	Moss	Vanwall	95.55	153.74

PORTUGUESE GRAND PRIX

Year	Driver	Car	Speed mph	km/h
Oporto				
1958	Moss	Vanwall	105.30	168.99
Monsanto				
1959	Moss	Cooper T51	95.32	153.37
Oporto				
1960	Brabham	Cooper T53	109.27	175.81

SWEDISH GRAND PRIX

Year	Driver	Car	Speed mph	km/h
Anderstorp				
1973	Hulme	McLaren M23	102.63	165.13
1974	Scheckter	Tyrrell 007	101.11	162.68
1975	Lauda	Ferrari 312T	100.45	161.62
1976	Scheckter	Tyrrell P34	100.90	162.38
1977	Laffite	Ligier JS11	100.87	162.33
1978	Lauda	Brabham BT46B	104.15	167.61

SWISS GRAND PRIX

Year	Driver	Car	Speed mph	km/h
Bremgarten				
1950	Farina	Alfa Romeo 159	92.76	149.28
1951	Fangio	Alfa Romoe 159	89.05	143.31
1952	Taruffi	Ferrari 500	92.78	149.31
1953	Ascari	Ferrari 500	97.16	156.36
1954	Fangio	Mercedes-Benz W196	99.20	159.64

INDIANAPOLIS 500 MILES

Year	Driver	Car	Speed mph	km/h
1950	Parsons	Wynn's Friction Proof Special	124.00	199.55
1951	Wallard	Balanger	126.24	203.16
1952	Ruttman	Agajanian	128.92	207.47
1953	Vukovich	Fuel Injection Special	128.74	207.18
1954	Vukovich	Fuel Injection Special	130.84	210.56
1955	Sweikart	John Zink Special	128.21	206.33
1956	Flaherty	John Zink Special	128.49	206.78
1957	Hanks	Belond Exhaust Special	135.60	218.22
1958	Bryan	Belond Exhaust Special	133.79	215.31
1959	Ward	Leader Card Special	135.86	218.64
1960	Rathmann	Ken Paul Special	138.77	223.32
1961	Foyt	Bowes Seal Fast Special	139.13	223.90
1962	Ward	Leader Card Roadster	140.29	225.77
1963	Jones	Agajanian	143.14	230.36
1964	Foyt	Sheraton-Offenhauser	147.35	237.13
1965	Clark	Lotus-Ford	150.60	242.36
1966	Hill	Lola-Ford	144.32	232.25
1967	Foyt	Coyote-Ford	151.21	243.34
1968	B. Unser	Eagle-Offenhauser	152.88	246.03
1969	Andretti	Hawk-Ford	156.87	252.45
1970	A. Unser	Colt-Ford	155.75	250.65
1971	A. Unser	Colt-Ford	157.74	253.85
1972	Donohue	McLaren-Offenhauser	162.96	262.25
1973	Johncock	Eagle-Offenhauser	159.04	255.94
1974	Rutherford	McLaren-Offenhauser	158.59	255.22
1975	B. Unser	Eagle-Offenhauser	149.21	240.12
1976	Rutherford	McLaren-Offenhauser	148.73	239.35
1977	Foyt	Coyote-Ford	161.30	259.58
1978	A. Unser	Chapparral	161.36	259.68
1979	Mears	Penske PC6	119.39	192.13
1980	Rutherford	Chapparral-Cosworth 2K	142.86	229.90

GRAND PRIX FORMULAE

1948-53 Maximum engine capacities: unsupercharged, 4.5-litres; supercharged, 1.5-litres. (The 1952-53 Championship Grands Prix were run to Formula Two regulations, admitting supercharged engines of up to 500 cc and unsupercharged engines up to 2-litres.)

1954-60 Maximum engine capacities: unsupercharged, 2.5-litres; supercharged, 750 cc. During the life of this formula the use of AvGas (100-130 octane) fuel became obligatory in 1958, and from 1959 open-wheeled cars were stipulated.

1961-65 Maximum engine capacity: 1.5-litres (minimum 1.3-litres and supercharged engines were not admitted). Fuel specifically pump grade as available to the public. Replenishment with oil was not permitted during a race. Roll-over bars, self starters and dual braking systems were required. Minimum weight of car with oil and water, but without fuel was 450 kg (991 lb).

1966- Maximum engine capacities: unsupercharged, 3-litres; supercharged (or turbocharged), 1.5-litres. From 1972, the maximum number of cylinders was twelve. Initial maximum weight was 500 kg (1102 lb), and was then increased to 530 kg (1168 lb) in 1970, to 550 kg (1213 lb) in 1972, to 575 kg (1268 lb) in 1973 and to 585 kg (1290 lb) in 1981. These weight changes were nominally to allow for additional safety equipment, such as obligatory on-board fire extinguishers and deformable structures with impact-resistant material around fuel tanks, and this effectively excluded spaceframes. Fuel tank capacity was restricted to 250 litres. In 1969 aerofoils were restricted and any form of moveable or driver-adjustable aerofoil was banned. For 1981, to counter a form of aerodynamic aid unthought of when these rules were framed, a static ground clearance of 6 cm (2$\frac{1}{3}$ in) was stipulated, hopefully to exclude the sliding skirts which were felt to be a form of moveable aerofoil. Measurements of fixed aerofoils were subsequently specified. As far as the rear wing is concerned a maximum width of 110 cm (50 in) was stipulated, with the rear edge of such a wing not projecting more than 80 cm (31 in) behind the centre line of the rear wheels. High airboxes (engine air intakes) were banned from 1976. The maximum overall width of cars, including the entire wheels was set at 215 cm (84$\frac{1}{2}$ in).

THE CONSTRUCTORS' CHAMPIONSHIP

The Formula One Constructors' Championship was introduced in 1958, but has never attracted the same public interest as the Drivers' Championship. A similar points system has been used, except that for several years the specified number of best results to count has varied (e.g., the five best results achieved in the nine scoring races in 1959) and until 1979 only the highest-placed car of a marque in the first six scored points (any points "freed" under this arrangement did not become available to cars which finished lower than sixth in a race). Subsequently, every car in the first six scored. Only three times—in 1958, 1973, and 1976—has the Constructors' Championship failed to go to the team which fielded the Champion Driver.

THE DRIVERS' CHAMPIONSHIP

The World Championship of Drivers was introduced in 1950. The results were to be decided on a cumulative points system. Until 1961, eight points were awarded for a win, and only the first five drivers in a race scored, but then the scoring system still in use today was introduced:

1st	9 points
2nd	6 points
3rd	4 points
4th	3 points
5th	2 points
6th	1 point

One point was awarded for the fastest lap until 1959, while points gained in shared drives were divided between the drivers concerned. In rare cases when races have been stopped prematurely, half the number of points have been awarded (4$\frac{1}{2}$ points, 3 points, 2 points, 1$\frac{1}{2}$ points, 1 point and $\frac{1}{2}$ point). Until 1960 the Indianapolis 500 was a Championship race, but since then only Grands Prix have been scoring events.

The basic points system has been criticized, because it has, and still can, disproportionately reward a driver who is consistently well placed, although he might win few races. An example of this was the 1958 season when Mike Hawthorn became World Champion, although he won only one race, but was second five times, while Stirling Moss won four races.

A specified number of best scores have always been allowed to count towards a driver's total. In an attempt to keep the championship open to the last race of the series, in 1979 the season was divided into two eight-race halves, and drivers were allowed to count their best four scores from each half. As it transpired, that year the championship would have been settled by the penultimate race, irrespective of which system was used.

THE CHAMPION DRIVERS

1950	Giuseppe Farina (I), Alfa Romeo
1951	Juan Manuel Fangio (RA), Alfa Romeo
1952	Alberto Ascari (I), Ferrari
1953	Alberto Ascari (I), Ferrari
1954	Juan Manuel Fangio (RA), Maserati and Mercedes-Benz
1955	Juan Manuel Fangio (RA), Mercedes-Benz
1956	Juan Manuel Fangio (RA), Ferrari
1957	Juan Manuel Fangio (RA), Maserati
1958	J.M. Hawthorn (GB), Ferrari
1959	J.A. Brabham (AUS), Cooper
1960	J.A. Brabham (AUS), Cooper
1961	P. Hill (USA), Ferrari
1962	G. Hill (GB), BRM
1963	J. Clark (GB), Lotus
1964	J. Surtees (GB), Ferrari
1965	J. Clark (GB), Lotus
1966	J.A. Brabham (AUS), Brabham
1967	D. Hulme (NZ), Brabham
1968	G. Hill (GB), Lotus
1969	J. Stewart (GB), Matra
1970	J. Rindt (A), Lotus
1971	J. Stewart (GB), Tyrrell
1972	E. Fittipaldi (BR), Lotus
1973	J. Stewart (GB), Tyrrell
1974	E. Fittipaldi (BR), McLaren
1975	N. Lauda (A), Ferrari
1976	J. Hunt (GB), McLaren
1977	N. Lauda (A), Ferrari
1978	M. Andretti (USA), Lotus
1979	J. Scheckter (ZA), Ferrari
1980	A. Jones (AUS), Williams

INDEX

223

ACKNOWLEDGEMENTS

The publishers gratefully acknowledge the assistance of the following individuals and organizations: Alfa Romeo SpA; Toshio Ashizawa, Honda Motor Company (Japan) Ltd.; Jurgen Barth, Porsche (Germany); Peter Biro, Long Beach Grand Prix Association; Rod Campbell, Team Ensign (Motor Racing Ltd.); Gerry Cannon; John Cooper; Michael Cotton, Porsche (Germany); Yvette d'Arcy, Renault (U.K.) Ltd.; Colin Doeg, Brooke Bond OXO Ltd.; Essex Motorsport; Andrew Ferguson, Team Lotus International Ltd.; Ferodo Ltd.; Robert G. Fox, Rubery Owen Holdings Ltd.; Geoff Goddard; Goodyear Tyre and Rubber Company (G.B.) Ltd.; Angela Hart, Yardley of London Ltd.; Mike Harting, HW Motors Ltd.; C.A. Heafey, John Player and Sons Ltd.; John Hogan, Charles Stewart & Co. (Kirkaldy) Ltd.; Ron McQueeney, Indianapolis Motor Speedway Corporation; Peter Mackintosh, Fittipaldi Automotive Ltd.; March Engineering Ltd.; Josie Matthews, Public Relations Counsel Ltd.; Jackie Oliver, Arrows Racing Team; W. Pratt, Dunlop Technical Film Unit; Simon Pearson, Fiat (U.K.) Ltd.; Daniel Schildge, Martini Racing; Shell (U.K.) Photographic Library; Jon Simpson, Vandervell Products Ltd.; Skyphotos Ltd.; John Surtees; Baron Fritz Huschke von Hanstein; Brenda Vernor, Ferrari; Colin Wilson.

Index: Jack Haigh

Artists
Jim Bamber drew all the cars on pages 19-47 and 52-118, as well as pages 2-3 and 4-5.
Neil Breeden did the portraits on pages 52-118.
Harry Clow drew the circuits on pages 180-216.
Jim Robins drew the historical race, pages 8-16.
Craig Warwick illustrated the section on the drivers, pages 122-175, and drew the portraits of the authors on the jacket.
Trevor Scobie: front cover
Roy Flooks: back cover